*The Cambridge Guide to
Blended Learning for Language Teaching*

THE CAMBRIDGE GUIDES SERIES

Authoritative, comprehensive and accessible guides, addressing both the theoretical and the practical aspects of key topics in second language teaching and learning.

For more information on these titles, please visit: www.cambridge.org/elt

Other titles in this series:

The Cambridge Guide to Research in Language Teaching and Learning
Edited by James Dean Brown and Christine Coombe

The Cambridge Guide to Second Language Assessment
Edited by Christine Coombe, Peter Davidson, Barry O'Sullivan and Stephen Stoynoff

The Cambridge Guide to Pedagogy and Practice in Second Language Teaching
Edited by Anne Burns and Jack C. Richards

The Cambridge Guide to Second Language Teacher Education
Edited by Anne Burns and Jack C. Richards

The Cambridge Guide to Teaching English to Speakers of Other Languages
Edited by Ronald Carter and David Nunan

The Cambridge Guide to Blended Learning for Language Teaching

Edited by
Michael McCarthy

CAMBRIDGE
UNIVERSITY PRESS

University Printing House, Cambridge CB2 8BS, United Kingdom

Cambridge University Press is part of the University of Cambridge.

It furthers the University's mission by disseminating knowledge in the pursuit of education, learning and research at the highest international levels of excellence.

www.cambridge.org
Information on this title: cambridge.org/9781316505113

© Cambridge University Press 2016

This publication is in copyright. Subject to statutory exception and to the provisions of relevant collective licensing agreements, no reproduction of any part may take place without the written permission of Cambridge University Press.

First published 2016

A catalogue record for this publication is available from the British Library

Library of Congress Cataloging-in-Publication Data
Names: McCarthy, Michael, 1947– editor.
Title: The Cambridge Guide to blended learning for language teaching /
Edited by Michael McCarthy.
Description: Cambridge : Cambridge University Press, [2016] |
Series: The Cambridge Guide Series | Includes index.
Identifiers: LCCN 2015029490| ISBN 9781316505113 (pb) |
ISBN 9781316505137 (google ebook) |
ISBN 9781316505144 (apple ibook) |
ISBN 9781316505151 (kindle ebook) |
ISBN 9781316505168 (ebooks.com ebook)
Subjects: LCSH: Language and languages – Study and teaching. |
Blended learning. | Teaching. | Language and education.
Classification: LCC P53 .C26 2016 | DDC 418.0071–dc23
LC record available at http://lccn.loc.gov/2015029490

ISBN 978-1-316-50511-3 Paperback
ISBN 978-1-316-50514-4 Apple iBook
ISBN 978-1-316-50513-7 Google ebook
ISBN 978-1-316-50515-1 Kindle ebook
ISBN 978-1-316-50516-8 eBooks.com ebook

Cambridge University Press has no responsibility for the persistence or accuracy of URLs for external or third-party internet websites referred to in this publication, and does not guarantee that any content on such websites is, or will remain, accurate or appropriate.

CONTENTS

Acknowledgements			*page* vii
Introduction		Blended Learning *Michael McCarthy*	1
Section 1		**Connecting Theories and Blended Learning**	**5**
Chapter	**1**	Issues in Second Language Acquisition in Relation to Blended Learning *Michael McCarthy*	7
Chapter	**2**	Educational Technology: Assessing its Fitness for Purpose *Scott Thornbury*	25
Chapter	**3**	The Role of Interaction in a Blended Learning Context *Steve Walsh*	36
Section 2		**Implications for Teaching**	**53**
Chapter	**4**	The Flipped Classroom *Christopher Johnson and Debra Marsh*	55
Chapter	**5**	Blended Teaching and the Changing Role of the Language Teacher: The Need for a Review of Teacher Professional Development *Anna Comas-Quinn*	68
Chapter	**6**	Teaching as Learning: '*Des professeurs – pour écouter*' *Anny King*	83
Section 3		**Rethinking Learner Interaction**	**105**
Chapter	**7**	Oral Output in Online Modules vs. Face-to-Face Classrooms *Susan Hojnacki*	107
Chapter	**8**	Reconceptualising Materials for the Blended Language Learning Environment *Freda Mishan*	123
Chapter	**9**	Developing Activities and Materials to Support Effective Interaction Online *Ildikó Lázár*	139
Section 4		**Case Studies**	**161**
Chapter	**10**	Blending Pedagogy, Technology, Skills and Food: The French Digital Kitchen Project *Paul Seedhouse, Anne Preston and Patrick Olivier*	163

| Chapter | 11 | A Case Study in Language Teacher Education
David Moloney and Anne O'Keeffe | 176 |
| Chapter | 12 | A Case Study in Blended Learning Course Design
Jeanne McCarten and Helen Sandiford | 200 |

Section 5		**The Future of Blended Learning**	**217**
Chapter	13	Blended Learning in a Mobile Context: New Tools, New Learning Experiences? *Gavin Dudeney and Nicky Hockly*	219
Chapter	14	Adaptive Learning *Maria Ofelia Z. San Pedro and Ryan S. Baker*	234
Chapter	15	Where We Are and Going Forward *Michael McCarthy*	248

List of contributors   267
Index   271

ACKNOWLEDGEMENTS

THE EDITOR

I would like to thank Debra Marsh for her editorial support and close collaboration during the early stages of the book's development. I would also like to thank Bryan Fletcher for his pioneering work on blended learning courses and for inspiring me to learn more and to become involved in the world of BL. Jo Timerick played an especially important role in bringing the manuscript together; without her dedicated work the book would not be what it is today. Thanks also go to Karen Momber, Helen Freeman, and Sue Ullstein for their expert guidance and support through the whole project.

Michael McCarthy

THE EDITOR AND PUBLISHERS

The authors and publishers acknowledge the following sources of copyright material and are grateful for the permissions granted. While every effort has been made, it has not always been possible to identify the sources of all the material used, or to trace all copyright holders. If any omissions are brought to our notice, we will be happy to include the appropriate acknowledgements on reprinting and in the next update to the digital edition, as applicable.

TEXT ACKNOWLEDGEMENTS

A. Aycock, C. Garnham, and R. Kaleta for the text on p. 18 adapted from 'Lessons Learned from the Hybrid Course Project' by A. Aycock, C. Garnham, and R. Kaleta, *Teaching with Technology Today*. Copyright © 2002 by A. Aycock. Reproduced by kind permission of A. Aycock; John Wiley & Sons Inc for the text on p. 38 adapted from 'From Language Proficiency to Interactional Competence' by Claire Kramsch, *The Modern Language Journal*. Copyright © 1986 John Wiley & Sons. All rights reserved. Distributed by the Copyright Clearance Center; International House London for the text on p. 46 adapted from 'Teacher Training DVD Series' by David Carr. Copyright © 2006 International House London. Reproduced with permission of International House London; SAGE Publications for the text on p. 55 adapted from 'What We Know About Second Language Acquisition: A Synthesis From Four Perspectives' by L. Quentin Dixon et al., *Review of Educational Research*, 01.02.12. Reproduced with permission of SAGE Publications; Taylor and Francis Group for the text on p. 70 adapted from *Understanding Language Teaching: from Method to Post-Method* by B. Kumaravadivelu. Copyright © 2006 Taylor and Francis Group. All rights reserved. Distributed by the Copyright Clearance Center; Dunedin Academic Press Ltd. for the text on p. 72 adapted from *Language Teaching in Blended Contexts* by Margaret Nicolson, Linda Murphy and Margaret Southgate. Copyright © 2011 Dunedin Academic Press Ltd. Reproduced with permission of Dunedin Academic Press Ltd; Routledge for the text on p. 110 adapted from *Second Language Acquisition: An Introductory Course* by

Susan M. Gass and Larry Selinker. Copyright © 2008 Routledge, an imprint of Taylor and Francis Group. Distributed by the Copyright Clearance Center; Edinburgh University Press for the text on p. 130 adapted from *Materials Development for TESOL* by Freda Mishan and Ivor Timmis. Copyright © 2015 Edinburgh University Press. Reproduced with permission of Edinburgh University Press; Taylor Mali for the quote 'What Teachers Make' from *What Learning Leaves*. Austin, TX, published by Write Bloody Publishing, 2012. Reproduced with permission; Jonathan Feinberg for the Word Cloud on p. 131 created in Wordle application. Reproduced by the kind permission of Jonathan Feinberg; Jossey-Bass for the text on p. 182 adapted from *Deep Learning for a Digital Age* by Van B. Weigel. Copyright © 2002 Jossey-Bass, an imprint of John Wiley & Sons Inc. Distributed by the Copyright Clearance Center; Cambridge University Press for the text on p. 202 adapted from *Touchstone Second Edition Student's Book 3* by Michael McCarthy, Jeanne McCarten and Helen Sandiford. Copyright © 2014 Cambridge University Press. Reproduced with permission of Cambridge University Press; Cambridge University Press for the text on p. 203 adapted from *Touchstone Second Edition Student's Book 3* by Michael McCarthy, Jeanne McCarten and Helen Sandiford. Copyright © 2014 Cambridge University Press. Reproduced with permission of Cambridge University Press; Cambridge University Press for the text on p. 210 adapted from *Touchstone Online* by Michael McCarthy, Jeanne McCarten and Helen Sandiford. Copyright © 2010 Cambridge University Press. Reproduced with permission of Cambridge University Press; Palgrave Macmillan for the text on pp. 220–221 adapted from *Mobile Learning: Languages, Literacies and Culture*. Copyright © 2014 Palgrave Macmillan. Reproduced with permission of Palgrave Macmillan; Nicky Hockly for the text on p. 226 adapted from the IATEFL 2013 conference presentation 'Moving with the times' by Nicky Hockly. Reproduced with permission; Nicky Hockly for the text on pp. 226–227 adapted from 'E-moderation Station blog' by Nicky Hockly. Reproduced with permission; Delta Publishing for the text on pp. 226–227 adapted from *Going mobile: Teaching with hand-held devices* by N. Hockly and G. Dudeney. Copyright © 2014 Delta Publishing. Reproduced with permission of Delta Publishing; Palgrave Macmillan for the text on p. 228 adapted from *Mobile Learning: Languages, Literacies and Culture*. Copyright © 2014 Palgrave Macmillan. Reproduced with permission of Palgrave Macmillan; Pfeiffer for the text on pp. 249–250 adapted from *The Handbook of Blended Learning: Global Perspectives, Local Designs* by Curtis J. Bonk and Charles R. Graham. Copyright © 2006 Pfeiffer, an imprint of John Wiley & Sons Inc. Distributed by the Copyright Clearance Center; Routledge for the text on p. 254 adapted from 'Online teacher development: collaborating in a virtual learning environment' by Pauline Ernest et al., *Computer Assisted Language Learning*. Copyright © 2013 Routledge, an imprint of Taylor and Francis Group. Distributed by the Copyright Clearance Center.

PHOTO ACKNOWLEDGEMENTS

p. 164: Paul Seedhouse; p. 164: LanCook Logo © Anne Preston; p. 167: Paul Seedhouse; p. 168: Paul Seedhouse; p. 169: Paul Seedhouse; p. 170: Paul Seedhouse.

INTRODUCTION

Blended Learning

Michael McCarthy

For centuries teachers the world over have sought to provide the conditions in which their learners can learn. Opinions and practices may differ; what constitutes 'good' conditions and effective learning has long been a matter for lengthy discussion and debate. Today, with the rapid development in the use of technology in our everyday lives and increasingly in teaching and learning, the debate continues to be long and protracted. This said, there is some agreement that technology and globalisation have changed the way people – especially young people – think and learn. There is also agreement that technology does, and indeed should, have a role to play in learning and teaching. However, there are some who see technology as the only solution to all current educational problems, while there are others who are completely opposed to this view and see technology as the major threat to civilisation as we know it and an agent of the 'dumbing-down' of quality education.

This book is about blended learning, and attempts to place the use of technology in language learning and teaching within a context which we hope reassures the sceptics but at the same time illustrates the benefits. This book also aims to curb the, at times, over-enthusiastic embrace of technology and stresses the need to revisit the pedagogical foundations of our understanding of what it means to learn and teach a language.

In a sense, various blends of ways of learning languages have existed side-by-side for a very long time. Learners and teachers look for the best conditions in which to foster learning. Ever since the first student carried around a notebook and continued working outside of class hours, we have been engaging in blended learning. The notebook, the pen and paper were the technologies which enabled learning to continue outside of class time. The components of the blend were called 'classwork' and 'homework', and this type of blended learning has served us well for generations. In the mid-twentieth century, new technologies came along which made it possible to extend learning in different ways outside of the classroom. In the 1960s, language laboratories came to the fore, enabling students to practise listening and speaking in the private environment of the laboratory booth, to imitate models and to work at their own pace. This mix of learning modes had much in common with what we now term blended learning. Later, the development of portable video technologies added the potential of visual learning to existing audio technologies in the multimedia lab. But, generally speaking, these technologies were bolt-on extras that did not have any major effect on what happened during class time.

It was the massive growth in the use of computers in the 1980s and 1990s, and more particularly the arrival of the internet, which took blended learning into completely new territory. The emergence of CALL (computer-assisted language learning) was game changing. The early days of simple programmes allowing learners to complete closed tasks and practice exercises of various kinds soon transformed into the world of sophisticated screen displays, high-definition video, enhanced audio and the ability to do things online, either in real time or in a fashion whereby the student's work could be recorded and monitored electronically (the update, as it were, of the notebook). The expansion of computational power and the ubiquity of the internet subsequently led educational practitioners to envision fundamental and radical changes to the way teaching and learning could be delivered. No longer was it necessary to cram everything in the curriculum into the precious hours of class time. In the case of foreign and second language learning, courses could now be planned in a way that maximised the potential of face-to-face classroom interaction. Elements of 'classroom' work which could equally well or, perhaps even more effectively, be carried out in a computer-mediated environment, were identified and shifted, most typically online and outside of class hours. Thus, what we now understand as blended learning (and hybrid courses, as they are often termed) is not simply a technological issue. Depending on the blend chosen, that is to say depending on the balance between what students do in class and what they do outside of class on computers and online, the pedagogy itself is being rethought.

It is this last preoccupation which is at the heart of this book. Technologies develop at breathtaking speed, particularly in the world of computers and their allied programmes and applications. Human beings also change in their ways of doing things, though probably at a slower pace than the changes which take place in computer technologies. Some things remain stubbornly (or perhaps reassuringly) constant: human beings struggle to learn foreign languages, to break the habits of a lifetime ingrained by their first language, to overcome the seemingly insurmountable obstacles of confronting a new grammar and thousands of new words in the target language, along with new ways of pronouncing words and new challenges in communicating through the medium of the target language and its associated culture(s).

Fortunately, language educators have at their disposal centuries of collective expertise, and, as a student, if you're lucky enough to have a good teacher, such expertise can considerably ease the burden of mastering a new tongue, and the classroom is a good place to concentrate your efforts. Good classrooms are places where human beings collaborate and support each other, where expertise is shared in a humane environment, where pedagogical intervention can offer real shortcuts to knowledge and skill. They are places where teachers and learners react to one another in a moment-by-moment fashion as social animals. The computer and the internet have no such delicate feelings and, at the time of writing, operate dispassionately and with little regard to whether the user is feeling tired, has a headache, is daydreaming, is bored rigid or is struggling and really needs a great deal of sympathy as well as practical help and informational input. Such is the messy, all-too-human world of learning a language in the face-to-face classroom. This brings us squarely to the thorniest of our preoccupations: can the computer-mediated world of online study replicate either partly, wholly or not at all the interactive and sociable world of a good classroom lesson? To answer this question, we must clearly go beyond an obsession with technology and not spend all our time in hot pursuit of what the 'next big thing' or technical buzzword might be.

First and foremost, to achieve best practice in blended language learning, we need to understand, insofar as we can, the complexities of how people acquire second and foreign languages. We may well conclude that some of the aspects of acquiring a second language are best left to happen within the walls of the face-to-face classroom. We may equally conclude that some types of learning, for example the more transmissive types, where new knowledge dominates (for example, accessing the meaning of a new word, reading a set text) can be done quite well outside of the classroom. After all, we have already witnessed widespread abandonment of paper dictionaries in favour of electronic and online dictionaries and people are becoming more and more accustomed to doing their reading on a screen. On the other hand, key elements of acquiring a second language successfully, such as developing strategies for effective learning and the nurturing of motivation and positive attitudes towards the language may be something which the human teacher can do best in direct, face-to-face interaction with students. Yet even here, technology has partly caught up. The advent of social networking in the online environment has meant that teachers and students can continue the conversations which they have in classrooms in online forums, blogs, chat rooms and the like, without time running out and putting an end to things just when they are becoming interesting. All of these issues feed into the decisions which have to be made in designing blended learning programmes. What we stress throughout this book is that such decisions should be pedagogy-led rather than technology-led. We see the technology as facilitating pedagogy, not vice-versa.

Classrooms, therefore, are one of the main focuses of this book, not only from the perspective of teachers and learners interacting but also from the fact that most language learning, whether in class or outside of class, is mediated through language teaching materials of some kind or another. It is therefore not just a problem of recreating in the online environment the kinds of verbal interactions that take place between teachers and students in classrooms, but also one of recreating materials and their use, and, above all, exploiting technology to create new types of materials, new types of interaction and new types of learning experience. In this regard, mobile technology and adaptive learning systems are good examples. On the one hand, smartphones and tablets could simply function as the latest version of the notebook or as a platform for the on-screen display and manipulation of coursebooks and other printed materials. On the other hand, a more fruitful way of viewing mobile technology is to see it as an opportunity for taking learning into new environments, new activities, new ways of generating learning resources, new ways of experiencing the world and new ways of learning. Similarly, adaptive learning systems are becoming more than just automatic error-correcting programmes that instruct the user to do this or that next, but are learning about their users and becoming more and more sensitive to their situations, emotions and needs. The machine is no longer the cold, soulless metal box or hand-held device, but becomes a 'participant' in the interaction that generates new and enhanced learning experiences.

We hope that the chapters of this book will both inform and reassure language teaching professionals of the benefits of blended learning and will offer food for thought for those involved in the design and implementation of blended learning programmes. The book cannot hope to cover everything: if your particular preoccupation is absent from its pages, we apologise, as we do for any shortcomings that remain within it.

SECTION I

CONNECTING THEORIES AND BLENDED LEARNING

A programme of blended learning can provide effective learning and teaching if built on a sound understanding of what constitutes best practice in language learning and teaching in general. Technology can support various learning environments and conditions if integrated seamlessly and in a way that allows pedagogy and technology to support one another smoothly. In this section of the book, we consider broader issues of language learning and teaching in relation to blended learning, considering what we know about language teaching and learning in conventional, face-to-face classrooms and exploring the questions this raises when language learning is transferred to the online and computer-mediated environment.

In **Chapter 1**, McCarthy considers the relevance to blended learning of certain key aspects of second language acquisition (SLA) and examines the question of which features of SLA can be conceived of as operating with equal, greater or lesser efficacy outside of the classroom in a computer-mediated and online environment. SLA not only focuses on strictly linguistic constraints but also recognises the role of psychological, social and cultural factors such as motivation, identity, individual styles and abilities and the effectivity of learning strategies, noticing and the value of feedback. The chapter seeks to lay out the territory for a consideration of how blended learning might be conducted if informed by key concepts in SLA. McCarthy focuses on some of the more challenging insights of SLA, for example, the importance of noticing, the importance of enhanced input, the role of motivation and attitudes and individual differences in language learning. None of these provides straightforward recipes or simple solutions for blended learning, but all should be in the minds of curriculum and materials designers when embarking upon blended programmes and entering into the delicate decisions that have to be made as regards the distribution of resources and activities. McCarthy also stresses the central significance of what happens in typical face-to-face classrooms, where moment-by-moment interaction is skilfully steered by expert, sensitive teachers, and how this mirrors the interactive world outside of the classroom, as evidenced in language corpora. The chapter concludes that some of the less mechanical aspects of language learning may well be replicable in the world of social media, while success in blended learning programmes will undoubtedly depend on collaboration between technology experts and educators, with neither alone holding the key to success.

In **Chapter 2**, Thornbury draws up a 12-point checklist for assessing the 'fitness for purpose' of blended learning programmes. His list expands upon and makes more specific the broader areas of SLA discussed by McCarthy in Chapter 1. He looks at questions such as the existence of a natural order of acquisition, the complexity of language as a system, the nature of input and output, the concept of noticing, the learner's sociocultural context, feedback, peer collaboration, automaticity and fluency, vocabulary learning and retention and the time needed for working on tasks. Every point in Thornbury's list raises challenges for the choices that have to be made in blended learning programmes. For instance, given the unpredictable and non-linear nature of SLA, does the technology take this into account and accommodate learners' goals and pathways? And if language is a complex system, can the technology embrace that complexity and offer learners input that reflects that complexity and possibilities for engaging in output that reflects the system in all its aspects (vocabulary, grammar, phonology, etc.)? Additionally, does the technology foster noticing, and does it offer the support and scaffolding which underpins good learning? The system should also be capable of providing a degree of personalisation, adequate feedback and error correction and remediation of any problems the learner might encounter. Ideally, too, the technological context should include ways of encouraging automatic production and fluency. Thornbury's chapter essentially sets the tone for the ethos of this book: technology should be judged against what we know about language learning and should be the servant of best practice grounded in good learning theory and practice, rather than dominating the learning process.

In **Chapter 3**, Walsh looks at what constitutes the heart of effective classroom interaction and the skills with which good teachers exploit the classroom environment. For Walsh, the interaction which occurs within the classroom is the object of study. The classroom is seen as a conversational world in which interaction and learning are closely tied to one another. It is not just the targeted 'conversation activities' that matter in class, but every exchange between teachers and learners. Walsh argues that the role of teachers is to enhance learning and in order to do this, they need to understand the complex relationship between language, interaction and learning, and their responsibility for aligning the language used and the pedagogical goals, and maximising learning opportunities within that relationship. The interaction that takes place in good classrooms is a sensitively orchestrated conversation which adjusts moment-by-moment and which grasps learning opportunities as they arise. The chapter provides us with strong arguments for carefully considering the when and why of technology use for language learning and provides an excellent pedagogical basis on which content developers for the blended learning context can build and develop their learning resources, as well as acting as a blueprint for the place of blended learning in teacher education programmes. Walsh concludes that some aspects of teacher–pupil interaction can be reflected in computer-mediated learning (e.g., variable wait-time), while other aspects (e.g., the careful scaffolding of learners' speaking turns) may be less suited to the computer-mediated environment.

CHAPTER 1

Issues in Second Language Acquisition in Relation to Blended Learning

Michael McCarthy

INTRODUCTION

This chapter aims to forge links between what is often seen as the more theoretical and/or experimental tradition in applied linguistics and the practical concern of this book: how to combine the best of technology and the best of classroom practice in the environment of Blended Learning (BL) (see also King, Chapter 6, and McCarten and Sandiford, Chapter 12, this volume). The study of Second Language Acquisition (SLA) is a long-established field that has concerned itself with finding out as much as possible about how second languages are acquired, the underlying processes, the problems, the success or failure of encounters with the target language in natural settings or through pedagogical intervention, within the context of the learner. In the design and implementation of BL, the more we can utilise relevant insights from SLA and other sub-disciplines of applied linguistics, the more likely we are to construct the balance within BL programmes (as between class work and computer-mediated work) on firm foundations.

Within the realm of SLA, there is a considerable body of research into what happens in classrooms, how learners interact with their teachers and peers and how this underpins language learning. These considerations lead us to examine, on the one hand, what the prospects are for recreating the classroom-interactive world in a computer-mediated environment and, on the other, which aspects of classroom interaction are best left in the classroom. Additionally, technology has not only made BL possible in terms of learning platforms and computer-mediated language teaching but it has also enabled us to learn more about how language is used and how learners perform in the target language through different types of language corpora. It is the contention of the present chapter that SLA studies, classroom interaction studies and insights from corpus linguistics can assist us greatly in deciding the balance in BL between classroom activity and computer-mediated work.

In bringing in discussion of corpus linguistics, the present chapter acknowledges both the pros and cons of applying corpus information to language pedagogy (for further discussion, see McCarthy, 1998; O'Keeffe et al., 2007). On the positive side, there has been a transition from the days when corpora were considered to be an obscure pursuit with few practical applications outside of the creation of dictionaries to the present when insights from corpus linguistics are having an ever-increasing influence on the design of teaching materials, from grammar- and vocabulary-learning materials to whole courses, and where learner corpora are more and more being seen as valuable sources of evidence for language development. Written corpora are highly influential and written texts will continue to play a big role in BL programmes as the online world is still dominated by written media (emails, blogs, web pages, chat, social media postings, etc.). However, the greatest transformation in our understanding of and attitudes towards language use has come from spoken corpora, and as communicative language teaching places great emphasis on speaking, the question is: can we incorporate truly interactive speaking into the online element of a BL programme? For this reason, the focus of the present chapter will be more towards the challenges of online speaking and the possibilities and (current) limitations of 'flipping' (moving things typically done in the face-to-face classroom to the online environment) classroom speaking so that it can be done outside of class via online work.

What spoken corpora reveal in terms of the nature of human-to-human interaction both outside and inside classrooms is most relevant to this particular discussion. The greatest challenge is how information extracted from spoken data (both conversational and classroom-originated) can be transferred and transformed from face-to-face contexts to technology-mediated ones, an issue which McCarten and Sandiford (Chapter 12, this volume) address directly. Technology is important in two ways to language learning, since it is not only driving developments in language learning, but also spoken language is in general, at a quickening pace, becoming mediated through technologies such as smartphones, video calling and conferencing, vlogs, and so on. We can still rely on a great deal of e-learning being carried out in the form of writing (online assignments, quizzes, blogs, and so on), but it would be complacent to downplay the growing importance of spoken communication on a global scale, a trend which will only become stronger. The age of the carefully-crafted business letter delivered on good-quality paper is rapidly receding from our collective memory as speaking skills make ever-increasing demands on the language teaching agenda.

As well as insights from corpus linguistics, we now have the benefit of more than two decades of experience of computer-assisted language learning (CALL), a broad term covering any situation in which language-learning activities are carried out on computers, and what happens at the human-machine interface (see Chambers, 2010, and the articles in Thorne and Payne, 2005, respectively). Despite technological limitations, CALL practitioners were interested from early days in recreating human interaction as far as possible via student-computer activity (Fischer, 2008). Although early CALL may now appear impoverished in terms of its screen displays, speed and restricted range of activities, the backroom technologies that facilitated it have since progressed in leaps and bounds. The introduction of tablets, smartphones and their associated apps has transformed the potential for machine-based, mobile language learning, creating new types of learning experiences in addition to transferring existing ones to mobile devices (see Patten et al., 2006; Mueller et al., 2012; Dudeney and Hockly, Chapter 13, this volume). CALL has also joined forces with corpus linguistics in the development of data-driven learning (DDL), i.e., activities where learners are directly exposed to corpus material, through which inductive learning (where learners are presented with particular examples and asked to make rules or generalisations about usage) is fostered.

DDL, like other technology-based approaches to language teaching, has its advantages and disadvantages (Allan, 2006; Boulton, 2009). Nonetheless, it is still relevant to certain domains of BL in terms of the types of acquisition it promotes or underpins and will need to be considered as a potential feature of the 'flipped' classroom (the system of choices whereby activities traditionally done in classrooms are 'flipped' or transferred to the domain of homework and self-study, and vice versa – see Johnson and Marsh, Chapter 4, this volume). In this case, broadly speaking, DDL presents a new way of studying (i.e., reading and interpreting computer-generated concordances) and an increased awareness of how language works in real contexts. However, at the very least, DDL demands considerable training and practice in a novel way of thinking about language before students can work comfortably and independently with it. Success in DDL is often related to student level, with higher-level and academically-oriented students tending to benefit most (e.g., Poole, 2012).

We have, therefore, a potential triangulation of evidence with which to inform decisions about BL (see Figure 1.1).

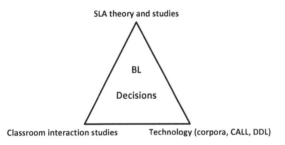

Figure 1.1 Triangle of Evidence to Inform Decisions about Blended Learning

At one point of the triangle we have a range of SLA research and theories; at another we have classroom interaction studies, which share some common ground with mainstream SLA but which rest on their own paradigms, often rooted in discourse analysis (the study of language beyond the sentence-level) and conversation analysis (the study of how conversations develop, how speakers take turns, and so on). The third point of the triangle is what we know about spoken interaction both outside and inside classrooms from corpus analysis and technology-mediated language learning (e.g., CALL and DDL). Trading these three points off against one another will, it is hoped, give us a clearer picture of what the criteria for best practice in BL might look like.

APPROACHES TO SLA IN RELATION TO BL

Late-twentieth century SLA researchers were often wedded to the belief that SLA should be a natural-scientific endeavour, with rigorous laboratory-style experimentation, control of variables, pre-testing and post-testing and rational interpretation of empirical data based on objective statistical analysis (for further discussion, see the special issue of the journal *Studies in Second Language Acquisition,* 1997, 19, (2). Many such studies reported on the incremental acquisition of grammatical morphemes (e.g., verb-tenses, articles) (Pica, 1983; Larsen-Freeman and Long, 1991) and vocabulary growth (Coady and Huckin, 1997; Laufer, 1998; Milton, 2009, 2010), two areas considered to be (readily) measurable and at the core of SLA. Additional factors that have come under scrutiny include:

- whether instruction is explicitly or only implicitly focused on language forms (Doughty and Williams, 1998; Ellis, 2002);
- the efficacy of corrective feedback (what the teacher or the machine can give back to students in response to their efforts) (Lyster and Ranta, 1997; Russell, 2009);
- attention and 'noticing' as a first step to acquisition (Schmidt, 1990, 1993);
- cross-linguistic transfer effects (Sharwood Smith and Kellerman, 1986);
- how L1 and L2 systems interrelate (Cook, 2008).

All of these go hand in hand with factors affecting the design and balance of BL programmes and what can be done outside of classrooms or inside them and what can be 'flipped' from one to the other.

As well as the question of whether fixed orders of acquisition of grammatical morphemes are a reality, scholars have attempted to ascertain whether there is a relationship between learning fixed formulaic expressions and later emergence of rule systems (see the discussion in Ellis and Shintani, 2013: 63ff.). However, the sequence of acquisition of grammatical morphemes is complex with a number of factors influencing the sequence, e.g., frequency of input and exposure to the target morphemes, semantic complexity and L1 influences (Goldschneider and DeKeyser, 2002). Thornbury (Chapter 2, this volume) urges considerable caution in this matter, bringing to bear evidence that acquisition need not be linear and can be quite varied, sometimes going backward as well as forward. By their nature, individual differences make it difficult/risky to make generalisations, although it may become apparent through careful analysis that there might be some suggestive trends which could be more reliably taken advantage of (Cook, 2008). Concrete evidence of a transition from the learning of fixed formulae to rule formation may be even more elusive.

INDIVIDUAL LEARNER DIFFERENCES

Individual differences are of great relevance to BL and have both positive and negative implications for how BL proceeds. On the positive side, as we have noted, individuals can do things successfully in their own way and own time outside of the collective pressures of the face-to-face classroom. However, individual differences among learners are numerous, and may include:

- age and gender;
- learning styles and strategic abilities (Dörnyei, 2006), including learning techniques and communicative strategies such as guessing, requesting clarification, avoidance of the use of what are perceived as difficult forms;
- emotional factors such as motivation, stress and anxiety;
- a sense of personal identity (for a detailed survey of these factors, see Ehrman et al., 2003).

These factors may present overwhelming obstacles to the designer of the out-of-class elements of a BL programme, in that computer-mediated activity by an individual working without a teacher cannot be monitored and responded to with the same sensitivity as would be second nature to the good, caring classroom practitioner, even though machine-based adaptive intelligent tutoring systems designed to maximise individual feedback will undoubtedly develop and be refined in the future (Wang and Liao, 2011; San Pedro and Baker, Chapter 14, this volume).

The literature on individual differences frequently stresses learning strategies and learning styles and the superiority of interlocked and targeted strategies. Learning strategies, it is held, can be taught, whether directly and separately or embedded in other language learning activities. O'Malley and Chamot (1990), who give a most detailed account of learning strategies and strategy training, highlight the importance of teachers and students interacting, with teachers providing scaffolding for the successful development of strategies. This suggests that the most successful strategy training will take place in face-to-face classrooms but it does not exclude the potential for well-constructed strategy training programmes for computer-mediated use (Kohler, 2002). The importance of consideration of the individual learner working outside of the class and his or her strengths and weaknesses is reflected in the fact that even relatively closed computer-mediated exercises may fall foul of lack of motivation, lack of preparedness, poorly developed learning strategies and lack of understanding of the learning opportunities provided by the technology on the part of the learner.

THE CONCEPT OF 'NOTICING'

One area clearly of relevance to the world of the student working either in class or alone, online, out of class with no 'live' or face-to-face encounters with a teacher, or in computer-mediated interaction with peers, is the value of 'noticing' (observing important features and consciously paying attention to the forms and meanings of the language one is working with) and attention in enhancing language acquisition. The idea of noticing is usually discussed within the more general umbrella of the role of consciousness in language learning and its related notions of explicit versus implicit knowledge. Mid-twentieth-century face-to-face classrooms typically cast the teacher in the role of transmitter of explicit knowledge about grammatical rules and the meanings and uses of language forms. Latter twentieth-century methodologies such as communicative teaching via 'notional-functional' (an emphasis on meaning and communicative function) or task-based pedagogy often played down the role of such conscious attention to language input and production, with the assumption that a good deal of learning would simply occur implicitly, though in reality, most common-sense teaching never adhered to one extreme or the other. Thornbury, in Chapter 2 of this volume, sees potential for software development to enhance the potential for noticing in computer-mediated environments where the student cannot rely on a teacher to direct and guide the noticing activity.

Recent decades have seen a reassessment of explicit focus on language and the advocacy of consciousness-raising activities in the classroom alongside more implicit types of syllabuses. Ellis (1993) argues for such a combination and sees the learner's task as noticing the gap between formal features of the language and those they use themselves. In Schmidt's (1990; 1993) view of consciousness, a distinction is drawn between 'intentionality' (put simply, the learner's desires/aims to find out about the target language whether inside or outside of the class) and 'incidental learning', which may occur without intent. What the learner notices in the input becomes the 'intake', which is the raw material upon which the acquisition processes operate. Schmidt himself famously kept a journal of what he noticed while learning Brazilian Portuguese, and what he noticed correlated well with what could be shown as that which he had learnt. But noticing also requires attention in second language learning, not just spotting things randomly, and what can be noticed depends on the nature and amount of input the learner experiences. What is noticed is then taken in to become part of hypothesis formation and induction.

Noticing is another of those activities which would seem to function best when assisted and scaffolded by good teachers in conventional classrooms helping learners towards learning opportunities. Walsh (2006: 30) sees 'quality interaction' in the classroom as enhancing opportunities for noticing and suggests that the richest moments for noticing are when the teacher is directing the class in what he terms 'skills and systems mode' (Ibid.: 74), where there is a direct focus on target language forms (see below).

THE LEARNER'S SOCIAL AND CULTURAL CONTEXT

Criticism of natural-science-driven, positivist approaches to SLA has come from scholars who view SLA as a humanistic discipline, one in which the learner and the processes of acquisition cannot and should not be detached from the social and cultural context. This sociocultural approach to SLA has been led by scholars such as Lantolf, Appel and Thorne (Lantolf and Appel, 1994; Lantolf, 2006; Lantolf and Thorne, 2006; Lantolf and Poehner, 2014) and goes hand in hand with theories of language socialisation (Duff and Hornberger, 2008). In these paradigms, the language learner cannot be perceived and treated as a laboratory subject but is a social being who builds upon existing knowledge and thrives under guidance and scaffolding during the experience of acquiring a language as a social and cultural resource. What we need a fuller understanding of is the nature of the computer-mediated world as a social and cultural environment and how its sociocultural practices may differ from (but not necessarily be inferior to) the sociocultural practices of the conventional face-to-face world.

The importance of the learner's sense of social and cultural identity and the role of classrooms in nurturing that sense are not to be underestimated. That humans are defined by a single identity has been challenged in the social sciences, with identity increasingly seen as made of multiple aspects which are flexible, dynamic and continuously reconstructed through interaction. National and ethnic identities are proposed as existing alongside identities such as those that can be triggered by language use (Spolsky, 1999: 181). Additionally, it is interesting to observe whether individuals feel comfortable with particular group-identities or prefer to distance themselves from them, a question relevant to classroom communities, online communities and wider social communities (Norton, 2000; Toohey, 2000; Maybin, 2006; Block, 2007). Motivation may also be affected by sense of self, a preoccupation addressed in the papers in Dörnyei and Ushioda (2009). Thus, activities such as noticing and giving attention cannot be seen as taking place in a mental space divorced from the sociocultural context of the learner, from the situations in which language is mediated within and without classrooms, from the scaffolding provided by teachers and peers and from the very sense of self and the aspirational self that the learner possesses. These values need to be retained in good language pedagogy and are probably best nurtured in the face-to-face classroom or at least in the context of online social networking among teachers and learners, rather than in the isolated domain of the student working alone on a task that merely gives machine-driven feedback.

To conclude this discussion of some of the preoccupations of SLA, we might say that what we know about learners is that they are complex beings who bring to the language learning task a mixture of factors, some relating to knowledge, skills and abilities and some related to personal, social, cultural and emotive aspects. Classrooms and student communities possess accumulated contexts and identities, manifested in an ability to deal with issues face-to-face, through sensitive, real-time adjustments to the responses and reactions of teachers and peers (see Thornbury, Chapter 2, this volume, for further discussion).

SLA IN RELATION TO COMPUTER-MEDIATED LANGUAGE LEARNING

PROCESS OR PRODUCT?

SLA scholars are concerned with how people acquire second languages and how best we can understand the underlying processes of language acquisition (VanPatten and Benati, 2010: 2). While not everything that falls within the domain of SLA may be relevant to the concerns of BL, issues such as typical patterns of grammatical acquisition, rates of vocabulary growth, the role of noticing in language learning and the role of feedback influence the choice of the balance of activity between the classroom and out of class computer-mediated study and what should and should not be 'flipped' in flipped classrooms.

We might begin by looking at the fundamental question of what it is that SLA quantitative experiments or qualitative studies observe. Is it the processes of acquisition or only the products? And how does one get from conscious processes to unconscious ones that may occur during acquisition? Clearly, the more we can understand processes, the better we can inform our decisions as regards which processes can be recreated in the online world. Some commonly used ways of attempting to access process include classroom observation protocols (where a researcher observes a class, perhaps with a checklist of things to record), concurrent think-aloud protocols (where learners speak aloud the thoughts going through their minds as they grapple with the language), interrupting students during tasks to find out what they are doing or thinking and retrospective verbal reports after task completion (Færch and Kasper, 1987). Yet such self-reporting can be criticised as separating what should really be considered as unified: thinking about and acting in a second language may be part of a unitary process (as Seedhouse et al., in Chapter 10, this volume, may well lead us to conclude). For example, there is considerable debate over whether concurrent thinking aloud during tasks can actually change mental processes rather than merely articulate them (Bowles, 2010). Furthermore, in sociocultural approaches to SLA (which stress the integration of social and cultural elements in learning), 'private speech' (speaking aloud to oneself to regulate one's own thoughts and actions) and 'inner speech' ('thinking' language rather than pronouncing it), as discussed by de Guerrero (2005) and Lantolf and Thorne (2006: Chapter 4), are considered no less important than 'social speech' (speech directed at others). Private speech data provide a window on thought processes that think-aloud language directed at someone else may complicate and can provide information concerning learners' attention to a task both in experimental settings and in classrooms. Private speech is thus seen as a crucial element in the process whereby features of the target language are internalised (Ohta, 2001: Chapter 2; Lantolf and Thorne, 2006; Lee, 2008). But can BL practice capitalise upon such insights and, by the same token, can data from BL environments contribute new insights to our understanding of acquisition processes inherent in different kinds of language-learning experiences?

USING TECHNOLOGY TO 'UNCOVER' THE PROCESSES OF SLA

The various types of thinking aloud (whether directed at someone else or private) can be observed both in the verbal world of the classroom but also in a proxy form in synchronous computer-mediated chat (SCMC, which are real-time exchanges of online chat activities) and in the writing of learner journals and blogs. Furthermore, these elements might offer invaluable evidence of self-regulated behaviour in the computer-mediated elements of the flipped classroom. Unlike traditional classroom-observation protocols, these provide a comprehensive and permanent record of activity.

Another avenue to potentially access learning processes is via the capability of learning platforms to monitor in real time and in fine detail what students do when working with materials (Chun, 2013; Collentine, 2013). A complete record can be had of how long students spend on each item in an exercise or task, how many times they repeat it, how often they get things right or wrong, how long they devote to each study session and so on, all of which may shed light on ongoing, underlying processes during learning activity. However, interpretation of such data must proceed with care. Weinberg (2007), for example, shows that students spending least time on activities are not necessarily the lowest achievers and, vice versa, those dedicating most time are not necessarily high achievers. Nonetheless, such information can provide extra insight that might be difficult or impossible to obtain through face-to-face classroom observation or conventional experimental protocols. The time-stamped evidence of activity on the computer or mobile device may not be sufficient in itself to elucidate the processes of acquisition but it is a robust addition to other available instruments for observing learners at work, grappling with the language and recording learning outcomes.

Time-stamped evidence of activity will, however, tell us little about affective factors (factors to do with feelings and emotions), learning styles and motivation (Barrs, 2010; Lai and Gu, 2011), but it may provide indications of points where motivation and concentration have possibly flagged or increased and information about which activities seem to have presented greatest difficulty. Difficulty of processing is a key topic in SLA and is considered to be among the factors which hinder acquisition (see Han, 2004: 116–118). Thus, indications of possible difficulty provided by time-stamped evidence of numerous students working online may point to an underlying issue in the teaching materials that will need further investigation. If difficulties persist, then the input probably needs some kind of remedial attention, or 'input enhancement' (modifying the material to make it more accessible), an important concept in SLA (Sharwood Smith, 1993; Chapelle, 1998). Such enhancement might involve adding greater emphasis to target items or increased practice material, but, once again, decisions should not be taken on the evidence of computer-mediated work only. Hwu (2004), who offers practical examples of technology-based input enhancement in video materials, states the importance of taking into account learner difficulty as observed in the face-to-face classroom too. One of the advantages of BL is that it offers researchers two different but complementary windows through which to observe learning.

Online work also offers the possibility of gathering evidence from the broader social networking that often accompanies it, including SCMC data, learner journals, blogs and vlogs, text messages, emails, chat rooms and forums. Students reluctant to offer up their observations, feelings and opinions in class or in an experimental setting may well feel less inhibited in the online world (though see Stevenson and Liu, 2010, for a discussion of the pluses and minuses of social networking in online language learning). SCMC data, in particular, offer the possibility of observing input-output loops as students negotiate meaning and solve problems during task activity and modify their own output, offering a potential window on real-time learning processes (Blake, 2000; Collentine, 2013).

LIMITATIONS OF USING TECHNOLOGY TO REVEAL PROCESSES IN SLA

A further difficulty in observing SLA processes in computer-mediated environments is the fact that CALL practitioners have pointed out the lack of a one-to-one correspondence between technological literacy and the ability to maximise the use of technology for learning and positive learning outcomes (Kirkwood, 2004, 2006; Kirkwood and Price, 2005). There is evidence at the time of writing that, when given the choice, learners utilise technology for a limited range of language-learning activities, such as listening, writing and vocabulary exercises (Stevenson and Liu, 2010; Çelik et al., 2012) and that they under-use or prefer not to use at all some capabilities of online learning and participation (Hampel and Pleines, 2013), though this may change in the future as the population becomes more adept and at ease with technology.

The basic problem, therefore, would seem to be that technological capabilities may assist us in measuring the amount of time and effort spent on learning activities and the success or otherwise in completing activities but may yet not give us enough insight into SLA processes intrinsic in computer-mediated language-learning activity, especially in relation to affective, strategic and motivational factors and attitudes towards technology-based learning. What data we can obtain with relative ease may not provide a full picture in relation to language learning activities beyond the basic ones of grammar and vocabulary, especially in areas such as the development of interactional competence (see Walsh, Chapter 3, this volume) or rhetorical (above-sentence-level) skills in writing. The combination of technology-based data and other, more conventional types of data and observation offered by BL programmes may, nonetheless, provide richer insight than any one type of data alone.

CLASSROOM INTERACTION AND SPOKEN CORPORA

Ever since the early days of the development of classroom discourse analysis (Sinclair and Coulthard, 1975), scholars have attempted to tease out the relationship between the discourse of teachers and learners and what, if anything, is being learnt and how. Although learners may well practise and learn a great deal through written work (whether conventionally on paper or computer-mediated), for most school-based learners in the world, what is said in the classroom remains central to the learning experience. By examining classroom transcripts, researchers have attempted to gauge the degree to which language learning in the classroom can represent an authentic encounter with the language of the world outside and to what extent teacher-student dialogue and student-student dialogue promote language acquisition. Studies have often focused on the degree to which negotiation for meaning in student-student tasks promotes acquisition (Wong-Fillmore, 1982, 1985; Johnson, 1995). It is clear that learners can assist one another in the process of language development (e.g., Ohta 2001: 124), even though lower-level learners may remain particularly dependent upon teachers before they can efficiently and effectively carry out peer-to-peer tasks (Ibid.: 269).

MODES OF INTERACTION WITHIN THE SECOND LANGUAGE CLASSROOM

The question of how teachers manage and run their classes and how that affects and promotes learning is a crucial one (Johnson, 1995; Kumaravadivelu, 1999; Seedhouse, 2004; Walsh, 2006, 2011 and Chapter 3, this volume). Effective teachers make moment-by-moment decisions about what is happening and what should happen in classes and switch, with sensitivity and aplomb, from one mode of interaction with their students to another, back and forth in a carefully choreographed performance designed both to manage with efficiency and efficacy the available learning time and to spot and exploit learning opportunities. Thornbury (Chapter 2, this volume) sees the teacher as providing just the right amount of support on a 'just in time' basis.

Walsh (2006), basing his study on a corpus of some 100,000 words of transcribed EFL classroom interactions, sees the different strategic behaviours of teachers as falling into four distinct 'modes' of interaction, whose purpose is to align language use with pedagogical goals to optimise teaching and learning (see also Seedhouse, 1994; Evison, 2013). Sometimes, the teacher will choose to engage in managing and organising the classroom, other times the focus is on the materials and their exploitation, other times the teacher may choose to focus on the system of the target language itself, its rules and ways of using them, and yet other times the teacher will encourage the students in genuine interaction. In this last mode, students can express themselves and their experiences and practise fluent production within the context of the classroom rather than in the outside world, where opportunities for interaction in the target language may be rare. The good teacher is also constantly monitoring the overall classroom situation and takes action to ensure that it creates an enjoyable and motivating environment (Dörnyei, 2007).

The movements from one classroom mode to another are made moment-by-moment and are principally controlled by the teacher; there is not necessarily a pre-ordained script and fluidity is all. This fluidity of interaction is best observed through discourse analyses (looking for patterns and structure in the interaction) and/or conversational analyses (focusing on the turn-by-turn unfolding of the interaction) of classroom transcripts, wherein classroom language is seen, like non-classroom conversations, to unfold turn-by-turn between speakers and listeners, where the construction of the discourse manifests as a joint activity, is goal-oriented and is organised on the content and interpersonal plains simultaneously. In such 'live' interactions, social and cultural contexts are both created and reinforced, jointly, by all the participants, sharing common goals.

COMPARISON OF CLASSROOM INTERACTION MODES WITH GENERAL INTERACTION

Insights from the analysis of classroom interaction share common ground with insights from general conversational studies, and indeed Markee (2008) has argued that conversation analysis techniques are key to understanding how linguistic competence and interactional competence emerge in second language classrooms. In adding the power of large-scale corpus data to the analysis of talk, spoken corpus studies reveal time after time the hard work that interactants engage in, the way conversational flow is created and maintained and how relationships among speakers are forged and reinforced to create successful communication.

Corpus studies reveal how speakers construct their turns to acknowledge and link them with previous speakers' turns (Tao, 2003; McCarthy, 2010), how speakers signal and project assumed shared worlds (O'Keeffe, 2006; Evison et al., 2007), how they draw on a repertoire of response tokens that simultaneously acknowledge and engage socially and emotionally with the contributions of other speakers (McCarthy, 2003; O'Keeffe and Adolphs, 2008), how they co-construct utterances in an apparently seamless way (Clancy and McCarthy, 2014), how discourse markers and other common, small words organise talk into coherent and meaningful segments (Aijmer, 2002), and so on. In casual conversations, the goals may be purely social; in classrooms, the goals are pedagogically focused but are often achieved more readily if participants put one another at their ease. Recreating in the computer-mediated world the conditions under which human beings typically converse in their daily lives is clearly a serious challenge to educators, especially where the machine is the 'listener/recipient'.

CAN 'MODE-SWITCHING' BE EXPLOITED ONLINE?

It is not easy to see at a glance how the out-of-class elements of language learning in BL can recreate such moment-by-moment responsiveness to the immediate context, especially that which is triggered through the teacher's experienced antenna, telling him/her to shift the focus to another mode, or else to persist within a mode, or to spot and exploit a golden learning opportunity and generally to promote an enjoyable experience. In this respect, it is perhaps over-simplistic to say that managerial, materials and systems and skills modes may best be transferred to the non-classroom zone of learning in order to ease up time for engagement in genuine interaction in the face-to-face classroom.

The point about mode-switching is that it responds to real-time events and the pedagogical opportunities which they offer; relocating any mode to a computer-mediated world may weaken its potential, though practical and institutional demands may, in the final analysis, rule the day. Once more though, the more fluid interactional world of social networking and SCMC may provide scope for recreating the liveliness and real-time feel of classrooms in cyberspace, especially where teachers are present as interactants. Successful teacher-student chat forums and blog-/vlog-spaces often possess positive features of the animated, scaffolded and fluid dialogue of the well-managed physical classroom (see Yang, 2009; McHaney, 2011: 101–103). Additionally, websites where users can create virtual worlds and alternative identities for themselves using avatars (sometimes called multi-user virtual environments or MUVEs) offer an immersive experience which teachers and learners can exploit for language learning. Voice chat, instant messaging and text chat can be utilised in virtual worlds and the liveliness of the classroom can, in some senses at least, be recreated, along with a keen sense of identity and community (de Freitas, 2008; Wang et al., 2012). Alongside the creation of an immersive experience and the sheer fun of virtual worlds and the motivation they create, sound pedagogical principles and intervention are still important. In cyberspace, the teacher has a particular role and responsibility in fostering learning opportunities as well as supporting a sense of community among learners (Hampel and Stickler, 2005).

Conclusion

This chapter has attempted to bring various disparate threads together. Examining key areas of SLA has led to the general conclusion that some aspects of language learning may work satisfactorily within the range of choices that have to be made in the design of BL programmes and decisions as to what can be 'flipped' one way or another as between class work and computer-mediated work, especially homework and self-study. Input enhancement, feedback and noticing can all be conceptualised in some way or another in the computer-mediated world within the scope of controlled materials. Meanwhile, the more socio-culturally and personally-oriented aspects of language acquisition may best be retained within the face-to-face classroom or else fostered via the opportunities generated by social networking and, in the (near?) future, via increased sophistication of intelligent adaptive feedback systems, which will 'learn' the behaviours of the system's users, will become sensitive to their interests, their strengths and weaknesses and their moods and emotions (see San Pedro and Baker, Chapter 14, this volume).

The chapter has also considered what happens in language classrooms where teachers manage their lessons with sensitivity and build an efficient world where organisational concerns operate side-by-side with the humane objectives of raising and maintaining motivation, creating good interaction, good relationships and opportunities for learning through the careful merging of classroom interaction with pedagogical goals. It was also argued that the successful classroom is essentially a conversational world which reflects what non-classroom spoken corpora tell us about how human beings interact and engage with one another.

Recreating the best of classroom practices, the best of insight into language acquisition processes and the best of person-to-person communication in the computer-mediated time of the flipped classroom is clearly neither an easy nor a straightforward task. But technology may provide both hope and solutions, in two ways. Firstly, educators are becoming increasingly engaged with the potential of online social networking and may see as yet unforeseen opportunities to exploit it in the service of recreating interaction, fostering learning and building educational communities. Secondly, as Aycock et al. (2002) suggest, simply trying to replicate classroom courses in blended courses will not produce the breakthroughs that are needed to address the challenges we have discussed; these will come when teachers and educators collaborate with technology experts to explore and create new learning modes and experiences. The project embarked upon by Seedhouse et al. (Chapter 10, this volume) is a good example of such collaboration leading to a novel outcome while still constrained by the parameters of language pedagogy (in their case, task-based learning) and SLA principles (e.g., noticing). Mobile learning is one such area where the learning experience and acquisition processes will certainly be transformed into new domains and not just simply be an opportunity to dump the course book onto a phone or tablet screen (Dudeney and Hockly, Chapter 13, this volume). Adaptive learning (San Pedro and Baker, Chapter 14, this volume) will undoubtedly also have a great transformational impact on both areas.

From the evidence we do currently have, it appears that the face-to-face classroom context, is (currently) still the best place to develop and deal with humanistic aspects of language learning such as motivation, attention and noticing, giving tactful and carefully phrased individual as well as group feedback, underpinning the growth of learning strategies and respecting the learner's emotional space, aspirations and identity, all under the guidance of sensitive, experienced teachers. However, cyberspace offers three potential additions to the language-teaching armoury:

- opportunities for learners to work at core features of the language at their own pace, albeit with automatic feedback or limited adaptive feedback, with everything time-stamped and recorded for later appraisal;
- contexts in which learners can negotiate meaning and develop and modify hypotheses about the target language (e.g., through SCMC);
- a space where learners can explore more intra-personal and interpersonal aspects of the learning experience and can forge identities and membership to greater or lesser degrees within online communities, whether tutor-mediated or not.

Aycock et al. (2002) end their account of BL (or 'hybrid courses' as they and others refer to such programmes) on an optimistic note that echoes some of the conclusions of this chapter, that is to say that classrooms and the computer-mediated world can benefit from one another. What we know about classroom interaction and what we know about peer interaction and teacher-student interaction in social networking may complement each other in unexpected ways. They conclude thus:

> Contrary to many instructors' initial concerns, the hybrid approach invariably increases student engagement and interactivity in a course. One of the primary fears expressed by faculty about hybrid courses is that they will lose contact with their students. Just the opposite occurs. Hybrid courses encourage instructors to develop new ways to engage their students online and foster online communities. This greater online interaction will emerge in the classroom as well.

Indeed, one thing which is emerging from research into BL environments is how peer-to-peer interaction in the social space of task-completion, blogs/vlogs, chat and SCMC creates and maintains a strong sense of community, distinct but perhaps as strong as the camaraderie of the face-to-face classroom (Brooks, 2013). There is evidence, too, in broad SLA terms, to suggest that more effective language learning may occur when students work together in small groups on computer-mediated activities than if they work alone or in large groups on the same tasks (Lin et al., 2013). These and other issues are further touched upon in the concluding chapter of this book, where we look again at factors that might underpin best practice in BL in the coming years.

Institutional pressures to expand BL may tempt us to abandon the quest to understand face-to-face classrooms and the SLA processes that take place within them, and to modify our research manifestos to concentrate upon the online world, but that would be a mistake. Continuing awareness and development of our understanding of the processes underlying SLA and the character of everyday human interaction in and outside of classrooms, along with an expanded research agenda in the area of spoken corpora must go hand in hand with technological developments and our observations of what happens when students sit down in front of the computer to tackle the computer-mediated elements of their courses. In that way and that way only will BL successfully evolve.

Suggested Resources

Dörnyei, Z., & Ushioda, E. (Eds.) (2009). *Motivation, Language Identity and the L2 Self*. Bristol: Multilingual Matters.

Ellis, R., & Shintani, N. (2013). *Exploring Language Pedagogy Through Second Language Acquisition Research*. London: Routledge.

Lantolf, J. P., & Poehner, M. E. (2014). *Sociocultural Theory and the Pedagogical Imperative in L2 Education. Vygotskian Praxis and the Theory/Practice Divide*. New York: Routledge.

O'Keeffe, A., McCarthy, M. J., & Carter, R. (2007). *From Corpus to Classroom. Language Use and Language Teaching*. Cambridge: Cambridge University Press.

VanPatten, B., & Benati, A. G. (2010). *Key Terms in Second Language Acquisition*. London: Continuum.

Walsh, S. (2006). *Investigating Classroom Discourse*. Abingdon: Routledge.

Discussion Questions

1. Do your students have enough speaking time in class? Does everyone get a chance to speak? How could BL help improve speaking time for you?

2. How important is language awareness and 'noticing'? Do you try to foster it in your lessons? How?

3. Do you use any of the following to communicate with your students? Why? Why not?

- email
- blogs/vlogs
- text messages
- social media platforms
- Twitter
- Skype
- chat rooms

4. What types of exercises, tasks or other activities are best suited for online work for your students?

References

Aijmer, K. (2002). *English Discourse Particles. Evidence from a Corpus*. Amsterdam/Philadelphia: John Benjamins.

Allan, R. (2006). *Data-driven Learning and Vocabulary: Investigating the Use of Concordances with Advanced Learners of English*. Trinity College, Dublin: Centre for Language and Communications Studies.

Aycock, A., Garnham, G., & Kaleta, R. (2002). Lessons learned from the Hybrid Course Project. *Teaching with Technology Today*, 8(6), 9–21.

Barrs, K. (2010). What factors encourage high levels of student participation in a self-access centre? *Studies in Self-Access Learning Journal*, 1(1), 10–16.

Blake, R. (2000). Computer mediated communication: A window on L2 Spanish interlanguage. *Language Learning & Technology*, 4(1), 120–136.

Block, D. (2007). *Second Language Identities*. London: Continuum.

Boulton, A. (2009). Testing the limits of data-driven learning: Language proficiency and training. *ReCALL*, 21(1), 37–54.

Bowles, M. (2010). *The Think-Aloud Controversy in Second Language Research*. London: Routledge.

Brooks, C. F. (2013). 'Don't even trip, u did your part': Analysing community in online student talk. *Classroom Discourse*, 4(2), 168–189.

Çelik, S., Arkin, E., & Sabriler, D. (2012). EFL learners' use of ICT for self-regulated learning. *The Journal of Language and Linguistic Studies*, 8(2), 98–118.

Chambers, A. (2010). Computer-Assisted Language Learning: Mapping the territory. *Language Teaching*, 43(1), 113–122.

Chapelle, C. (1998). Multimedia CALL: Lessons to be learned from research on instructed SLA. *Language Learning & Technology*, 2(1), 22–34.

Chun, D. (2013). Contributions of tracking user behavior to SLA research. *CALICO Journal*. Special issue, Learner-Computer Interaction in Language Education: A Festschrift in Honor of Robert Fischer, 256–262.

Clancy, B., & McCarthy, M. J. (2014). The pragmatics of co-constructed turn taking. In C. Rühlemann & K. Aijmer (Eds.), *Corpus Pragmatics: A Handbook*. Cambridge: Cambridge University Press.

Coady, J., & Huckin, T. (Eds.) (1997). *Second-Language Vocabulary Acquisition: A Rationale for Pedagogy*. Cambridge: Cambridge University Press.

Collentine, K. (2013). Using tracking technologies to study the effects of linguistic complexity in CALL input and SCMC output. *CALICO Journal*. Special issue, Learner-Computer Interaction in Language Education: A Festschrift in Honor of Robert Fischer, 46–65.

Cook, V. (2008). *Second Language Learning and Language Teaching*. Abingdon: Routledge.

Dörnyei, Z. (2006). Individual differences in second language acquisition. *AILA Review*, 19, 42–68.

Dörnyei, Z. (2007). Creating a motivating classroom environment. In J. Cummins & C. Davison (Eds.), *The International Handbook of English Language Teaching* (pp. 639–651). New York: Springer.

Dörnyei, Z., & Ushioda, E., (Eds.) (2009). *Motivation, Language Identity and the L2 Self*. Bristol: Multilingual Matters.

Doughty, C., & Williams, J., (Eds.) (1998). *Focus on Form in Classroom Second Language Acquisition*. Cambridge: Cambridge University Press.

Duff, P. A. (2008). Language socialization, participation and identity: Ethnographic approaches. In N. H. Hornberger, M. Martin-Jones & A. de Mejía (Eds.), *Encyclopedia of Language and Education, 2nd edition, Volume 3: Discourse and Education* (pp.107–120). Boston: Springer.

Ehrman, M. E., Leaver, B. L., & Oxford, R. L. (2003). A brief overview of individual differences in second language learning. *System*, 31(3), 313–330.

Ellis, R. (1993). The structural syllabus and second language acquisition. *TESOL Quarterly*, 27(1), 91–113.

Ellis, R. (2002). Does form-focused instruction affect the acquisition of implicit knowledge? *Studies in Second Language Acquisition*, 24(2), 223–236.

Ellis, R., & Shintani, N. (2013). *Exploring Language Pedagogy Through Second Language Acquisition Research*. London: Routledge.

Evison, J. (2013). Turn openings in academic talk: Where goals and roles intersect. *Classroom Discourse*, 4(1), 3–26.

Evison, J. M., McCarthy, M. J., & O'Keeffe, A. (2007). Looking out for love and all the rest of it: Vague category markers as shared social space. In J. Cutting (Ed.), *Vague Language Explored* (pp. 138–157). Basingstoke: Palgrave Macmillan.

Færch, C., & Kasper, G. (Eds.) (1987). *Introspection in Second Language Research*. Clevedon: Multilingual Matters.

Fischer, R. (2008). Introduction to the special issue. *CALICO Journal*, 25(3), 377–384.

de Freitas, S. (2008). *Serious Virtual Worlds: A Scoping Study*. Online at: http://webarchive.nationalarchives.gov.uk/20140702233839/http://www.jisc.ac.uk/media/documents/publications/seriousvirtualworldsv1.pdf

Goldschneider, J. M., & DeKeyser, R. M. (2002). Explaining the 'natural order of L2 morpheme acquisition' in English: A meta-analysis of multiple determinants. *Language Learning*, (51)1, 1–50.

de Guerrero, M. (2005). *Inner Speech – L2: Thinking Words in a Second Language*. New York: Springer.

Hampel, R., & Stickler, U. (2005). New skills for new classrooms: Training tutors to teach languages online. *Computer Assisted Language Learning*, 18(4), 311–326.

Hampel, R., & Pleines, C. (2013). Fostering student interaction and engagement in a virtual learning environment: An investigation into activity design and implementation. *CALICO Journal*, 30(3), 342–370.

Han, Z. (2004). *Fossilization in Adult Second Language Acquisition*. Bristol: Multilingual Matters.

Hwu, F. (2004). On the applicability of the input-enhancement hypothesis and input processing theory in multimedia CALL: The case of Spanish preterite and imperfect instruction in an input application. *CALICO Journal*, 21(2), 317–338.

Johnson, K. (1995). *Understanding Communication in Second Language Classrooms*. New York: Cambridge University Press.

Kirkwood, A. (2004). Networked learning in context: What does e-learning offer students working independently, and what do they bring to it? In D. Murphy, R. Carr, J. Taylor & T. Wong (Eds.), *Distance Education and Technology: Issues and Practice* (pp. 217–229). Hong Kong: Open University of Hong Kong Press.

Kirkwood, A. (2006). Getting networked learning in context: Are on-line students' technical and information literacy skills adequate and appropriate? *Learning, Media and Technology*, 31(2), 117–131.

Kirkwood, A. T., & Price, L. (2005). Learners and learning in the twenty-first century: What do we know about students' attitudes towards and experiences of information and communication technologies that will help us design courses? *Studies in Higher Education*, 30(3), 257–274.

Kohler, D. B. (2002). The effects of metacognitive language learning strategy training on lower-achieving second language learners. Unpublished doctoral dissertation, Brigham Young University, Provo, Utah.

Kumaravadivelu, B. (1999). Critical classroom discourse analysis. *TESOL Quarterly*, 33(3), 453–484.

Lai, C., & Gu, M. (2011). Self-regulated out-of-class language learning with technology. *Computer Assisted Language Learning*, 24(4), 317–335.

Lantolf, J. P. (2006). Sociocultural theory and second language learning: State of the art. *Studies in Second Language Acquisition*, 28, 67–109.

Lantolf, J. P., & Appel, G. (Eds.) (1994). *Vygotskian Approaches to Second Language Research*. Norwood, NJ: Ablex.

Lantolf, J. P., & Poehner, M. E. (2014). *Sociocultural Theory and the Pedagogical Imperative in L2 Education. Vygotskian Praxis and the Theory/Practice Divide*. New York: Routledge.

Lantolf, J. P., & Thorne, S. L. (2006). *Sociocultural Theory and the Genesis of L2 Development*. Oxford: Oxford University Press.

Larsen-Freeman, D., & Long, M. H. (1991). *An Introduction to Second Language Research*. London: Longman.

Laufer, B. (1998). The development of passive and active vocabulary in a second language: Same or different? *Applied Linguistics*, 12, 255–271.

Lee, J. (2008). Gesture and private speech in second language acquisition. *Studies in Second Language Acquisition*, 30(2), 169–190.

Lin, W.-C., Huang, H.-T., & Liou, H.-C. (2013). The effects of text-based SCMC on SLA: A meta-analaysis. *Language Learning and Technology*, 17(2), 123–142.

Lyster, R., & Ranta, L. (1997). Corrective feedback and learner uptake: Negotiation of form in communicative classrooms. *Studies in Second Language Acquisition*, 20, 37–66.

Markee, N. (2008). Toward a learner behavior tracking methodology for CA-for-SLA. *Applied Linguistics*, 29(3), 404–427.

Maybin, J. (2006). *Children's Voices: Talk, Knowledge and Identity*. London: Palgrave Macmillan.

McCarthy, M. J. (2010). Spoken fluency revisited. *English Profile Journal* 1 (1) e4. Online at: http://journals.cambridge.org/action/displayIssue?decade=2010&jid=EPJ&volumeId=1&issueId=01&iid=7908256

McCarthy, M. J. (1998). *Spoken Language and Applied Linguistics*. Cambridge: Cambridge University Press.

McCarthy, M. J. (2003). Talking back: 'Small' interactional response tokens in everyday conversation. *Research on Language in Social Interaction*, 36(1), 33–63.

McHaney, R. (2011). *The New Digital Shoreline: How Web 2.0 and Millennials are Revolutionizing Higher Education*. Sterling, VA: Stylus Publishing.

Milton, J. (2010). The development of vocabulary breadth across the CEFR levels. In I. Bartning, M. Martin & I. Vedder (Eds.), *Communicative Proficiency and Linguistic Development: Intersections Between SLA and Language Testing Research*. Eurosla Monographs Series, 1 (2010) (pp. 211–232). Online at: http://eurosla.org/monographs/EM01/211-232Milton.pdf

Milton, J. (2009). *Measuring Second Language Vocabulary Acquisition*. Bristol: Multilingual Matters.

Mueller, J. L., Wood, E., De Pasquale, D., & Cruikshank, R. (2012). Examining mobile technology in higher education: Handheld devices in and out of the classroom. *International Journal of Higher Education*, 1(2), 43–54.

Norton, B. (2000). *Identity and Language Learning: Gender, Ethnicity and Educational Change*. Harlow: Longman.

Ohta, A. S. (2001). *Second Language Acquisition Processes in the Classroom: Learning Japanese*. Mahwah, NJ: Lawrence Erlbaum Associates.

O'Keeffe, A. (2006). *Investigating Media Discourse*. Abingdon: Routledge.

O'Keeffe, A., McCarthy, M. J., & Carter, R. (2007). *From Corpus to Classroom. Language Use and Language Teaching*. Cambridge: Cambridge University Press.

O'Keeffe, A., & Adolphs, S. (2008). Using a corpus to look at variational pragmatics: Response tokens in British and Irish discourse. In K. P. Schneider & A. Barron (Eds.), *Variational Pragmatics* (pp. 69–98). Amsterdam: John Benjamins.

O'Malley, J. M., & Chamot, A. U. (1990). *Learning Strategies in Second Language Acquisition*. Cambridge: Cambridge University Press.

Patten, B., Arnedillo Sánchez, I., & Tangney, B. (2006). Designing collaborative, constructionist and contextual applications for handheld devices. *Computers and Education*, 46, 294–308.

Pica, T. (1983). Adult acquisition of English as a second language under different conditions of exposure. *Language Learning*, 33(4), 465–497.

Poole, R. (2012). Concordance-based glosses for academic vocabulary acquisition. *CALICO Journal*, 29(4), 679–693.

Russell, V. (2009). Corrective feedback, over a decade of research since Lyster and Ranta (1997): Where do we stand today? *Electronic Journal of Foreign Language Teaching*, 6(1), 21–31.

Schmidt, R. (1990). The role of consciousness in second language learning. *Applied Linguistics*, 11, 129–158.

Schmidt, R. (1993). Awareness and second language acquisition. *Annual Review of Applied Linguistics*, 13, 206–226.

Seedhouse P. (1994). Linking pedagogical purposes to linguistic patterns of interaction. *International Review of Applied Linguistics*, 32(4), 309–326.

Seedhouse, P. (2004). *The Interactional Architecture of the Language Classroom: A Conversation Analysis Perspective*. Oxford: Blackwell.

Sharwood Smith, M. (1993). Input enhancement in instructed SLA: Theoretical bases. *Studies in Second Language Acquisition*, 15, 165–179.

Sharwood Smith, M., & Kellerman, E. (1986). Crosslinguistic influence in second language: an introduction. In E. Kellerman & M. Sharwood Smith (Eds.), *Crosslinguistic Influence in Second Language Acquisition* (pp. 1–9). Oxford: Pergamon.

Sinclair, J. McH., & Coulthard, R. M. (1975). *Towards an Analysis of Discourse*. Oxford: Oxford University Press.

Spolsky, B. (1999). Second-language learning. In J. Fishman (Ed.), *Handbook of Language and Ethnic Identity* (pp. 181–192). Oxford: Oxford University Press.

Stevenson, M. P., & Liu, M. (2010). Learning a language with Web 2.0: Exploring the use of social networking features of foreign language learning websites. *CALICO Journal*, 27(2), 233–259.

Studies in Second Language Acquisition, 1997, 19(2).

Tao, H. (2003). Turn initiators in spoken English: A corpus-based approach to interaction and grammar. In P. Leistyna & C. F. Meyer (Eds.), *Corpus Analysis: Language Structure and Language Use* (pp. 187–207). Amsterdam: Rodopi.

Thorne, S. L., & Payne, J. S. (Eds.) (2005). Computer-mediated communication and foreign language learning: Context, research and practice. *CALICO Journal*, 22(3), 369–370.

Toohey, K. (2000). *Learning English at School: Identity, Social Relations and Classroom Practice*. Cleveland: Multilingual Matters.

VanPatten, B., and Benati, A. G. (2010). *Key Terms in Second Language Acquisition*. London: Continuum.

Walsh, S. (2006). *Investigating Classroom Discourse*. Abingdon: Routledge.

Walsh, S. (2011). *Exploring Classroom Discourse*. Abingdon: Routledge.

Wang, Y., & Liao, H-C. (2011). Adaptive learning for ESL based on computation. *British Journal of Educational Technology*, 42(1), 66–87.

Wang, F., Burton, K., & Falls, J. (2012). A three-step model for designing initial second life-based foreign language learning activities. *Journal of Online Learning and Teaching* 8(4). Online at: http://jolt.merlot.org/vol8no4/wang_1212.htm

Weinberg, A. (2007). Web tracking and students' work patterns in online language-learning activities. *CALICO Journal*, 25(1), 31–47.

Wong-Fillmore, L. (1982). Instructional language as linguistic input: Second language learning in classrooms. In L. C. Wilkinson (Ed.), *Communication in the Classroom* (pp. 283–294). New York: Academic Press.

Wong-Fillmore, L. (1985). When does teacher talk work as input? In S. Gass & C. Madden (Eds.), *Input in Second Language Acquisition* (pp. 17–50). Rowley, MA: Newbury House.

Yang, S.-H. (2009). Using blogs to enhance critical reflection and community of practice. *Educational Technology and Society*, 12(2), 11–21.

CHAPTER 2

Educational Technology: Assessing its Fitness for Purpose

Scott Thornbury

INTRODUCTION

Blended learning (BL), like any model of pedagogic intervention, must be grounded in some coherent theory of learning, a theory that should, in turn, be informed by a body of empirical research (see McCarthy, Chapter 1, this volume). This is arguably even more pressing a need when, as in the case of BL, technologies play a prominent role. Whereas the probity of traditional, 'low tech' teaching approaches might be taken on trust, reinforced as they are by generations of accepted 'best practices', the introduction of (often very new) technological tools into this equation suggests that their usefulness should be subject to a degree of scrutiny that is both rigorous and impartial. If not, their adoption might simply be ascribed to faddishness and their effects trivial or even counterproductive. As Postman (1996: 41) long ago remarked: 'The role that new technology should play in schools or anywhere else is something that needs to be discussed without the hyperactive fantasies of cheerleaders.'

In short, the adoption of any aid to language learning (whether print or digital, and, in the case of the latter, whether app, program, game or the software that supports these) must be dependent on some assessment of its fitness for purpose, that is to say whether it is suitable for use with learners and whether it might fulfil the aims expected of it. As Selwyn (2011: 88) argues: 'Digital technology will not automatically support and enhance learning processes unless some thought is given to the "goodness of fit" between the learning task and the learning technology.' In short, does the tool facilitate learning? Drawing on the ever more extensive literature on second language acquisition (SLA), I will propose some principles that might help address that question.

HYPE, HOPE AND DISAPPOINTMENT

'The hyperactive fantasies of cheerleaders' might well be an accurate characterisation of some of the claims made, in promotional materials and on websites, for language teaching technologies. As often as not, no evidence at all is offered for an item's efficacy, it being sufficient, apparently, just to invoke the technology that is used, whether speech recognition software, 'big data' or video games, to name but a few.

Exaggerated claims for the efficacy of educational tools and methods have, of course, long pre-dated the advent of digital technologies, but it seems that technology inflates these claims exponentially, motivated in part, perhaps, by the financial investment involved in designing, producing and promoting new programs and devices, but also compelled by an ideological commitment to what Selwyn (2014: 37) calls 'techno-fundamentalism', i.e., 'a straightforward enchantment with technology and desire to benefit from continued technological progress'.

At the same time, the promise of new technologies is seldom, if ever, fulfilled – such that the history of educational technology has been characterised as a continuous cycle of 'hype, hope, and disappointment' (Selwyn, 2011: 59). Those with long memories will recall the enthusiasm that greeted the widespread adoption of the language laboratory, and the subsequent disappointment when it allegedly failed to deliver, prompting Wilga Rivers (1981) to ask: 'Has the language learning laboratory failed?' Concluding that it had, Rivers drew several lessons from the experience, one of which was that, before embracing a new technology, 'we must be able to demonstrate in a convincing way, through *improved student learning*, that the cost of the equipment is justified' (Rivers, 1981: 428, emphasis in original).

Three decades down the line, the goal of 'improved student learning' seems as elusive as ever. As Selwyn goes on to observe, 'at best the "evidence" over the influence of digital technology on mental and cognitive development and performance is mixed and inconclusive. At worst the debates descend into the realms of what can be termed uninformed conjecture' (Selwyn, 2011: 86).

GOING BEYOND THE HYPE

One obvious way of rising above the realms of 'uninformed conjecture' and assessing a product's fitness for purpose is to test it by, for example, comparing pre- and post-test results between matched groups of learners, some using the learning aid, others not. While many such studies have been done (see Zhao, 2003, Kern, 2006, and Levy, 2009, for reviews), the problem of controlling for variables, such as the time spent on the learning task or the technological skills of the learners, often means that the results are at best inconclusive. Moreover, any claims made by the manufacturer of the item in question, whether or not based on independent research, must be treated cautiously.

But even if positive effects for an educational tool or procedure can be established beyond doubt, it will not necessarily be clear as to what specific design features were responsible for these effects: given the number of factors that impact positively on language learning, which was it that the tool activated? Nor would it be obvious how to 'reverse engineer' these positive effects (i.e., use the positive effect of existing products as input to the design of new ones), if there is no way of knowing what caused them in the first place.

Arguably, however, enough is now known about instructed SLA to be able to extrapolate some core principles according to which any existing tool can be judged and claims for its efficacy reasonably evaluated. At the same time, such a set of principles might offer designers and programmers a rubric for the informed design and trialling of new products.

Extrapolating such principles, of course, is easier said than done, as there is (still) little real consensus on how the extensive research into SLA should be interpreted. This is partly due to the invisibility of most cognitive processes, but is also a consequence of the huge range of variables that SLA embraces: different languages, different aspects of language, different learners, different learning contexts, different learning needs, different learning outcomes, different instructional materials, and so on. Generalising from research context A to learning context B is fraught with risks. It is for this reason that Spada (2015) urges caution in deriving classroom applications from the SLA literature.

Nevertheless, the temptation to infer pedagogical principles from research findings has proved irresistible, and – cautiously or not – a number of scholars (e.g., Lightbown, 2000; VanPatten and Williams, 2007; Long, 2011; Ellis and Shantini, 2014) have ventured into this terrain, compiling checklists of criteria which, they argue, should guide and inform pedagogical practices. Still others have focused exclusively on the implications of SLA research for the design and use of educational technology (Chapelle, 2001; Kervin and Derewianka, 2011). Inevitably, the research that these scholars draw on is necessarily selective, and the conclusions they derive are no doubt coloured by their own particular concerns and predispositions. Moreover, the domain of SLA is neither static nor impermeable. Indeed, it has never been less so, with rival theoretical paradigms (such as information processing theory, sociocultural theory, conversation analysis, dynamic systems theory and emergentism) competing for centre stage, and even, on occasions, colliding and merging. Hence, no single checklist can claim to be definitive. Nor (as Kern, 2006, argues) should any single theory of SLA guide decisions as to how technology should be selected and implemented. In short, the need for revised criteria of assessment drawn from an eclectic theoretical base is ongoing.

So, motivated by the wish to anchor the educational uses of technology to a bedrock of empirically-based theory, but conscious that developments not only in technology but also at the level of learning theory are in a state of flux, even turbulence, this chapter offers a provisional list of 'observations' (to borrow a term from VanPatten and Williams, 2007) about the nature of second language learning. On the basis of these observations, and inspired by Long (2011), a set of twelve questions are framed that can be asked of any teaching aid (tool, device, program, or whatever) in order to calculate its capacity for facilitating learning – what Chapelle (2001) terms its 'language learning potential'.

WHAT CAN SLA RESEARCH TELL US?

Here, then, are the twelve observations:

1. *The acquisition of an L2 grammar follows a 'natural order'.* Moreover, this order is roughly the same for all learners, independent of age, L1, instructional approach, etc., although there is considerable variability in terms of the rate of acquisition and of ultimate achievement (Ellis, 2008). In addition, 'a good deal of SLA happens incidentally' (VanPatten and Williams, 2007: 10). Dynamic systems theorists (e.g., Larsen-Freeman and Cameron, 2008) go further, arguing that: 'Learning linguistic items is not a linear process – learners do not master one item and then move on to another. In fact, the learning curve for a single item is not linear either. The curve is filled with peaks and valleys, progress and backslidings.' (Larsen-Freeman, 1997: 151) It is worth noting that the way that most traditional (i.e., print) materials deal with the notion that there is a natural order of acquisition has been largely to ignore it. Designers of textbook syllabuses seem to subscribe to the view that – if there is such a thing as a natural order – too little is known about it to justify aligning a syllabus to it, and/or that the

natural order can be overridden by explicit teaching and concentrated practice. Moreover, such a syllabus would, strictly speaking, require teachers to adopt the untenable position of having to tolerate, if not actively teach, non-standard interlanguage forms (i.e., forms that learners typically produce but which are considered incorrect). On a more practical level, the linear and incremental nature of textbooks, plus the need to standardise programs for assessment purposes, is simply not conducive to an approach that respects the more organic, even random pathways of natural acquisition.

2. *'The learner's task is enormous because language is enormously complex.'* (Lightbown, 2000: 450). Lightbown expands upon this observation by noting that many learners have limited access or exposure to both formal and incidental learning opportunities (although, arguably, and thanks to the internet, opportunities for incidental learning have increased hugely, even since 2000). Moreover, if learners are aiming for native-like proficiency and they are already adults, the probability of achieving this goal, outside of a total immersion context, is virtually zero. However, it is increasingly the case that such a goal is not only unachievable but unrealistic, given that many learners require a level of communicative competence sufficient only to cope with the demands of 'English as a lingua franca' (ELF) use – a goal that, while as yet uncodified (and even, arguably, resistant to codification; see MacKenzie, 2014), is unlikely to be as exacting as that of native-speaker-like competence. Nevertheless, the complexity of language, even of a lingua franca variety, is not in doubt, and materials or methods that focus almost exclusively on the teaching of grammar (as has often been the case) seriously under-represent this complexity.

3. *'Exposure to input is necessary.'* (VanPatten and Williams, 2007: 22). The necessity (as opposed to the sufficiency) of feedback as a prerequisite for language acquisition is not in doubt, and attention is now focused on identifying the optimal quality and quantity of that input. Research into vocabulary acquisition, for example, suggests that learners need several encounters with a word in order to learn it (Nation, 2001) which, for low frequency words, would require exposure to several millions of words of text, a strong argument for extensive reading. A revival of interest in the role of the frequency of encounters of 'constructions' and the effect of these on associative learning underpins so-called 'usage-based' theories of SLA, which argue that 'the acquisition of grammar is the piecemeal learning of many thousands of constructions and the frequency-biased abstraction of regularities within them' (N. Ellis, 2003: 67). This 'piecemeal learning' assumes exposure to 'many millions of utterances' since 'fluent language users have had tens of thousands of hours on task' (Ibid.: 82). Corpus linguistics has lent support to the view that cumulative exposure to authentic text 'primes' learners to the phraseological regularities of language out of which an emergent grammar might be generalised (Hoey, 2005).

4. *'Language learners can benefit from noticing salient features of the input.'* (Tomlinson, 2011: 7). For input to become intake, conscious attention to form-function matches seems not only desirable, but, as a guard against fossilisation, even imperative. Noticing features of the input can, arguably, accelerate acquisitional processes and thereby lighten the input requirement. In classrooms, noticing activities are typically teacher-directed, but consciousness-raising by means of 'input enhancement' (Sharwood Smith, 1993) would seem to be an option available to designers of learning software.

5. *Learners benefit when their linguistic resources are stretched to meet their communicative needs.* In formulating the 'output hypothesis', by analogy with Krashen's (1985) input hypothesis, Swain (1995) retrieves the notion that production is a necessary condition for language acquisition, since it forces the learner to engage in syntactic processing. Output is optimal when it is 'pushed', i.e., 'pushed towards the delivery

of a message that is not only conveyed, but that is conveyed *precisely, coherently* and *appropriately'* (Swain, 1985: 248–9, emphasis in original). (Re-)asserting the importance of accuracy is also consistent with research that suggests that accuracy contributes to the *perception* of fluency (Segalowitz, 2010).

6. *Learning is a mediated, jointly-constructed process, enhanced when interventions are sensitive to, and aligned with, the learner's current stage of development.* This observation is consistent with a sociocultural view of learning (e.g., Lantolf and Thorne, 2006), which foregrounds the importance of instruction that takes account of the learner's 'zone of proximal development'. It is also consistent with a sociocognitive view (Batstone, 2010; Atkinson, 2011) in which learning is seen as being an adaptive and participatory process, embedded in its contexts of use: 'We learn languages through using them to act – to interact – with/in the world' (Atkinson, 2011: 157) and language learning is therefore a process 'of continuously and progressively fitting oneself to one's environment, often with the help of guides' (Atkinson, 2010: 611). The notion of 'assisted performance' (Tharp and Gallimore, 1988) captures the responsive nature of this kind of guidance well: as van Lier (2004: 224) describes it, 'The teacher provides assistance, but only just enough and just in time (in the form of pedagogical scaffolding), taking the learners' developing skills and interests as the true driving force of the curriculum.' How such 'just-in-time' interventions might be engineered via technology would seem to be a challenge, given that such interventions assume a degree of intersubjectivity, i.e., the teacher's capacity to 'get into the mind' of the learner, which is arguably a uniquely human trait (Zlatev et al., 2008). On the other hand, Gee (2007) makes the case that well-designed video games can adapt themselves to the user's current level of competence, while providing 'just in time' support when needed.

7. *'There is clear evidence that corrective feedback contributes to learning.'* (R. Ellis, 2008: 885) and that 'negative evidence plays an important role in L2 acquisition' (Ibid.) Moreover, such feedback is best provided 'at the point of need' (Nelson, 1991) if it is to be of optimal use. Lyster (2007: 137), reviewing a number of studies on corrective feedback, concludes that 'providing feedback "in the heat of the moment" may be the most efficient and effective technique'. CALL software is capable of providing immediate feedback on error, but the nature of the feedback has been criticised as seldom being 'intelligent', in that it focuses primarily on formal features of the output, and fails to offer guidance as to how learners might restructure their interlanguage (Chapelle, 2001).

8. *'Learners can learn from each other during communicative interaction.'* (Swain et al., 2003). The extent to which peer teaching occurs in classroom contexts is under-researched, but belief in the efficacy of pair and group work activities, not just as opportunities for practice, but as sites for co-constructed learning, is a core principle of the 'strong' communicative approach. The 'interactionist' hypothesis (Long, 1996) argues that, if classroom learners 'negotiate for meaning' when engaged in information-gap tasks, input is made comprehensible and thereby available as intake. Evidence that classroom learners actually do this is not extensive, despite an unswerving commitment on the part of some scholars to task-based learning. However, the growing acceptance of sociocultural theory (Lantolf, 2000) has given interactionist learning theories a new boost, albeit reconfigured as processes by which learners 'appropriate' the mediations of 'better others' and use them to regulate their own behaviours.

9. *Automaticity in language processing is a function of 'massive repetition experiences and consistent practice'.* (Segalowitz, 2003: 402), practice, furthermore, that is best experienced in 'real operating conditions' (Johnson, 1996). That is to say, the optimal conditions for practice are those that replicate the psychological demands of authentic

language use, including real-time processing and a communicative imperative. These conditions are absent from the kinds of drill-type practice activities often associated with traditional classrooms: 'Drill and practice are usually boring, reduce motivation, and tend to involve highly artificial, non-communicative uses of language' (Segalowitz, 2003: 402). Nevertheless, these are exactly the kinds of activities often favoured by the designers of language learning software: as Beatty (2003: 11) complains, 'Many programs being produced today feature little more than visually stimulating variations on the same gap-filling exercises used 40 years ago.' Judging by the language learning apps that are currently popular, little seems to have changed in the 15 years since Beatty wrote those words.

10. *A precondition of fluency is having easy access to a large store of memorised sequences or chunks.* (Nattinger and DeCarrico, 1992; McCarthy, 2010; Segalowitz, 2010). Although associated with 'the lexical approach' (Lewis, 1993), the idea that fluency is largely a phrase-combining skill goes back at least to Palmer's (1925 [1999: 187]) contention that 'No amount of sentence-constructing ingenuity can replace the patient daily repeating and reviewing of foreign-word groups.' More recently, Skehan (1998) proposes a 'dual processing system' of language competence: a lexicon of memorised words and phrases, on the one hand, and a rule-based 'grammar', on the other, and that spontaneous, real-time processing draws mainly on the former. More recently still, from an emergentist position, the rule-based grammar may itself have been assembled lexically, as multiword fragments coalesce, become entrenched and 'release' their grammar (see Observation 3 above).

11. *Learning, particularly of words, is aided when the learner makes strong associations with the new material.* (See Sökmen, 1997: 241). Arguably, the strength of these associations is a function of the perceived relevance of the new material and the extent to which it engages the learner, cognitively, affectively and even physically. Theories of identity suggest that motivation alone is insufficient to ensure engagement. Norton (2013) argues that learners need to be 'invested' in the learning process, implying not only that they have 'agency' and are granted a 'voice', but that their 'histories and lived experiences' are acknowledged, valued and integrated into the curriculum. Kramsch (2009: 191) concurs: 'While other classes in the curriculum activate mostly the brain, the language class engages the whole body, its emotions, feelings, desires, and projections.' The extent to which such situated and embodied 'identity construction' is feasible in online learning is debatable. Brumfit (2001: 125), for one, argues that 'The internet cannot be a substitute for the holistic understanding that comes from direct meetings with individuals; knowledge transfer cannot be a substitute for seeing, smelling, hearing and walking through unfamiliar settings.' On the other hand, a study by Lam (2000) that reports a Chinese teenager's empowerment by means of social networking might suggest otherwise.

12. *The more time (and the more intensive the time) spent on learning tasks, the better.* (See Muñoz, 2012, for an extended discussion). While the value of 'time-on-task' is uncontroversial, the factors that serve to sustain effort and attention over a prolonged period of time are less easily identifiable. 'Positive affect', e.g., in the form of 'fun', is often argued to be a strong motivator. Tomlinson (2011: 7), for example, claims that 'Learners who achieve positive affect are much more likely to achieve communicative competence.' This seems to be a 'received wisdom' that derives from Krashen's (1981) hypothesised 'affective filter' that acts as a barrier to acquisition. Long (1990: 657) takes a more cautious line: 'The role of affective factors appears to be indirect and subordinate to more powerful developmental and maturational factors, perhaps influencing such matters as the amount of contact with the L2, or time on task.'

Indeed, as with motivation generally, it is often difficult to decide whether positive affect (or 'fun') is a cause of task engagement, or its result. This is where Csikszentmihalyi's (1990) construct of 'flow' – the peak engagement that occurs when challenge and skill are optimally balanced – is perhaps more useful. Reporting an empirical study of flow in a language classroom, Egbert (2003) concludes that flow is achieved:

(a) when the learners' skills are equal to the task;
(b) when the task requires sustained and focused attention;
(c) when the task is intrinsically interesting, echoing Breen's (1987: 349) contention that 'learners will invest effort in any task if they perceive benefit from it'; and
(d) when the learners perceive that they have control over the task and its outcomes.

It may be significant that there is no mention of the 'fun' element that is so often highlighted in the marketing of learning technologies.

TWELVE PRINCIPLES

On the basis of the above observations, I have derived twelve principles that might inform the decision as to whether or not to adopt a new learning tool:

1. ADAPTIVITY

Does the tool accommodate the non-linear, unpredictable, incidental and idiosyncratic nature of learning, e.g., by allowing the users to set their own learning paths and goals?

2. COMPLEXITY

Does the tool address the complexity of language, including its multiple interrelated subsystems (e.g., grammar, lexis, phonology, discourse, pragmatics)?

3. INPUT

Is there access to rich, comprehensible and engaging reading and/or listening input? Are there means by which the input can be made more comprehensible? And is there a *lot* of input (so as to optimise the chances of repeated encounters with language items, and of incidental learning)?

4. NOTICING

Are there means whereby the user's attention is directed to features of the input so that their usefulness is highlighted?

5. OUTPUT

Are there regular opportunities for language production? Are there means whereby the user is pushed to produce language at or even beyond his/her current level of competence?

6. SCAFFOLDING

Are learning tasks modelled and mediated? Are interventions timely and supportive, and adjusted to take account of the learner's emerging capacities?

7. FEEDBACK

Do users get focused and informative feedback on their comprehension and production, including feedback on error?

8. INTERACTION

Is there provision for the user to collaborate and interact with other users (whether other learners or proficient speakers) in the target language?

9. AUTOMATICITY

Does the tool provide opportunities for massed practice, and in conditions that replicate conditions of use? Are practice opportunities optimally spaced?

10. CHUNKS

Does the tool encourage/facilitate the acquisition and use of formulaic language?

11. PERSONALISATION

Does the tool encourage the user to form strong personal associations with the material?

12. FLOW

Is the tool sufficiently engaging and challenging to increase the likelihood of sustained and repeated use? Are its benefits obvious to the user?

Conclusion

As noted above, this list is provisional. And it is not exhaustive. Nor is it sensitive to local contexts, where the culture of the institution and, indeed, of the broader community will inevitably influence the acceptability or not of any innovation, technological or otherwise. Nor are more pragmatic issues addressed such as: Will the tool *work?* (Recall the massive adoption of interactive whiteboards in Mexico a decade ago, where many rural schools still did not have access to electricity.) And: what special training will be required of both teachers and students in order to make it work?

While not exhaustive, the questions I have posed are nevertheless quite demanding, and it is unlikely that a single learning aid (whether print or digital) could ever aspire to answer all of them. This would seem to make a good case for using technologies in combination, and, especially, in combination with classroom teaching: a case, in fact, for BL. What the learning tool is not able to provide independently may be compensated for by face-to-face teaching. Teachers, after all, are probably still best placed to provide the scaffolded learning opportunities at the point of need (Principle 6), while the physical presence of other learners may be a better incentive than an online presence for engaging in authentic interaction (Principle 8).

In the end, the question is not so much about whether a learning tool meets any of the criteria listed above, but whether it does so in a way that outperforms existing means and resources. As Hattie (2009: 18) argues, 'Instead of asking "What works?" we should be asking "What works best?" as the answers to these two questions are quite different.'

Suggested Resources

A useful summary of SLA research and its application to pedagogy is Ellis, R., & Shantini, N. (2014). *Exploring Language Pedagogy Through Second Language Acquisition Research*. London: Routledge.

Also very readable is Cook, V., & Singleton, D. (2014). *Key Topics in Second Language Acquisition*. Bristol: Multilingual Matters.

A useful survey of the effectiveness of online learning in general, and including blended learning, is Means, B., Bakia, M., & Murphy, R. (2014). *Learning Online: What Research Tells Us about Whether, When and How*. London: Routledge.

Discussion Questions

1. Why should one be 'cautious' when applying the results of SLA research to pedagogy?

2. Which of the twelve principles does current educational technology already support? How? Which, do you think, are least well served by current technology?

3. Can you think of ways that the local context, including the institutional culture, might impact on the extent to which a new technology might 'fit'?

4. How applicable are the 'twelve observations' (see What Can SLA Research Tell Us?, p. 27 above) to traditional classroom materials, such as textbooks? Can you apply them to a textbook or other learning aid that you are familiar with?

5. Can you think of specific ways that a BL approach might incorporate some or even all of the 'twelve principles' into its overall design?

6. How might you design an experimental study to determine 'what works best?', as opposed to simply 'what works?'

References

Atkinson, D. (2010). Extended, embodied cognition and second language acquisition. *Applied Linguistics*, 31(5), 599–622.

Atkinson, D. (2011). A sociocognitive approach to second language acquisition: How mind, body, and world work together in learning additional languages. In D. Atkinson (Ed.), *Alternative Approaches to Second Language Acquisition*. London: Routledge.

Batstone, R. (Ed.) (2010). *Sociocognitive Perspectives on Language Use and Language Learning*. Oxford: Oxford University Press.

Beatty, K. (2003). *Teaching & Researching Computer-Assisted Language Learning*. London: Longman.

Breen, M. P. (1987). Learner contributions to task design. Republished in K. van den Branden, M. Bygate & J. Norris (Eds.) (2009), *Task-based Language Teaching: A Reader*. Amsterdam: John Benjamins.

Brumfit, C. (2001). *Individual Freedom in Language Teaching*. Oxford: Oxford University Press.

Chapelle, C. A. (2001). *Computer Applications in Second Language Acquisition*. Cambridge: Cambridge University Press.

Csikszentmihalyi, M. (1990). *Flow: The Psychology of Optimal Experience*. New York: Harper & Row.

Ellis, N. (2003). Constructions, chunking and connectionism. In C. Doughty & M. Long, (Eds.), *The Handbook of Second Language Acquisition*. Oxford: Blackwell.

Ellis, R. (2008). *The Study of Second Language Acquisition* (2nd edition). Oxford: Oxford University Press.

Ellis, R., & Shantini, N. (2014). *Exploring Language Pedagogy through Second Language Acquisition Research*. London: Routledge.

Egbert, J. (2003). A study of flow theory in the second language classroom. *Modern Language Journal*, 87(4), 499–518.

Gee, J. P. (2007). *What Video Games Have To Teach Us About Learning and Literacy*. New York: Palgrave Macmillan.

Hattie, J. (2009). *Visible Learning: A Synthesis of Over 800 Meta-Analyses Relating to Achievement*. London: Routledge.

Hoey, M. (2005). *Lexical Priming: A New Theory of Words and Language*. London: Routledge.

Johnson, K. (1996). *Language Teaching and Skill Learning*. Oxford: Blackwell.

Kern, R. (2006). Perspectives on technology learning and teaching languages. *TESOL Quarterly*, 40(1), 183–210.

Kervin, L., & Derewianka, B. (2011). New technologies to support language learning. In B. Tomlinson (Ed.), *Materials Development in Language Teaching* (2nd edition). Cambridge: Cambridge University Press.

Kramsch, C. (2009). *The Multilingual Subject*. Oxford: Oxford University Press.

Krashen, S. (1981). *Second Language Acquisition and Second Language Learning*. Oxford: Pergamon.

Krashen, S. (1985). *The Input Hypothesis: Issues and Implications*. London: Longman.

Lam, W. S. E. (2000). L2 literacy and the design of the self: A case study of a teenager writing on the Internet. *TESOL Quarterly*, 34(3), 457–482.

Lantolf, J. P. (Ed.) (2000). *Sociocultural Theory and Second Language Learning*. Oxford: Oxford University Press.

Lantolf, J. P., & Thorne, S. L. (2006). *Sociocultural Theory and the Genesis of Second Language Development*. Oxford: Oxford University Press.

Larsen-Freeman, D. (1997). Chaos/complexity science and second language acquisition. *Applied Linguistics*, 18(1).

Larsen-Freeman, D., & Cameron, L. (2008). *Complex Systems and Applied Linguistics*. Oxford: Oxford University Press.

Levy, M. (2009). Technologies in use for second language learning. *Modern Language Journal, Focus Issue: Technology in the Service of Language Learning*.

Lewis, M. (1993). *The Lexical Approach*. Hove: Language Teaching Publications.

Lightbown, P. M. (2000). Classroom SLA research and second language teaching. *Applied Linguistics*, 21(4), 431–462.

Long, M. H. (1990). The least a theory of second language acquisition needs to explain. *TESOL Quarterly*, 24(4), 649–666.

Long, M. H. (1996). The role of the linguistic environment in second language acquisition. In W. Ritchie & T. Bhatia (Eds.), *Handbook of Second Language Acquisition*. San Diego: Academic Press.

Long, M. H. (2011). Methodological principles for language teaching. In M. H. Long & C. Doughty (Eds.), *The Handbook of Language Teaching*. Oxford: Blackwell.

Lyster, R. (2007). *Learning and Teaching Languages Through Content: A Counterbalanced Approach*. Amsterdam: John Benjamins.

McCarthy, M. J. (2010). Spoken fluency revisited. *English Profile Journal*. Inaugural issue. Online at: http://journals.cambridge.org/action/displayJournal?jid=EPJ

MacKenzie, I. (2014). *English as a Lingua Franca: Theorizing and Teaching English*. London: Routledge.

Muñoz, C. (Ed.) (2012). *Intensive Exposure Experiences in Second Language Learning*. Bristol: Multilingual Matters.

Nation, I. S. P. (2001). *Learning Vocabulary in Another Language*. Cambridge: Cambridge University Press.

Nattinger, J. R., & DeCarrico, J. S. (1992). *Lexical Phrases and Language Teaching*. Oxford: Oxford University Press.

Nelson, M. W. (1991). *At the Point of Need: Teaching Basic and ESL Writers*. Portsmouth, NH: Heinemann.

Norton, B. (2013). *Identity and Language Learning: Extending the Conversation*. Bristol: Multilingual Matters.

Palmer, H. (1925). Conversation. Re-printed in R. Smith (1999), *The Writings of Harold E. Palmer: An Overview*. Tokyo: Hon-no-Tomosha.

Postman, N. (1996). *The End of Education: Redefining the Value of School*. New York: Vintage Books.

Rivers, W. M. (1981). *Teaching Foreign Language Skills* (2nd edition). Chicago: University of Chicago Press.

Selwyn, N. (2011). *Education and Technology: Key Issues and Debates*. London: Continuum.

Selwyn, N. (2014). *Distrusting Educational Technology: Critical Questions for Changing Times*. London: Routledge.

Segalowitz, N. (2003). Automaticity and second languages. In C. J. Doughty & M. H. Long (Eds.), *The Handbook of Second Language Acquisition*. Oxford: Blackwell.

Segalowitz, N. (2010). *Cognitive Bases of Second Language Fluency*. London: Routledge.

Sharwood Smith, M., (1993). Input enhancement in instructed SLA. *Studies in Second Language Acquisition*, 15, 165–179.

Skehan, P. (1998). *A Cognitive Approach to Language Learning*. Oxford: Oxford University Press.

Sökmen, A. J. (1997). Current trends in teaching second language vocabulary. In N. Schmitt & M. McCarthy (Eds.), *Vocabulary: Description, Acquisition and Pedagogy*. Cambridge: Cambridge University Press.

Spada, N. (2015). SLA research and L2 pedagogy: Misapplications and questions of relevance. *Language Teaching*, 48(1), 69–81.

Swain, M. (1985). Communicative competence: Some roles of comprehensible input and comprehensible output in its development. In S. Gass & C. Madden (Eds.), *Input in Second Language Acquisition* (pp. 235–256). Rowley, MA: Newbury House.

Swain, M. (1995). Three functions of output in second language learning. In G. Cook & B. Seidlhofer (Eds.), *Principle and Practice in Applied Linguistics: Studies in Honour of H.G.W. Widdowson*. Oxford: Oxford University Press.

Swain, M., Brooks, L., & Tocalli-Beller, A. (2003). Peer-peer dialogue as a means of second language learning. *Annual Review of Applied Linguistics*, 23, 171–185.

Tharp, R. G., & Gallimore, R. (1988). *Rousing Minds to Life: Teaching, Learning, and Schooling in Social Context*. Cambridge: Cambridge University Press.

Tomlinson, B. (2011). Introduction: Principles and procedures of materials development. In B. Tomlinson (Ed.), *Materials Development in Language Teaching* (2nd edition). Cambridge: Cambridge University Press.

van Lier, L. (2004). *The Ecology and Semiotics of Language Learning: A Sociocultural Perspective*. Norwell, MA: Kluwer.

VanPatten, B., & Williams, J. (Eds.) (2007). *Theories in Second Language Acquisition: An Introduction*. Mahwah, NJ: Lawrence Erlbaum Associates.

Zhao, Y. (2003). Recent developments in technology and language learning: A literature review and meta-analysis. *CALICO Journal*, 21(1), 7–27.

Zlatev, J., Racine, T. P., Sinha, C., & Itkonen, E. (Eds.) (2008). *The Shared Mind: Perspectives on Intersubjectivity*. Amsterdam: John Benjamins.

CHAPTER 3

The Role of Interaction in a Blended Learning Context

Steve Walsh

INTRODUCTION

One of the most important challenges facing materials writers, curriculum designers and organisations who adopt a blended learning (BL) approach is the need to develop an understanding of how learning actually 'works' in a face-to-face classroom so that at least some elements of the learning process might be adapted for online use or 'flipped' to the opposite environment. It is clear that certain classroom practices, processes and procedures facilitate learning, while others may hinder learning (Walsh, 2002). For advocates of a BL approach, this proposition raises questions such as: what features of a typical language classroom are central to learning? Which of these features could be transferred to the online environment? Should a BL approach attempt to replicate those features which promote learning in a 'normal' classroom? In this chapter, I argue that the prime role of the language teacher is to enhance learning, which, I suggest, occurs most effectively when teachers understand the complex relationship between language, interaction and learning. The problem which is addressed is how to sensitise language teachers to the centrality of interaction to teaching and learning, which requires a detailed understanding of their local context and accompanying roles. In this chapter, I propose that teachers and learners need to acquire 'Classroom Interactional Competence' (CIC), defined as 'teachers' and learners' ability to use interaction as a tool for mediating and assisting learning' (Walsh, 2011: 130). For teachers working in a BL context, understanding CIC might be regarded as the first step in designing and using materials which facilitate learning, whether for in-class use or in an out-of-class computer-mediated environment. If CIC is indeed central to the learning process, then its core elements of real-time interaction in exploring the language, negotiating meanings, monitoring learning and seeing learning opportunities must be considered for their potential or otherwise to be 'flipped' out of the face-to-face classroom into the online world.

The assumption is that by first understanding and then developing CIC, there will be greater opportunities for learning: enhanced CIC results in more learning-oriented interactions. Teachers, by varying their roles in order to ensure that language use and pedagogic goals are aligned, may demonstrate CIC using a variety of methods, discussed in this chapter in some detail. These methods include the use of extended 'wait-time' (the time that passes before a student responds to a prompt and before the teacher intervenes) to bring about more dialogue in teaching, extending learner responses by careful management of the interaction, scaffolding contributions when necessary and paraphrasing a learner's utterance. Achieving CIC will only happen if teachers are able to understand interactional processes and make changes to the ways in which they manage classroom interaction.

L2 Classroom Interaction

When we reflect on language classes, we quickly realise that classroom communication is both highly complex and central to all classroom activity. In the rapid flow of classroom interaction, it can be difficult to comprehend what is happening since the interaction is both very fast and involves many people and has multiple focuses. Classroom interaction may be performing several functions at the same time: seeking information, checking learning, offering advice, and so on. Given its complexity and centrality to the classroom, it is fair to say that any endeavour to improve teaching and learning should begin by looking at classroom interaction. Crucially, in a classroom, it is through interaction that we access new knowledge, acquire and develop new skills, identify problems of understanding, deal with 'breakdowns' in communication, establish and maintain relationships, and so on. Interaction, quite simply, lies at the heart of everything.

Yet despite its obvious importance, until recently, little time has been given to helping teachers understand classroom interaction. While researchers have gone to great lengths to describe the interactional processes of the language classroom, this knowledge has not properly been exploited as a way to help teachers improve their practices. Most teacher education programmes devote a considerable amount of time to teaching methods and to subject knowledge. Few, I suggest, devote nearly enough time to developing understandings of interactional processes and the relationship between the ways in which language is used to establish, develop and promote understandings. Teachers and learners need to acquire CIC (Walsh, 2011) if they are to work effectively together. Put simply, teachers and learners must make use of a range of appropriate interactional and linguistic resources in order to promote active, engaged learning. Naturally, it is to be hoped that such an active (and *inter*active) form of learning can be recreated online, or at least that online components of BL courses can complement in an interactive way the face-to-face interactions of the physical classroom.

Key Competences within Communication

One of the most important and central constructs underpinning current language teaching methodologies is *communicative competence*, a term first coined by Dell Hymes in 1972. Communicative competence looks at the ways in which speakers use linguistic, semantic, discoursal (communication beyond the sentence-level, e.g., telling an extended story), pragmatic (using and understanding the appropriate uses of language in different contexts) and strategic resources in order to convey meaning. It has, to a large extent, been a focal point of Communicative Language Teaching (CLT) and the more recent 'versions' of CLT, broadly couched under Task-Based (Language) Learning and Teaching (TBLT).

While the notion of communicative competence has certainly furthered our understandings of spoken communication and contributed greatly to advances in language teaching methodology, especially concerning the teaching of speaking, it tends to operate at the level of the individual and focuses on solo performance rather than joint competence. Communication in the classroom, as in any other context, is a joint enterprise which requires collective competence by all parties (McCarthy, Chapter 1, this volume). And yet, teachers often spend a great deal of time assessing and evaluating learners' ability to produce accurate, fluent and appropriate linguistic forms, rather than their ability to interact with another learner or with the teacher. The feedback from teachers is typically at a linguistic rather than an interactional level.

Of course, it is evident that one reason for this position is that a solo performance is easier to teach and easier to test than a joint, collective one. Most teaching and testing materials focus primarily on individual performance and help learners to become more accurate and more fluent; they do not, usually, help learners to become better *interactants* (e.g., to be good, active listeners, to show engagement with other speakers, etc.) – and yet this is what is needed in the 'real world', where effective communication rests on an ability to interact with others and to collectively reach understandings. Being accurate or fluent, in themselves, are, I suggest, insufficient. Speakers of an L2 must be able to do far more than produce correct strings of utterances. They need to be able to pay attention to the local context, to listen and show that they have understood, to clarify meanings, to repair breakdowns, and so on. Interactional competence, then, is what is needed in order to 'survive' most communicative encounters.

DEFINITIONS OF INTERACTIONAL COMPETENCE

Against this backdrop, then, lies the notion of interactional competence (IC), first coined by Kramsch (1986: 370) who says: 'I propose (…) a push for interactional competence to give our students a truly emancipating, rather than compensating foreign language education.'

Kramsch's main argument is that the focus of language education should be directed towards helping learners to use their existing skills and knowledge to interact by making IC the focus of attention. Thirty years ago, then, Kramsch was arguing that a focus on interactional competence would allow teachers to concentrate more on the ability of learners to *communicate* intended meaning and to establish joint understandings. This central claim should never be forgotten in deciding what can or cannot work in an online environment.

Essentially, IC is concerned with what goes on *between* interactants and how that communication is managed. Rather than fluency, we are concerned with what McCarthy (2010) terms *confluence*: the act of making spoken language flow together with another speaker or other speakers. Confluence is highly relevant to the present discussion since it highlights the ways in which speakers attend to each other's contributions and focus on collective meaning-making. It is also a concept which lies at the heart of most classroom communication, where interactants are engaged in a constant process of making sense of each other's contributions, negotiating meanings, assisting, clarifying, and so on. We might say that, both inside and outside the classroom, being confluent is more fundamental to effective communication than being mono-fluent. In the same way, we might suggest that there is a need to teach interactional competence rather than just communicative competence. Although many have seen learning benefits for learners of online interactions using social media, email, chat, etc. (e.g., Stockwell and Harrington, 2003), these are not, as such, modes that permit the *teaching* of interactional competence, and new ways of thinking about materials will be needed for the online environment (see Mishan, Chapter 8, this volume).

FEATURES OF INTERACTIONAL COMPETENCE

More recent studies of interactional competence have looked at the ways in which learners use a range of resources to interact proficiently and participate competently in different L2 encounters. In one of the most comprehensive and convincing recent accounts of interactional competence, Kelly-Hall et al. (2011) start from the position that learners, rather than being 'deficient', have a range of interactional competencies which need to be described and understood. Using socially grounded methodologies such as conversation analysis, researchers in that edited collection demonstrate how learners develop interactional competence in a diverse range of contexts and across a number of second languages, including English, German, French, Danish and Icelandic. Other studies, brought together under the sub-discipline now known as CA-SLA (or CA-for-SLA, i.e., Conversation Analysis for Second Language Acquisition), have considered phenomena such as the influence of task-type on learners' use of interactional resources (Mori, 2002); features of participant frameworks between speakers of English and German (Kasper, 2004); and the interactional resources used by teachers to create learning opportunities (e.g., Hellermann, 2008; Koshik, 2002; Walsh, 2002). All of these studies share a number of perspectives on IC. For example, they emphasise the fact that IC is context-specific and concerned with the ways in which interactants construct meanings *together*. They acknowledge, for example, that different interactional resources are needed in a context where the emphasis is on a transaction of goods or services, such as ordering a coffee, to those required to participate in a multi-party conversation. Clearly, in the first context, a basic knowledge of English will allow you to order a coffee with minimal interactional competence. In the second, however, and in most classroom contexts, much more sophisticated interactional resources will be required if you are to successfully compete for the floor, gain and pass turns, attend to what the speaker has said, interrupt, clarify, create and maintain social relations, and so on. We can see, from these two examples, that IC is highly context-specific and related very closely to speaker intent and to audience. These contextual factors will be no less important in the design of any materials for online teaching of communicative skills, as well as for teachers' and learners' understandings of the potential of online forms of communication for offering learning opportunities, and for how to take advantage of them.

In an attempt to identify specific features of interactional competence, Young (2003) points to a number of 'interactional resources' including specific interactional strategies like turn-taking, topic management, signalling boundaries, and so on. Markee (2008) proposes three components, each with its own set of features:

- language as a formal system, including grammar, vocabulary, pronunciation;
- semiotic systems, including turn-taking, repair, sequence organisation;
- gaze and paralinguistic features.

As Markee remarks (2008: 3), developing IC in a second language involves learners 'co-construct[ing] with their interlocutors locally enacted, progressively more accurate, fluent, and complex interactional repertoires in the L2'. It seems that while this definition does advance our understanding of what IC actually is, it does rely to some degree on more traditional measures of spoken proficiency such as accuracy and fluency. It should be noted that a person who demonstrates a high degree of interactional competence may not be an accurate user of the language, while the converse is also true.

Young (2008: 100) offers this definition of IC: 'Interactional competence is a relationship between participants' employment of linguistic and interactional resources and the contexts in which they are employed.'

Here then, Young focuses on the relationship between 'the linguistic and interactional resources' used by interlocutors (people addressing one another in a conversation) in specific contexts. Clearly, this relationship is an important one and includes, for example, interlocutors' ability to take turns, interrupt politely, acknowledge a contribution, in addition to their ability to make appropriate use of vocabulary, intonation, verb forms, and so on. It is the relationship between linguistic and interactional resources which is crucial to effective communication. Consider, for example, the effect of a mistimed turn or a misplaced word stress; either can cause 'conversational trouble' and result in the need for repair.

The implications of the research to date on IC suggest the need for a very different perspective on teacher roles, on language and on learning. Any understanding of IC in a classroom setting should be concerned to develop fine-grained understandings of the ways in which social actions, interactional and linguistic resources combine to create microcontexts in which understanding and learning can occur. Such understandings can only be attained when we have a clear idea of the context under scrutiny and can relate the actions and interactions of the participants to their intended goals. In a language classroom, IC will be determined by the extent to which linguistic, social and interactional resources are used to bring about learning. This, in turn, is highly dependent on the teacher's ability to ensure that pedagogic goals and the language used to achieve them are working together. We therefore have to conclude that reproducing such scenarios online represents a huge challenge. Simply relying on social media and other forms of online communication to fill the gap left by a lack of real-time, face-to-face teaching and learning will not be sufficient. The sensitive, experienced classroom teacher will still have a role in fostering good communication and exploiting the learning opportunities that arise from it, whether in-class or online.

CLASSROOM INTERACTIONAL COMPETENCE

Turning now to a conceptualisation of Classroom Interactional Competence (CIC), defined here as 'teachers' and learners' ability to use interaction as a tool for mediating and assisting learning' (Walsh, 2011: 130), the starting point is to acknowledge the centrality of interaction to teaching and learning; some would even go as far as to say that the interaction which takes place *is* the learning – they are one and the same thing (see, for example, Lantolf, 2000; van Lier, 2004). CIC focuses on the ways in which teachers' and learners' interactional decisions and subsequent actions enhance learning and learning opportunities. In the discussion which follows, together with extracts of classroom data, I present a conceptualisation of CIC and consider how this might be used to promote teacher development.

While it is true to say that CIC is highly context-specific, not just to the particular class, but to a specific moment in the discourse, there are a number of features of CIC which are common to all contexts. First, teachers may demonstrate CIC through their ability to use language which is both convergent to the pedagogic goal of the moment and which is appropriate to the learners. As mentioned previously, language use and pedagogic goals must work together. Essentially, this entails an understanding of the interactional strategies which are appropriate to teaching goals and which are adjusted in relation to the co-construction of meaning and the unfolding agenda of a lesson. This position assumes that pedagogic goals and the language used to achieve them cannot be separated and are constantly being readjusted (see, Walsh, 2003; Seedhouse, 2004). Any evidence of CIC must therefore demonstrate that interlocutors are using discourse which is both appropriate to specific pedagogic goals and to the agenda of the moment. This is what I mean by micro-context: micro-contexts or modes are created through the use of specific interactional features and pedagogic goals which are in turn linked to a particular agenda (for a fuller discussion on modes, see Walsh, 2006).

To demonstrate this alignment between pedagogic goal and language use, consider Figure 3.1, which presents an extract from data collected using a stimulated recall methodology, where teachers are asked to look at a transcript, to recall the lesson and what they believe was going on at that moment: on the left we see the actual classroom interaction and on the right we have the teacher's commentary on his teaching. The class in Extract 1 is of intermediate ability and the students, all adults, are recalling amusing experiences from their school days. A guide to the transcription symbols can be found in the Appendix (see p. 52).

1. T: what was the funniest thing that happened to you at school (1) NAME? 2. S1: funniest thing? 3. T: the funniest 4. S1: the funniest thing I think out of school was go to picnic 5. T: go on a picnic? So what happened what made it funny? 6. S1: go to picnic we made playing or talking with the teacher more closely because in the school we have a line you know he the teacher and me the student= 7. T: =so you say there was a gap or a wall between the teacher and the students so when you= 8. S1: if you go out of the school you went together with more (**gestures 'closer' with hands**)= 9. T: =so you had a closer relationship [outside the school] 10. L1: [yeah yeah]	*Basically he's explaining that on a picnic there wasn't this gap that there is in a classroom – psychological gap – that's what I'm drawing out of him. There's a lot of scaffolding being done by me in this monitoring, besides it being managerial, there's a lot of scaffolding because I want to get it flowing, I want to encourage them, keep it moving as it were. I'm clarifying to the class what he's saying because I know in an extended turn – a broken turn – and it's not exactly fluent and it's not articulate – I try to re-interpret for the benefit of the class so that they're all coming with me at the same time and they all understand the point being made by him.*

Figure 3.1 Extract Using Stimulated Recall

A brief analysis of this extract reveals, I believe, the extent to which this teacher's pedagogic goals and the language used to achieve them are aligned, or working together. Essentially, his comments on the right indicate quite clearly why certain interactional decisions were taken. For example, in the interaction, we see evidence of the teacher constantly seeking clarification, affirming and re-affirming and helping the learner to articulate a full response (in lines 5, 7 and 9). Each of these responses is designed, according to the teacher to 'get it flowing' and 'to reinterpret for the benefit of the class'. Not only is he helping the learner to articulate his ideas more clearly, he is helping the rest of the class to understand what is being said. For example, in his own analysis, the teacher refers to the extent to which he uses 'scaffolding' and 'monitoring' as a means of keeping the class together ('so that they're all coming with me at the same time'). He also comments on the need to 'clarify' and 'reinterpret' and we see evidence of this in the classroom interaction data: 'So what happened, what made it funny?'; 'So you say there was a gap...'; 'So you had a closer relationship'. This teacher displays CIC from the evidence presented here. It is apparent that not only are his pedagogic goals and the language used to achieve them at one, but also that this teacher knows *why* he has made certain interactive decisions. He is able to articulate quite clearly the interactive decisions taken with this group of learners, a key element of CIC.

INTERACTIONAL SPACE

Turning now to a second feature of CIC, and one which, I believe, is common to all language teaching contexts, let us consider the extent to which it facilitates interactional 'space': learners need space for learning to participate in the discourse, to contribute to class conversations and to receive feedback on their contributions. In short, CIC creates 'space for learning' (Walsh and Li, 2012). A brief discussion of what I mean by 'space for learning' now follows before we turn to an example using classroom data.

The starting-point for this discussion is to acknowledge the significant developments which have occurred over the last 15 years or so and which challenge traditional and long-standing views of both the nature of language and the nature of learning. Perhaps the starting-point for these developments was the seminal paper by Firth and Wagner (1997, 2007) which questioned existing conceptualisations of learning, arguing instead that learning should be seen as a social process and that language should be viewed as a complex, dynamic system which is locally managed by interactants in response to emerging communicative needs. It is a view of learning which resonates with much more established sociocultural theories which emphasise its social nature; learners interact with the 'expert' adult teacher 'in a context of social interactions leading to understanding' (Röhler and Cantlon, 1996: 2). Learning, under this perspective, entails dialogue, discussion and debate as learners collectively and actively construct their own understandings in and through interactions with others who may be more experienced. This view of learning owes its origins to the influential work of the Russian philosopher Lev Vygotsky (1978), whose theories have been applied to language learning contexts by researchers such as Lantolf (2000) and Lantolf and Thorne (2006).

SPACE FOR LEARNING

The work of another sociocultural researcher, Leo van Lier, has considerable relevance to the present discussion. Van Lier's (2000, 2004) work on ecological approaches to learning stresses its emergent nature and attempts to explain learning in terms of the verbal and nonverbal processes in which learners engage. If we want to understand learning, we should begin by looking at the interactions which take place; by gaining a closer understanding of these interactions, we are gaining a closer understanding of learning itself. Central to this view of learning is what van Lier terms 'affordance': the relationship between learners and particular features in their environment which have relevance to the learning process. One such affordance in the language classroom is the interaction which takes place between all parties, but especially between teacher and learners. 'Space for learning' in the present context is presented as a specific example of the theoretical construct 'affordance' and my aim is to demonstrate how particular interactional features may create opportunities for learning, or, indeed, influence the learning which takes place. Further, the aim is to demonstrate how teachers can play a pivotal role in creating space for learning by the ways in which they use specific interactional practices and by gaining a closer understanding of the relationship between intended pedagogical goals and the language used to achieve them.

There are a number of ways in which space for learning can be maximised. These include increasing wait-time, by resisting the temptation to 'fill silence' (by reducing teacher echo), by promoting extended learner turns and by allowing planning time. By affording learners space, they are better able to contribute to the process of co-constructing meanings – something which lies at the very heart of learning through interaction. Note that this does not necessarily mean simply 'handing over' to learners and getting them to complete pair and group work tasks. While this may facilitate practice opportunities and give learners a chance to work independently, it will not, in itself, necessarily result in enhanced learning. The same point has been made by others (cf. Rampton, 1999). These spaces for learning may be harder to conceptualise in the flipped classroom where interaction may be with a machine or via a social network platform, but, nonetheless, they should be a part of our conception of the BL environment and not forgotten. Until adaptive feedback is developed to a high state of sophistication, i.e., until the machine learns that student B typically needs more time for recording his/her responses than student A, frustration and demotivation may result.

What is needed is a rethinking of the role of the teacher so that interaction is more carefully understood, and so that the teacher plays a more central role in *shaping* learner contributions. Shaping involves taking a learner response and doing something with it rather than simply accepting it. For example, a response may be paraphrased, using slightly different vocabulary or grammatical structures; it may be summarised or extended in some way; a response may require scaffolding so that learners are assisted in saying what they really mean; it may be recast (Lyster, 1998): 'handed back' to the learner but with some small changes included. By shaping learner contributions and by helping learners to really articulate what they mean, teachers are performing a more central role in the interaction, while, at the same time, maintaining a student-centred, decentralised approach to teaching. At the present time, it is difficult to see how a machine could feed back on student activity to achieve the results that shaping is capable of in classrooms. A good classroom teacher, for example, can spot when a topic seems to inspire or excite a student and will encourage the student to say more, to explore the topic, as well as helping that student to make their contribution more accurate/more effective. Machines are not good at sensing 'excitement' or 'inspiration', yet.

Turning now to an illustration of space for learning, let us consider Figure 3.2, an extract taken from a secondary English language class in China. This is a large class of around 40 students aged 15–16 and of intermediate ability. The class is organised in a 'traditional' way, with students sitting in individual desks in rows. Roles too are traditional, and most of the interaction which takes place goes through the teacher. In this extract, the teacher is preparing the class to do a reading activity and is eliciting from them their experiences of visiting museums. (See Appendix, p. 52, for the guide to the transcription symbols.)

In the extract, a number of interactional strategies are used by this teacher to create space for learning. First, there is evidence of an extensive use of pausing, some of which are quite extensive (lines 1, 3, 6 and 17, for example). This use of wait-time is quite unusual in most classrooms where teachers typically wait for less than one second after asking a question (Rowe, 1986). Here, we see pauses of 2–4 seconds, a feature which has a number of functions:

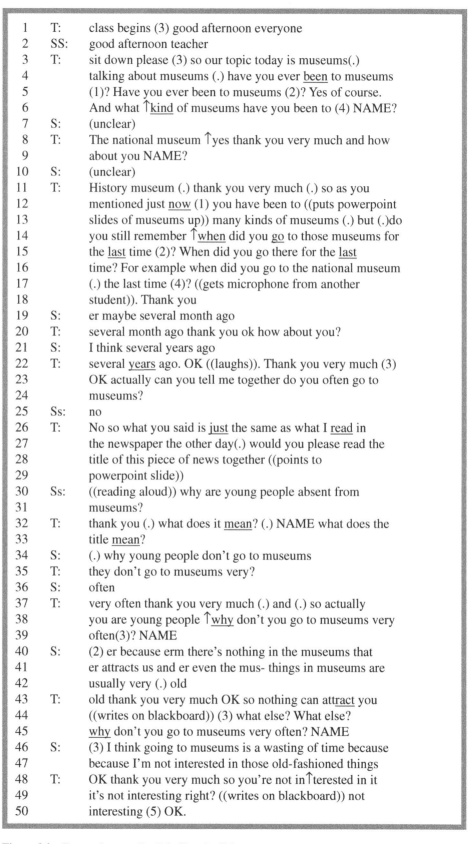

```
1    T:    class begins (3) good afternoon everyone
2    SS:   good afternoon teacher
3    T:    sit down please (3) so our topic today is museums(.)
4          talking about museums (.) have you ever been to museums
5          (1)? Have you ever been to museums (2)? Yes of course.
6          And what ↑kind of museums have you been to (4) NAME?
7    S:    (unclear)
8    T:    The national museum ↑yes thank you very much and how
9          about you NAME?
10   S:    (unclear)
11   T:    History museum (.) thank you very much (.) so as you
12         mentioned just now (1) you have been to ((puts powerpoint
13         slides of museums up)) many kinds of museums (.) but (.)do
14         you still remember ↑when did you go to those museums for
15         the last time (2)? When did you go there for the last
16         time? For example when did you go to the national museum
17         (.) the last time (4)? ((gets microphone from another
18         student)). Thank you
19   S:    er maybe several month ago
20   T:    several month ago thank you ok how about you?
21   S:    I think several years ago
22   T:    several years ago. OK ((laughs)). Thank you very much (3)
23         OK actually can you tell me together do you often go to
24         museums?
25   Ss:   no
26   T:    No so what you said is just the same as what I read in
27         the newspaper the other day(.) would you please read the
28         title of this piece of news together ((points to
29         powerpoint slide))
30   Ss:   ((reading aloud)) why are young people absent from
31         museums?
32   T:    thank you (.) what does it mean? (.) NAME what does the
33         title mean?
34   S:    (.) why young people don't go to museums
35   T:    they don't go to museums very?
36   S:    often
37   T:    very often thank you very much (.) and (.) so actually
38         you are young people ↑why don't you go to museums very
39         often(3)? NAME
40   S:    (2) er because erm there's nothing in the museums that
41         er attracts us and er even the mus- things in museums are
42         usually very (.) old
43   T:    old thank you very much OK so nothing can attract you
44         ((writes on blackboard)) (3) what else? What else?
45         why don't you go to museums very often? NAME
46   S:    (3) I think going to museums is a wasting of time because
47         because I'm not interested in those old-fashioned things
48   T:    OK thank you very much so you're not in↑terested in it
49         it's not interesting right? ((writes on blackboard)) not
50         interesting (5) OK.
```

Figure 3.2 Extract from an English Class in China

- It creates 'space' in the interaction to allow learners to take a turn-at-talk.
- It allows thinking or rehearsal time (cf. Schmidt, 1990) enabling learners to formulate a response (see lines 44 and 46 where a teacher pause is followed by a learner pause).
- It enables turn-taking to be 'slowed down', helping to make learners feel more comfortable and less stressed.
- Increased wait-time often results in fuller, more elaborated responses, as in lines 40ff and 46ff. It may also result in the kind of dialogic classroom interaction advocated by researchers such as Mercer (2004) and Alexander (2008).

A second strategy used by this teacher to create space for learning is a distinct lack of repair. Although students make some mistakes in this extract (line 34, word order; line 46, verb form 'wasting of time'), they are ignored since they do not impede communication. Importantly, error correction is not the focus of attention in this micro-context where the teacher is concerned to elicit and share sharing personal experiences. This condition can be recreated online in the world of blogs and voice recordings deposited by students (see Hojnacki, Chapter 7, and McCarten and Sandiford, Chapter 12, this volume), where error-correction is not part of the process of writing or speaking and can be attended to later. Less confident students may often feel more at home without such immediate pressure.

A third feature of space for learning is extended learner turns. In Figure 3.2, Extract 2, there are several examples of this feature (in lines 40–42 and 46–47, for example), where the teacher allows learners to complete a turn and make a full and elaborated response. Often teachers interrupt and close down space when learners are attempting to articulate something quite complicated. Here, she does the opposite and allows the student space in the interaction to make a full and useful contribution. Providing the time and space for this to occur are essential; too often teachers may be concerned to move on to the next item on their teaching agenda and may inadvertently interrupt or complete learner turns.

The discussion so far has identified two features of CIC: the extent to which language use and pedagogic goals converge, and space for learning. A third feature is what I am calling *shaping*: a teacher's ability to accept a learner's contribution and improve it in some way by scaffolding, paraphrasing, reformulating or extending it. Essentially, through shaping the discourse, a teacher is helping learners to say what they mean by using the most appropriate language to do so. The process of 'shaping' contributions occurs by seeking clarification, scaffolding, modelling or repairing learner input. In a decentralised classroom in which learner-centredness is a priority, these interactional strategies may be the only opportunities for teaching and occur frequently during the feedback move (cf. Cullen, 1998). Elsewhere (see, for example, Jarvis & Robinson, 1997), the process of taking a learner's contribution and shaping it into something more meaningful has been termed *appropriation;* a kind of paraphrasing which serves the dual function of checking meaning and moving the discourse forward.

Looking at the notion of shaping in some data now, we turn to Figure 3.3, an extract from a class in which the teacher is working with a group of upper-intermediate learners, studying at a private language school in the UK and preparing to do a listening comprehension about places of interest. There are a number of features in the extract which show evidence of CIC, especially this teacher's ability to manage feedback in a more open and more effective way.

From our knowledge of classrooms and from previous experience, we can ascertain that the teacher's main concern here is to elicit from the students which places of interest they have already visited during their stay in the UK. As a micro-context, the pedagogic goal is to establish a context using students' personal experiences and the main interactional feature is the use of referential (or genuine) questions.

1	T:	okay, have you have you ever visited any places ↑outside London?=
2	L1:	=me I stay in (.) Portsmouth and er:: in Bournemouth
3	T:	[where've you been?
4	L1:	[in the south
5	T:	[down (.) here? (pointing to map)
6	L1:	yeah yeah
7	T:	↑why?
8	L1:	er my girlfriend live here and (.) I like this student
9		place and all the people's young and a lot (.) er go out
10		in the (.) evening its very [good
11	T:	[right
12	T:	anybody else? (4) Have you been anywhere Tury?
13	L2:	Yes I have been in er (.) Edinbourg ((mispronounced)),
14		(())=
15	T:	=so here here ((pointing to map))=
16	L2:	=yes er Oxford (.) Brighton (.) many places (())=
17	T:	=and which was your favourite?=
18	L2:	=my favourite is London
19	T:	(.) ↑why?
20	L2:	because it's a big city you can find what what you [want
21	T:	[mmhh
22	L2:	and do you can go to the theatres (1) it's a very (.)
23		cosmopolitan [city
24	L:	[yes
25	L2:	I like it very much=
26	T:	=do you all (.) agree=
27	LL:	=yes (laughter)
28	T:	((3)) laughter)
29	T:	has anybody else been to another place outside London?
30	L:	no not outside inside
31	T:	(.)mm? Martin? Anywhere?
32	L3:	=no nowhere=
33	T:	=would you like to go (.) [anywhere?
34	L3:	[yes yes
35	T:	[where?
36	L3:	well Portsmouth I think it's very (.) great=
37	T:	=((laughter)) cos of the students [yes (.) yes
38	LL:	[yes yes
39	L3:	and there are sea too
40	T:	Pedro?
41	L4:	it's a (.) young (.) place
42	T:	mm anywhere else? (3) no well I'm going to talk to
43		you and give you some recommendations about where you
44		can go in (.) England (.) yeah

Figure 3.3 Extract from D. Carr (Ed.) (2006), *Task-based Learning*, DVD 12 in Teacher Training DVD Series

One of the most striking features, again, is the lack of repair, despite the large number of errors throughout the extract (see, for example, lines 2, 8, 13, 36, 39), the teacher chooses to ignore them because error correction is not conducive to allowing learners to have space to express themselves. Second, the questions she asks are often followed with expansions such as 'why'? (see, for example, lines 7 and 19) which result in correspondingly longer turns by learners (in lines 8 and 20). Again, I would suggest that both the teacher's questioning strategy and the longer learner turns are evidence of CIC since they facilitate opportunities for both engaged interaction and learning opportunity. Third, we note that there are several attempts to 'open the space' and allow for wider participation of other learners. This occurs, for example, in line 12 (*anybody else* plus a 4-second pause), in line 26 (*do you all agree?*), in line 42 (*anywhere else* plus a 3-second pause). On each of these occasions, the teacher is attempting to include other students in the interaction in a bid to elicit additional contributions. Again, her use of language and pedagogic goals are convergent, ensuring that learning opportunities are maximised.

Other features which show evidence of CIC include:

- the use of extended wait-time, pauses of several seconds (in lines 12 and 42) which allow learners time to think, formulate and give a response. Typically, teachers wait less than one second after asking a question (see, for example, Rowe, 1986), leaving learners insufficient time to respond.
- the use of requests for clarification (in lines 3, 5, 15) which serve to ensure that understandings have been reached. Not only do such requests give important feedback to the students, they allow the teacher to ensure that the other students are included by clarifying for the whole class.
- minimal response tokens which tell the other speaker that understandings have been reached without interrupting the 'flow' of the interaction (see, for example, line 11 [*right*], line 21 [*mmhh*]). Again, the use of such feedback is further evidence of convergence of pedagogic goals and language use.
- evidence of content feedback by the teacher who responds to the message and not the linguistic forms used to articulate a particular message. In extract 3, for example, the teacher responds in an almost conversational way to almost all of the learners' turns. She offers no evaluation or repair of learner contributions, as would be the 'norm' in many classroom contexts. Instead, she assumes an almost symmetrical role in the discourse, evidenced by the rapid pace of the interaction (note the overlapping speech in lines 3–5, lines 33–35, and latched turns in lines 14–18 and 25–27).

In the same extract, there are a number of features of CIC which we can highlight from the learner's perspective. First, there is recognition on the part of L1 during the interaction that the appropriate reaction to a question is a response, as evidenced in lines 2, 4, 6, 8. Not only does L1 answer the questions posed by the teacher, he is able to recognise the precise type and amount of response needed, ensuring that his contributions are both relevant and timely. He is also sufficiently competent to appreciate that a question like 'why' in line 7 almost always requires an extended response, which he provides in line 8. His CIC is sufficiently advanced to appreciate that the teacher's focus here is on eliciting personal experiences – while his responses are adequate and appropriate, they are certainly not accurate; yet this is of little or no concern given the pedagogic focus of the moment. This learner has correctly interpreted the teacher's question as a request for further information where accuracy is less important than the provision of that information.

L1 also displays CIC in terms of his ability to manage turns, hold the floor and hand over his turn at a particular point in the interaction. He responds quickly to the teacher's opening question, as indicated by the latched turn in line 2 and turn continuation in line 4, indicated by the overlapping speech. As well as being able to take a turn and hold the floor, this learner (L1) also recognises key signals which mark a transition relevance place – the teacher's 'right' and accompanying overlap in lines 9 and 10 signal to this learner that it is time to relinquish his turn at talk and hand over to another learner. While it is the teacher who 'orchestrates the interaction' (Breen, 1998), nonetheless, L1 has to be able to take cues, observe key signals and manage his own turn-taking in line with what is required by the teacher. He must also recognise that his own contributions are largely determined by the teacher's and by the specific pedagogic goals of the moment.

Conclusion

In this chapter, we have seen how CIC might be described and characterised across a range of classroom settings. By studying in some detail the interactions which take place in second language classrooms, we have seen how the interactional and linguistic resources used by teachers and learners will vary considerably according to specific teaching and learning goals at a particular point in time. There is no 'one-fits-all' recipe, which is often a problem with technology-led learning, where machine limitations and institutional constraints impose more homogeneous solutions. Three broad features of CIC were discussed and then analysed in some detail:

- alignment between pedagogic goals and language use;
- creating space for learning;
- shaping learner contributions in feedback.

These interactional strategies help to maintain the flow of the discourse and are central to effective classroom communication. They offer a different but complementary view of learning through interaction to that provided by a conversation analytic perspective which focuses mainly on turn design, sequential organisation and repair. The notion of CIC has direct relevance to both teacher educators and language teachers and should be regarded as a key means of enhancing learning by developing more complex understandings of both local context and teacher roles. To ignore the insights provided by the study of CIC when designing and implementing BL programmes is to condemn students to a reduced environment where the best and most effective pathways to learning are at best fewer or at worst are absent.

The relevance and applicability of CIC to a BL or online learning context should not be forgotten. Having raised a number of problems in connection with CIC vis-à-vis BL programmes, it is nonetheless the case that certain features of CIC can be integrated into the computer-mediated environment, where, for the most part, technology performs many of the roles and responsibilities of the teacher or tutor. For example, in straightforward gap-fill tasks and individual writing tasks, wait-time can be extended for students working online, since, at least most of the time, learners respond in their own time. Indeed, it may be argued that, in an online or BL context, wait-time could be enhanced since it can be deliberately incorporated into materials design so that, for example, more advanced learners are given less time to respond to a particular task than elementary or intermediate learners. However, we have already noted how wait-time could be problematic for more instantaneous forms of response such as the time-gap allowed between the speakers when students are taking one of the parts in a conversation and recording their voices. In the face-to-face classroom, teachers and student peers can develop greater sensitivity to individuals' needs.

There are other aspects of CIC which may be more problematic to recreate in a BL environment. For example, as I have argued previously in this chapter, in a face-to-face classroom, the role of the teacher in *shaping* learner contributions (see above) is central to facilitating learning. But how does the process of shaping arise in a BL or online context where there may be no teacher present? Are there opportunities, in a technology-enhanced learning environment, to design materials where student online contributions are mediated in some way by the technology and where this mediation acts as a substitute for shaping? Consider, for example, the value of pull-down menus which guide learners to a correct response. There is a sense in which this scaffolded support performs a very similar function to that of a teacher prompting and guiding learners to a correct response through particular questioning, paraphrasing and clarifying strategies, even though it is hardly a full substitute for the real thing.

The challenge for designers of BL materials is to adequately acknowledge the importance of CIC and ensure that its features are either adapted or replaced for online use, and above all, that what is best done in the physical classroom stays there and is given the benefit of the extra time released by 'flipping' other elements of the classroom course into the online environment. It is by studying interaction in a face-to-face classroom and comparing it to the interactions which take place in a BL or online context that our understandings of CIC in both learning environments will be enhanced (de Leng et al., 2010). By enhancing interaction, and the potential for interaction, opportunities for a more engaged learning environment will be maximised, and decisions about what can be flipped from one environment to another can best be made. Furthermore, once teachers and materials designers understand that pedagogic goals and the language used to achieve them must be convergent, it becomes easier to design tasks and materials with specific learning outcomes. For example, it is not difficult to imagine how, in a BL or online setting, students are given a task which gets them to rewrite a text in a different genre: from email to report, or from a verbal transcript to the minutes of a meeting. In such cases, an understanding, under CIC, of the important relationship between language use and pedagogic goal will greatly facilitate both task design and online delivery.

Suggested Resources

Kelly-Hall, J., Hellermann, J., & Pekarek-Doehler, S. (Eds.) (2011). *L2 Interactional Competence and Development*. Bristol: Multilingual Matters.

Markee, N. (2008). Toward a learning behavior tracking methodology for CA-for-SLA. *Applied Linguistics*, 29, 404–427.

Walsh, S. (2013). *Classroom Discourse and Teacher Development*. Edinburgh: Edinburgh University Press.

Young, R. (2008). *Language and Interaction: An Advanced Resource Book*. London: Routledge.

Discussion Questions

1. How might interaction be improved or increased in a BL context, when there may be little or no face-to-face teaching?
2. What would be the key features of CIC in a BL context (a) for a teacher, (b) for learners?

3. One of the key features of CIC outlined in this chapter is *shaping*, where teachers take a learner response, improve it in some way and then hand it back. How would this strategy work in an online setting?

4. To what extent is interactional competence (IC) achievable in an asynchronous learning environment, when responses to students do not take place in real time?

References

Alexander, R. J. (2008). *Towards Dialogic Teaching: Rethinking Classroom Talk* (4th edition). York: Dialogos.

Breen, M. P. (1998). Navigating the discourse: On what is learned in the language classroom. In W. A. Renandya & G. M. Jacobs (Eds.), *Learners and Language Learning. Anthology Series 39*. Singapore: SEAMEO Regional Language Centre.

Carr, D. (Ed.) (2006). *Teacher Training DVD Series* (Set of 15 DVDs). London: International House.

Cullen, R. (1998). Teacher talk and the classroom context. *English Language Teaching Journal*, 52, 179–187.

Firth, A., & Wagner, J. (1997). On discourse, communication, and (some) fundamental concepts in SLA research. *Modern Language Journal*, 81, 285–300.

Firth, A. & Wagner, J. (2007). Second/foreign language learning as a social accomplishment: Elaborations on a reconceptualized SLA. *Modern Language Journal*, (Special Focus Issue on: The impact of the ideas of Firth & Wagner on SLA), 91, 798–817.

Hellermann, J. (2008). *Social Actions for Classroom Language Learning*. Bristol: Multilingual Matters.

Hymes, D. (1972). Models of the interaction of language and social life. In J. Gumperz & D. Hymes (Eds.), *Directions in Sociolinguistics: The Ethnography of Communication* (pp. 35–71). New York: Holt, Rinehart and Winston.

Jarvis, J., & Robinson, M. (1997). Analysing educational discourse: An exploratory study of teacher response and support to pupils' learning. *Applied Linguistics*, 18, 212–228.

Kasper, G. (2004). Participant orientations in German conversations-for-learning. *The Modern Language Journal*, 88, 551–567.

Kelly-Hall, J., Hellermann, J., & Pekarek Doehler, S. (Eds.) (2013). *L2 Interactional Competence and Development*. Bristol: Multilingual Matters.

Koshik, I. (2002). Designedly incomplete utterances: A pedagogical practice for eliciting knowledge displays in error correction sequences. *Research on Language and Social Interaction*, 3(5), 277–309.

Kramsch, C. (1986). From language proficiency to interactional competence. *The Modern Language Journal*, 70(4), 366–372.

Lantolf, J. P. (2000). *Sociocultural Theory and Second Language Learning*. Oxford: Oxford University Press.

Lantolf, J. P., & Thorne, S. (2006). *Sociocultural Theory and the Genesis of Second Language Development*. Oxford: Oxford University Press.

de Leng, B. A., Dolmans, D. H., Donkers, H. H., Muijtjens, A. M., & van der Vleuten, C. P. (2010). Instruments to explore blended learning: Modifying a method to analyse online communication for the analysis of face-to-face communication. *Computers & Education*, 55(2), 644–651.

Lyster, R. (1998). Recasts, repetition and ambiguity in L2 classroom discourse. *Studies in Second Language Acquisition*, 20, 51–81.

Markee, N. (2008). Toward a learning behavior tracking methodology for CA-for-SLA. *Applied Linguistics*, 29, 404–427.

McCarthy, M. J. (2010). Spoken fluency revisited. *English Profile Journal*, 1(1). Online at: http://journals.cambridge.org/action/displayIssue?decade=2010&jid=EPJ&volumeId=1&issueId=01&iid=7908256

Mercer, N. (2004). Sociocultural discourse analysis: Analysing classroom talk as a social mode of thinking. *Journal of Applied Linguistics*, 1(2), 137–168.

Mori, J. (2002). Task design, plan, and development of talk-in-interaction: An analysis of a small group activity in a Japanese language classroom. *Applied Linguistics*, 23(3), 323–347.

Rampton, B. (1999). Dichotomies, difference and ritual in second language learning and teaching. *Applied Linguistics*, 20, 316–340.

Röhler, L. R., & Cantlon, D. J. (1996). Scaffolding: A powerful tool in social constructivist classrooms. In K. Hogan & M. Pressley (Eds.), *Scaffolding Student Learning: Instructional Practices and Issues* (pp. 6–42). Cambridge, MA: Brookline Books.

Rowe, M. B. (1986). Wait-time: Slowing down may be a way of speeding up! *Journal of Teacher Education*, 37, 43–50.

Schmidt, R. W. (1990). The role of consciousness in second language learning. *Applied Linguistics*, 11(2), 129–158.

Seedhouse, P. (2004). *The Interactional Architecture of the Language Classroom: A Conversational Analysis Perspective*. Oxford: Blackwell.

Stockwell, G., & Harrington, M. (2003). The incidental development of L2 proficiency in NS-NNS email interactions. *CALICO Journal*, 20(2), 33–359.

van Lier, L. (2000). From input to affordance: Social-interactive learning from an ecological perspective. In J. P. Lantolf (Ed.), *Sociocultural Theory and Second Language Learning*. Oxford: Oxford University Press.

van Lier, L. (2004). *The Ecology and Semiotics of Language Learning: A Sociocultural Perspective*. Dordrecht: Kluwer Academic.

Vygotsky, L. S. (1978). *Mind in Society: The Development of Higher Psychological Processes*. Cambridge, MA: Harvard University Press.

Walsh, S. (2002). Construction or obstruction: Teacher talk and learner involvement in the EFL classroom. *Language Teaching Research*, 6, 3–23.

Walsh, S. (2003). Developing interactional awareness in the second language classroom. *Language Awareness*, 12, 124–142.

Walsh, S. (2006). *Investigating Classroom Discourse*. London: Routledge.

Walsh, S. (2011). *Exploring Classroom Discourse: Language in Action*. London: Routledge.

Walsh, S., & Li, L. (2012). Conversations as space for learning. *International Journal of Applied Linguistics*, 23(2), 247–266.

Young, R. (2003). Learning to talk the talk and walk the walk: Interactional competence in academic spoken English. *North Eastern Illinois University Working Papers in Linguistics*, 2, 26–44.

Young, R. (2008). *Language and Interaction: An Advanced Resource Book*. London: Routledge.

Appendix

A guide to the transcription symbols:

:	Stretching, where one sound is noticeably longer than the others
((2))	Indecipherable from recording with the number indicating time in seconds
(2)	a pause of 2 seconds
(.)	a micro pause of less than 1 second
<u>been</u>	said with heavy emphasis
↑	high rising intonation
[]	overlapping speech
=	latched turn – indicates no pause between turns

SECTION 2

IMPLICATIONS FOR TEACHING

In this section, we consider significant ways in which blended learning impacts upon teaching. Not least of the considerations is the fact that technology-enhanced teaching allows for the complete rethinking of how classrooms operate and how the curriculum can be organised.

Chapter 4, by Johnson and Marsh, begins with an outline of the typical mismatch between the ideal conditions for language learning and the reality of most language learners' situations. While we know, from SLA studies and the accumulated experience of the language teaching profession, that opportunities for interaction, authentic tasks, adequate time, good feedback, low anxiety levels, and so on are important features of good language learning environments, the reality for many learners is that time and opportunity to use the target language are usually severely restricted. Technology (e.g., the internet) offers wider opportunities for some of the ideal conditions to be enhanced, but the technology alone is not sufficient; it is the quality of decision-making in bringing blended learning into being which is important. The biggest benefit that technology offers is the opportunity to 'flip' the classroom. What this means is that work which often consumes time in conventional, face-to-face classrooms can be 'flipped' out into the domain of homework. This might include task preparation, reading and vocabulary tasks and the like, which then releases time in the classroom for more genuine interaction. Johnson and Marsh report on a blended learning project which set out to address the problems of restricted time and resources and which implemented the flipped classroom as a response. Central to the chapter is the qualitative study of the impact upon the teachers involved and how they saw their roles in the new setting. Teachers felt the flipped classroom helped their students to be better prepared and enabled more student interaction and less teacher talk in the classroom.

In **Chapter 5**, the most immediately telling remark by Comas-Quinn is her final sentence: 'Research need no longer be something that researchers do on teachers, but an activity that is an integral part of the professional development choices available to teachers.' The theme of the changing role of the teacher is central to the chapter, but Comas-Quinn goes further than seeing just the teacher's role in the classroom as changing; not only do teachers need to feel comfortable with current technologies, they also need to be flexible and ready to adapt as new means of communication are introduced with increasing rapidity. These developments should be seen not only as tools for teaching learners in new ways, but should be an integral part of the teacher's own quest for professional development and can be successfully harnessed to improve and transform teacher education. Comas-Quinn argues for a fundamental change in the way we approach teacher professional development towards an approach which encourages collaboration and a sharing of resources and experiences, facilitated through the same technologies that have brought about the changes in teaching. In encouraging and supporting teachers to take full responsibly for their own professional development, we can ensure that teachers receive exactly the training they personally need and desire within the requirements of their professional context and individual experiences. Crucially, the motivation, or lack of it, in teachers to participate constructively in teacher training depends greatly on the degree to which they share the values and beliefs immanent in the training programme and the extent to which their sense of identity matches the experience. In short, both the classroom and the new technologies within it and outside of it are seen as areas for the teacher's pursuit of professional and personal development.

Chapter 6 closes the section by bringing us back with a thump to some fundamental questions about the nature of teaching and learning. King reminds us that the ancients can still teach us a thing or two about what good teaching and learning should be and how we should never forget what we are aiming to achieve as theoretical frameworks for pedagogy come and go, and as the tide of technological change breaks over us. King reflects on the notion of blended learning and prefers to refer to integrated learning for contexts where the activities that take place in the classroom and those that take place online are in close complementarity. Although she describes successful online programmes created and used in her own institution, she argues that technology will never replace the need for a human teacher, given the fundamental importance of the teacher's role in developing and supporting the learner, because only the teacher can help the learner understand and appreciate the surrounding context of form, function and culture required when learning a language. For King, the good teacher is above all a listener, a person with sensitive antennae akin to the teacher as described and advocated by McCarthy and by Walsh in their chapters in Section 1. King discusses in detail the role the teacher has to play in today's technology-driven world and argues that teaching and learning should be seen as complementary to one another and not as two distinct entities or in opposition to each other. Her position is, above all, a humanistic one and her message is basically that the never-changing human context of teaching and learning should always inform our perspective, whether we are dealing with the face-to-face interaction between teachers and learners or the online world of integrated/blended teaching and learning.

CHAPTER 4

The Flipped Classroom

Christopher Johnson and Debra Marsh

INTRODUCTION

Learning a foreign language presents diverse challenges for different people in varied contexts, and the reasons for learning a foreign language are as diverse as the ways individuals approach the tasks of learning new vocabulary, figuring out new grammar rules, listening, reading and speaking in a language other than their native language (Dörnyei, 2006, Ehrman et al., 2003). Research tells us that there is no single 'best' way to master a second language, other than perhaps to be born to mixed nationality parents and brought up in a totally bilingual environment. Nevertheless, there is research to suggest that it is possible to identify 'optimal' conditions for effective second language learning (Dixon et al., 2012), and among these conditions are the following:

- Learners interact in the target language with an authentic audience.
- Learners are involved in authentic tasks.
- Learners are exposed to and are encouraged to produce varied and creative language.
- Learners have opportunities to interact socially and negotiate meaning.
- Learners have enough time and feedback.
- Learners are guided to attend mindfully to the learning process.
- Learners work in an environment with an ideal stress/anxiety level.
- Learner autonomy is supported.

With these 'optimal' conditions in mind, we have to recognise that most second language learning still takes place in a face-to-face classroom context and language teachers the world over experience daily the challenge of creating, at least in part, these 'optimal' conditions. These teachers use a range of methods and approaches to introduce new language, and employ a variety of classroom management techniques to maximise learning opportunities (Walsh, 2006, and Chapter 3, this volume). But, the reality is such that time is limited in the classroom, and although teachers are well aware of the need to provide their students with opportunities to practise the language in different and varied contexts, this is sometimes just not feasible given timetabling constraints. Equally, the reality is such that the majority of students have relatively limited opportunities to actively engage in using the target language. Often surrounded by speakers of their own L1, students rarely have the opportunity to enter the world of the target language, despite teachers' best efforts to introduce communicative, authentic language tasks into the classrooms.

This said, with the arrival of the internet, language learners today do have more immediate access to communities of native language speakers and to authentic resources than the language learner of 30 years ago. With computers and technology so much part of our everyday lives, digitally supported learning and teaching are often key components in many a language curriculum both in and out of the classroom. However, the impact of technology has not been as significant as we would expect given the promised potential, and there is still a fair degree of reserve, indeed scepticism, among educators as to the benefits of using technology in language learning. This in fact has little to do with the technology itself, but far more to do with the pedagogy applied when integrating technology into language teaching and learning. As Hubbard has noted: 'As computers have become more a part of our everyday lives – and permeated other areas of education – the question is no longer whether to use computers but how.' (Hubbard, 2009:1). And it is this 'how' which requires our attention.

The Need for Research into the Pedagogy of Blended Learning

Blended learning (BL, i.e., integrating the use of technology into classroom-based learning and teaching) is not a new concept, but the terminology was not firmly established until the beginning of the 21st century. There are an ever-increasing number of research studies into the efficacy of BL, a number of which suggest that when 'appropriately' implemented, BL can significantly improve the learning experience (Peña-Sánchez and Hicks, 2006; Stracke, 2005; and Stracke, 2007). But, what exactly do we mean by 'appropriately implemented' in the context of language learning and teaching?

BL, when well understood and implemented, has the potential to support deep and meaningful learning (Garrison and Vaughn, 2007), but simply mixing information technologies with face-to-face learning is not sufficient to exploit the potential of BL (Marsh, 2012). When considering BL, there is no single perfect blend, nor is there a set or simple formula for making a 'good' blend. The most important aim of a BL design is: 'to find the most effective and efficient combination of learning modes for the individual learning subjects, contexts, and objectives. The focus is not to choose "the right" or "the best", "the innovative" as opposed to "the traditional"; but to create a learning environment that works as a whole.' (Neumeier, 2005: 164–65).

McCarthy (Chapter 1, this volume) takes a similar stance, emphasising the need for decisions on BL pedagogy to be grounded in a number of constraints and parameters based on our knowledge of second language acquisition and language use, both within and outside of the classroom.

This chapter will discuss the results of a study conducted by the present authors in 2013 with a group of teachers in higher education institutions around the world. The study set out to explore teachers' experiences implementing a BL model, and the results were significant in identifying a model of BL appropriate to language learning. This model is what is often termed the 'flipped classroom'.

BACKGROUND TO THE RESEARCH

The Laureate English Program (LEP) started in 2007 when English Department leaders from institutions within the Laureate International Universities programme (two from Chile, one from Spain and one from Mexico) came together in a working group to build a programme that would connect network schools and bring value to its students. The stated objective of the Laureate English Program is to provide all students with an opportunity to reach a 'sufficient' level of English language proficiency while attending a Laureate institution. This 'sufficient level' is identified as B1 (threshold or intermediate level) according to the *Common European Framework of Reference for Languages* (CEFR) standards (Council of Europe, 2001).

However, in order to reach the B1 target, 400–500 hours of guided instruction is a recommended minimum and most Laureate programmes allow for an average maximum of 50–60 hours of face-to-face instruction over the course of an academic period. It was therefore considered unrealistic to require universities to introduce eight terms of English language instruction, into what was an already fully programmed curriculum, in order to ensure students had enough face-to-face instruction time to reasonably attain the B1 goal. As a result, the proposal was for a blended teaching/learning solution to address the issues of time and resource limitations. The blend was conceived in terms of a three-part whole: class time, online time and a social networking platform for students to interact with their peers from other Laureate International Universities (LIUs). This platform is seen as a way to strengthen the usefulness of English as a common language medium and to promote the sense of belonging to an international higher education consortium (see Johnson and Marsh, 2013 for full description).

The Laureate network (see http://www.laureate.net/AboutLaureate) consists of institutions across the world with differing academic and regional cultures, differing resource availability, and time constraints on class scheduling. The advantage of BL is its very flexibility and, as such, institutions have been encouraged to implement a blend appropriate to the local context. The rollout of the Laureate English Program has been steady over the past five years and today the LIUs network has BL programmes for ELT across more than 40 institutions worldwide, and thousands of students and hundreds of teachers engaged on a day-to-day basis in a range of different BL contexts (for further information, see http://lnps.laureate.net/languages/).

The online content has been designed specifically to allow for complete flexibility (see McCarten and Sandiford, Chapter 12, in this volume for a full description) and includes presentation of language through video and audio, and practice of language through automated feedback (grammar, vocabulary and pronunciation). The students are able to record their voices and compare with native speaker models, role play dialogue through specially created templates which provide a talking-head partner with whom they can turn-take, and undertake listening and reading activities and controlled writing and speaking practice. All student activity can be tracked and monitored by the teacher, and students are encouraged to work in their own time and at their own pace (see McCarthy, Chapter 1, this volume, for a discussion of these parameters).

Research into BL is of critical importance to the LIUs network in order to develop and further understand the impact and benefits of BL and the study discussed in this chapter is part of a larger collaborative initiative between Laureate Education and Cambridge University Press. This initiative involves multiple projects, with different objectives and expected outcomes over an extended minimum period of five years, and aims to develop a research-informed understanding into the effective implementation of blended language learning (BLL) with the objective of identifying key pedagogical principles to support learning and teaching in different blended contexts. The emphasis is on teaching and learning outcomes in a BL environment, not primarily on the technology incorporated into the blend.

PHASES OF THE RESEARCH

The present authors led this research programme, phase one of which was completed in 2012. This first study reported on the different blends within the Laureate Network and concluded that there was 'a need for these different blends to be buttressed by pedagogical principles' (Johnson and Marsh, 2013: 50). They also concluded that it was 'too early to determine exactly what constitutes the "most effective" or the "most appropriate" blend', but what is clear is the importance of not losing sight of fundamental language learning and teaching principles when introducing technology into the curriculum' (Johnson and Marsh, 2013: 51–52).

The second phase of the research, completed in 2013, aimed to explore further the conclusions from phase one and set out to identify 'effective' and 'appropriate' best practice BL models within the network. A study was set up with 36 teachers, all experienced ELT teachers with differing levels of experience in blended language teaching, who took part in extended focus groups where discussion sessions were prompted by a series of questions (see Appendix: Interview Protocol, p. 66). These teachers teach in institutions in the following countries: Honduras, Spain, Peru, Chile and Thailand, and represent a range of academic and regional cultures.

THE STUDY

As with any qualitative research project design, the present authors set out with certain assumptions and expectations. It was expected that the teachers would identify changes in their role in the BL context, although the full detail and impact on teaching would, it was assumed, be variable depending on relative experience in BL, along with the cultural and academic context. Similarly, it was expected that teachers would identify changes in the classroom dynamic (i.e., in the types of pedagogical interaction discussed in Walsh, Chapter 3, this volume), again depending on the variables identified previously. However, what was not anticipated was the emerging model of BL common across the groups in different parts of the world. This study revealed that the teachers, quite independently of each other in the different institution groups had considered the same issues to determine their blend. The key issues for these teachers were time constraints (i.e., how to make best use of available face-to-face classroom contact hours to achieve stated learning outcomes) and appropriacy of task (i.e., which activity types were best suited for online study and which activities were best facilitated by the teacher).

FIGURING OUT THE 'BLEND'

The teachers, in considering the question, 'How would I like to make best use of time in class?', all came to the same conclusion: 'getting my students to use the language communicatively'. This is not really a surprising answer given that this tends to be the principal objective of present-day language learning, and yet one so often difficult to achieve in the limited time available in the classroom. Activities which require learners to use language communicatively involve interaction between pairs and/or groups of students, but in order to successfully take part in such activities learners need adequate control of language structures and vocabulary. As a result much of classroom time is often predominantly taken up with presenting and practising new language so that the learner is prepared to take part in the final production activity, but the teacher faced with a class composed of a range of language levels and abilities, which may require language to be presented and reviewed in different ways, more often than not finds that time runs out before the communicative activity for which the lesson is preparing has been attempted. Time and opportunity to create possibilities to engage in the shaping and exploitation of learning opportunities as discussed in Walsh (Chapter 3, this volume) are typically at a premium. Having identified the need to use classroom time for communicative activities, the teachers also considered how the online elements could best support the classroom activity. In other words, they had to consider how the online content could support the learning objectives.

The teachers recognised that the ability to extend the amount of time for practice with the online course content through guided practice outside of the classroom brought a number of clear advantages, but simply putting EFL content for students to access 'out there' on the learning platform was not sufficient in terms of good blended course design. They recognised that online content needs to become an integral part of the overall course in order to more readily achieve the learning aims of instruction and that they, the teachers, had to play a leading role in this integration and change their teaching methods in ways that promote student engagement (Johnson, 2014). On this basis, the teachers in the focus group reported that they had decided to allocate the online content to prepare and practise language before the classroom session and that students were expected to complete the presentation and controlled practice activities in the Learning Management System (LMS). For, as one teacher explained:

The actual presentation part doesn't need to be done by a human being.
[Teacher D]

HOW DID THE 'BLEND' TURN OUT?

The teachers in *'analysing what technology can do and what teachers bring to the equation which technology cannot bring'* [Teacher C] have, as a result, implemented a model of BL in which the online focus is on presentation and practice and the classroom focus is on communication, thus distributing the activity types in accordance with the grounding principles advocated by McCarthy, Chapter 1, and by Walsh, Chapter 3, in the present volume. According to this group of teachers, this model has brought significant advantages to the learning experience, the most notable of which are:

1. Increased interaction and participation in class:
   '[It's] now better since we are asking students to come prepared [...] when they come prepared they see that this is [...] something different the class becomes more interactive [...] and participative.' [Teacher H]

   'I think that one of the greatest benefits [...] is that since students have already prepared at home they come to class already knowing some of the vocabulary and some of the grammar points that they need to know.' [Teacher L]

2. Consequent reduction in teacher talk time:
   'I would say that one of the greatest [...] benefits of the blended programme is that since the students have already been introduced to the language and to the grammar that reduces [the] teacher's talking time.' [Teacher K]

3. Much more student-centred learning:
   'When you're in a classroom with thirty students with books and nothing else [...] it's really quite hard to have the student-led classroom. I've had to not take the lead. The students definitely take the lead now in the classroom. And it's exactly what we always say we should be doing. But using blended learning has really made it easier and possible to do that hundred percent.' [Teacher P]

The teachers in this study have implemented a BL environment which carefully integrates the two components of the course, face-to-face and online. They recognise that the online platform does not replace the need for face-to-face teaching and learning (see also So and Bonk, 2010) and that some types of learning activities, tasks or experiences are better suited to online interactions than face-to-face (McCarthy, Chapter 1, this volume), and that they do not need to replicate or 'teach the same thing twice'. As Senior (2010) described in her work, these teachers, instead of trying to cover everything face-to-face, have instead focused on more general pedagogical outcomes and used technology as a means of virtually extending the classroom.

The teachers, in taking the important principle that language learning requires some basic level of human-to-human interaction, and recognising that 'some [EFL] skills can be acquired through self-study … other skills need to be learned through the experience of interacting with other people along with the guidance of a teacher' (Nakazawa, 2009: 406), have implemented a model of BL which firmly places the focus of classroom activity on communication skills development and the online activity on language presentation and practice, and which allows for more effective use of classroom time, and as defined by these teachers, 'effective' means a focus on communication.

Although none of the teachers actually used the term, it is clear that these teachers were in fact 'flipping' their classroom. For these teachers, 'flipping' the classroom has emerged as a 'logical extension of blended learning' (Roger and Tingerthal, 2013), because it made sense in terms of their own understanding of best practice language teaching within the constraints of their allocated classroom time with their students.

An Emerging Model of Blended Learning for Language Learning: the Flipped Classroom

'Flipping the classroom' has become something of a buzzword, but the concept has in fact been around for some years. Walvoord and Anderson (1998) described the use of this approach in their book *Effective Grading*; Lage, Platt, and Treglia (2000) labelled a similar approach as the 'inverted classroom'; and Mazur (2009) describes a modified form of the flipped classroom using the term 'peer instruction'. Flipping the classroom has been driven in part by high profile exposure in publications such as the *New York Times* (Fitzpatrick, 2012), *The Chronicle of Higher Education* (Berrett, 2012) and *Science* (Mazur, 2009), and also by a recognition on the part of educators that this model can embody best practice principles for teaching and learning and the integration of technology.

The flipped model originally defined as 'students watching pre-recorded lectures online', and first associated with maths and science classes, at first sight does not appear to offer much to language learning. However, Bergmann, Overmeyer and Wilie (2013) are at pains to stress that flipping is not a synonym for watching online videos and is not all about technology (also Bergmann, 2012). As he explains, 'The "Flipped Classroom" starts with one question: what is the best use of my face-to-face class time?' (Ibid.) The answer appears to be: 'One of the major benefits of the flipped concept is that it frees up class time in which teachers can create engaging learning experiences for the students.' (Saxena, 2013).

A Revolution in Pedagogy, not Technology

Often in discussions around the use of technology in education, the focus is on the student and student motivation, interest and achievement (issues raised by McCarthy, Chapter 1, this volume, as potential difficulties for BL contexts). What was interesting from this study was the extent to which the teachers reported that flipping the classroom has generally

had a positive impact on their teaching and teaching experience. Participants indicated that the model can make lesson planning easier; reduce their planning time; provide more flexibility in face-to-face class sessions; and allow them to focus on student needs. Teacher K believes his approach to teaching, in his own words, has been 'revolutionised':
'I have been a teacher for a long time now and this has definitely revolutionised my preparation and also the way I look at things [...] I think for me personally ... if I was to go back [or] to take another job [...] I'd actually find it quite difficult to go back now to just teaching with a book. I would really feel that I'm not benefiting students as I should be.' [Teacher K]

When questioned further about the extent to which his teaching had been 'revolutionised', it was clear that this teacher did not consider this in terms of the technology. For as Bergmann (2012), commented, 'Many people think the flipped class is all about the technology. In fact, this is not correct. It is about changing the pedagogy with the aid of technology.'

THINKING THE CLASSROOM FROM THE 'END'/WHERE DO THE CHALLENGES COME FROM?

It is widely recognised that blended teaching represents a complex and challenging new model for many teachers, (So and Bonk, 2010), and although there is a growing body of research into the role of the teacher in the online environment (Artino, 2008; Doughty et al., 2009; Fang, 2010; Salcedo, 2010, Senior, 2010; Vlachopoulos and Cowan, 2010; Yuksel, 2009), equal attention needs to be paid to the role of the teacher and the changing dynamics in the face-to-face context. For many teachers, the classroom is no longer the familiar environment of their learning experiences, nor is it the familiar environment for which they have been trained. A flipped class approach to teaching is difficult and risky work. Flipping the classroom requires that the instructor start with the end in mind, asking questions like: Where do you want to lead the students?; What, 'exactly', do you want your student to be able to do or know? Effective flipping means planning the class with 'good practice in mind'. (Roger and Tingerthal, 2013).

The teachers in this study, while embracing change, readily recognised the challenges it presents not only for themselves but also for their colleagues. The challenges identified by the teachers were not related to the technology, in fact this was seen as the 'easy' part. The challenges all relate to the pedagogy:

'One of the problems I had is giving up the power that we had as a traditional teacher where you were in command of the class. And now you're like letting your students do their learning. They [...] take over. And it's a difficult transition because as we said we want our students to learn. And maybe we think we have the way for them to learn but [...] today we [understand] that they can help themselves. And it's a step that has to be taken but it's difficult to kind of start losing control.' [Teacher G]

'When you're feeling like your powers are being taken you have to let go of that power and it's not easy. It's like trying to compare it as parents when your children grow up you just have to realise that it's going to happen. You're not going to like it but you have to let go and I don't think that's been easy at least not for me.' [Teacher J]

The teachers recognised the need for training as they felt ill-prepared for BL due to the following factors: lack of control over the learning process; the changing role of teacher; changing instructional paradigms; and teacher/student resistance to change.

'I would also say from the perspective of [...] just the teaching and starting to use blended learning one of the challenges has definitely been that because not many of us has actually been educated as teachers [...] using blended learning uh when we went to university so it's been quite a handful to adapt to it.' [Teacher L]

Teacher training programmes are often criticised for failing to prepare their teachers to integrate technology into their teaching (Sayadian et al., 2009), and those that do include a technology element in the programme tend to focus on the technical *what* rather than the pedagogical *how*. Walsh (Chapter 3, this volume) asserts that understanding classroom interaction should be at the heart of decision-making over BL but also notes an absence of attention to classroom interaction in teacher education programmes, so we potentially have a double problem in this regard. Just considering some of the key characteristics of an effective flipped classroom, we begin to realise the extent to which the 'traditionally' trained language teachers face change in their classrooms, and these have little to do with the technology itself.

In an effectively flipped classroom, active student engagement is encouraged (indeed required) and student-led discussions, collaborative work, problem solving, and critical thinking arise spontaneously. Student ownership of the learning process – and a felt responsibility for how their knowledge is applied in a flipped classroom – leads to lively peer-to-peer dialogue and the freedom to explore issues and questions beyond a set scope and sequence of course content without teacher-directed prompting. Student involvement in the classroom, where the traditional presentation and practice of core content happens online with or without teacher support, leads to real-world, realia-based interactions around topics of their own interests and to student-led discussions that expand upon the course content and challenges all towards further learning.

Many pre-service or in-service teacher training programmes often fail to prepare their students to integrate technology into their teaching in order to promote more autonomous engagement and learner involvement. Lack of training, lack of a thoughtful blended course design, and a lack of hands-on practice with technological innovations for learning leave teachers unprepared for the challenges of computer-based or blended instruction (Johnson, 2014).

Conclusion

The concept of flipped learning is gaining interest in language learning and teaching, and there now exist an increasing number of documented successes in the field, such as The Flipped Language Classroom – Resources (see http://www.miscositas.com/flipped.html), but what is notable in findings from the present study is the extent to which a flipped model was developed by teachers based on need and understanding of best practice principles rather than on the desire to follow the latest trend. The research study by the present authors provides evidence that the concept of flipping the classroom can provide a pedagogically sound model recognised and embraced by language teachers themselves.

This study also indicates that the most significant change engendered by flipping the classroom takes place in the classroom itself, and impacts directly on the role of the teacher. The role of the teacher remains central to this 'flipped' model of BL, for 'technology is nothing without a teacher and a plan' (Lewis, 2009: 9), but the consequent need for change in pedagogical approach can not to be underestimated. One of the most encouraging aspects of the present study is that teachers remain empowered in their central role, as Walsh (Chapter 3, this volume) outlines.

A flipped model will not overnight provide the 'optimal' learning environment as identified at the start of this chapter. However, the literature and the research demonstrate that the ability to extend student access to course content outside of the classroom through the technology (and in so doing increase opportunities for meaningful student-to-teacher and student-to-student interaction in the classroom) does offer a potentially exciting model. As Gojak (2012) noted: the right question now is not whether or not to flip our classroom, instead, we should seek the 'how', the technologies and the content to support the model.

Suggested Resources

TNTP (2014). *Reimaging Teaching in a Blended Classroom*. Working Paper from TNTP, Brooklyn, NY. Online at: http://tntp.org/assets/documents/TNTP_Blended_Learning_WorkingPaper_2014.pdf

Johnson, L., Adams Becker, S., Estrada, V., & Freeman, A. (2015). *NMC Horizon Report: 2015 Higher Education Edition*. Austin TX: The New Media Consortium. Online at: http://www.nmc.org/publication/nmchorizon-report-2015-higher-education-edition/

City and Guilds Kineo and e.learning age (2014). *Learning Insights Report 2014*. Online at: http://www.kineo.com/resources/papers-and-guides/learning-insights-report-2014

Flipped Learning Network (FLN) (2014). *The Four Pillars of F-L-I-P™ What is flipped learning?* Online at: http://flippedlearning.org/cms/lib07/VA01923112/Centricity/Domain/46/FLIP_handout_FNL_Web.pdf

Discussion Questions

1. If you were asked to describe the skills required of the teacher BEFORE reading this chapter what would you have said?
2. To what extent has your answer to this question changed having read this chapter?
3. What skills do you think you need further development in?
4. Where can you obtain the appropriate development to acquire these skills?
5. Is the flipped classroom the same as or different to BL?
6. To what extent is the flipped language classroom the same as or different to the flipped classroom in other subjects?

References

Artino, A. R. (2008). Promoting academic motivation and self-regulation: Practical guidelines for online instructors. *TechTrends*, 52(3), 37–45. doi:10.1007/s11528-008-0153-x

Bennett, B., Kern, J., Gudenrath, A., & McIntosh, P. (2012). The flipped class revealed. *The Daily Riff*. Online at: http://www.thedailyriff.com/articles/the-flipped-class-what-does-a-good-one-look-like-692.php

Bergmann, J. (2012). The 'Flipped Classroom' starts with one question: What is the best use of my face-to-face class time? *Daily edventures*. Online at: http://dailyedventures.com/index.php/2012/05/22/the-flipped-classroom-starts-with-one-question-what-is-the-best-use-of-my-face-to-face-class-time/

Bergmann, J., Overmeyer, J., & Wilie, B. (2013). The flipped class: Myths vs. reality. *The Daily Riff*. Online at: http://www.thedailyriff.com/articles/the-flipped-class-conversation-689.php

Berrett, D. (2012). How 'flipping' the classroom can improve the traditional lecture. *The Chronicle of Higher Education*, Feb. 19, 2012. Online at: http://chronicle.com/article/How-Flipping-the-Classroom/130857/

Chambers, A. (2010). Computer-assisted language learning: Mapping the territory. *Language Teaching*, 43(1), 113–122.

Council of Europe (2001). *Common European Framework of Reference for Languages: Learning, Teaching, Assessment*. Cambridge: Cambridge University Press.

Dixon, L. Q., Zhao, J., Shin, J.-Y., Wu, S., Su, J.-S., Burgess-Brigham, R., Gezer, M. U., & Snow, C. E. (2012). What we know about second language acquisition: A synthesis from four perspectives. *Review of Educational Research*, 82(1), 5–60. doi: 10.3102/0034654311433587 (SSCI; Impact Factor: 3.127)

Dörnyei, Z. (2006). Individual differences in second language acquisition. *AILA Review*, 19, 42–68.

Doughty, H. A., Meaghan, D. E., & Barrett, R. V. (2009). The political economy of educational innovation. *College Quarterly*, 12(2), 1. Online at: http://www.collegequarterly.ca/2009-vol12-num02-spring/doughty_meaghan_barrett.html

Ehrman, M. E., Leaver, B. L., & Oxford, R. L. (2003). A brief overview of individual differences in second language learning. *System*, 31(3), 313–330.

Fang, Y. (2010). Perceptions of the computer-assisted writing program among EFL college learners. *Educational Technology & Society*, 13(3), 246–256. Online at: http://www.ifets.info/journals/13_3/22.pdf

Fitzpatrick, M. (2012). Classroom lectures go digital. *The New York Times*, June 24, 2012. Online at: http://www.nytimes.com/2012/06/25/us/25iht-educside25.html?_r=0

Garrison, D., & Vaughan, N. (2007). *Blended Learning in Higher Education: Framework, Principles, and Guidelines*. San Francisco: Jossey-Bass.

Gojak, L. (2012, October). To flip or not to flip: That is not the question! *National Council of Teachers of Mathematics*. Online at: http://www.nctm.org/News-and-Calendar/Messages-from-the-President/Archive/Linda-M_-Gojak/To-Flip-or-Not-to-Flip_-That-Is-NOT-the-Question!/

Hubbard, P. (Ed.) (2009). *Computer Assisted Language Learning: Critical Concepts in Linguistics*, Volumes I–IV. London & New York: Routledge.

Johnson, C. P. (2014). *Increasing Students' Academic Involvement: Chilean Teacher Engagement with Learners in Blended English as a Foreign Language Courses*. (Doctoral dissertation). Available from ProQuest/UMI. (waldenu14174).

Johnson, C. P., & Marsh, D. (2013). The Laureate English Program: Taking a research informed approach to blended learning. *Higher Learning Research Communications*. Online at: http://journals.sfu.ca/liu/index.php/HLRC/article/view/103

Lage, M. J., Platt, G. J., & Treglia, M. (2000). Inverting the classroom: A gateway to creating an inclusive learning environment. *The Journal of Economic Education*, 31, 30–43.

Lewis, G. (2009). *Bringing Technology into the Classroom*. New York: Oxford University Press.

Marsh, D. (2012). *Blended Learning: Creating Learning Opportunities for Language Learners*. New York: Cambridge University Press.

Mazur, E. (2009). Farewell, lecture? *Science*, 323, 50–51. Online at: http://www.sciencemag.org/content/323/5910/50.full

Nakazawa, K. (2009). Student engagement in online language learning: A case study examining the online delivery of tertiary language courses. *The International Journal of Learning*, 16(7), 405–414. Online at: http://ijl.cgpublisher.com/product/pub.30/prod.2308

Neumeier, P. (2005). A closer look at blended learning – parameters for designing a blended learning environment for language teaching and learning. *ReCALL*, 17, 163–178.

Peña-Sánchez, R., & Hicks, R. C. (2006). Faculty perceptions of communications channels: A survey. *International Journal of Innovation and Learning*, 3(1), 45–62.

Roger, T., & Tingerthal, J. (2013). Blended learning and 'flipping' the construction management classroom for improved teaching and learning. *ASC International Proceedings of the 49th Annual Conference*. California Polytechnic State University, San Luis Obispo, CA. Online at: http://ascpro0.ascweb.org/archives/cd/2013/paper/CEUE40002013.pdf

Salcedo, C. S. (2010). Comparative analysis of learning outcomes in face-to-face foreign language classes vs. language lab and online. *Journal of College Teaching & Learning*, 7(2), 43–54. Online at: http://journals.cluteonline.com/index.php/TLC/article/view/88/85

Saxena, S. (2013). How to best use the class time when flipping your classroom. *EdTech Review*. Online at: http://edtechreview.in/news/news/trends-insights/insights/726-how-to-best-use-the-class-time-when-flipping-your-classroom

Sayadian, S., Mukundan, J., & Baki, R. (2009, October). Exploring the factors influencing UPM English language faculty members' adoption and integration of web-based instruction (WBI). *Journal of College Teaching & Learning*, 6(6), 31–38. Online at: http://journals.cluteonline.com/index.php/TLC/article/view/1132/1116

Senior, R. (2010). Connectivity: A framework for understanding effective language teaching in face-to-face and online learning communities. *RELC Journal*, 41(2), 137–147. doi:10.1177/0033688210375775

So, H.-J., & Bonk, C. J. (2010). Examining the roles of blended learning approaches in computer-supported collaborative learning (CSCL) environments: A Delphi study. *Educational Technology & Society*, 13(3), 189–200. Online at: http://www.ifets.info/journals/13_3/17.pdf

Stracke, E. (2005). Conflicting voices: Blended learning in a German university foreign language classroom. In M. Dúill, R. Zahn, & K. D. C. Höppner (Eds.), *Zusammenarbeiten: Eine Festschrift für Bernd Voss* (pp. 403–20). Bochum: AKS-Verlag. Also published in L. Miller (Ed.), *Learner Autonomy 9: Autonomy in the classroom* (pp. 85–103). Dublin: Authentik.

Stracke, E. (2007). A road to understanding: A qualitative study into why learners drop out of a blended language learning (BLL) environment. *ReCALL*, 19(1), 57–78.

Vlachopoulos, P., & Cowan, J. (2010). Choices of approaches in e-moderation: Conclusions from a grounded theory study. *Active Learning in Higher Education*, 11(3), 213–224. doi:10.1177/1469787410379684

Walsh, S. (2006). *Investigating Classroom Discourse*. Abingdon: Routledge.

Walvoord, B. E., & Anderson, V. J. (1998). *Effective Grading: A Tool for Learning and Assessment*. San Francisco: Jossey-Bass.

Yuksel, I. (2009). Instructor competencies for online courses. *Procedia Social and Behavioral Sciences*, 1, 1726–1729. doi:10.1016/j.sbspro.2009.01.305

Appendix

INTERVIEW PROTOCOL FOR LAUREATE ENGLISH PROGRAM RESEARCH
INTRODUCTORY REMARKS

Good (morning, afternoon, evening). We want to thank you all again for taking the time to do this focus group interview with us today. As we mentioned before, we'd like to talk with you about:

- your experiences as an TEFL practitioner and your role within the LEP BL courses at your university.
- your perceptions of the role of students in BL and online settings and,
- your opinions about the changing nature of the 'classroom' (face-to-face and virtual) in BL environments.

We would like to ask you a few questions related to these topics. The interview should take less than an hour.

We are soliciting the perspectives of TESOL professionals as part of an ongoing research project about blended EFL teaching and learning in an **effort to identify best practices that can be put forward in the Laureate network**. Your input is invaluable and will be used as part of the primary data from which conclusions and recommendations can be made.

The information you provide during this interview will be used for this purpose only and will remain strictly confidential. This means that your input will only be shared with the members of research team and that anything used in the final summary report will not identify you specifically as respondents.

We would like this to be a conversation and therefore not have to interrupt the flow of our discussion by taking detailed notes while we talk. In order to do this, we will be audio recording the interview, with your permission, so that we do not miss anything that you say and can accurately document the insights you convey. Please speak as clearly as possible. We do not want to misunderstand any of your valuable comments during later analysis of the transcript.

Please know that there are no particular right-or-wrong answers to any of these questions. We are simply looking for your sincere views and opinions on the issues involved. If you feel that you are unsure of, uncomfortable with, or merely unable to respond to a particular question, please just tell us so and we will move on. You may also ask to end the focus group interview at any time.

In your responses to any of the questions, please feel free to elaborate or illustrate in any way you like. Your personal examples will be very helpful.

Some of the questions may be interpreted in different ways. If we ask a follow up question to something you have said, we are only trying to clarify the original question or seeking to fully understand your response. Please feel free to ask us to clarify any question or comment that you may not understand as well.

Do you have any questions before we start about what I have just said?

At this time, then, I remind you of your signed consent to participate in this study. Both of us have signed and dated copies of the consent form which certifies we agree to proceed with this interview. You will receive one of the copies of this document and the other will be kept, by me, in a secure location, separate from the transcript of your responses.

With your permission then, let us begin the interview.

QUESTIONS

BLENDED LANGUAGE LEARNING

1. Which online activities did you usually ask students to complete before class? Why?
2. Which activities did you usually use in the classroom? Why?
3. Which online activities did you usually ask students to complete after class? Why?

THE ROLE OF THE TEACHER

1. What do you consider to be the major benefits to **language teaching** in blended EFL courses?
2. What do you consider to be the major challenges to **language teaching** in blended EFL courses?
3. To what extent has a blended instructional format changed the way you approach teaching?

THE ROLE OF THE LEARNER

1. What do you consider to be the major benefits to **language learning** in blended EFL courses?
2. What do you consider to be the major challenges to **language learning** in blended EFL courses?
3. How have your students adapted to the change in content delivery format?

THE CHANGING NATURE OF THE 'CLASSROOM'

1. To what extent is the teaching experience in the 'blended' classroom different from the 'traditional' teaching experience in class?
2. What did you like about the changes in the classroom teaching experience?
3. What did you NOT like about the changes in the classroom teaching experience?

Before we conclude this interview, are there any final comments you would like to add or questions you would like to ask me?

*** If any participants wish to discontinue the interview, ask if they would be willing to share why.
Thank the participants for their participation.

CHAPTER 5

Blended Teaching and the Changing Role of the Language Teacher: The Need for a Review of Teacher Professional Development

Anna Comas-Quinn

INTRODUCTION

It is widely accepted that the role of the online language teacher is different to that of the classroom teacher (Baumann et al., 2008; Murphy et al., 2011; Comas-Quinn et al., 2012). With language teaching moving increasingly toward blended modes of delivery, incorporating online teaching and learning inevitably changes the function of the so-called traditional classroom and its place in the educational system (Moore and Kearsley, 2011). The new elements added to the mix may be tools (instructional, conferencing or social media, for example), activities (telecollaboration, forum discussions) or approaches (flipped classroom, open pedagogy, student-generated content). In this context, teachers need to understand how to perform their roles, not just online, but in relation to each of the elements of the new blended learning (BL) environment.

As technological innovation speeds up, the number and variety of tools is ever-increasing and rapidly changing, so a key challenge for teachers, and a fundamental aim of professional development, has to be understanding how to harness the various tools and modes of teaching to deliver the learning outcomes and meet the learners' needs. Additionally, teachers have to be made aware that a blended teaching approach, being multimodal (including a combination of media, visual, audio and textual, both online and face-to-face), will require them to engage with learners and peers in a variety of ways, some of which will be new and, at least initially, more demanding (Gallardo et al., 2011: 219).

Professional development cannot just focus on the technical aspect of mastering tools and skills, but needs to place more emphasis on the pedagogical aspect of understanding what these new technologies enable us to do and how we can effectively apply them to teaching and learning. This distinction between technical and pedagogical knowledge and skills (Hubbard and Levy, 2006), at the core of much professional development for online language learning, still falls short of accounting for the transformational impact that learning to teach within a BL context can have on teachers. Wang, Chen and Levy (2010) recommend a more 'holistic approach', that is, one that looks not just at the teacher but at the whole person, taking into consideration the cognitive and the affective, the personal and the professional. This approach should place particular emphasis on identity formation and personal development if training and professional development are to support teachers adequately in their transition to becoming online language teachers, able to deliver the appropriate blend of online and traditional teaching.

It may be argued that encouraging a deeper understanding and acceptance of the new ways of performing their roles will have a positive influence on the learning process of both teachers and learners, as teachers are often instrumental in shaping learners' perceptions of the function and value of the different elements of a course. McPherson and Nunes (2004) claimed that online teachers were 'a critical success factor in learner acceptance of elearning', a claim supported by later research (Comas-Quinn, 2011 and Nissen and Tea, 2012), which has shown that the success in the implementation of online language learning is influenced to a large extent by how well teachers understand their own role and make the transition to the new system.

This chapter examines what constitutes an effective approach to professional development for blended teaching. The second section starts with a review of the literature including some key underpinning concepts: how learning and the role of the teacher are understood and conceptualised, and the effect these can have on the design of the professional development on offer; the centrality of the individual and the impact that teachers' values, identity and conception of self has in their engagement with professional development; and the affective issues, particularly motivation, that impact on teachers' readiness to engage with professional development initiatives designed to change their practice. This section also includes a description of the main characteristics of an effective approach to professional development.

The third section presents a case study of professional development for BL provided for language teachers at The Open University, UK. Firstly, it describes the evolution of the training provision for online teaching through synchronous audio-graphic conferencing. Secondly, it reports on initiatives to encourage collaborative working, and the sharing of good practice and resources. Finally, it explores further ways of promoting deeper learning and understanding through open practices, and the evaluation of teaching practice through self-reflection and creative engagement with scholarship and research.

The Analysis and Discussion section includes some reflections on how the approaches detailed in the previous section match, or otherwise, the key principles identified in the literature review. The conclusion offers examples from other language teaching and learning contexts in which some of the approaches to professional development presented in the main case study and the literature can also be found to operate successfully.

LITERATURE REVIEW

In this chapter teachers are regarded as practitioners, developers, trainers and researchers (Freeman, 1998). They need not necessarily be the CALL specialists defined by Hubbard (2009) but they are certainly professionals who are capable of extending their own knowledge, skills and understanding of a variety of teaching modes and technological tools.

Johnson (2006) highlights the need to redraw the boundaries of professional development to accommodate the learning, often informal, situated and unplanned, in which these professionals engage. She argues that teachers should be able to direct their own professional development and that this can take place in new spaces of learning such as informal social and professional networks or even their own classrooms, reconceptualised as sites for professional learning. In this way, second language teacher education can be aligned with more current conceptions of teacher learning, and become a more self-directed, collaborative, inquiry-based learning activity directly relevant to teachers and their practice. New technologies make it easier for teachers to take control of their own learning by experimenting with the kind of learning activities they might want their learners to engage with, and to access virtual communities where they can co-construct their personal understanding of online learning through discussions with peers. McCarthy (Chapter 1, this volume) discusses the value of social networks for students; many of those aspects are equally relevant to teachers.

Professional development for BL needs to offer teachers freedom to experiment according to their own interests and priorities, and to treat change, innovation and continuous learning as integral parts of their professional practice. Kumaravadivelu (2008: 225) expresses it very clearly:

> Change produces anxiety, particularly if it involves a move from the comfortable climate of familiarity to an unpredictable arena of uncertainty. But, such a change can be less disorienting if it develops within a context in which the participants themselves play a role in making decisions and in implementing those decisions. In the context of educational change, this means making change part of the learning process itself.

In the following sections we examine how the conceptualisation of learning and the role of the teacher influence the approach taken when designing professional development initiatives, and how issues related to identity and motivation can play a big role in determining the success or failure of professional development.

APPROACHES TO LEARNING AND THE TEACHER'S ROLE

A widely accepted view of learning is that it is 'a dynamic social activity that is situated in physical and social contexts, and distributed across persons, tools, and activities' (Johnson, 2006: 237). Learning often takes place as a result of participation in human practices or communities of practice (Lave and Wenger, 1991) and its effect is transformational in a way that is 'practical, physical and emotional as well as cognitive' (Hager and Hodkinson, 2009: 633). Nevertheless, learning as acquisition, in which learners are expected to absorb a defined body of knowledge and skills to become competent in a relevant field or practice, is still widely used and accepted in many contexts, and is particularly common in much of the training offered in the workplace.

This view of learning ignores the fact that the 'skillful practice of occupations is both holistic and significantly contextual' (Ibid.: 625), an idea that is fundamental to Kumaravadivelu's (2008) concept of 'particularity'. This concept stresses that teachers perform their roles not in the abstract, but in concrete situations where they respond to the needs of a particular group of students at a particular point in time and in a particular context. Therefore, training and professional development systems must equip teachers with techniques or 'macrostrategies' for blended teaching and rely on their ability to develop their own 'microstrategies' to cope with particular teaching situations, thus developing their own personal theory of practice (Kumaravadivelu, 2003).

IDENTITY AND MOTIVATION

White and Ding (2009) argue that the most crucial challenge for teachers engaging in online learning is that to their teacher 'identity' and teacher 'self'. The concept of 'identity' describes the interpretation of oneself as a certain kind of person which is recognised as such in a particular context and in relation to others, whilst the concept of 'self' represents the collection of beliefs and attitudes a person has about oneself and can include past, present and future selves (see also McCarthy, Chapter 1, this volume and Lave and Wenger, 1991). Dörnyei (2009) explores this notion of possible selves as a way of understanding motivation in his L2 Motivational Self System, which Kubanyiova (2009) applies and extends using the following categories: an *Ideal Language Teacher Self,* the teacher that one aspires to become; an *Ought-to Language Teacher Self,* the teacher they feel they should become to comply with external rules and expectations; and a *Feared Language Teacher Self,* which the teacher feels they might become if they cannot fulfil their ideals or meet what is expected or required of them.

In two studies that used Dörnyei's framework to explore how language teachers might or might not see themselves as online teachers, White and Ding (2009) and Kubanyiova (2009) concluded that teachers' motivation to engage constructively with training is largely dependent on the extent to which they share the values and beliefs on which the training is based. If the training helps the teacher move forward towards achieving their Ideal Language Teacher Self, they are more likely to engage with and benefit from it. Conversely, if the values and beliefs on which the training is based do not match the teacher's own, the teacher will comply with the training but reluctantly and without much interest, and may even resist it, resulting in poor learning and performance.

Consequently, it is essential to refocus professional development on identity formation and personal transformation, to prompt teachers to examine and question their beliefs and assumptions about their role and their practice, and 'to persuade them of the value of online teaching and the desirability of becoming online teachers' (Comas-Quinn, 2011: 229).

EFFECTIVE PROFESSIONAL DEVELOPMENT FOR LANGUAGE TEACHING

Models of professional development for online learning have often been based on teaching the technical and pedagogical skills required to master certain tools or environments (Hampel and Stickler, 2005; Hubbard and Levy, 2006; Compton, 2009). These are no doubt essential, but focusing solely on particular tools and the skills, technical or pedagogical, required to use them is of limited use, since technological innovation happens at an increasingly fast pace and specific tools can quickly become outdated. Understanding the functions of particular components in blended teaching and how each fits into the overall learning design, what Kirkwood and Price (2005) simply explained as knowing *why* as well as *how*, needs to become an integral part of professional development. Equally important is the realisation that 'traditional teaching + online tools ≠ online teaching', i.e., that learning to be an effective online teacher is not just learning how to teach online but requires a substantial revision and transformation of the role of the teacher and their approach to teaching.

Nissen and Tea's study on the challenges for language tutors of delivering a blended course showed that competence in the use of the technology was just one of many factors that teachers identified as important in helping them feel truly involved and comfortable with their role as blended teachers (2012: 155–159). More importantly, Nissen and Tea pointed out that 'the majority [of teachers in their study] had trouble understanding the function of the online part of the courses, and their own role within the online part' (Ibid.: 159). This vague view of the online component of the course was shared, implicitly or explicitly, with learners, who were therefore less likely to engage with it, as its function and value had not been properly communicated to them. These conclusions echo those reported by Comas-Quinn (2011) who examined teachers' limited success in understanding how to perform their teaching role through asynchronous tools (forums and blogs) and highlighted the need for training to include further opportunities for teachers to 'construct their own personal understanding of what online teaching [is]' (p. 229).

Wang, Chen and Levy (2010) propose a holistic approach that is built on practice, reflection and collaboration. For them, 'a pedagogy of teacher education should go beyond the mere transmission of knowledge and focus on identity formation and personal growth' (Ibid.: 777). A holistic approach to teacher education should include the professional aspects but also the personal aspects of learning such as self-awareness, confidence and personal transformation.

Ernest and Hopkins (2006) list awareness raising, teacher reflection, construction of knowledge and community as the pillars on which effective training and professional development must be based. Gallardo et al. (2011: 224–226) expand these into a list of basic requirements for effective training and professional development for online teaching. Such a programme would need to:

- provide opportunities for sharing knowledge and for teachers to compare their existing experience with the new role and practice.
- explore what different tools and modes of delivery allow or facilitate, to develop an understanding of their pedagogic usefulness and function in the learning design.
- use an experiential approach (learning by doing) to training and careful modelling of practice in an environment that mirrors the learning environment in which teachers will have to perform their roles.
- encourage teachers to view their classroom as a 'site of professional learning' (Johnson, 2006: 243) and to engage in some form of practitioner research or 'exploratory practice' (Allwright, 2005) to reflect on their own teaching practice (Schön, 1983).

In the following case study I describe how the Department of Languages at The Open University, UK, organises its professional development programme for language teachers. I then go on to discuss how this provision matches or otherwise the key principles described above.

CASE STUDY: PROFESSIONAL DEVELOPMENT FOR BLENDED LANGUAGE TEACHING AT THE DEPARTMENT OF LANGUAGES, THE OPEN UNIVERSITY, UK

CONTEXT

The Open University is a distance learning institution of Higher Education teaching over 200,000 students in the UK. The Department of Languages offers languages qualifications including English, Spanish, French, German and Italian, as well as English for Academic Purposes, and beginners' Welsh and Chinese. Some 300 part-time associate lecturers (here referred to as teachers) support the learning of approximately 10,000 part-time students, who study using audio-visual, online and print materials produced by a team of around 30 full-time academic staff (referred to as lecturers) working as course developers and course coordinators. Teachers are line managed and supported by 12 regional language academic coordinators (referred to as regional academic managers) who have responsibility for groups of language teachers and learners in designated geographical areas.

In 2007 the Department of Languages adopted a blended teaching approach for all its language courses. This meant that all courses had an online component including most of the following: asynchronous teaching through forums (and sometimes blogs and wikis), synchronous teaching through an audio-graphic conferencing tool (Blackboard Collaborate at the time of writing), a course website with a study calendar to guide learners through the teaching and assessment resources, and online multimedia content to complement the customary print and audio-visual materials on which the language courses had traditionally relied.

The following subsections focus on four ways in which professional development for online and blended language teaching is organised at this institution. The assumptions and choices made are then discussed in the Analysis and Discussion section in relation to the theoretical issues presented earlier.

TRAINING LANGUAGE TEACHERS FOR ONLINE SYNCHRONOUS TEACHING

The move to blended teaching brought with it the challenge of having to train all existing language teachers to operate in this new environment. An additional challenge was that some of them had experience of teaching online while others were totally new to this mode of delivery, and occasionally they were reluctant or doubtful of its ability to support effective language teaching.

The initial training focused on knowledge and skills, and attempted to separate the technical aspects of using the different tools from their pedagogical application. Initially, technical training was provided by a central training unit, although soon a dedicated languages training team was created, substantially improving the relevance of the training programme. Pedagogical training was left to lecturers coordinating particular courses, and was confined to one session before the start of the course, followed by more personalised support through the teacher forum for each course. Regional academic managers were responsible for providing further professional development in their regions, and this often took the shape of face-to-face workshops in which trainers delved more deeply into the technical and pedagogical aspects of the tools.

Progressively, the training moved online, as it was realised that this was more effective in mirroring the online teaching that teachers would have to engage in. The choice of trainers also changed, with more experienced online teachers asked to develop a more coherent training programme for those new to, or less experienced in online teaching. Eventually, the department consolidated all training provision in an internal training website with space for creating online classrooms, discussion forums, wikis, resource areas, etc. Since 2010 most training activities for language teachers have taken place in this space, and materials have been archived here for reference by those who did not attend specific training events or by new teachers joining the institution.

The current professional development provision for synchronous online teaching includes a variety of optional sessions that deal with aspects such as managing mixed abilities in the online classroom, the use of more advanced features of the tools, creating and adapting resources and creative uses of the tools to enhance interactivity and increase learner engagement. The principles underpinning this training programme are described in Warnecke and Lominé (2011) and Lominé, Warnecke and St. John (2011).

SHARING TEACHING RESOURCES

Many teachers have shared the teaching materials they produce or find, often on an informal or ad hoc basis, with close colleagues or particular groups of teachers. The benefits of this practice for professional development have long been recognised by regional academic managers at the institution, responsible for teacher professional development. Over the years, these managers have encouraged a more systematic approach to sharing and come up with a range of systems to facilitate it, from paper and CD compilations of resources to curated websites. These partial solutions were limited, and it was evident that a simple, open and easily accessible system to allow sharing across the whole community was needed to more effectively support teachers as they developed their online teaching practice (Comas-Quinn et al., 2011, Section 3.2).

A repository, an online space for managing and storing digital content, was identified as the best solution to this challenge, and in 2009 the department was awarded some funding from the Joint Information Systems Committee (JISC) to create and populate LORO (Languages Open Resources Online, http://loro.open.ac.uk), a repository of Open Educational Resources for language teaching and learning. Initially, LORO hosted the 800+ resources created by course developers to support teachers as they incorporated online teaching into their practice. Being an open repository, it also allowed for teachers at The Open University and beyond to upload their own materials to share openly with the rest of the language teaching community beyond the institution. LORO currently contains over 2,500 resources for language teaching and the professional development of language teachers.

There is substantial evidence that language teachers at The Open University make use of the resources provided through LORO. Data from usage surveys indicates that around 80% of respondents use LORO to find resources for the course/s they teach, while about a third also browse for and download resources for other courses beyond those they teach (Comas-Quinn, 2013: 3). Ongoing research on the use and reuse of resources (Beaven, 2013; Pulker and Calvi, 2013; Winchester, 2013) is slowly uncovering the complex decisions taken by teachers in terms of the suitability of the materials they have available and the modification they feel these require when preparing and delivering an online language lesson, and the ways in which teachers are inspired by available resources which they use, adapt, repurpose or recreate to meet the needs of their learners and their own individual teaching styles.

SHARING GOOD PRACTICE, COLLABORATION AND THE MOVE TOWARDS OPEN PRACTICES

Regional academic managers have responsibility for organising training and development opportunities where teachers can exchange knowledge and practice. The traditional annual face-to-face encounters (where time was limited and non-attenders missed out) have increasingly been supplemented by online events, which can be recorded and archived for the benefit of those who cannot attend or new teachers joining the institution, to provide more regular and varied development opportunities. Moving professional development largely online has also encouraged the creation of a wider community of teachers (no longer restricted by the regional groupings) who can collaborate and support each other. The very successful programme of online peer observation (Harper and Nicolson, 2013) is a good example of the potential of linking this wider teacher community.

Sharing teaching resources through an open online repository has encouraged increased transparency and paved the way for further initiatives to promote collaboration and the sharing of good practice. Several projects have embedded online discussion and collaboration, peer review and open online publishing of resources (Duensing et al., 2013, and Calvi et al., 2013). These have often been just one aspect of activities that had another main focus like the application of drama techniques to the language classroom (Álvarez et al., 2013) or the exploration of the challenges associated with dyslexia for those teaching and learning languages (Gallardo and Arias-McLaughlin, 2013).

Modelling open practices in the professional development of teachers has started some changes in the way teachers approach the creation of resources, increasing, for example, their awareness of good practice in attribution (referencing sources and acknowledging original authors) when reusing materials created by others, and of copyright issues, particularly in relation to the use of images. Through the projects mentioned above, open publishing of teaching resources is slowly becoming a valid alternative for promoting professional reflection and starting pedagogical conversations amongst language teachers.

DEEPENING LEARNING: TRAINERS, CHAMPIONS AND RESEARCHERS

The institution encourages deeper learning and engagement with online teaching in a variety of ways. More technologically competent teachers and those who show a better grasp of the demands and challenges of designing and delivering online teaching might be invited to act as mentors for those who are new to the institution, or to work as 'champions' who can provide more individualised support for colleagues. The training programme for online synchronous teaching is designed, delivered and evaluated by language teachers employed to act as trainers and training designers. These are ways of publicly recognising and rewarding the accumulated experience and expertise of language teachers who work hard to become effective online teachers. At the same time, engaging in these activities promotes further exploration and deeper understanding, which can in turn only benefit their own practice.

Professional development activities for language teachers at this institution are firmly based on the concept of the teacher as a reflective practitioner (Schön, 1983). Action research as described by Burns (2003) or Allwright's 'exploratory practice' (2005) are seen as naturally complementing teachers' practice, and teachers are therefore supported and encouraged to engage in scholarship activities to further their understanding of language teaching and learning using new tools and modes of delivery. Opportunities are available for teachers who show an interest to collaborate on (or originate) research or scholarship projects designed to evaluate their own practice and the learning experiences of students. For example, the institutional scheme leading to external recognition from the UK Higher Education Academy (HEA) is based on practitioners undertaking an investigation into their own practice (a practitioner inquiry/action research approach) and is available to anybody involved in teaching and supporting learning.

DEVELOPING FURTHER LEARNING, PRESENTING AND WRITING FOR PUBLICATION

Further study is also possible as teachers might be sponsored by the institution to take undergraduate and postgraduate courses that are of interest or relevant to their roles, like the Doctorate in Education or the Master in Open and Distance Education, or any of the courses offered by the institution, where they can experience online and blended teaching from the learner point of view.

The institution provides opportunities for teachers to present their work internally to their department or elsewhere in the institution, and externally, by offering financial help for travel and conference attendance. This helps teachers view their work as valued and relevant to the wider teaching community.

The opportunities created by the ease with which content can now be published, particularly online, further contribute to this, and empower teachers to add their voices to the academic discussions in their field. Some examples of work *by* practitioners *for* practitioners can be found in Nicolson et al. (2011), Beaven et al. (2013) and Borthwick, Corradini and Dickens (2015).

ANALYSIS AND DISCUSSION

Effective training for online and blended teaching needs to start by encouraging teachers to be agents in their own learning and by providing them with opportunities to challenge and reconstruct their existing understanding of their role as teachers. The above case study has exemplified how the training provision at one particular institution has evolved to offer teachers increased choice and responsibility for their own learning.

Unfortunately, even the best provision cannot guarantee that teachers will be interested in and committed to making the most of the training and professional development opportunities provided. Some teachers will be more willing and ready to take up what is on offer than others, and this has a lot to do with the strength of internal and external motivators, their individual dispositions and attitudes, life histories and preferences (Billet and Somerville, 2004). Performance issues may arise as a consequence of resistance to change, and the institution will have to find supportive ways of encouraging teachers to re-evaluate their beliefs and values, and embrace new ways of working. Hampel and Stickler (2005: 324) hold institutions ultimately responsible for encouraging good practice, devising effective training programmes and persuading teachers to fully benefit from them. Tait (2002) suggests that involving teachers in the design and delivery of professional development is an effective way of encouraging them to own and shape the training and, therefore, to engage with it more successfully. The case study presented here includes several examples of how teachers have been invited to be partners in the process of creating and delivering training for online teaching.

The strength of teachers' beliefs and attitudes, and the impact that these have on their whole practice, cannot be underestimated and has been shown to determine to a large extent how successfully teachers engage with training and professional development. For example, when adapting resources for reuse, the decisions made by teachers appear to be firmly rooted in their beliefs, values and individual perceptions of their role as teachers (Pulker and Calvi, 2013). Consequently the resulting resources are perceived by some teachers to be highly customised to particular teaching events and groups of learners, and therefore of limited value for resharing (Beaven, 2013), in spite of institutional encouragement to share good practice and resources.

What the case study has shown is that the online medium is ideal to support a distributed community of language teachers, and to replicate the environment in which they need to operate to support their own students when teaching in an online and/or blended context. Embedding online working, collaboration, open practices and practitioner inquiry into the professional development activities of language teachers, as seen here, has proven to be an effective way of modelling good practice, which teachers can then transfer to their own teaching practice. An increasing number of contributions to the literature describe and advocate an experiential, situated approach to learning as the most successful in training teachers to teach online (Ernest and Hopkins, 2006; Johnson, 2006; Hampel, 2009; Motteram, 2009; Wang et al., 2010; Gallardo, Heiser and Nicolson, 2011; Capellini, 2013, amongst others).

Conclusion

Understanding that teachers can be, and generally are, agents in their own learning, choosing their own professional development paths according to their own needs and preferences, is leading to a substantial change in the way in which professional development is conceived. For example, recognising that much learning takes place in a bite-size, informal manner has resulted in channelling efforts into providing learning resources in formats that help pressed-for-time teachers to learn about tools, practices and their application to the language classroom. Stannard's (2006–2011) Teacher Training Videos are a good example of how a relatively modest endeavour (a screen capture of the author talking us through how to use a particular tool) was spectacularly successful in meeting teachers' needs. A similar approach was taken in the Developing Online Teaching Skills (DOTS) project (Beaven et al., 2010), which provided concise learning objects on how to use selected ICT tools in language teaching, and was aimed at part-time or freelance teaching professionals, whose access to training opportunities is often limited.

Also with these communities in mind, several projects and initiatives have been developed at the time of writing to encourage the sharing of resources and good practice. The creation of resource repositories similar to The Open University's LORO repository, specifically Humbox and Language Box for the language teaching community in the UK and beyond, are opening the way for these teacher communities to engage in sharing as an integral part of professional development (Borthwick, 2011; Borthwick and Dickens, 2013; King, 2013; Martínez-Arboleda, 2013; Nelson and Pozo-Gutiérrez, 2013; and Watson, 2013 amongst others). There are other repositories designed to support teacher communities such as Jorum for the Higher and Further Education community in the UK, the Re:Source platform that hosts content from Scotland's colleges to support their further education (FE) sector, and resource-sharing platforms primarily aimed at the school sector, like the Teaching Resources bank in the TESConnect website, or the resources area of *The Guardian*'s Teacher Network. All of these contain languages sections although they are not discipline-specific repositories like Language Box, Humbox or LORO.

Open collaboration and sharing are finally making teachers' work more visible, whilst online tools and social media increase their opportunities for presenting their work and telling their own story (see Voices for Openness, Center for Open Educational Resources and Language Learning COERLL, 2013). This increased exposure to the experiences of others should encourage teachers to become more engaged in examining, reflecting on and evaluating their own practice. Research need no longer be something that researchers do on teachers, but an activity that is an integral part of the professional development choices available to teachers.

Suggested Resources

Dörnyei, Z., & Ushioda, E. (Eds.) (2009). *Motivation, Language Identity and the L2 Self*. Bristol: Multilingual Matters.

DOTS (Developing Online Teaching Skills) (2011). Online at: http://dots.ecml.at

Gallardo, M., Heiser, S., & Nicolson, M. (2011). Teacher development for blended courses. In M. Nicolson, L. Murphy & M. Southgate (Eds.), *Language Teaching in Blended Contexts* (pp. 219–231). Edinburgh, Dunedin Academic Press.

Guardian Teacher Network (2013). Online at: http://www.guardian.co.uk/teacher-network

HumBox. Online at: http://humbox.ac.uk

Johnson, K. E. (2006). The sociocultural turn and its challenges for second language teacher education. *TESOL Quarterly*, 40(1), 235–257.

Jorum. Online at: http://www.jorum.ac.uk/

Kumaravadivelu, B. (2006). *Understanding Language Teaching: From Method to Post-Method*. Taylor and Francis e-Library. Online at: http://www.tandfebooks.com/action/showBook?doi=10.4324/9781410615725&queryID=15%2F290481769

LanguageBox. Online at: http://languagebox.ac.uk

LORO (Languages Open Resources Online). Online at: http://loro.open.ac.uk

Re:Source. Online at: http://resource.blogs.scotcol.ac.uk/

Stannard, R. (2006–2011). Teacher Training Videos. Online at: http://www.teachertrainingvideos.com/

TESConnect (2013) Teaching Resources. Online at: http://www.tes.co.uk/teaching-resources/

Wang, Y., Chen, N-S., & Levy, M. (2010). The design and implementation of a holistic training model for language teacher education in a cyber face-to-face learning environment, *Computers & Education*, 55, 777–788.

Discussion Questions

1. Think of examples of spaces of learning (including professional networks and virtual communities) where teachers may find support for developing their online teaching practice.

2. Examine a particular teacher training or professional development programme, and identify what approach to learning underpins this provision. Is it based on the acquisition of knowledge and competences? Is the approach experiential? Is it situated?

3. Using Dörnyei's L2 Motivational Self System (2009), think of what your Ideal Teacher Self, your Ought-to Teacher Self and your Feared Online Language Teacher Self would look like.

4. What would a teacher training or professional development programme that is built on practice, reflection and collaboration (Wang et al., 2010) look like?

References

Álvarez, I., Beaven, T., & Comas-Quinn, A. (2013). Performing languages: An example of integrating open practices in staff development for language teachers. *Journal of e-Learning and Knowledge Society*, 9(1), 85–92.

Allwright, R. (2005). Developing principles for practitioner research: The case of exploratory practice. *The Modern Language Journal*, 89(3), 353–66.

Baumann, U., Shelley, M., Murphy, L., & White, C. (2008). New challenges: The role of the tutor in the teaching of languages at a distance. *Distances et Savoirs*, 6, 364–392.

Beaven, A., Comas-Quinn, A., & Sawhill, B. (Eds.) (2013). *Case Studies of Openness in the Language Classroom*. Dublin: Voillans, Research-publishing.net. Online at: http://research-publishing.net/publications/2013-beaven-comas-quinn-sawhill/

Beaven, T. (2013). Use and reuse of OER: professional conversations with language teachers. *Journal of e-Learning and Knowledge Society*, 9(1), 59–71.

Beaven, T., Emke, M., Ernest, P., Germain-Rutherford, A., Hampel, R., Hopkins, J., Stanojevic, M. M., & Stickler, U. (2010). Needs and challenges for online language teachers – the ECML project DOTS. *Teaching English with Technology: A Journal for Teachers of English*, 10(2), 5–20.

Billet, S., & Somerville, M. (2004). Transformations at work: Identity and learning, *Studies in Continuing Education*, 26(2), 309–326.

Borthwick, K. (2011). What HumBox did next: Real stories of OERs in action from users of a teaching and learning repository for the humanities. In *Proceedings of OpenCourseWare Consortium Global 2011: Celebrating 10 Years of OpenCourseWare*. Cambridge, MA.

Borthwick, K., Corradini, E., & Dickens, A. (2015). *10 Years of the LLAS elearning Symposium: Case Studies in Good Practice*, Dublin: Voillans, Research-publishing.net. Online at http://research-publishing.net/10-years-of-the-llas-elearning-symposium-case-studies-in-good-practice/

Borthwick, K., & Dickens, A. (2013). The Community Café: Creating and sharing open educational resources with community-based language teachers. *Journal of eLearning and Knowledge Society*, 9(1), 23–25.

Burns, A. (2003). *Collaborative Action Research for English Language Teachers*. Cambridge: Cambridge University Press.

Calvi, A., Motzo, A., & Silipo, A. (2013). Designing OERs to teach Italian pronunciation in an open educational environment: A case study. In A. Beaven, A. Comas-Quinn & B. Sawhill (Eds.) (2013), *Case Studies of Openness in the Language Classroom* (pp. 70–84). Dublin: Voillans, Research-publishing.net. Online at: http://research-publishing.net/publications/2013-beaven-comas-quinn-sawhill/

Capellini, M. (2013). When learner autonomy meets open educational resources: A study of a self-learning environment for Italian as a foreign language. In A. Beaven, A. Comas-Quinn & B. Sawhill (Eds.), *Case Studies of Openness in the Language Classroom* (pp. 205–216). Dublin: Voillans, Research-publishing.net. Online at: http://research-publishing.net/publications/2013-beaven-comas-quinn-sawhill/

Center for Open Educational Resources and Language Learning (COERLL) (2013). *Voices for Openness in Language Learning*. Online at: http://sites.la.utexas.edu/voices/

Comas-Quinn, A., de los Arcos, B., & Mardomingo, R. (2012). Virtual Learning Environments (VLEs) for distance language learning: Shifting tutor roles in a contested space for interaction. *Computer Assisted Language Learning*, 25(2), 129–143.

Comas-Quinn, A. (2011). Learning to teach online or learning to become an online teacher: an exploration of teachers' experiences in a blended learning course. *ReCALL*, 23(03), 218–232.

Comas-Quinn, A., Beaven, M., Pleines, C., Pulker, H., & de los Arcos, B. (2011). Languages Open Resources Online (LORO): Fostering a culture of collaboration and sharing. *The EuroCALL Review* (18).

Comas-Quinn, A., & Fitzgerald, A. (2013). *Open Educational Resources in Language Teaching and Learning*. Higher Education Academy (HEA), York. Online at http://oro.open.ac.uk/37550/

Compton, L. (2009). Preparing language teachers to teach language online: A look at skills, roles, and responsibilities. *Computer Assisted Language Learning*, 22(1), 73–99.

Dörnyei, Z. (2009). The L2 motivational self system. In Z. Dörnyei & E. Ushioda (Eds.), *Motivation, Language Identity and the L2 Self*. Bristol: Multilingual Matters.

Duensing, A., Gallardo, M., & Heiser, S. (2013). Learning to share and sharing to learn – professional development of language teachers in HE to foster open educational practices. In A. Beaven, A. Comas-Quinn & B. Sawhill (Eds.), *Case Studies of Openness in the Language Classroom*. Dublin: Voillans, Research-publishing.net. (pp. 121–133). Online at http://oro.open.ac.uk/38590/

Ernest, P., & Hopkins, J. (2006). Coordination and teacher development in an online learning environment. *CALICO Journal*, 23, 551–568.

Freeman, D. (1998). *Doing Teacher Research: From Inquiry to Understanding*. Boston: Heinle.

Gallardo, M., Heiser, S., & Nicolson, M. (2011). Teacher development for blended courses. In M. Nicolson, L. Murphy & M. Southgate (Eds.), *Language Teaching in Blended Contexts* (pp. 219–223). Edinburgh: Dunedin Academic Press.

Gallardo, M., & Arias-McLaughlin, X. (2013). Developing professional expertise using online communication tools: Teachers' considerations when designing online activities for dyslexic language students. Paper presented at the EUROCALL 2013 conference, University of Évora, Portugal.

Hager, P., & Hodkinson, P. (2009). Moving beyond the metaphor of transfer of learning. *British Educational Research Journal*, 35(4), 619–638.

Hampel, R. (2009). Training teachers for the multimedia age: Developing teacher expertise to enhance online learner interaction and collaboration. *Innovation in Language Learning and Teaching*, 3(1), 35–50.

Hampel, R., & Stickler, U. (2005). New skills for new classrooms: Training tutors to teach languages online. *Computer Assisted Language Learning*, 18, 311–326.

Harper, F., & Nicolson, M. (2013). Online peer observation: Its value in teacher professional development, support and well-being. *International Journal for Academic Development*, 18(3), 264–275.

Hubbard, P., & Levy, M. (2006). The scope of CALL education. In P. Hubbard & M. Levy (Eds.), *Teacher Education in CALL*, 3–20. Amsterdam, PA: John Benjamins.

Hubbard, P. (2009). Educating the CALL specialist. *Innovation in Language Learning and Teaching*, 3(1), 3–15.

Johnson, K. E. (2006). The sociocultural turn and its challenges for second language teacher education. *TESOL Quarterly*, 40(1), 235–57.

King, T. (2013). The 'Onstream' project: Collaboration between teachers in mainstream and supplementary schools. In A. Beaven, A. Comas-Quinn & B. Sawhill (Eds.), *Case Studies of Openness in the Language Classroom* (pp. 110–120). Dublin: Voillans, Research-publishing.net. Online at: http://research-publishing.net/publications/2013-beaven-comas-quinn-sawhill/

Kirkwood, A., & Price, L. (2005). Learners and learning in the twenty-first century: What do we know about students' attitudes towards and experiences of information and communication technologies that will help us design courses? *Studies in Higher Education*, 30, 257–274.

Kumaravadivelu, B. (2003). *Beyond Method: Macrostrategies for Language Teaching*. New Haven, CT: Yale University Press.

Kumaravadivelu, B. (2006). *Understanding Language Teaching: From Method to Post-Method*. Taylor and Francis e-Library. Online at: http://www.tandfebooks.com/action/showBook?doi=10.4324/9781410615725&queryID=15%2F290481769

Kubanyiova, M. (2009). Possible selves in language teacher development. In Z. Dörnyei & E. Ushioda (Eds.), *Motivation, Language Identity and the L2 Self* (pp. 314–332). Bristol: Multilingual Matters.

Lave, J., & Wenger, E. (1991). *Situated Practice: Legitimate Peripheral Participation*. Cambridge: Cambridge University Press.

Lominé, L., Warnecke, S., & St. John, E. (2011). Delivering synchronous online teaching. In M. Nicolson, L. Murphy & M. Southgate (Eds.), *Language Teaching in Blended Contexts* (pp. 140–153). Edinburgh: Dunedin Academic Press.

Martínez-Arboleda, A. (2013). Discovering Spanish voices abroad in a digital world. In A. Beaven, A. Comas-Quinn & B. Sawhill (Eds.), *Case Studies of Openness in the Language Classroom* (pp. 176–188). Dublin: Voillans, Research-publishing.net. Online at: http://research-publishing.net/publications/2013-beaven-comas-quinn-sawhill/

McPherson, M. A., & Nunes, J. M. B. (2004). The role of tutors as an integral part of online learning support. *European Journal of Open and Distance Learning*. Online at: http://www.eurodl.org/materials/contrib/2004/Maggie_MsP.html

Moore, M. G., & Kearsley, G. (2011). *Distance Education: A Systems View* (2nd edition). Belmont, CA: Wadsworth.

Motteram, G. (2009). Social computing and teacher education: An agenda for course development. *Innovation in Language Learning and Teaching*, 3(1), 83–97.

Murphy, L. M., Shelley, M. A., White, C. J., & Baumann, U. (2011). Tutor and student perceptions of what makes an effective distance language teacher. *Distance Education*, 32(3), 397–419.

Nelson, I., & Pozo-Gutiérrez, A. (2013). The OpenLIVES Project: Alternative narratives of pedagogical achievement. In A. Beaven, A. Comas-Quinn & B. Sawhill (Eds.), *Case Studies of Openness in the Language Classroom* (pp. 162–175). Dublin: Voillans, Research-publishing.net. Online at: http://research-publishing.net/publications/2013-beaven-comas-quinn-sawhill/

Nicolson, M., Murphy, L., & Southgate, M. (2011). *Language Teaching in Blended Contexts*. Edinburgh, UK: Dunedin Academic Press.

Nissen, E., & Tea, E. (2012). Going blended: New challenges for second generation L2 tutors. *Computer Assisted Language Learning*, 25(2), 145–163.

Pulker, H., & Calvi, A. (2013). The evaluation and re-use of Open Educational Resources in language teaching – a case study. *OER13: Creating a Virtuous Circle*, 26–27 March 2013, Nottingham, UK. Online at: http://oro.open.ac.uk/38056/

Schön, D. (1983). *The Reflective Practitioner*. London: Temple Smith.

Stannard, R. (2006–2011). *Teacher Training Videos*. Online at: http://www.teachertrainingvideos.com/

Tait, J. (2002). From competence to excellence: A systems view of staff development for part-time tutors at a distance. *Open Learning*, 17(2): 153–166.

Wang, Y., Chen, N-S., & Levy, M. (2010). The design and implementation of a holistic training model for language teacher education in a cyber face-to-face learning environment. *Computers and Education*, 55, 777–788.

Warnecke, S., & Lominé, L. (2011). Planning and preparing for synchronous online teaching. In M. Nicolson, L. Murphy & M. Southgate (Eds.), *Language Teaching in Blended Contexts* (pp. 126–139). Edinburgh: Dunedin Academic Press.

Watson, J. (2013). FAVORing the part-time language teacher: The experience and impact of sharing open educational resources through a community-based repository. In A. Beaven, A. Comas-Quinn & B. Sawhill (Eds.), *Case Studies of Openness in the Language Classroom* (pp. 85–95). Dublin: Voillans, Research-publishing.net. Online at: http://research-publishing.net/publications/2013-beaven-comas-quinn-sawhill/

White, C., & Ding, A. (2009). Identity and self in e-language teaching. In Z. Dörnyei & E. Ushioda (Eds.), *Motivation, Language Identity and the L2 Self*, (pp. 333–349). Bristol: Multilingual Matters.

Winchester, S. (2013). Repurposing open educational resources: Creating resources for use and reuse. In A. Beaven, A. Comas-Quinn & B. Sawhill (Eds.), *Case Studies of Openness in the Language Classroom* (pp. 57–69). Dublin: Voillans, Research-publishing.net. Online at: http://research-publishing.net/publications/2013-beaven-comas-quinn-sawhill/

CHAPTER 6

Teaching as Learning: *'Des professeurs – pour écouter'*[1]

Anny King

INTRODUCTION

It is interesting to note that in French 'apprendre' (from the Latin 'apprehendere', meaning 'to grasp with the mind, to understand/comprehend') is the basic word for both 'teach' and 'learn'. If you learn something – say 'I'm learning Chinese' – you would say in French 'J'apprends le chinois'. However, if you're teaching Chinese to (say) Isabelle, then you would say 'J'apprends le chinois à Isabelle.' In other words you (the teacher) are helping Isabelle learn Chinese. And in this action, the learner is understood to be at the centre of your teaching.

In this chapter my premise is that 'teaching' and 'learning' should be viewed as complementary to one another. In Blended Learning (BL) this premise not only is still valid but is even more important because part of the 'teaching' and part of the 'learning' do not necessarily happen synchronously. This proposition is based on my extensive experience (some 40 years) in many Higher Education institutions, not just in the UK, but also other countries such as China, Oman, Malaysia, India and recently Georgia, as a teacher, a teacher-trainer, an external examiner and an adviser.

Teaching and learning is a constant dialogue between the teacher (the 'expert') and the learner (the 'searcher') (Plato, 1955 edition). The teacher is someone who is an expert in their field and whose job is to guide the learner through his or her learning journey 'sometimes opening the way to him, and sometimes leaving him to open it for himself' (Montaigne, 1595). Teaching and learning are primarily social interactions and as such the teacher should encourage learners to 'draw less from books and more from their interactions with the world, with an emphasis on developing the senses, and the ability to draw inferences from them' (Rousseau, 1762). One could say that this approach is an underlying concept in BL.

This view of 'teaching' and 'learning' is not new but somehow with the advent of the democratisation of education after the Second World War (1939–1945), this complementarity, this constant dialogue, this guidance, this interaction with the real world seems to have been lost. Emphasis was more on what to teach rather than on how to teach; more on what to learn rather than how to learn. And yet, this centuries' old view, which is at the core of Plato's, Montaigne's and Rousseau's philosophy on education, was never so important as it is today.

Why it is so important will be explained throughout this chapter which will look at teaching and learning as it was 'then' (as advocated by Plato, Montaigne and Rousseau and many other philosophers and educationalists of the past) and as it generally is 'now'. I feel that this historical perspective will help shape the framework within which 'teaching' and learning' will be discussed and how this historical perspective relates to BL. Furthermore, three key questions will be asked in this chapter:

- What kind of teaching supports and promotes learning?
- What is the role of technology in helping teachers support and promote learning?
- What is the role of today's teacher?

In order to answer these fundamental questions, this chapter will then consider a variety of language learning environments from 'traditional' classrooms to 'blended learning'. Examples taken from the University of Cambridge Language Centre's experience with CULP (Cambridge University Language Programme, see http://www.langcen.cam.ac.uk/culp/culp.php?c=10) and CUTE (Chinese University Teacher Training in English, see Marsh et al., 2007) will illustrate this. The chapter will conclude by looking at the role of the teacher and asking whether the teacher's role has changed/must change in a 'blended' environment (see also Walsh, Chapter 3, this volume).

TEACHING AS LEARNING

Teaching cannot be defined separately from learning. It is 'guiding and facilitating learning, enabling the learner to learn' (Brown, 2000: 18). One could therefore conclude that the key to teaching is 'understanding how the learner learns' (Ibid.). Ultimately this will determine a teacher's philosophy of education, their teaching style, their teaching approach, their methods and classroom techniques. It is a truism to say that one cannot *not* learn. We learn by looking, by imitating, by listening, by reading, by doing, by practising. We learn intentionally and through serendipity. We learn through well-organised graded programmes of study and through random encounters. Life is about learning and learning means life. So, this seems to beg the questions: Is teaching necessary?; Do we really need teachers? My answer is an unequivocal 'yes'. We need teachers as mediators, as facilitators, as experts, as guides, as support. Above all we need teachers as listeners.

BACKGROUND TO PEDAGOGY

This section will briefly look at Plato's, Montaigne's and Rousseau's views on education (see *Pedagogical philosophy* section below) as they are particularly pertinent to today's educational theories and teaching methodologies. This will be followed by a mention of the major linguistic theories of the last 50 years that have influenced the latest teaching methodologies in order to give a context to today's teaching. It will conclude by looking at the difficulty many teachers have in implementing these latest methodologies (see *Putting theory into practice* section below) and will examine the most frequent reasons why this is so.

PEDAGOGICAL PHILOSOPHY

If one looks back at Plato's, Montaigne's and Rousseau's views on education, then it would seem that learner centredness and learner autonomy, not just as an end goal but also as a process, had already been considered to be the cornerstone of education. In Plato's works, for example *The Republic*, we see that at the basis of education are the Socratic dialogues. Through these dialogues the learner (the 'searcher' in Plato's terms) questions the teacher (the 'expert' in Plato's terms) and it is through these dialogues (based primarily on questions and answers) that the learner will gain knowledge: *knowledge will not come from teaching but from questioning*. One of the significant features of this dialogic method is that it emphasises collective, as against solitary, activity. It is through the to and fro of argument with experts and amongst peers that understanding grows (or is revealed). It is clear that Plato viewed learning as a social activity.

In Montaigne's *Essays* we see that the teacher guides the learner through his learning journey. The teacher also encourages his learner to apply what he has learned to his own use: 'Let him make him put what he has learned into a hundred several forms, and accommodate it to so many several subjects.' (Montaigne, 1595) By doing so, the learner will take more responsibility for his own learning. The aim is clear: 'To see if he yet rightly comprehends it, and has made it his own, taking instruction of his progress by the pedagogic institutions of Plato.' (Ibid.). And Montaigne illustrates this vividly by saying "Tis a sign of crudity and indigestion to disgorge what we eat in the same condition it was swallowed; the stomach has not performed its office unless it has altered the form and condition of what was committed to it to concoct.' (Ibid.)

In Rousseau's *Emile* we see that for Rousseau education should be derived less from books and more from interactions with the world, with an emphasis on developing the senses, and the ability to draw inferences from them. Rousseau was one of the first to point out that 'Every mind has its own form' (Rousseau, 1762). He emphasised the importance of encouraging students to develop ideas for themselves, to make sense of the world in their own way, to reason for themselves and draw their own conclusions and not rely on the authority of the teacher: this is what is known today as 'discovery learning'. For Rousseau the role of the teacher ('educator' in Rousseau's term) is to facilitate opportunities for learning. Rousseau put great emphasis on 'the environment'. For him it was crucial that educators pay attention to the environment because for Rousseau the more they were able to control it, the more effective would be the education.

For Plato, Montaigne and Rousseau, the journey is as important (if not more important) as the end goal. It is the journey – the process – which allows learners to develop at their own speed, taking into account their own experiences, digesting new knowledge, making it their own and then applying it to new knowledge domains. In this process the role of the expert/tutor/educator is crucial. They are there to guide, encourage, facilitate and support the learner on his journey.

So has nothing changed? Well, the answer is both 'Yes' and 'No'. In terms of listening to learners, giving them a helping hand, supporting them and letting them go – in this sense nothing has changed because this is the basis of learner centredness and learner autonomy (see also Walsh, Chapter 3, this volume). In terms of catering for the many and not for an elite (as in Plato's, Montaigne's and Rousseau's times) and thus adapting to new needs and new environments, in order to control them and, in so doing, facilitate and support learning – in this sense much needs to change and is changing.

The key question to consider here is whether Plato's, Montaigne's and Rousseau's ideas on education, elaborated for an elite few and which are at the root of learner centredness and autonomy, are applicable today for the many in the age of mass education. And if they are, how can they be applied? In other words, how can the teacher go back to basics?

How can they guide, encourage, facilitate and support the learner on his or her journey and, in particular, on his or her language learning journey? And how, if at all, is this changed by the use of technology?

Before looking at the 'how', we should first consider the 'what', in other words what constitutes language teaching.

KEY MODERN PEDAGOGICAL APPROACHES IN ELT

In teaching two things are inter-related: first what to teach, then how to teach it. The linguistic theories of the last 50 years have shed light on 'what to teach' and applied linguists have given us help with 'how to teach it'.

Before looking at the theories of the last 50 years or so, spearheaded by Chomsky and Hymes, it might be interesting to mention the three most prominent and prevalent methods in language teaching in the first half of the twentieth century: the Grammar-Translation Method (which lasted up to the 1940s); the Direct Method (which lasted up to the 1970s) and the Audiolingual Method (which lasted up to the mid-1960s).

The Grammar-Translation Method (GTM) was based on a way of teaching Latin and Greek which focused on grammatical rules, memorisation of vocabulary, declensions and conjugations and obviously on translation of texts from the second language (L2) into the native language (L1). This method had no theoretical underpinning and it is interesting to note that criticisms from educators date as far back as the sixteenth or seventeenth century as concerns were raised about the importance given to form (grammar) over content in language teaching, and the place given to literary texts in a language curriculum. There were calls for an inductive and active approach where concrete examples of 'language in use', or the use of the target language as the medium of instruction was used to help learners find 'rules' for themselves (Comenius, 1648).

The Direct Method (also known as the 'Berlitz' Method), based on L1 acquisition, was at the other end of the language teaching/learning spectrum from GTM. The Direct Method claimed that the key to language learning is to transform perceptions into understanding ('conceptions'), that learners must be taught directly (hence the name of the method), e.g., without translation, and conceptually, i.e., without any grammatical rules or explanations.

The Audio-Lingual Method was firmly grounded on Contrastive Analysis Hypothesis (CAH, a linguistic and psychological theory developed by Lado, 1957). CAH claimed that the principal barrier to L2 learning is the interference of the L1 linguistic system. Therefore the Audio-Lingual Method advocated conditioning and habit-formation models of learning which were translated into drills and pattern practices.

Chomsky (1965) distinguished between 'competence and performance' in language learning. This distinction had previously been made by De Saussure (1916) 'Langue et parole'. Competence is 'the knowledge and rules that are necessary to produce speech', (Chomsky, 1965: 3) whereas performance is 'the way speech functions when contaminated with external factors' (Ibid.). In other words, Chomsky drew a distinction between the linguistic system of a language (competence) and its use (performance). Applied linguists started to see that learning an L2 means primarily learning to *comprehend it and to speak it* (my emphasis). So it became clearer that teaching must involve both comprehension and production. Hymes' communicative competence (1972) took this distinction one step further by expanding the notion of competence to embrace what a speaker needs to know about how a language is used in particular situations for effective and appropriate communication (McCarthy and Carter, 1994).

The notion of discourse competence put forward by Halliday and Hasan (1976) encompassed the inter-relationship of Chomsky's grammar system with Hymes' language systems in use. This inter-relationship enables the language user to be discourse competent (in either spoken or written texts) through the choices he or she makes (as speaker or writer) at all stages of production (which take into account how the receiver will experience the message, what speech-acts are necessary and desirable, which patterns of interaction or which registers of language are appropriate, in other words 'realising the value of language elements in contexts of use', Widdowson, 1979: 248) to have an effective and appropriate discourse.

During this period of fertile methodological development the Council of Europe made the case for a communicative approach to language teaching through Van Ek's *The Threshold Level* (1976). A communicative approach promotes language learning as a social activity. It has a primarily functional view of language learning and emphasises the social roles of both the speaker and the listener. A communicative approach has been interpreted as being based on three fundamental principles:

- the first and central one is that of learners' needs, i.e., an identification of learners' needs, desires and interests;
- the second one is that of learner centredness which is linked to the first principle and informs teaching; and
- the final principle is the primacy of the functionality of language use over its form.

Whereas some teachers continued to focus their teaching on the traditional goals of grammar and accuracy to the detriment of fluency, others interpreted this to mean that fluency was more important than accuracy and this led to grammar teaching and accuracy to be downplayed in some versions of Communicative Language Teaching. Moreover, the primacy of the functionality of language use over its form advocated by *The Threshold Level* established a dichotomy between communicative-based teaching, which has over the years been the preserve of non-specialist teaching, whilst the more traditional grammar/translation-based teaching is still favoured by teachers teaching specialist language learners.

In the 1990s the Council of Europe's *Common European Framework of Reference for Language Learning and Teaching* (CEFR) developed the understanding of what constitutes communication. It does not talk of 'the four language skills' as such, but refers to 'communicative language competence' needed to engage in 'communicative language activities' through six scales of proficiency (from A1–C2 where A1 is beginner learner whereas C2 is very proficient learner/near-native speaker proficiency). By 2001 this scale provided a systematic description of what a learner/user of a language 'can do' at a given level in *any* language. The CEFR clearly views grammatical competence as 'integral to all language skills' (Council of Europe, 2001: 114). The CEFR explains what grammatical competence within a communicative approach is by emphasising that 'grammatical competence is the ability to understand and express meaning by producing and recognising well-formed phrases and sentences in accordance with these principles' (as opposed to memorising and reproducing them as fixed formulae) (Council of Europe, 2001: 113).

The Council of Europe's communicative approach and the CEFR have been decisive in helping teachers design courses appropriate to learners' needs: in other words 'what to teach'. The learner centredness of the communicative approach together with the increased interest in learner autonomy in the 80s – in Holec's words the 'ability to take charge of one's own learning' (Holec, 1981: 3) – highlighted the fact that teachers should look at teaching more from a learner's point of view than from a teacher's perspective as this would help with 'how to teach'.

PUTTING THEORY INTO PRACTICE

Putting theory into practice is not easy. It took many years for syllabuses to reflect this functional, communicative approach of the Council of Europe, and often fluency has been promoted at the cost of accuracy in the process. This has denied learners a deep understanding of how language works: how its patterns, its structural systems can help them develop their language further in a more autonomous way. This was a simplistic view of the communicative approach which did not grasp that primacy of the functionality of language use over its form is a question of balance between content and form, between competence and performance dictated by the learner's interests and needs, in other words dictated by the purpose and objectives of a particular learner's vocation.

If traditional language teaching often resulted in limited fluency, communicative approaches could often lead to fluency with poor accuracy. In the 1990s researchers in SLA started to present potential solutions to this dilemma by trying to bridge the false dichotomy between content and form through concepts such as 'noticing' and 'focus-on-form'. By emphasising 'attention' in learning or 'noticing', the teacher helps learners convert input into intake (Schmidt, 1990; see also McCarthy, Chapter 1, this volume). In 'focus-on-form' a teacher overtly draws students' attention to linguistic elements *as they arise incidentally* in lessons whose overriding focus is on meaning or communication (Doughty and Williams, 1998, my emphasis). In both cases the balance between content and form is respected. The focus-on-form or the 'noticing' help learners to understand linguistic elements consciously; thus helping them process these elements, making them their own with a view to producing their own text.

The CEFR was conceived as an attempt to help teachers to devise syllabuses according to learners' needs by providing guidance on what should be taught. Whilst some teachers may feel that they must follow the CEFR rigidly (or may be told to do so), this runs counter to the intention of the framework and all notions of teachers as good listeners who solely can be aware of their learners' interests, learning objectives and needs. As Trim[2] emphasised: 'We did not wish to impose a top-down system on all adult learners across Europe, but rather to empower teachers and learners to plan courses as close to the point of learning as possible, in light of the needs, motivations, characteristics and resources of the particular learners involved in their local situations.' (Trim, 2012: 25)

It is undeniable that the linguistic theories on language teaching and learning of the last 50 years and their application in the classroom have helped teachers worldwide. There are a number of pressures from beyond the classroom situation which impact upon the modern classroom teacher and can endanger their ability to constantly connect with their learners. This can in turn mean that they may lose the ability to listen to their students, to engage in dialogue in teaching, to give learners a chance to discover for themselves and in doing so become truly autonomous learners. In my experience of teaching in a range of higher education language classrooms I found that the teacher-student ratio in the Higher Education language classroom tends to be around 1 to 20, which is not conducive to communication in the form of dialogue. Furthermore, some teachers find it easier (although in my experience some are compelled) to follow a syllabus with an eye mainly fixed on the end-of-course examinations, thus allowing learners little time and space for serendipity, for unexpected random diversions and therefore denying them incidental learning (and the kind of moment-by-moment adjustments to the learning context discussed by McCarthy, Chapter 1, and Walsh, Chapter 3, this volume). Some teachers who have embraced technology readily have, unfortunately, not had the chance or enough time to analyse its strengths and weaknesses, thus sometimes not using either the quantitative elements of technology (e.g., giving learners the freedom to listen to a text as many times as necessary whenever and wherever they like) or the qualitative ones (e.g., just-in-time support for learners whenever and wherever they need it). And finally others may still find technology too daunting to make it part of their teaching, thus depriving learners of a flexible, just-in-time learning support, a powerful tool helping learner-learner and teacher-learner communication outside the classroom.

These reasons partly explain why some teachers tend to stand in front of their class teaching the whole class instead of mingling with their learners and helping them learn. Given these kinds of challenges, it is not surprising that some teachers feel unable to employ the communicative approach wholeheartedly within their classroom and are forced to spend more time than they might wish on the receptive rather than the productive skills. Even when they try to implement it fully, they are left with little time for listening to learners' production once the new language has been introduced, its comprehension checked and its grammar explained and/or inductively understood. Teaching communication is not an easy task as there is so much to consider, so little time and so many students to listen to. Indeed, it can be a thankless task, leaving teachers feeling that, despite their hard work and efforts, not much has been accomplished. And yet teaching communication is vital, possible and achievable. It is vital because what learners the world over want and need is to be able to communicate. It is possible if we (as teachers) take time to look at teaching from the learner's point of view. It is achievable if we (as teachers) take advantage of technology and use technology not for technology's sake but appropriately. So in this sense, much needs to change and teachers in particular will need to change and adapt to new environments, in order to control them and, in so doing, facilitate and support learning.

The question thus to ask ourselves is: 'How can we use technology appropriately?' A major part of the answer lies in us (as teachers) understanding what technology as a learning environment can do better than the classroom environment and indeed vice versa: what the classroom environment can do better than technology (McCarthy, Chapter 1, this volume). So let us now go back to the question of whether Plato's, Montaigne's and Rousseau's ideas on education related to the privileged few are applicable and if they are, how they can be applied in today's democratisation of education with its greater diversity of learners with many differing needs. In other words, how can today's teachers, faced with a greater diversity of learners with differing needs, 'go back to basics'? How can they guide, encourage, facilitate and support learners on their journey and in particular on their language learning journey?

LEARNING ENVIRONMENTS

This section will start with an analysis of the characteristics associated with the 'traditional' vs. the 'flipped' language classroom. Then what is meant by 'blended learning' will be considered and examples illustrating this will be given.

THE 'TRADITIONAL' VS. THE 'FLIPPED' LANGUAGE CLASSROOM

At first glance the 'traditional' classroom is about teaching and the teacher. Teaching is often interpreted as the teacher talking in front of the class whilst the learner is passively sitting listening to the teacher (or more likely actively dreaming) or repeating what has been said[3] – thus inducing 'passive learning'. This is somewhat nonsense, because if a learner is not actively engaged in their learning, learning cannot happen; 'passive' learning as such does not exist. In a 'traditional' classroom teachers tend to spend more time on teaching the receptive skills than the productive skills for the reasons outlined in the previous section, *Putting theory into practice*. Therefore the majority of class time is spent on checking input comprehension and explaining grammar 'rules' and not much time is spent on listening to learners' production.

On the surface the 'flipped' classroom, where activities normally associated with in-class work are set for homework, and vice versa, is about learning and learners (see Johnson and Marsh, Chapter 4, this volume). Learners are requested to work on a specific subject matter on their own (outside the classroom) by (for example) viewing a video before coming into the classroom. This format can be particularly favourable to language learning because while watching a video (say, at home), the students can work at their own pace, in their own time, viewing the video as many times as necessary, so when they go back into the classroom, they are better prepared and feel more inclined to ask questions, solve problems and interact with their peers. In other words, learners take charge of their learning; they feel empowered to direct their own learning. This, it is said, improves their proficiency dramatically. So is 'active' learning linked to the format of the learning environment? And is the role of the teacher more important in the 'traditional' rather than the 'flipped classroom'? Before answering these questions let us consider what is meant by blended learning and how this relates to the environments mentioned above.

'BLENDED' LEARNING, I.E., 'INTEGRATED', LEARNING ENVIRONMENT

The term blended learning (BL) is used to describe learning systems that 'combine face-to-face instruction with computer mediated instruction' (Bonk and Graham, 2006). In other words it refers generally to a programme of study which is delivered within two different learning environments; partly online and partly face-to-face. The term 'blended' to my mind misses a vital point which is the specificity of each learning environment; the 'classroom' environment and the 'online' environment. It fails to distinguish what is best delivered in the classroom and what is best delivered online. It is not apt at describing precisely what teachers and learners should be doing in the classroom and what they should be doing online. I therefore prefer to call it 'integrated' learning. In 'integrated' learning the teacher's role is primarily to support learners inside and outside the classroom – both in a synchronous and asynchronous way (see the Examples from Practice section on CUTE, p. 94). In an 'integrated' (blended) learning environment the teacher's role should be one of equilibrium, whereby no less attention is paid to supporting learners than in conventional classrooms; in other words, the growth of online learning does not alter the challenge, so a teacher's thinking should be one where his/her task is integrated across the 'blend'. The teacher must analyse and determine how to 'integrate' classroom teaching with online learning. In other words, they must take the following into account: learners' needs and wishes, their previous language learning experience, their learning styles and motivations and any constraints imposed by the institution. They must also use each medium appropriately, maximising their strengths and minimising their weaknesses in order to facilitate learning and support learners. In language learning terms, this also means that the teacher's role is to analyse and determine which skills are best 'learned' in the classroom and which skills are best 'learned' online. Later on I will be looking at what is best dealt with in the classroom and what is best done online. In brief my belief is that only BL can be flexible enough in helping teachers design programmes that are specifically tailored to learners' individual needs.

However, one must take into account the level of the learners when devising an integrated (blended) course as it is my experience that learners at the lower levels need more classroom time than those at the higher levels (see the Examples from Practice section on CULP, p. 92). Let us now analyse the characteristics of each learning environment.

CLASSROOM ENVIRONMENT

The classroom environment offers the social space where communication as a social activity can be best served. By communication is meant not only the usual reference to two people engaged in a dialogue (teacher-learner or learner-learner), but also to the teacher 'communicating' with learners, either through brief presentation of input, through explanations of language points learners find difficult, through the advice/feedback/encouragement given to their learners or indeed through listening intently to their learners which makes them at times throw away their carefully prepared plan and respond appropriately to their learners' needs at a specific moment in time (Walsh, Chapter 3, this volume). As this dialogic interaction through turn taking, sequence and repair develops, the teacher's intended pedagogy is transformed into actual pedagogy (Seedhouse, 2004). It is through this interaction that teachers can best support learners to learn as they adapt their pedagogic discourse to what is needed.

Within an integrated approach, the teacher often takes a back seat in this social environment which is particularly well suited to learners taking centre stage: by producing their own language, asking questions of clarification on some language points, indeed (at times) on taking on the role of the teacher/facilitator and helping their peers with some aspects of language. It is this reflexive relationship between pedagogy and interaction, between language use and interaction that is at the heart of good teaching and learning (Walsh, 2006).

ONLINE ENVIRONMENT

By 'online' environment we include not only the online course or material at the disposal of the learners (as in the Languages at Your Fingertips or L@YF and English at Your Fingertips or E@YF packages, exemplified below) but also any website, forum, conferencing and chat room incorporated in the delivery of a programme of study. What is key is that the online environment must be learner driven and not technology driven (Salaberry, 2001). An appropriate online environment must be conceived and developed to provide support to learners learning online and thus must focus on learners' needs and use technology appropriately to support these needs (Colpært, 2004). As Chinnery (2006: 1) clearly states: 'technologies, mobile or otherwise, can be instrumental in language instruction. Ultimately, though, they are not of themselves instructors; rather, they are very powerful tools for the transmission and distribution of linguistic information' (Fox, 1994: 27), in other words aids to communication rather than a means of instruction. And the effective use of any tool in language learning requires the thoughtful application of second language pedagogy. Indeed we must not view 'online' as an instructor, as a teacher. Online, if conceived and designed with learning and learners in mind, can offer very good learning support tools, such as vocabulary on demand or subtitles for visual texts, that will help learners in their learning and help them become independent learners who are confident enough to decide on the learning choices appropriate to their needs and interests (see section on E@YF, p. 93). This in turn will make them 'independent users' of the language who can for example 'understand the main points of input on familiar matters regularly encountered in work, school, leisure' (B1); or who can 'interact with a degree of fluency and spontaneity with native speakers' (B2); or who can 'produce simple connected text on topics which are familiar or of personal interest' (B1); or who can 'produce clear, detailed text on a wide range of subjects' (B2), (Council of Europe, 2001).

The major assets of the online environment are its flexibility (non-linearity), its richness and its just-in-time support. An online environment is particularly appropriate for language learning: its inherent flexibility allows learners to choose their entry points within an online course through a 'Learning Map' (see section on E@YF, p. 93) according to their needs and interests. Rich input is accessed through authentic video, audio and texts providing meaningful content relevant to learners' needs either preselected by the teacher (lower levels) or discovered by learners when surfing the internet (higher levels) (see section on L@YF, p. 92). Support is offered (both in a synchronous and asynchronous way) by giving immediate feedback to maximise learning (within the online course/material), by putting many learning tools[4] at learners' disposal and incorporating website, forum, chat room, conferencing as appropriate (see section on CUTE, p. 94; see also McCarthy, Chapter 1, this volume).

EXAMPLES FROM PRACTICE

I will now consider how these key principles have been applied in the specific context of The University of Cambridge Language Centre (http://www.langcen.cam.ac.uk/lc/index.html). The Centre has had over 14 years' experience of not only developing online multimedia material and courses but also using integrated learning environments for the delivery of some of its courses within the Cambridge University Language Programme (CULP) from 2000 onwards and for its CUTE (Chinese University Teacher Training in English) project (within the Higher Education Funding Council for England eChina/UK initiative) between 2003–2007.

CAMBRIDGE UNIVERSITY LANGUAGE PROGRAMME (CULP)

In 2000 the University of Cambridge Language Centre launched a new programme called Cambridge University Language Programme (CULP: see http://www.langcen.cam.ac.uk/culp/culp.php?c=10) whose specification was that it was delivered 30% online and 70% face-to-face. Its other specificity was that the online material was developed in-house and conceived in such a way that it put learners firmly at the centre, concentrating on developing listening and reading skills whilst at the same time helping learners with speaking (and writing) skills by offering preparatory activities that helped learners 'perform' in the classroom. As CULP developed and learners' needs became better identified, the delivery of the programme became more flexible. By B2/C1 we put the onus of learning on learners by:

- negotiating the programme with them[5];
- letting them make suggestions that corresponded better to their wishes/needs; and
- making sure that most bi-weekly classes be learner-led by having learners presenting a topic of their choice to their peers.

The 30% online/70% face-to-face split of the first years was kept for lower levels (corresponding to CEFR A1–A2), but then the split slowly changed to 70% online and 30% face-to-face for higher levels (CEFR B2–C1). This not only made sense in terms of resources (i.e., using teacher resource where it was most needed) but helped learners gradually become independent of the classroom environment as they became more proficient. This resulted in learners becoming more confident in their language and more independent in their learning whilst at the same time having the safety net of not only the online support (website/chat room, etc.) but also the bi-monthly classroom environment where they could come and produce their own language and get the feedback/advice/support needed from the teacher.

LANGUAGES AT YOUR FINGERTIPS (L@YF)

As the technology developed the Centre went on to adapt its online courses to better meet learners' needs and wishes. This is exemplified by Languages At Your Fingertips (L@YF) in French and Spanish, an innovative online language programme developed between 2002 and 2005 by the University of Cambridge Language Centre in partnership with BBC Worldwide. The programme is aimed at basic (A1–A2) and intermediate (A2–B1) level students in Further or Higher Education. It is structured into two levels that are accessed in a totally flexible and non-linear fashion.

The non-linearity and just-in-time qualities of the online medium were used fully to develop a rich, flexible and supportive learning environment for learners at all stages of their learning experience. Learning support tools are put at the disposal of learners who are further supported in their learning through graded and scaffolded activities (see Appendix 1, p. 100). L@YF focuses mainly on receptive skills because they are best served by the online medium. The materials for listening/speaking are based on authentic multimedia resources already produced by the BBC or specially recorded for this purpose by the BBC. L@YF also has many activities that help learners prepare for their productive skills.

Both online levels, together with online material developed specifically for CULP in other languages (Chinese, German, Italian and Russian) are used within CULP integrated courses that are delivered partly online and partly face-to-face to about 2,000 students and staff of the university every year. Every year, student feedback is positive about this form of delivery and most make the comments that having the online element allowed them to catch up (if they had been ill or away on field or research trips), to better prepare for the face-to-face classroom interaction and to revise more efficiently for the end of year examinations.

Within CULP, A1–B1 level students tend to rely more on classroom teaching/support than B1–C1 level students, whose higher linguistic ability allows them to widen their sphere of support from teacher to peer to the internet. This reinforces Ohta's clear demonstration of how in the classroom setting learners seek help/corrective information not only from the teacher but also from their peer partners (Ohta, 2001). In 2004, as technology developed, the Centre was able to refine its online learner support methodology as exemplified by E@YF.

ENGLISH AT YOUR FINGERTIPS (E@YF)

English At Your Fingertips (E@YF) is a multimedia, interactive online English course developed by the University of Cambridge Language Centre over ten years ago. It is offered at three levels:

- E@YF Advanced (B2–C1) which is aimed at private/public sector professionals operating in English at an international level;
- E@YF Higher (B1–B2) aimed at 18+ students wishing to continue their postgraduate studies in an English-speaking country; and
- E@YF Intermediate (A2–B1) aimed at 16 to 18+ year-old students wishing to be fully operational on a day-to-day basis in English.

Like L@YF, it is learner driven and not technology driven, concentrating on learners' needs, and it uses technology appropriately to support these needs. Unlike L@YF, E@YF has been conceived and developed to provide support to learners learning primarily online, since the course was aimed at university students worldwide.

E@YF is learner-centred, not teacher-led. It empowers learners whilst supporting them through its graded and scaffolded approach and uses the online characteristics of flexibility, non-linearity and just-in-time support to help learning at any time. Through both its Learning Map, which works as a navigation tool and also as a tracking device, and its just-in-time Learning Support Tools, E@YF uses technology to support and enhance learning every step of the way (see section on E@YF characteristics in Appendix 2, p. 100).

CHINESE UNIVERSITY TEACHER TRAINING IN ENGLISH (CUTE)

E@YF Advanced[6] was developed for and used in the CUTE project[7] (part of the eChina/UK eLearning Initiative funded by the Higher Education Funding Council for England), a project undertaken in partnership with Tsinghua University[8] whose aims were to support Chinese academics to improve their English language capabilities for teaching and for participating in academic exchange. In her main findings, the external evaluator commented[9] that the CUTE programme and approach were 'sufficiently flexible to meet the needs of a wide range of different trainees' (Holmes, 2008: 4). She went on to say that: 'The benefits of a coherent integrated face-to-face and online programme of learning have been fully recognised by the majority of Chinese academics involved in the project and the positive response to this approach is reflected in the evidence from the evaluation of the trainees' learning experience.' (Holmes, 2008: 5) But perhaps the most significant finding is that two out of every three trainees agreed or agreed strongly that: 'They now felt confident and able to deliver a paper at an international conference; deliver a lecture or presentation in English in their specialist subject and draft a conference paper.' (Ibid.) In other words, two thirds of our trainees felt that the CUTE programme fulfilled their needs (thus delivering on all its aims).

However, it is not insignificant that the CUTE trainees were at least at B1 level, which is labelled as 'Independent User' in the CEFR. As the course developed, their confidence in their linguistic ability developed and they were thus able to fully benefit from their integrated course. One of the most striking developments was how the dynamics of teacher/learners in the classroom changed from reliance on classroom teaching to increased participation of trainees on the CUTE website – be it for exchange of information, comments or advice – and all in English.

EVALUATION OF THE BLENDED ENVIRONMENT

The beauty of an integrated approach is that both environments are not considered at opposite ends of the learning/teaching process (i.e., online vs. classroom) but, on the contrary, as complementing one another. Each environment brings its own strengths into supporting learning. The classroom environment cannot offer the flexibility, rich input and non-linearity of online. Nor can it cater as successfully to individual learners' needs. As teachers, we all know that in the little time available to us we tend to aim for the needs of the majority (middle ground representing about 70%–80% of our learners) and therefore both extremes tend to be left behind. Online is particularly apt at catering for all abilities. On the other hand online cannot replicate the dynamics of the classroom, the ability of the teacher (the good listener) to react immediately to their learners' needs having realised that some of their learners need extra support in order to move forward (see McCarthy, Chapter 1, and Walsh, Chapter 3, this volume, for further discussion). This is particularly significant for learners at lower levels of proficiency who rely more heavily on their teacher than those at higher levels. And finally, if integrated learning environments are to live up to their potential, then an understanding of the role of the teacher is paramount to this success.

THE (CHANGING?) ROLE OF THE TEACHER

This section will start by asking the question 'What is a good teacher?' It will then move on to consider how a (good) teacher can best promote and support learning and what role technology plays in this.

LISTENING TO LEARNERS

What is a good teacher? Over my many years providing teacher training, most course participants have answered that it is someone who has a deep knowledge of their topic, who prepares their lessons well, maintains discipline in the classroom, fulfils the syllabus and prepares learners well for their examinations. They would also add that it is someone who is patient, open minded and sympathetic to their needs.[10]

However, very few teachers would see that a good teacher is by definition a good listener. Yves Châlon, a French educationalist considered by many to be the father of autonomy in language learning, famously asked the question: 'Des professeurs – pour quoi faire?' And he answered: 'Des professeurs – pour écouter.' He then goes on to say that the most important role of teachers is not to transfer their knowledge onto their learners, it is primarily to find out what their learners know and want to know (Châlon, 1970). By stating this, Châlon clearly emphasised the importance of listening in teaching: listening to learn. By listening, teachers learn about their students' needs and wishes, their students' strengths and weaknesses, about what to repeat and what to consolidate, what to ask and what not to ask, how and when to support learners and when 'to let them go', to use Brian Page's (1992) words, i.e., when to let them discover for themselves. And listening to learners also entails giving them the means for self-analysis and the tools for true communication. A good teacher is also a good communicator and a good communicator is primarily a good listener actively engaged in the dialogic exchange at hand, at times enhancing the effectiveness of communication and at other times compensating for breakdowns in communication. Researchers such as Markee (2000), Seedhouse (2004) and Walsh (2006 and Chapter 3, this volume) have rightly argued that a good teacher is one who has the knowledge and skills to be able to align classroom interaction with pedagogical goals. For a good teacher, quality interaction in the classroom is paramount because it is primarily through quality interaction that pedagogical goals are met. The teacher-learner dialogic interaction is at the basis of good teaching and learning.

PROMOTING AND SUPPORTING LEARNING

Facilitating or helping learners 'produce' their own language, promoting learning and supporting them throughout the learning process have always been the hallmarks of a good teacher who listens to their learners, to their needs and wishes, who mediates between the learner and learning, who makes learners induce 'rules' rather than stating them. A good teacher helps learners reflect on their learning thus promoting deep learning. A good teacher also understands how their learners learn best and does not impose their own learning style. Finally a good teacher encourages their learners to take more responsibility for their learning whilst always providing advice and support.

The role of a teacher is determined and defined by their learners. It exists in association and partnership with a learner. Is the same true for a learner? Does a learner exist in association and partnership with a teacher or can they exist on their own? In the great majority of cases, and certainly at the beginning of the learning process, a learner also exists in association and partnership with a teacher. But whereas a teacher's role will always be determined and defined by learners, learners will slowly but inevitably move away from the teacher as they become more proficient, and therefore more confident and independent, learners. Indeed the success of a teacher is ultimately measured not by the needs their learners have of them but, on the contrary, by the lack of them. The best teacher/learner relationship is one that tends to fade away because that means that both teacher and learner have fulfilled their roles – the teacher by supporting their learners' needs and wishes and the learner by taking responsibility for their learning, becoming an independent learner and, having 'digested' knowledge (to use Montaigne's terminology), being able to produce their own language, to be in Hymes' (1972) terminology 'communicatively competent', that is to say using language competently in order to be efficient communicators.

And finally, a good teacher faced with technology will first analyse their learners' needs and, taking into account their wishes and any constraints there may be (linked to for example the institution, the syllabus or the facilities), will develop a programme of study that will use technology appropriately. This means using technology for its strengths in terms of helping learners prepare for the classroom session or revise what has been learned or support learners' communication with peers (student as teacher) and/or the teacher in their own time, at their own speed whenever they wish and wherever they can. Technology must become part of the teacher's everyday range of support tools, not an exception or an after-thought. Today's learners' tablets and smartphones are part of their everyday life and this must be used to the full by the teacher because learning happens everywhere, not just in the classroom and this is particularly true in this digital age of ours. (See Dudeney and Hockly, Chapter 13, this volume.)

CONCLUSION

So what are we to conclude on our three key questions?

1. What kind of teaching supports and promotes learning?
2. What is the role of technology in helping teachers support and promote learning?
3. What is the role of today's teacher and should it change?

On question 1 the kind of teaching that supports and promotes learning, it is my experience that teaching as listening is best suited to respond to learners' needs, to help learners at every turn of their learning journey, to let go when appropriate and support them when necessary. It is teaching as listening that gives teachers both the framework of what needs to be taught and the freedom of diverging from it. It is teaching as listening that fosters the dialogic interaction between the teacher and their learners, which allows the teacher's intended pedagogy to be transformed into actual pedagogy (Seedhouse, 2004) and ultimately can lead to autonomous learning.

On question 2 the role of technology in helping teachers support and promote learning, it is my experience that it is not the format of the learning environment (be it 'traditional' or 'integrated') where the teacher operates that impedes or supports learning as such. The format of the learning environment supports learning only if the teacher (as a listener) fulfils their supportive role of facilitator and mediator. The format of the learning environment supports learners in their learning only if technology is used appropriately, i.e., used as cognitive tools for learning. The role of the teacher in choosing the appropriate learning environment according to the task at hand (or skill to be practised) is crucial. Technology gives learners extra tools to support their learning whenever and wherever it suits them. It allows learners to learn both formally (through a blended programme) and informally (through incidental learning). Technology gives teachers extra tools to cater for differing learners' needs. So the role of technology in supporting language learning and helping the teacher fulfil their mediator role is vital.

On question 3 the role of today's teacher and whether it should change, it is my experience that the answer is a dual one: *Yes and No*. 'No' it shouldn't change because the teacher's role in terms of its essentiality, importance and support in the learning process has not changed over the centuries. 'No' because the teacher's relationship[11] to learners, be it as an 'expert' (Plato), a 'tutor' (Montaigne) or an 'educator' (Rousseau), has not changed over the centuries. 'No' because teaching is fundamentally and ultimately about supporting learning and making learners more and more independent of their support – and this has not changed over the centuries.

And 'Yes', because what has changed is that education is now available to a greater number of learners with differing and varied needs. 'Yes' because what has changed is learners' entitlement to the best education – i.e., teaching/learning support. And 'Yes' because what has changed is the omnipresence of technology in today's world. And because of this relatively new environment – new usually for teachers and education systems that generally tend to lag behind – the teacher's role (crucial in supporting learning) must change and is changing. After all, today's learners are increasingly children of the digital age who breathe technology and for whom 'electronically mediated communication' in their day-to-day lives (Crystal in King, 2011: 27) is the norm, not something exceptional.

However, in wider educational (humanistic) terms the role of technology has its limits whereas the role of the language teacher is paramount. The teacher is the one who can help learners develop their 'other' personality as some learners put it. The CEFR mentions 'le savoir-être' (existential competence) as an important element amongst the competences learners need to develop to be communicatively competent. The CEFR defines this as 'attitudes and personality factors [which] greatly affect not only the language users'/learners' roles in communicative acts but also their ability to learn' (CEFR: 5.1.3). Indeed any language learner (as independent user) is aware of developing an 'intercultural personality' that gives them the confidence to operate appropriately in a foreign language knowing that not only the right utterances (competence) have been chosen but that they have been delivered competently (performance). And to achieve this not only linguistic knowledge is important but so are knowledge of the world and sociocultural knowledge. Of equal importance is intercultural awareness defined as 'knowledge, awareness and understanding of the relation – similarities and distinctive differences – between the "world of origin" and the "world of the target community"' (CEFR: 5.1.1.3).

I would like to conclude by saying that not only Plato's, Montaigne's and Rousseau's (and indeed many other philosophers and educationalists of the past) ideas on education are applicable today but they are crucial in today's globalisation in preparing our young people to become the citizens of the world. Only the teacher can help learners understand/appreciate – and I would add 'critically' – the relationship between the 'world of origin' and the 'world of the target community'. By doing this the teacher can help them become, in Verlaine's words, 'not completely the same, not completely different'.[12]

Suggested Resources

Holec, H. (1981). *Autonomy and Foreign Language Learning*. Oxford: Pergamon. (First published 1979, Strasbourg: Council of Europe.)

Marsh, D., Brewster, E, Cavaleri, N., & King, A. (2007). CUTE: A flexible approach to the integration of online and face-to-face support for language learning. In H. Spencer-Oatey (Ed.), *E-learning Initiatives in China: Pedagogy, Policy and Culture* (pp. 95–107). Hong Kong: Hong Kong University Press.

McCarthy, M., & Carter, R. (1994). *Language as Discourse: Perspectives for Language Teaching*. London: Longman.

Montaigne, Michel de (1595). *Les Essais*, Livre I, Chapitre XXV, 'De l'Institution des enfants'. HTML version from 1595 publication. Online at: http://www.bribes.org/trismegiste/montable.htm

Plato (1955). *The Republic*. Harmondsworth: Penguin Classics.

Rousseau, J. J. (1762). *Emile ou De l'Education*, Book II. The Project Gutenberg EBook; HTML version. Online at: http://www.gutenberg.org/cache/epub/5427/pg5427.html

Trim, J. L. M. (2012). The Common European Framework of Reference for Languages: A case study of cultural politics and educational influences. In M. Byram & L. Parmenter (Eds.), *The Common European Framework of Reference: The Globalisation of Language Education Policy* (pp. 14–34). Bristol: Multilingual Matters.

Discussion Questions

1. Yves Châlon famously said 'Teachers – what for? Teachers – to listen'. Would you agree/disagree with this and why?

2. It is more and more customary nowadays to talk of a teacher as 'a guide', 'a facilitator', as someone 'supporting learning'. How does your experience in the classroom tally with this? If it does not, explain why not.

3. 'A good teacher is a good communicator and a good communicator is primarily a good listener.' Would you agree/disagree with this and why?

4. 'A good teacher is one who has the knowledge and skills to be able to align classroom interaction with pedagogical goals.' Could you give one or two examples of your teaching that would prove this statement?

5. 'Technology must become part of the teacher's everyday range of support tools, not an exception or an after-thought.' Would you agree/disagree with this and why?

References

Bonk C. J., & Graham, C. R. (2006). *The Handbook of Blended Learning Environments: Global Perspectives, Local Designs*. San Francisco: Jossey-Bass/Pfeiffer.

Brown, H. D. (2000). *Principles of Language Learning and Teaching*. White Plains, NY: Addison Wesley Longman Inc.

Châlon, Y. (1970). *Pour Une Pédagogie Sauvage*. Mélanges: CRAPEL.

Chinnery, G. M. (2006). Emerging technologies going to the MALL: Mobile assisted language learning. *Language Learning and Technology*, 10(1), 9–16.

Chomsky, N. (1965). *Aspects of the Theory of Syntax*. Cambridge, MA: MIT Press.

Colpært, J. (2004). From courseware to coursewear? *Computer Assisted Language Learning*, 17(3–4), 261–266.

Comenius, J. A. (1648). *Novissima Linguarum Methodus. La Toute nouvelle méthode des langues*. French translation by Honoré Jean, Genève/Paris: Librairie Droz (2005).

Council of Europe (2001). *Common European Framework of Reference for Languages: Learning, Teaching, Assessment*. Cambridge: Cambridge University Press.

Crystal, D. (2011). Multilingualism and the internet. In L. King et al., *Languages in Europe – Towards 2020*. London: The Languages Company.

Doughty, C., & Williams, J. (Eds.) (1998). *Focus on Form in Classroom Second Language Acquisition*. Cambridge: Cambridge University Press.

Fox, J. (1994). Demystifying IT. In E. Esch (Ed.) *Self-Access and the Adult Language Learner* (p. 27). London: CILT.

Halliday, M. A. K., & Hasan, R. (1976). *Cohesion in English*. London: Longman.

Holec, H. (1981). *Autonomy and Foreign Language Learning*. Oxford: Pergamon. (First published 1979, Strasbourg: Council of Europe).

Holmes, B. (2008). *Executive Summary Report* (unpublished).

Hymes, D. H. (1972). On communicative competence. In J. B. Pride & J. Holmes (Eds.), *Sociolinguistics. Selected Readings* (pp. 269–280). Harmondsworth: Penguin.

Lado, R. (1957). *Linguistics Across Cultures*. University of Michigan Press, Foreign Language Study.

Markee, N. (2000). Conversation analysis. *Second Language Analysis Research Series*. Mahwah, NJ: Lawrence Erlbaum Associates.

Marsh, D., Brewster, E, Cavaleri, N., & King, A. (2007). CUTE: A flexible approach to the integration of online and face-to-face support for language learning. In H. Spencer-Oatey (Ed.), *E-learning Initiatives in China: Pedagogy, Policy and Culture* (pp. 95–107). Hong Kong: Hong Kong University Press.

McCarthy, M., & Carter, R. (1994). *Language as Discourse: Perspectives for Language Teaching*. London: Longman.

Montaigne, Michel de (1595). *Les Essais*, Livre I, Chapitre XXV, 'De l'Institution des enfants'. HTML version from 1595 publication. Online at: http://www.bribes.org/trismegiste/montable.htm

Ohta, A. S. (2001). *Second Language Acquisition Processes in the Classroom: Learning Japanese*. Mahwah, NJ: Lawrence Erlbaum Associates.

Page, B. (1992). *Letting Go – Taking Hold: A Guide to Independent Language Learning by Teachers for Teachers*. London: CILT.

Plato (1955). *The Republic*. Harmondsworth: Penguin Classics.

Rousseau, J. J. (1762). *Emile ou De l'Education*, Book II. The Project Gutenberg EBook; HTML version. Online at: http://www.gutenberg.org/cache/epub/5427/pg5427.html

Salaberry, M. R. (2001). The use of technology for second language learning and teaching: A retrospective. *The Modern Language Journal*, 85(i), 39–56.

Saussure, Ferdinand de (1916). *Cours de Linguistique Générale*. C. Bally and A. Sechehaye (Eds.). Paris: Librairie Payot & Cie.

Schmidt, R. (1990). The role of consciousness in second language learning. *Applied Linguistics*, 11, 129–158.

Seedhouse, P. (2004). *The Interactional Architecture of the Language Classroom: A Conversation Analysis Perspective*. Oxford: Blackwell.

Trim, J. L. M. (2012). The Common European Framework of Reference for Languages: A case study of cultural politics and educational influences. In M. Byram & L. Parmenter (Eds.), *The Common European Framework of Reference: The Globalisation of Language Education Policy* (pp. 14–34). Bristol: Multilingual Matters.

Van Ek, J. A. (1976). *The Threshold Level*. Strasbourg: Council of Europe.

Walsh, S. (2006). *Investigating Classroom Discourse*. London and New York: Routledge.

Widdowson, H. G. (1979). *Explorations in Applied Linguistics*. Oxford: Oxford University Press.

Appendix 1

L@YF (Languages at Your Fingertips)
CHARACTERISTICS

L@YF online material is based on authentic multimedia resources produced by the BBC or specially shot or recorded for this purpose by the BBC and is made available to students via an intranet platform.

There are two key stages to the programme. The first basic part of the programme (CEFR: A1–A2 level) is designed around a virtual town comprising eight locations. It provides the environment in which to learn and practise the functional language needed to communicate at a hotel, in a market, in a department store, in a bar, at a petrol station, at a campsite, in a restaurant and at a railway station.

In the intermediate part of the programme (CEFR: A2–B1) students navigate through the functional language needed for working, for dealing with health and for recalling past events.

L@YF features language functions; many different types of activities such as comprehension, manipulation of language, extension of vocabulary, production and reproduction, games; cultural notes; grammar notes (with practice); a glossary and a standalone section accessible at all times for basic needs such as numbers, time and date, phoning, greetings and talking about yourself.

L@YF has graded (from the simplest to the more complex) and scaffolded (supported) activities to help learners deconstruct the language stimuli (comprehension, vocabulary, grammar activities) and then reconstruct them (manipulation and production activities) according to their needs. These activities are conceived in such a way as to support learning. Hints are present so that learners can find the answer themselves and in the feedback to activities explanations are given to learners when answers are wrong so that learners learn from their mistakes.

L@YF is designed to be flexible and learners can decide what they want or wish to do: If they feel confident enough about their language, they can choose to test their knowledge in the first instance and according to how they do, decide either to go to some revision units before launching into the new learning units or, on the contrary, to access the learning units first, before accessing the topic-based units. Indeed, some might go straight to the topic-based units without even testing themselves. These topic-based units are being designed as a discovery path through the French/Spanish language and culture and use video/audio and texts as input in an integrated way.

Appendix 2

E@YF (English at Your Fingertips)
CHARACTERISTICS

E@YF benefits from three specific characteristics:

- It is learner-centred (and not teacher-led).
- It empowers learners whilst supporting their learning through its graded and scaffolded approach.
- It uses the online characteristics of flexibility, non-linearity and just-in-time support, to help learning whenever it is required.

E@YF uses technology to support and enhance learning at every step through:

- its Learning Map; and
- its just-in-time Learning Support Tools.

E@YF specific characteristics are:

- It is learner-centred and has been designed from a learner's point of view; it provides a context for and a purpose to learning. It captures learners' interest and gives them achievable targets – through purposeful and appropriate activities. This system of learning can offer a great deal that standard textbooks cannot. It can provide multimedia stimuli which help make it more responsive to different learning styles. Its interactive nature means that it can provide learners with instant feedback. But one of the greatest advantages is the fact that the content can be dynamic and relevant; so it can be changed, updated, revised and can address learners' needs quickly and efficiently.
- It empowers learners to learn without an intermediary; E@YF encompasses everything that learners need to self-teach. It has rich, video-based authentic (and not textbook-based) input – videos and/or audios and/or texts – i.e., the language stimuli so to speak. It has just-in-time learning support tools – transcripts, subtitles, glossary, grammar explanation and culture notes – which are available at the click of the mouse. It gives learners every help they need to learn and improve through graded (from the simplest to the more complex) and scaffolded (supported) activities. These activities help learners deconstruct the language stimuli (comprehension, vocabulary, grammar activities) and then reconstruct them (manipulation and production activities) according to their needs. These activities are conceived in such a way as to support learning. There are many pre-view/listening activities that build on learners' prior knowledge. Hints are present so that learners can find the answer themselves; in the feedback to activities explanations are given to learners when answers are wrong so that learners learn from their mistakes.
- It uses the online characteristics of flexibility, non-linearity and just-in-time support, to help learning at any time. Learners choose their pathway according to their needs and interests with the help of the Learning Map. Online with its combination of visuals, audio and written texts is a good environment for employing our various senses. Learners can choose whether to start watching a video or listening to an audio; they can choose whether to test their comprehension or go directly onto games designed to build their vocabulary or onto production activities designed to help them construct their own message. Help and learning support tools (such as glossary, culture notes, grammar explanations, hints) are always available.

APPROPRIATE USE OF TECHNOLOGY

1. E@YF has a Learning Map which works both as a navigation tool and as a tracking device.
2. E@YF offers just-in-time Learning Support Tools, such as 'Functions' (key language), a glossary, grammar explanations, culture notes, subtitles and transcript:
    - 'Functions' is a reference tool that helps students identify the key language introduced in the module they are studying.
    - The glossary lists all the words and phrases used in the course. A definition of each word/phrase is given followed by an example of its use. The glossary also highlights whether it is a 'noun', 'adjective', 'determiner', 'adverb', 'preposition' or a 'verb'.
    - Grammar arises from the key language to help deconstruct and reconstruct language and not for its own sake.
    - Culture notes explain the cultural dimension or connotation of the language.

- The subtitles functionality gives students the option to view or not to view the video subtitles. Once enabled, subtitles appear at the bottom of the video screen. This is a pedagogical tool that enables students to read the subtitles whilst at the same time listening to the audio, thus helping them with understanding the video content.
- The transcript functionality can be launched whilst the student is watching the video. A pop-up window opens displaying the relevant transcript. This useful function allows students to get the help they might need with the entire video content.

LANGUAGE CONTENT

1. E@YF Intermediate (CEFR: A2–B1) offers four function-based modules. Each module is divided into two to four units. Each unit explores the functional language needed for socialising, travelling, keeping fit and healthy and talking about personal experiences. Most units have two kinds of inputs – video-based and audio-based. Both inputs complement and reinforce one another as many of the functions, key language, grammar points and vocabulary words overlap and expand on one another.

2. E@YF Higher (CEFR: B1–B2) has been conceived in such a way as to integrate listening and reading skills. E@YF offers rich input. Most topics have two kinds of inputs – one aural (video/audio) and one written (text). Both inputs complement one another (one offers exposure to spoken language, the other to written language/discourse) and reinforce one another, as many of the functions, key language, grammar points and vocabulary words overlap and expand on one another. It offers two parallel paths through the topics and the activities – learners can either start with the video/audio input or the written text. It is recommended to learners to start the unit with the Getting Started Activities which help them assess their previous knowledge on the topic and hence on the language.

3. E@YF Advanced (CEFR: B2–C1) has been conceived to help university teachers and researchers improve their academic skills in English for publishing and for presentations. It offers two modules, English for Presentations and English for Publishing, representing 50 hours of online learning for each area. Both English for Presentations and English for Publishing have adopted integrated approaches in order to fulfil their learning objectives. In English for Presentations, the key learning objectives are to improve speaking skills and produce a cohesive presentation. In order to achieve this, learners are encouraged to deconstruct authentic presentations (Cambridge Lectures), and then reconstruct them paying attention not just to the language used, but also to the mode of delivery. English for Publishing aims to improve writing skills by asking learners to deconstruct authentic texts (abstracts, published articles), and then reconstruct them paying attention not only to the writing, but also to the structure and the process needed to write abstracts and articles.

Notes

[1] 'Teachers – what for? Teachers – to listen' (Châlon, 1970).

[2] John Trim, Director of the Council of Europe's Modern Languages projects from 1971 to 1997, played a key role in developing the Common European Framework of References for Languages (CEFR).

[3] ''Tis the custom of pedagogues to be eternally thundering in their pupil's ears, as they were pouring into a funnel, while the business of the pupil is only to repeat what the others have said,' Montaigne, 'De l'Instruction des enfants', Livre I, Chapitre XXV.

⁴ Such as language functions, many different types of activities (comprehension, manipulation of language, extension of vocabulary, oral or written production, reproduction, such as voice recording, games), cultural notes, grammar notes (with practice), a glossary and a standalone section accessible at all times for basic needs such as numbers, time and date, phoning, greetings and talking about yourself.

⁵ CULP caters for students across the university. At that level learners' interests may differ quite dramatically as some would want more 'cultural/literary' input and others would want topics more focused on their main area of study (i.e., economics, law, natural sciences, etc.).

⁶ E@YF Advanced was used in connection with a forum, conferencing and chat room incorporated in the delivery of the specific programme of study aimed at training teachers.

⁷ Phase 1 ran from March 2003–September 2004.

⁸ In Phase 2 of the project (September 2005–July 2007), the Centre for English Language Teacher Education, University of Warwick, joined the project.

⁹ Executive Summary Report, Bernardette Holmes, May 2008 (unpublished).

¹⁰ Characteristics listed by teachers over the years during teacher training.

¹¹ We feel that the teacher/learner relationship/partnership is one that starts on an unequal footing: Beginner language learners (at CEFR A1 to B1 level) are more dependent on the teacher's advice, help and direction than intermediate/advanced language learners (at CEFR B2 to C2 level) who have developed enough confidence in their learning techniques and have enough language knowledge not just to make informed and relevant choices in their learning pathways, but also to work more independently.

¹² 'Ni tout à fait la même, ni tout à fait une autre', Verlaine's poem *Mon Rêve Familier*, in Poèmes Saturniens (1866).

SECTION 3

RETHINKING LEARNER INTERACTION

Chapter 7, by Susan Hojnacki, focuses on one of the core problems of online second-language learning: whether speaking skills can effectively be developed in a computer-mediated environment, a preoccupation also taken up later in Chapter 12 of this volume by McCarten and Sandiford. Hojnacki begins with the observation that conventional conversation classes frequently offer students only scant amounts of actual talking time. Instead, she sees the potential of asynchronous computer-mediated communication for enabling students to produce more extensive output in the target language, by providing opportunities beyond the four walls of the classroom to practice and produce oral language. Her study appears to have found that such a blended approach, in which communication opportunities are provided outside of the classroom in an asynchronous environment, in particular benefited those students who may feel reticent in the classroom to speak in front of their peers. Interestingly, the students who spoke the least number of minutes during class showed the greatest gains in online speaking time. These students appear to gain confidence online and perform better in the face-to-face classroom. Hojnacki qualifies the positive results of her study with the following caveat: 'Provided that the online modules were well-developed and followed from sound SLA research, hybrid or blended courses could buy valuable instructor-monitored time on task while not robbing students of face-to-face instruction time.' Once again the recurring theme of this book, the need to put pedagogy before the technology, appears of paramount importance.

In **Chapter 8**, Mishan discusses how the harnessing of technology in language learning forces us to redefine what we mean by teaching materials: materials were once the static product held in the hand, the course book, the dictionary, the course-book CD-ROM, etc. and were used in class or at home by the teacher and students. Internet technologies open up the possibility for a dynamic view of materials, where interaction is potentially at the heart of the tools, the activities they make possible and the texts they offer. Tools such as social network platforms, wikis, blogs/vlogs, Twitter and other forms of interactive communication online can offer a positive way out of a static view that simply dumps the course book online, merely substituting a screen for printed paper. Mishan points to a content vs. process distinction: between materials seen as sources of information on the one hand and, on the other hand, materials as frameworks for learners to exercise their communicative abilities. Technology can support and effectively transform how we think about teaching materials, with the proviso that not all the bells and whistles of modern technology necessarily guarantee such a transformation. Through a series of case studies, Mishan leads us to her conclusion that there seems to be a disconnection between blended learning and its technology and language teaching in general. Institutional technologies such as learning management systems can sometimes dictate the pedagogy, instead of vice versa, which is a concern which should be borne constantly in mind.

Lázár, in **Chapter 9**, also discusses the need to engage in a process of designing and redesigning materials for blended contexts, not just for students, but in teacher education programmes as well, and in wider teacher/professional communities. Lázár recognises the challenge in creating materials and activities to support authentic interaction between learners in a blended environment, and her chapter provides details of the benefits and challenges of a five-month collaboration project between four classes in four different countries. International collaboration of this kind is facilitated by the borderless nature of technology but brings with it a great burden of organisational and logistic work. Lázár lets us into the details of such work, emphasising the role of teachers, facilitators, monitors and other engaged parties in the complexity of setting up online programmes across different countries and cultures. The projects she describes have their ups and downs but leave us with a positive conclusion that a judicious combination of face-to-face interaction with continent-wide online activity can enhance the learning experience not only for language learners, but also for teachers in the professional development context and in the creation and maintenance of international professional communities. Lázár argues the need to consider learning as something which takes place beyond the classroom; the classroom setting is ideal for setting the context, establishing the language needed and the overall focus but the real interaction takes place beyond this formal setting. The learning needs to 'go mobile' and be integrated into the daily lives and routines of the learners. Here the technology can come into its own and Lázár successfully provides the evidence to support this approach, while not shying away from the difficulties and setbacks involved.

CHAPTER 7

Oral Output in Online Modules vs. Face-to-Face Classrooms

Susan Hojnacki

INTRODUCTION

This chapter addresses the issue of oral output in the blended second language (L2) classroom. Speaking, or creating with the language, is a key component of a broad sociocultural theory of L2 learning (Lantolf and Beckett, 2009). As L2 instructors introduce more blended courses, which integrate online tools into the curriculum, in addition to existing face-to-face (F2F) class time, questions about second language acquisition (SLA) theory in computer-mediated instruction will need to be addressed (see also McCarthy, Chapter 1, this volume). Online learning can take many forms and is not always comparable to F2F learning (Smith et al., 2003). For example, synchronous computer-mediated communication (SCMC), such as video conferencing, creates different types of oral output from asynchronous computer-mediated communication (ACMC), such as text chat or virtual conversations. Studies have shown that the slowed down communication of asynchronous online communication can be beneficial for language learners (Smith et al., 2003). This chapter looks at differences in students' oral output while using ACMC for an L2 course in comparison with their oral output during F2F class time. Results showed that students produced significantly more of the L2 in the online modules than they did in the F2F classroom. Issues of class-time distribution and student personalities were both shown to play a role in these results.

RATIONALE

In the midst of the ever-expanding web connecting language pedagogy, online and blended course design, SLA theory and advancing technological capabilities sits the second language instructor, wondering how to connect them all. Whether that instructor is a recent graduate or seasoned instructor, digital native or tech-savvy early adopter, there are far more questions about online course design than there are accepted best practices and published success stories. While language pedagogy has had decades to develop, and SLA theory is entering its adolescent period, the newest generation of distance learning is in its relative infancy (Kraemer, 2008). While distance learning is not new (think correspondence courses through the mail as early as 1840), the introduction of the computer in the 1980s and of Web 2.0 tools in the 1990s has helped bring the newest generation of interactive, computer-mediated communication (CMC) into language courses (Godwin-Jones, 2003).

The traditional foreign language classroom was a predominantly text-based learning environment, and while the communicative approach to teaching brought oral input and output to the fore, time constraints and large class sizes proved ineffective and did not allow enough true interaction for proficiency to improve. In the present pilot study, for example, it was found that in a 90-minute intermediate German conversation class, the average student spoke for a mere 82 seconds. Research on computer-mediated communication (CMC) has found that it holds several advantages over the F2F classroom: it slowed down conversation, practice and planning time, there was democratisation of participation, an increase in language use, and an increase in time spent on language production. Unfortunately computer-mediated activities have logistical disadvantages such as time differences for native-speaking communication partners, differing levels of commitment to the partnership and technology breakdowns. Furthermore, text-based media have the disadvantage of avoiding issues of intonation and pronunciation while voice-based tools can reintroduce anxiety with the pressure to produce accurate language spontaneously. Hence, voice-based simulated conversation tools are being explored as part of asynchronous online lessons (ACMC).

The role of output in the SLA process has been well established in the past few decades (Swain, 1985, 1995, 2005). From a sociocultural theory of second language learning, language is a product of interaction and is based on the social context in which it is used. Can students interact with online tools to create more of the target language than in the F2F classroom and is there evidence of learning within this language production? A pilot study was carried out, comparing oral production in a F2F German conversation course in the USA with online modules in the same course. The study showed that students spent more time on language production and produced significantly more and more complex language when interacting with the online tools. 'Learner affect' is a term describing a student's general anxiety level and openness to learning a second language. If a student's emotions and anxiety are highly activated through embarrassment or confusion, these factors could limit their ability to pay attention to the forms and function of the language. Krashen ranked having a low 'affective filter' as one of the most important aspects for SLA in combination with comprehensible input in his monitor theory (Krashen, 1985). An emic perspective on student learning describes taking the student's needs and opinions into account when designing instruction models as opposed to teaching only what the instructor deems necessary. As these two topics are also crucial for language pedagogy, a student survey was completed at the end of the study, which yielded key information about the participants' views on online, computer-assisted language learning (CALL).

The implications of these results point towards a better understanding of blended course design in second language courses. If output is a significant aspect for improving proficiency, can blended learning (BL) increase output in meaningful ways? Is the output produced in ACMC settings comparable to the 'pushed output' produced through interaction and feedback in the F2F classroom (as described by Walsh, Chapter 3, this volume)? Are there ways that we, as instructors, can better design blended language courses so that the output produced there leads to higher proficiency levels and greater student satisfaction with the learning process? The implications for BL are clear and this study contributes answers to all of the aforementioned questions.

LITERATURE REVIEW

Ideas about output in the SLA process have undergone dramatic changes since the years of rote memorisation and repetition used in the Audiolingual teaching methods of the 1970s. First came Krashen's input (or i+1) hypothesis, stating that, 'Second language acquisition theory provides a very clear explanation as to why immersion works. According to current theory, we acquire language in only one way: when we understand messages in that language, when we receive comprehensible input.' (Krashen, 1985) This hypothesis cast speaking as a result of acquisition and not as its cause. This hypothesis was widely and promptly criticised for its lack of testability (i.e., what is 'i'? and how much is '+1'?). One of the early responders to Krashen was Swain, who undertook an in-depth look at bilingual French/English education programmes in Canada. An outline of the results of numerous studies (for early summaries, see Lambert and Tucker, 1972; Swain, 1978; Swain and Lapkin, 1981) led to her output hypothesis in 1985. The studies showed that the immersion students in French scored similarly to their Francophone peers in reading and listening comprehension but performed differently in speaking and writing. Swain correlates this gap in performance with a lack of output, specifically 'pushed output' in the immersion classrooms (Swain, 1985). The 'pushed output' hypothesis (Mackey, 2002) is illustrated when interlocutors ask specifically for clarification, pushing the speaker to use a more precise, coherent or appropriate form.

This 'pushed output' hypothesis is significant to the topic of BL, especially when comparing F2F interactions with computer-mediated or asynchronous exchanges, since the turns taken in online tools are often time-delayed (i.e., email or text chat) or in response to a task and not a human being. In a 2002 study, Izumi showed that 'Output, especially pushed output, promotes not only detection of forms but also integrative processing to conceive a coherent structure among the detected elements.' (Izumi, 2002: 571) Grammatical *encoding*, then, is quite different in its effect from grammatical *decoding*, which does not push learners to reorganise their form-meaning mappings. It is only through output that learners are pushed to move from the decoding to the encoding process.

McCarthy (Chapter 1, this volume) touches on input enhancement. However, Izumi (2002: 570) suggests that within this framework, 'Input enhancement may have caused mere recirculation or rehearsal at the same, relatively shallow, processing level, which led the learners to experience only a short-term retention of the attended form. On the other hand, the greater learning evidenced by the output subjects suggests that output triggered deeper and more elaborate processing of the form, which led them to establish a more durable memory trace.' Izumi, Bigelow, Fujiwara and Fearnow (Izumi et al., 1999) tested this hypothesis with a study in which students were exposed to written input. An experimental group was given a production task, in addition to the processing of the input. In a delayed post-test, participants who had produced output showed greater improvement on a written assignment than those who had not produced output, 'thereby suggesting that output may indeed be important for acquisition' (Gass and Selinker, 2008: 328).

Graf (Graf, 1994; Graf and Schacter, 1989) connected the ideas of output and integrative processing. Graf's point is that not only must one pay attention to the elements but also the relationships among them so as to connect and organise elements into a coherent whole. Students of second languages are familiar with the concept that it is a simpler cognitive task to understand a more complicated spoken or written text than it is to produce that same level of language themselves. This illustrates the concept of integrative processing that is at work in such tasks. While comprehension remains primarily at the semantic level, production moves the learner to the syntactic level, requiring a greater understanding and integration of the whole language process. Output, then, is an opportunity for the learner to produce the language, which leads to noticing. Learners can notice gaps between their language and that of native speakers and also notice gaps where they do not know how to produce certain semantic, syntactic, morphological and phonological aspects of the target language (see also McCarthy, Chapter 1, this volume). This noticing can compel the learner to seek out more input or more instruction from other sources.

The context for output amongst the other key aspects of language learning began to take shape in the mid-nineties as interactionist theory was developed. Long proposed the interaction hypothesis stating that: *'Negotiation for meaning,* and especially negotiation work that triggers *interactional* adjustments by the NS [native speaker] or more competent interlocutor, facilitates acquisition because it connects input, internal learner capacities, particularly selective attention, and output in productive ways.' (Long, 1996: 451–452) Gass stated that: 'Interaction research takes as its starting point the assumption that language learning is stimulated by communicative pressure and examines the relationship between communication and acquisition and the mechanisms (e.g., noticing, attention) that mediate between them.' (Gass, 2003: 224) According to Gass and Selinker (2008: 328), output serves four functions in the language learning process:

1. Receiving crucial feedback for the verification of hypotheses;
2. Testing hypotheses about the structures and meanings of the target language;
3. Developing automaticity in interlanguage (IL) production; and
4. Forcing a shift from more meaning-based processing of the second language to a more syntactic mode.

ACMC, such as the kind analysed in this pilot study, would seem to show benefits in the areas 3 and 4, but not so much in 1 and 2. Other studies which have looked at SCMC, be it text-based such as chatting or oral communication such as Skype, would be necessary for establishing the benefits of feedback and hypothesis testing (see Schenker, 2012).

Research that replaces F2F contact time with online time was practically non-existent until Adair-Hauck et al. (2000) set out to evaluate the effectiveness of integrating technology into a second-semester college-level French course. Since then, several other course redesigns have had success in achieving proficiency results equal to, or greater than, the proficiency measured in the non-blended courses (Bañados, 2006; Bauer et al., 2006; Chenowith and Murday, 2003). A review of the literature on BL reveals that, 'In general, the literature advocates the application of sound pedagogical and design principles, such as interactionist learning theory and learner-centred design guidelines and models.' (Young, 2008: 162).

Many studies into BL have been spurred by a need to either reduce costs or facilitate a growing number of language learners. When a university language requirement overflowed the Spanish classrooms at the University of Illinois in the USA, a study which converted 50% of classroom time into online learning allowed each teaching assistant to teach twice as many students each semester (Musumeci, 1999). This study fell into the 'no significant difference' theory (Twigg, 2001: 4), which coincides with the bulk of the studies done on online learning in the past ten years. These studies all found that online learners achieved a relatively equal level of proficiency when compared with their peers taught entirely in the classroom (Chenowith and Murday, 2003; Chenowith et al., 2006; Musumeci, 1999; Sanders, 2005; Young, 2008). The ongoing challenge to researchers in the field of BL is to find ways in which these tools can be used to produce more and greater proficiency to move beyond the 'no significant difference' hypothesis. The present study aims to look at ways in which CALL technology can be utilised to increase oral output within the same time and cost framework of an advanced level German course.

Firth and Wagner argued in an article in the *Modern Languages Journal* that SLA needs to expand to include sociocultural and socio-interactional as well as emic perspectives on L2 learning (Firth and Wagner, 1997). These emic perspectives can include more learner autonomy. Rather than replacing F2F instruction with completely online courses, BL seeks to expand upon instruction with more interactionist material and puts the focus of learning on the learner in negotiating the material (see also McCarten and Sandiford, Chapter 12, this volume). With the importance of output in the L2 learning process and the advantages for CMC in the L2 classroom having been proven, it would follow that integrating this type of learning into the curriculum would lead to benefits for the instructor and result in greater oral, written and cultural fluency on the part of the learner. The following pilot study aims to determine if a blended course format can not only equal, but also improve the amount of oral production provided in a given class and ascertain for which students this format is particularly useful.

THE PRESENT STUDY

Given the established role of output in the second language learning process and the growing number of blended and online courses being offered in that area, it seemed appropriate to look at the role of output in both the F2F and the computer-mediated classroom. F2F class time with native-speaking or advanced level instructors can provide valuable input but does not always allow time for each student to create with the language. Time constraints often mean that individual students only speak for a small fraction of the instruction time. Web 2.0 instruction tools are giving students the opportunity to access authentic texts, websites and videos, and spend more time speaking in the target language using ACMC tools such as email, texting, online gaming forums and simulated conversation tools in ways designed by a qualified instructor and guided by sound SLA theory. These individualised, online instruction modules can free up F2F class time for more comprehensible input, give students guided access to additional input outside of class time, and allow students who are more reserved about speaking in public the chance to gain more speaking experience. Through these online technologies, foreign language learners can be put in contact with the target culture (see for example the *Cultura* project, Bauer et al., 2006), students can spend more time creating with the language outside of the classroom, and the anonymous nature of online communication tools often encourages more equal participation and more open discussions (Warschauer, 1996). For these three reasons, a third-year German course was redesigned to incorporate online modules and this study served as a pilot study for the curriculum redesign.

The term Web 2.0 refers to web applications which increase user participation, collaboration and interaction (O'Reilly, 2005). Hybrid or blended courses create the opportunity for developing increased oral proficiency by utilising Web 2.0 tools to increase input and output while not sacrificing in-class instructional time. The term 'blended learning' has been used to describe the type of programme that provides synchronous classroom contact with asynchronous online learning for the purpose of replacing some of the synchronous classroom seat time (Albrecht, 2006).

This study investigated the amount of oral output produced by language learners in a F2F classroom and in online modules to determine which delivery format elicited more oral output. Participants in the pilot programme were six students enrolled in a German conversation and culture course at a small, liberal arts college in the USA during the spring semester of 2011. The course title was 'German Culture and Conversation'. The class members ranged in proficiency levels from advanced-beginner to intermediate-mid on the ACTFL[1] proficiency rating scale (comparable to an A2–B1 on the CEFR). The class, as it stood, followed a traditional F2F instruction format, meeting twice a week for 75 minutes at a time, and was taught by a full-time professor. The syllabus was arranged around the topics presented in the textbook *Anders Gedacht*, 2nd Edition (Motyl-Mudretzkyj and Späinghaus, 2010). Uses of technology in the F2F classroom included a course management system called 'Course Connect', viewing online videos and websites during class time and the use of online dictionary tools such as *dict.leo.org* and *dict.cc*.

RESEARCH QUESTIONS AND HYPOTHESES

This pilot programme sought to determine whether online teaching modules resulted in greater oral output when compared with the current class format of F2F teacher-led instruction. In addition, the study examined which students exhibited the largest increase in participation from the classroom to the online lessons. Research question (RQ) 1 tried to determine which delivery format would result in the most oral output. RQ 2 looked at which students benefited the most/least from the different delivery formats. RQ 3 investigated student attitudes about the online learning modules and computer-assisted language learning (CALL) through a post-assessment survey. This survey looked at learners' attitudes on BL to observe learner affect and determine if the course redesign could lead to increased learner motivation.

The hypotheses of the pilot programme were that:

1. the online modules would produce greater oral production.
2. the students who spoke the least in the classroom would show the largest gains in online performance.
3. student attitudes would be mixed in relation to the CALL tools. A post-assessment survey looked at learners' attitudes on BL to observe learner affect and determine if the course redesign could lead to increased learner motivation.

METHODS

The current syllabus of the class was analysed and four individual lessons were converted into an online delivery format. The topics chosen were: 'Grüne Politik' (Green Politics), 'Migration' (Migration), 'Vergangenheit' (The Past) and 'Anselm Kiefer und seine Kunst' (Anselm Kiefer and his Art). Each of these topics was taught in the traditional F2F classroom using the textbook and a teacher-led lecture format. These four lessons were videotaped. Additionally, four online 'Mashups' (interactive sites using various CALL applications) were developed to correlate with each in-class lesson. These Mashups were created using Michigan State University's CLEAR (Center for Language Education and Research) *Rich Internet Applications*. (See Instruments and Treatment, below, and Appendix, p. 122, for more information and links to online lessons.) To control for the effect of repetition of subject matter, the lessons were implemented first in the classroom and then online for the first two modules and then switched to first online and then in the classroom for the second two modules. By switching the order of the delivery format the students did not have the advantage of always being exposed to the content for a second time in either the traditional or online mode. For example, the Green Politics and Migration modules were first covered in class and then the students completed the online work, whereas with the Past and Anselm Kiefer modules, the students completed the online modules and then had in-class lessons on that material.

INSTRUMENTS AND TREATMENT

Primary instruments in the pilot project were the textbook, *Anders Gedacht*, used to choose thematic topics and to guide the in-class lessons and CLEAR (Michigan State University's Center for Language Education and Research). CLEAR has developed a full portfolio of *Rich Internet Applications* intended for use by language instructors and consisting primarily of online tools to facilitate language learning. The programmes include: *Mashups,* a type of online, interactive worksheet; *Conversations,* an asynchronous conversation recorded by the instructor and completed by students; audio dropboxes[2], a place for students to deposit recorded speech; and *Smile,* an assessment programme, which can be customised by the instructor. Other online tools included Google Docs, VoiceThread, YouTube and various websites. Each of these tools was used to elicit oral or written production. For the purposes of this pilot study only the oral production was analysed. The *Mashup* application allows for multiple online applications to be consolidated onto one webpage, which acts like an interactive worksheet. Each of the online modules was consolidated into one *Mashup* containing several Web 2.0 tools to elicit oral production. The *Conversation* application, which simulates a two-way conversation eliciting spoken answers or comments to recorded oral questions, was used in all four *Mashups*. VoiceThread, a program which allows students to record audio in response to visual images or videos, was used in the third and fourth *Mashups*. Additionally, authentic texts such as TV advertisements, music videos, political websites and images of paintings served as topics of conversation around culturally relevant themes. Audio dropboxes were also embedded into the *Mashups* so that students could leave longer, oral responses to prompts based on the online materials. In one dropbox assignment, students were asked to create their own political party with a poster and then talk about which aspects of that party were environmentally responsible or not. In the traditional classroom this would have been a written homework assignment and the students would have either presented their work in class (each student speaking for 1.5 minutes plus transition time, equalling approximately 12 minutes of class time taken for oral production) or not had the opportunity to create oral language around the assignment. With the use of the audio dropboxes, the students were able to plan their language production and submit it to the instructor without taking up valuable in-class instruction time. The instructor gave feedback on their language through a typed response and each student spent an average of 1.5 minutes on oral production for that task alone.

The VoiceThread assignments were similar to the dropbox tasks except that they were more closely related to visual cues. In a VoiceThread, images are presented on the page somewhat like a PowerPoint presentation and students are given either a written or oral prompt to which they must respond. All student responses are logged with an icon around the visual image so that anyone with access to the VoiceThread can listen and respond to each icon, resulting in a conversation thread based on a given topic. The instructor or native-speaker participant can be involved in this thread to give feedback or move the conversation in a different direction. These assignments generated even more oral output than the dropbox tasks, seemingly because they had more direct visual prompts and there was a level of interaction and feedback to elicit 'pushed output'.

DATA COLLECTION, ANALYSIS AND RESULTS

The videos of the in-class sessions were observed and the students' oral production timed. The online lessons were also timed and the length of oral output for each student in each format was compared. Students were given a post-assessment survey, which was completed anonymously. Speaking times for individual students were determined for individual online activities. These individual times were then combined to compare in-class oral production to online production. The percentage of increase in that production time was also calculated as well as the percentage of total talk time in each of the formats.

Results showed that there was a significant increase in oral production in the online lessons. The average percentage increase in oral production from in-class to online instruction was 299%. The percentage of students who showed an increase in oral production from in-class to online instruction was 100%. The results give a picture of total time spent on oral production as well as the type of language produced in each format. The anonymous survey also produced interesting opinions from the students regarding online work, learner affect and motivation.

Each of the three individual online speaking applications (CLEAR *Conversations*, audio dropboxes, and VoiceThread) resulted in a greater number of minutes spoken than the total amount of in-class speaking time for each student. When these three applications were combined into one *Mashup*, the time spent on oral production was more than tripled. This makes a strong case for the use of online speaking applications such as the ones used in this study to extend oral output in the BL environment. The individual nature of these tools allows each student to speak for more time than would ever be possible during in-class lessons. The following tables show the amount of oral production for each delivery format as well as the percentage of class speaking time taken by each student in each format. These numbers help to answer RQs 1 and 2, which examine the amount of language produced by each student and the distribution of that language amongst the students.

In the following tables, the amount of oral production in each format is reported. The first column in each format shows each student's total oral production in minutes. The second column shows the percentage of total group production taken up by each individual student. When a student was absent from a F2F class, that student's online oral production was not used in the online total, so as not to skew the comparison of total oral production in each format. In the percentage of total group production totals, all students' online contributions were used regardless of whether they were present in the F2F class since these totals represent a percentage of the total and were used to determine the distribution of talk time, not total amounts.

ANALYSIS

Topic: 'Grüne Politik' (Green Politics). F2F first, followed by online. Total class time: 1hr 05 min.

STUDENT	F2F ORAL PRODUCTION		ONLINE ORAL PRODUCTION	
	A F2F oral production	B Individual % of total group F2F talk (A/10.2 [total oral production time])	C Online oral production	D Individual % of total group online talk (C/23.8 [total oral production time]) (including absent F2F student for total talk time)
A	0.6 min	6%	4.6 min	19%
B	1.9 min	19%	2.1 min	9%
C	2.9 min	28%	4.5 min	19%
D	3.0 min	29%	3.8 min	16%
E	Absent	N/A	2.3 min (N/A)	10%
F	1.8 min	18%	6.5 min	27%
Totals	10.2 min	100%	21.5 min	100%

Figure 7.1 Lesson 1

Topic: 'Migration' (Migration). F2F first, followed by online. Total class time: 1hr 16 min.

STUDENT	F2F ORAL PRODUCTION		ONLINE ORAL PRODUCTION	
	A F2F oral production	B Individual % of total group F2F talk (A/7.9 [total oral production time])	C Online oral production	D Individual % of total group online talk (C/25 [total oral production time])
A	1.6 min	20%	3.3 min	13%
B	1.2 min	15%	2.1 min	8%
C	2.1 min	27%	3.8 min	15%
D	1.0 min	12%	4.3 min	17%
E	0.6 min	8%	3.6 min	15%
F	1.4 min	18%	7.9 min	32%
Totals	**7.9 min**	100%	**25 min**	100%

Figure 7.2 Lesson 2

Topic: 'Vergangenheit' (The Past). Online first, followed by F2F. Total class time: 55 min.

STUDENT	ONLINE ORAL PRODUCTION		F2F ORAL PRODUCTION	
	A Online oral production	B Individual % of total group online talk (A/37 [total oral production time])	C F2F oral production	D Individual % of total group F2F talk (C/5.9 [total oral production time]))
A	9.0 min	24%	0.7 min	12%
B	4.2 min	12%	0.9 min	15%
C	4.6 min	12%	1.4 min	24%
D	5.9 min	16%	1.1 min	19%
E	4.0 min	11%	0.7 min	12%
F	9.3 min	25%	1.1 min	19%
Totals	**37 min**	100%	**5.9 min**	100%

Figure 7.3 Lesson 3

Topic: 'Anselm Kiefer und seine Kunst' (Anselm Kiefer and his Art). Online first, followed by F2F. Total class time: 1hr 16 min.

STUDENT	ONLINE ORAL PRODUCTION		F2F ORAL PRODUCTION	
	A. Online oral production (including absent F2F student for total talk time)	B: Individual % of total group online talk (A/35.9 [total oral production time])	C F2F oral production	D: Individual % of total group F2F talk (C/6.3 [total oral production time])
A	5.9 min (N/A)	17%	Absent	N/A
B	4.4 min	12%	0.9 min	14%
C	6.2 min	17%	1.0 min	16%
D	9.0 min	25%	2.3 min	37%
E	3.5 min	10%	1.3 min	21%
F	6.9 min	19%	0.8 min	13%
Totals	**30 min**	100%	**6.3 min**	100%

Figure 7.4 Lesson 4

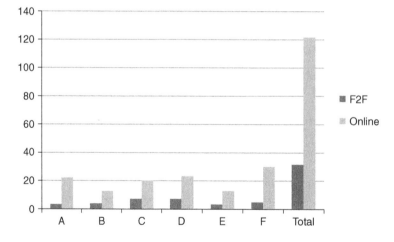

Figure 7.5 Amount of Total Oral Output in Online vs. F2F lessons (minutes)

RESULTS

Primarily, the students who spoke the least amount of minutes during class made the most gains in online speaking time. Figure 7.5 shows the total amount of oral output for each student, as well as the course totals, in each format. As the chart shows, students C and D tended to dominate the speaking time during class while students A and E spoke the least. In the online lessons students A and F spoke the most while B and E spoke the least. Students A and F seemed to benefit the most from the online units as they spoke the most online but were sometimes overpowered by students C and D in class. In several individual modules, such as Module 1 and Module 3, students A and F went from producing the

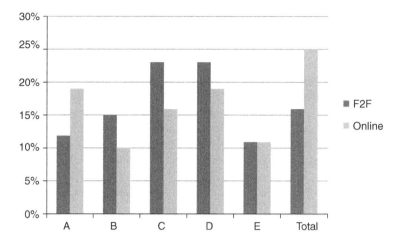

Figure 7.6 Average Individual % of Total Oral Production

least spoken language in class to the most online. This would support the hypothesis that students who are more shy speakers in class produce comparatively more language when given the planning time and privacy to create their language online. This finding also supports the idea that online talk is distributed more evenly and does not rely on factors such as gender, personality or perceived language ability. It also points to a recommendation for including both kinds of talk into a language curriculum, since different students benefit from each type of spoken format. While confident students with big personalities or those with previous experience of studying abroad may take up more F2F speaking time, quieter or less confident students may take the opportunity to make up that difference when speaking online. Figure 7.6 shows clearly how different students take the lead in oral production in both F2F and online environments. While students C and D dominated the F2F conversations, students A and D spoke the most in the online modules.

Examining the data from the in-class lessons reveals that an average of 60% of the spoken turns taken in class consisted of one second, one-word responses to questions. These could have been yes/no answers or simply factual responses used by most teachers to check comprehension and keep students on task. In comparison, students spoke for an average of 32 seconds in each of their online spoken turns, which equates to much more complex use of the language. When taking the one-word utterances out of the comparison, the increase in online oral language becomes even greater.

If in-class minutes are primarily spent on teacher talk and comprehensible input, then homework assignments of this sort can provide ways for students to create with the language during non-classroom hours. Given that these assignments are still monitored by a qualified professor and feedback is given either online or in class, this provides an extension of the reach of the instructor. Rather than replacing the instructor, hybridising the curriculum could allow qualified teachers more time to impact students' learning. While the scope of this trial study was small, it points to many possible applications which could allow students to benefit from more access to instructors and more interaction with cultural aspects, which are not available in the foreign language classroom. That would be a possible next step in the research in this area.

If positive learner affect and keeping the affective filter low are considerations in the effectiveness of the modules, then one must also take the learner's opinion into account when judging the success or failure of the study. In the learner survey, positive aspects of the online lessons were listed as: 'easy guidelines', 'time to prepare', 'being able to talk without anyone listening to me at first and being able to playback and hear myself'. Other positive comments included: 'I don't feel confident when I speak German, so being forced to practice was a positive thing for me.' '(Online) I was forced to speak German, whereas in class you can participate as much as you want to.' Or, 'I do believe it pushed me to speak more, which is great because I am usually a bit shy to talk in class.'

The main complaints about the online modules stemmed from the fact that the assignments were not graded (since they were completed for the purposes of this study) and came as additional work on top of their other German homework. Some students stated that they just rushed through the work to get it done because it was not for a grade; however, even rushing through the work, they still produced more oral output than in class. Obviously correcting the curriculum by making the assignments part of the graded work would help solve this problem.

Several students stated that they did not think it helped their spoken German because they wrote everything down and then read it out loud online. This is more of a concern if the goal of the lessons is truly spontaneous oral output. If the instructor is only concerned with oral output in general then this is not as much of a problem. Rather ironically, one student wrote, 'I think it's hard to take online learning seriously. I pay less attention when I am on the computer and I can spend a lot of time perfecting my German, *which is kind of cheating*' (my italics). The question then arises, what the goal of these blended lessons is. Obviously some of the modules, which were meant to produce spoken language, ended up producing large amounts of written language as well. This is something that should be addressed before the final curriculum redesign.

Conclusion

The hypothesis that the online learning modules would produce more oral output, was confirmed in this study. Each student increased his or her oral output in the online modules. On average, the students who spoke the least in class increased their oral output by a greater percentage than those who spoke the most in class. Students who identified themselves as 'shy' in class saw the most gains in oral output. The other aspect of this project aimed to assess students' attitudes about online learning. There were more positive than negative comments on the post-assessment surveys and the main complaints about the activities stemmed from the fact that they were not graded. The positive comments centred around the 'forced to speak' aspects of the modules and admitted that this was an upside of the design.

The main limitation for this pilot study was obviously the number of participants. While more students would have provided more breadth within the results, the fact that 100% of the students showed gains in oral production helps underscore the validity of the study. Questions of whether the students were actually creating with the language or writing first and then reading aloud are also a concern. This could potentially be addressed in the specific design of the online modules.

Based on the results of this pilot study, the next step in blended course design research could be the design and implementation of more online learning based on SLA theory. While this study shows that computer-mediated communication (CMC) can help students produce more oral output and that students who feel shy about speaking in class show greater gains in computer-mediated oral production, there needs to be more focus on proficiency levels to determine if this type of production can truly imitate the interaction which has been shown to improve proficiency in F2F classroom settings. The blended course designer should take from this study that online modules, in addition to F2F instruction, can be beneficial for their L2 students and look forward to future studies, which add to this body of inquiry.

Judging from this pilot study, moving classes from a traditional to a blended format could provide the opportunity to give students more access to teacher-led instruction, more oral production outside of the classroom, more interaction with the language and a format for noticing their own language production (McCarthy, Chapter 1, this volume). Provided that the online modules were well-developed and followed from sound SLA research, hybrid or blended courses could buy valuable instructor-monitored time on task while not robbing students of F2F instruction time, which can still be used for providing comprehensible input and instruction in other areas such as cultural studies and literacy. Instructors and course designers must choose the online tools for web-based instruction carefully and consider the pros and cons of different modalities for the goals of their specific language learners. While this study looked at asynchronous communication tools, synchronous communication brings its own advantages and disadvantages (see Abrams, 2003; Pérez, 2003; Schenker, 2012; Sotillo, 2000). Further studies might look at the differing effects of written and oral output on student proficiency levels. A thorough classification of online tool types (not specific tools, since the evolution of such tools moves much too quickly to keep a relevant database) could help course designers and instructors identify the most applicable online tool for their language learning goals. The slowed down nature of asynchronous communication could also be applied differently to beginning level students (who need time to plan their language and get easily overwhelmed with speedy, F2F communication) and to more advanced students (who can take in and produce more than just simple exchanges) by utilising the tools in different ways. These goals would all be interesting studies in the future.

Suggested Resources

Blake, R. (2013). *Brave New Digital Classroom: Technology and Foreign Language Learning*. Washington, DC: Georgetown University Press.

Warschauer, M. (1996). Comparing face-to-face and electronic discussion in the second language classroom. *CALICO Journal*, 13(2), 7–26.

Abrams, Z. I. (2003). The effect of synchronous and asynchronous CMC on oral performance in German. *The Modern Language Journal*, 87(2), 157–167.

Smith, B., Álvarez-Torres, M., & Zhao, Y. (2003). Features of CMC technologies and their impact on language learners' online interaction. *Computers in Human Behavior*, 19(6), 703–729.

Garrett, N. (2009). Computer-assisted language learning trends and issues revisited: Integrating innovation. *The Modern Language Journal*, 93, 719–740.

Discussion Questions

1. What role do you feel output plays in the learning of a second language? How does output help to develop a learner's language proficiency?

2. How much time have you (as an instructor or as a learner) generally spent on oral output during a typical language class? How much face-to-face class time do you feel should be devoted to the learners' oral output?

3. In what ways can the use of computer-mediated communication (CMC) help students produce more oral output? Which students do you feel would benefit most from online language production?

4. Are you familiar with any online tools with which students can record oral output or interact in the target language online? How can you imagine using those tools to enhance the language learning process?

5. Can you think of some aspects of oral output and interaction, which do not lend themselves to being moved online?

References

Abrams, Z. I. (2003). The effect of synchronous and asynchronous CMC on oral performance in German. *The Modern Language Journal*, 87(2), 157–167.

Adair-Hauck, B., Willingham-McLain, L., & Youngs, B. E. (2000). Evaluating the integration of technology and second language learning. *CALICO Journal*, 17(2), 269–306.

Albrecht, B. (2006). *Enriching Student Experience Through Blended Learning*. Boulder, CO: EDUCASE Centre for Applied Research.

Bañados, E. (2006). A blended-learning pedagogical model for teaching and learning EFL successfully through an online interactive multimedia environment. *CALICO Journal*, 23(3), 533–550.

Bauer, B., DeBenedette, L., Furstenberg, G., Levet, S., & Waryn, S. (2006). The Cultura Project. In J. Belz & S. L. Thorne (Eds.), *Internet-mediated Intercultural Foreign Language Education* (pp. 31–62). Boston: Heinle.

Chenowith, A. N., & Murday, K. (2003). Measuring student learning in an online French course. *CALICO Journal*, 20, 285–314.

Chenowith, A. N., Ushida, E., & Murday, K. (2006). Student learning in hybrid French and Spanish courses: An overview of language online. *CALICO Journal*, 24, 115–145.

Firth, A., & Wagner, J. (1997). On discourse, communication and (some) fundamental concepts of SLA research. *Modern Language Journal*, 81, 285–300.

Gass, S. (2003). Input and interaction. In C. Doughty & M. H. Long (Eds.), *The Handbook of Second Language Acquisition* (pp. 224–255). Oxford: Basil Blackwell.

Gass, S., & Selinker, L. (2008). *Second Language Acquisition: An Introductory Course* (3rd edition). New York: Routledge.

Godwin-Jones, R. (2003). Emerging technologies. Blogs and wikis: Environments for online collaboration. *Language Learning and Technology*, 7(2), 12–16.

Graf, P. (1994). Explicit and implicit memory: A decade of research. *Attention and Performance*, 15, 681–696.

Graf, P., & Schachter, D. L. (1985). Implicit and explicit memory for new associations in normal and amnesic subjects. *Journal of Experimental Psychology: Learning, Memory, and Cognition*, 11, 501–518.

Izumi, S. (2002). Output, input enhancement and the noticing hypothesis: an experimental study on ESL relativization. *Studies in Second Language Acquisition*, 24, 541–577.

Izumi, S., Bigelow, M., Fujiwara, M., & Fearnow, S. (1999). Testing the output hypothesis: Effects of output on noticing and second language acquisition. *Studies in Second Language Acquisition*, 21, 421–452.

Kraemer, A. (2008). Formats of distance learning. In S. Goertler & P. Winke (Eds.), *Opening Doors through Distance Language Education: Principles, Perspectives, and Practices*, CALICO Monograph Series, 7. San Marcos, TX: CALICO.

Krashen, S. (1985). *The Input Hypothesis: Issues and Implications*. London: Longman.

Lambert, W., & Tucker, R. (1972). *Bilingual Education of Children: The St. Lambert Experiment*. Rowley, MA: Newbury House.

Lantolf, J. P., & Beckett, T. G. (2009). Sociocultural theory and second language acquisition. *Language Teaching*, 42(4), 459–475.

Long, M. H. (1996). The role of the linguistic environment in second language acquisition. In W. C. Ritchie & T. K. Bhatia (Eds.), *Handbook of Second Language Acquisition* (pp. 413–468). San Diego, CA: Academic Press.

Mackey, A. (2002). Beyond production: Learners' perceptions about interactional processes. *International Journal of Educational Research*, 37, 379–394.

Motyl-Mudretzkyj, I., & Späinghaus, M. (2010). *Anders Gedacht: Text and Context in the German-Speaking World* (2nd edition). Boston: Heinle Cengage Learning.

Musumeci, D. (1999). *The Spanish Project*. From The National Center for Academic Transformation.

O'Reilly, T. (2007). What is Web 2.0: Design patterns and business models for the next generation of software. *International Journal of Digital Economics*, 65, 17–37.

Pérez, L. C. (2003). Foreign language and productivity in synchronous vs. asynchronous computer-mediated communication. *CALICO Journal*, 21(1), 89–104.

Sanders, R. (2005). Redesigning introductory Spanish: Increased enrollment, online management, cost reduction and effects on student learning. *Foreign Language Annals*, 38, 523–532.

Schenker, T. (2012). *The Effects of a Virtual Exchange on Language Skills and Intercultural Competence*. Doctoral dissertation, Michigan State University, East Lansing, Michigan.

Smith, B., Álvarez-Torres, M., & Zhao, Y. (2003). Features of CMC technologies and their impact on language learners' online interaction. *Computers in Human Behavior*, 19(6), 703–729.

Sotillo, S. M. (2000). Discourse functions and syntactic complexity in synchronous and asynchronous communication. *Language Learning and Technology*, 4(1), 82–119.

Swain, M. (1978). French immersion: Early, late or partial? *Canadian Modern Language Review*, 34, 577–585.

Swain, M. (1985). Communicative competence: Some roles of comprehensible input and comprehensible output in its development. In S. Gass & C. Madden (Eds.), *Input in Second Language Acquisition* (pp. 235–253). Rowley, MA: Newbury House.

Swain, M. (1995). Three functions of output in second language learning. In G. Cook & B. Seidlhofer (Eds.), *Principle and Practice in Applied Linguistics* (pp. 125–144). Oxford: Oxford University Press.

Swain, M. (2005). The output hypothesis: Theory and research. In E. Hinkel (Ed.), *Handbook on Research in Second Language Teaching and Learning* (pp. 471–484). Mahwah, NJ: Lawrence Erlbaum Associates.

Swain, M., & Lapkin, S. (1982). *Evaluating Bilingual Education*. Bristol: Multilingual Matters.

Swain, M., & Lapkin, S. (1981). *Bilingual Education in Ontario: A Decade of Research*. Toronto: Ontario Institute for Studies in Education.

Twigg, C. (2001). *Innovations in Online Learning: Moving Beyond No Significant Difference*. Retrieved March 21, 2013, from National Center for Academic Transformation.

Warschauer, M. (1996). Comparing face-to-face and electronic discussion in the second language classroom. *CALICO Journal*, 13(2), 7–26.

Young, D. J. (2008). An empirical investigation of the effects of blended learning on student outcomes in a redesigned intensive spanish course. *CALICO Journal*, 26(1), 160–181.

Appendix

1. MASHUP – GRÜNE POLITIK

http://clear.msu.edu/teaching/online/ria/mashup2/view.php?ID=8788

ORAL EXERCISES

a) CLEAR Conversation based on 'Bündnis 90/die Grünen' website.

b) Audio dropbox showing creation of students' own political party.

2. MASHUP – MIGRATION

http://clear.msu.edu/teaching/online/ria/mashup2/view.php?ID=8918

ORAL EXERCISES

a) CLEAR Conversation eliciting background knowledge on immigration in Germany and the USA.

b) Audio dropbox based on 'Zeit Online' article about immigrants to Germany.

3. MASHUP – VERGANGENHEIT

http://clear.msu.edu/teaching/online/ria/mashup2/view.php?ID=9379

ORAL EXERCISES

a) CLEAR Conversation with questions related to a music video by the rapper 'Dissziplin'.

b) VoiceThread – students comment on ten images from post WWII Germany.

4. MASHUP – ANSELM KIEFER UND SEINE KUNST

http://clear.msu.edu/teaching/online/ria/mashup2/view.php?ID=9493

ORAL EXERCISES

a) CLEAR Conversation based on the C.V. of the artist Anselm Kiefer

b) VoiceThread – students describe five paintings using vocabulary from the textbook.

Notes

[1] The ACTFL (American Council on the Teaching of Foreign Languages) scale corresponds approximately to the CEFR (Common European Framework of Reference) levels A2-B1. For further information, see http://www.actfl.org/sites/default/files/pdfs/public/ACTFLProficiencyGuidelines2012_FINAL.pdf.

[2] An internet application provided free by the Michigan State University CLEAR Center (Center for Language Education and Research), which is a US Department of Education Title VI Language Research Center.

CHAPTER 8

Reconceptualising Materials for the Blended Language Learning Environment

Freda Mishan

INTRODUCTION

The concept of language learning materials has been difficult to define ever since technology was added to the repertoire of media for language learning. This is partly because, historically, language teaching was rooted in print-based learning materials. The affordances (capabilities) of technology (and in particular, from the mid-2000s, Web 2.0 tools) made for shifting notions of 'authorship' together with a transition to materials in different media, with their variations in audio/audio-visual input and degrees of transience. These changes have broadened the scope of what were formerly understood as materials, but at the same time, have made for some ambiguity in the use of the term in the literature. For some, materials are still products created using technological applications (the word processor, podcasting software, and so on) or sourced from the web (e.g., YouTube videos). For others, technology has transformed materials from being products like this to being processes – of socialising, networking and collaborating (via tools such as social networking sites, wikis, etc.). Given these disparities, it would now seem time to reconcile these concepts of materials as regards technology and to look at how they are realised within the blended language learning (BLL) environments which increasingly characterise our educational landscape. In this endeavour, this chapter looks firstly at how the concept of materials has had to develop in line with the affordances of technology. It then consults frameworks for blended learning (BL) in the literature, focusing on the place of language materials within these, in order to evolve a conceptual model for materials in BLL contexts. In the second part of the chapter, samples from the author's practice and a cross-section of the contemporary literature are used to show how the model can be put into practice. The chapter closes by using the devised model as a measure to critically evaluate current parameters for BLL materials design.

REDEFINING MATERIALS FOR THE TECHNOLOGICAL/DIGITAL ENVIRONMENT

A logical starting point for this chapter is to explore definitions of the focus of the chapter, language learning material. A classic practical definition provided by Tomlinson is 'anything used by teachers or learners to facilitate the learning of a language' (2011: 2). Tomlinson goes on to list examples such as 'videos, DVDs, emails, YouTube, dictionaries, grammar books, readers, workbooks or photocopied exercises […] newspapers, food packages, photographs, live talks by invited native speakers, instructions given by a teacher, tasks written on cards or discussions between learners' (Ibid.: 2). In large part, this description represents materials as products or resources. Some descriptions of materials in the technological context leave materials rooted more or less within this tradition, representing technology chiefly as a tool for materials' production and/or delivery: 'Technology nowadays plays a prominent role in the development of language-learning materials, *both as a tool in support of their creation and as a means of delivering content.*' (Reinders and White, 2010: 58, my italics) The same view is represented in the chapter title 'Developing language-learning materials with technology' (Motteram, 2011). This might be characterised as a Web 1.0-era perspective, when onscreen/online materials were still identifiable with their print equivalents; they were still largely static and basically maintained the same mono-directional flow of information from provider to user.

However, even in the 'traditional' definition of materials above from Tomlinson, we see a gradual extension of the concept of materials from products to include interactions – in emails and 'discussions between learners' for instance. This is in line with a shift made possible by Web 2.0. tools – social networking sites, blogs and so on – which cultivate collaboration and interaction (Hojnacki, Chapter 7, this volume). Chapelle, one of the key figures in CALL (Computer Assisted Language Learning), implicitly identifies materials with interactivity; she talks of learning occurring during learner-computer interactions 'where the language and *interactions* have been designed for learning' (2009: 745, my italics).

This advances towards a more contemporary, technology-inclusive definition of materials; 'CALL materials, that is, artefacts produced for language teaching […] – can be taken to include tasks, websites, software, courseware, online courses, and virtual learning environments' (Reinders and White, 2010: 59). Intrinsic to these tools/platforms is interaction, and this is increasingly identified with materials in language learning in the digital environment, as are the tasks which act as the pedagogical framework for them (see Hojnacki, Chapter 7, and McCarten and Sandiford, Chapter 12, this volume). The task is arguably the 'natural' format for this environment: 'The characterisation of task as free-standing, goal-focused and learner-driven in nature, is perfectly in tune with the work modes which have come to be associated with using the internet.' (Mishan, 2010: 150) This synergy between the task concept and CALL is explained and developed in Thomas and Reinders' edited book *Task-Based Language Learning and Teaching with Technology* (2010). In the research reported in that volume, the 'learning material' can often be seen as the task, or more precisely, the interactions that occur within it, rather than the teaching material that merely sets the task (a distinction made in Doughty and Long, 2003, as well as Ellis, 2011). Chapelle, meanwhile, calls for a holistic (inclusive) view of materials in the CALL context, and, significantly, consistently pairs materials and tasks in writings on CALL and SLA (for example, 2009, 2010). Translating theory to practice, in the Web 2.0 setting, it is learner interactions within tasks, traced as social networking site (SNS), blog/vlog or wiki postings along with others, that increasingly constitute the 'learning material'.

We might, in sum, be talking of a content vs. process distinction similar to that between product and process in the learning of language skills (see McCarthy, Chapter 1, this volume). In the context of use of technology, this is a distinction between '*content* materials as sources of information and data and *process* materials that act as frameworks within which learners can use their communicative abilities' (Reinders and White, 2010: 59, italics in original). Fundamentally, as Hampel reminds us, it is the process-oriented features of technology, its interactive and collaborative affordances, which 'represent its best assets' (2006: 106). This expansion of the concept of materials to include process aspects – interactions and tasks – as well as the outcomes these can generate, is an essential one in a BLL environment, or, to use Gruba and Hinkelman's more holistic term, 'ecology' (Gruba and Hinkelman, 2012), and allows the concept to be situated within a broader theoretical framework.

Technology and Language Learning: the Theoretical Base

The learning philosophy traditionally most closely associated with CALL is sociocultural theory (originating from the works of Vygotsky, e.g., 1981), one aspect of which is the importance of tools in mediating and transforming action (see, for example, Warschauer, 2005 on CALL through the sociocultural lens). Technology is, of course, a tool that has mediated and transformed activity like no other since, perhaps, the invention of the telegraph. Learning materials can be seen as another tool, constituting a set ranging from the traditional textbook to the sorts of interactions described above, which 'direct behaviour and lead to higher mental processing' (Ducate et al., 2014: 72); the cognitive level which drives learning (see work on education and the cognitive domain, by Bloom et al., 1956). A view of learning as not only a cognitive effort at individual level but also as collaboratively created in social environments is offered by socio-constructivist theory which is commonly linked to BLL (see, for example, Delialioglu and Yildirim, 2007; Gruba and Hinkelman, 2012). The technologies available as part of BLL environments, notably Web 2.0 tools such as wikis, SNSs, blogs, etc., make this sort of 'collaborative knowledge-building' a reality – and continue to shift our notion of materials from learning from products to learning as a result of processes.

A Framework for Blended Language Learning Materials

Having provided the background for a reconceptualisation of materials in the digital environment, the next step is to look more closely at the place of materials within existing frameworks for BLL. As renowned early adopters (Crystal, 2001), the language teaching community have been swift to embrace BL, particularly at tertiary level (i.e., universities and college level) where it can be perceived as offering a financial 'quick-fix' by reducing teaching contact hours (see for instance Rubio and Thoms, 2014 and also the following section). This has caused a sudden burst of research and publication (summarised briefly in the following section), some of it voicing concerns about *ad hoc* methodological changes and stressing the need to 'provide a solid foundation for the design of BL contexts and the theoretical underpinnings that may justify their [technologies'] integration' (Rubio and Thoms, 2014: 1). This is not a new concern, but one that has been on the research agenda in tertiary education since the potential of technology began to be recognised, notably in seminal work by Laurillard originating from 1993 (*Rethinking University Teaching: A Framework for the Effective Use of Learning Technologies*, with a second edition in 2002).

Although predating BL by at least a decade, Laurillard's framework anticipated the BL model, challenging established 'transmission mode' (classically teacher-centred e.g., lecturing) teaching formats and moving to a position of more technology-facilitated, student-led learning, thus forming the theoretical foundation for much subsequent work in this area. Given its pedigree and its influence on BL theory (such as Bonk and Graham, 2006; Gruba and Hinkelman, 2012, see Figure 8.1 below), Laurillard's blueprint would seem a basic reference point for reimagining the role of materials within technology.

Laurillard conceptualised a set of teaching and learning 'actions' aligned with sample technologies. These 'actions' range along a continuum from 'narrative' at one end, to 'productive' at the other. Narrative actions, for example, range from transmission mode teaching, using tools such as presentation software suites (ones current at the time of writing include PowerPoint [PPT] and Prezi) or audio-visual media, through controlled interactivity, where students might work online with tutor or online feedback, to the other end of the pedagogy spectrum where students are 'productive', e.g., contributing to online media, with the teacher's role being 'facilitative'.

Of these, 'narrative' actions, consisting of conventional 'transmission mode' tools, approximate most closely to the traditional notion of materials as physical products. However, all the other actions, from 'interactive' through to 'productive', where material is student-generated, correspond to the enlarged 'digital-age' concept of materials being proposed in this chapter.

Among other influential frameworks for BL, Bonk and Graham's (2006) focuses on the distinctions between interactions in face-to-face contexts and in the technological environment, emphasising an interaction pattern where the interactions are between the learner and the materials and where the 'teacher' interface is absent. Neumeier's much-referenced model (2005), suggests parameters for designing BL environments, but likewise confines 'materials' to self-access online materials (used in her reported case study).

TYPES (LAURILLARD, 2002)	TEACHING ACTION	LEARNING ACTION (LAURILLARD, 2002)	EXAMPLE TECHNOLOGIES
Narrative	Presenting	Apprehending	Lectures, television, DVDs, printed textbooks, printed instructions
Interactive	Questioning	Exploring	Pairwork dialogues, hyperlinked texts, printed workbooks, quizzes with feedback
Adaptive	Modelling	Practising	Role plays, tutorial programmes, simulations, games, micro worlds
Communicative	Facilitating	Discussing	Discussion board, chat dialogues, messaging
Productive	Coaching	Expressing	Publishing, productions, conferences, websites, manuscripts

Figure 8.1 Pedagogical Actions and Dimensions of Technology (Gruba and Hinkelman, 2012: 18)

The only BL framework to explicitly incorporate a comprehensive materials dimension is Gruba and Hinkelman's (2012). Their framework consists of five core dimensions: actions (after Laurillard), groupings, timings, tools and texts. Three of these inform the conceptual basis for the notion of materials being built here: actions (as noted above), tools and texts. Texts are defined by Gruba and Hinkelman as 'communicative artefacts that have materiality and structure' (Ibid.: 25). These are 'generated' through the use of 'tools' (e.g., paintbrushes, pens), which today are frequently technologies (e.g., the digital camera, the word processor). Where texts are delivered physically, as printed photographs or documents, there is a clear distinction between them and the tools that create them. However, where interactivity is intrinsic to the tools/technologies (as in social networking sites such as Facebook, or micro-blogging tools running on mobile devices such as Twitter) the tool is inseparable from the text. Notably, too, the notion of text is broadened in line with the affordances of technology to include the audio-visual and graphic (Rossomondo, 2014: 221). This idea of the merging of the tool and text coincides with the extended notion of materials in technological environments where they are often interactively created, as discussed above.

In language pedagogy, interactive technological tools are not always used 'interactively' in this way, of course. Printing a transcript of a discussion forum on a social networking site, perhaps for a classroom discourse analysis task, removes its interactivity and renders it as 'passive' as a printed coursebook. This highlights that there is a fixed (or static) vs. dynamic dimension to materials, one which depends on their presentation, not on the technologies which generate or deliver them (see Mayer, 2005). This proves a core distinction in the conception and development of materials for the BLL context, adding another dimension to the materials model (see Figure 8.2 below). It also avoids the sort of 'tool-centric perspective' (Gruba and Hinkelman, 2012: 28) which links pedagogy with the tool itself, only to become obsolete as soon as the technology does (a historical case in point is the audio-lingual labs of the 1950s and 60s which embodied a behaviourist approach to language learning).

This 'multi-dimensional' concept of materials (Figure 8.2), in which the relationship between texts, actions and tasks is fluid and ever shifting, is crucially shaped by and for the BLL context. It is a conceptualisation which is realised within the platforms commonly used to support BL, learning management systems (LMSs, also known as Virtual Learning Environments or VLEs) such as Blackboard, WebCT and Moodle, all widely used systems

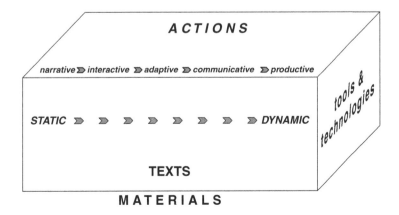

Figure 8.2 Materials in Blended Learning Contexts: a Multidimensional Concept ('Actions' after Laurillard, 2002)

at the time of writing. These can contain a broad variety of 'texts', interactive applications, set tasks and collaborative tools:

MATERIALS	SAMPLES/TOOLS*
Texts	Presentations using presentation software suites (e.g., PPT, Prezi), podcasts, screencasts, video clips (e.g., from YouTube).
Interactive applications	Online exercises using LMSs' own formats or external sites for creating quizzes and games.
Tasks	e.g., Webquests.
Collaborative tools	Blogs, micro-blogs (e.g., Twitter), chatrooms, videochat and conferencing applications (e.g., Skype), SNSs (e.g., Facebook).

*Please note tools mentioned here are in widespread use at the time of writing.

Figure 8.3 Tools and 'Materials'

While intended as descriptive, the model (Figure 8.2) can also function as a gauge for materials being designed for BL contexts, for assessing their range and variety across the dimensions.

Using the Blended Language Learning Materials Framework

In this section, examples of materials from BL situations are used to illustrate and operationalise (put into operation) this broader interpretation of materials. A couple of disclaimers are necessary first of all, however. The present author is aware that showing materials in isolation undermines the integrative philosophy of BL to an extent (see Johnson and Marsh, Chapter 4, and King, Chapter 6, this volume), so each example is contextualised within its curriculum or programme in order to cushion this. That there are risks involved in committing in print mode to technologies that change more rapidly than book editions goes without saying; it must be emphasised, therefore, that the case study materials illustrated here are only 'snapshots in time' as far as the tools they use are concerned.

In the interests of balance and representation, the materials' samples are drawn from both the author's practice and from a cross-section of the contemporary literature on BLL. As a relatively new approach, much of the research on BLL is empirical in nature, steadily generating a 'critical mass' of international practice in the area. Among current research collections, Tomlinson and Whittaker (2013) provide European and international perspectives and Nicolson et al. (2011) focus on British ones (the Open University in the UK). Volumes combining case studies with theoretical research include Rubio and Thoms (2014), giving 'hybrid language teaching' perspectives from the United States, and Gruba and Hinkelman (2012), which develops a principled framework for BLL and describes BLL programmes in Japan. The case studies reported in these volumes are from tertiary level with the exception of Tomlinson and Whittaker (2013), which also offers case studies on adult learning with various specialisms, EAP, ESP, teacher education, as well as EFL. Most of the case studies in Rubio and Thoms (2014) and some in Nicolson et al. (2011) are on the teaching of modern foreign languages.

A useful first illustration of the materials dimension diagram as an analytic tool is material from a Turkish ESP context with a fairly 'low tech' BLL framework in which teacher-produced podcasts for learner self-access were delivered via a blog platform and accessed via mobile phone (Kern, 2013). Podcasts like this would fall toward the 'narrative' and 'static' poles of the relevant dimensions (see Figure 8.2). Kern describes devising the BLL framework and materials as a solution to the typical problem faced by vocational students, in her case taxi-drivers, of availability for F2F class time. This typifies the application of BLL for 'life-long learners' (as also illustrated in Nicolson et al., 2011, writing on the use of BLL in the Open University, UK). The podcasts were designed through negotiation with the learners regarding their needs, and consisted of typical dialogues taking place between passengers and cab drivers, such as making recommendations for hotels or places of interest amongst others. In this case study, classroom work and self-access of the podcasts were interwoven, a structure which proved thoroughly suitable for the students in question; as Kern puts it 'taxi-drivers have a lot of down time' (2013: 134). The choice of mobile phones as the delivery medium in this situation is significant (see Dudeney and Hockly, Chapter 13, this volume), a growth area for BL particularly in 'emergent communities' lacking the technological infrastructure for internet-based systems (see also the following section).

The next case study is from tertiary education, and is a typical case of BLL originating as a practical, financial step for the reduction of F2F class time (see, for example, Rubio and Thoms, 2014; Young and Pettigrew, 2014). The context was a semester-long EFL programme for Erasmus (European exchange) students at the Common European Framework of Reference (CEFR) level C1 (advanced level), being run at the present author's institution in the Republic of Ireland.[1]

The BLL framework consisted of three F2F teaching hours per week plus a self-access/self-directed hour dedicated to extensive reading, and the undertaking of tasks on it, which were posted on the university LMS. The set novel, *Paddy Clarke Ha Ha Ha* (Roddy Doyle, 1993), was chosen as a critical introduction to cultural aspects of the students' host country. The diagram below illustrates a brainstorming session done

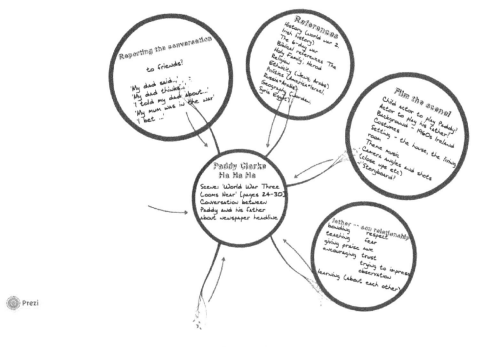

Figure 8.4 Brainstorming Activity (generated on Prezi)

in class which followed individual work reading and analysing a section of the novel. In the brainstorming activity, students worked in groups interpreting the passage from different viewpoints.

In contrast to the first case study, this second example illustrates how the materials 'dimensions' (see Figure 8.2) can and do operate independently; while the 'actions' dimension is productive, i.e., student-generated, the 'text' dimension remains towards the static pole. This activity also illustrates how the tool and the task are distinct. The tool, Prezi, was originally designed as a dynamic presentation tool but is ideal for brainstorming and mind-mapping type activities as well. Using it, students engage with the brainstorming activity in fully interactive mode; but as is often the case, when presented, this returns to 'narrative' and static poles on the respective dimensions.

The use of BLL for assessment is fairly well documented (see chapters in Nicolson et al., 2011; Gruba and Hinkelman, 2012; Rubio and Thoms, 2014) and fitted the parameters of this programme well. An end of semester assignment on the extensive reading was posted on the university LMS and used a blog about the author of the set book as its launching point:

> Look at this blog about Roddy Doyle:
>
> www.guardian.co.uk/books/booksblog/2010/may/30/falling-roddy-doyle
>
> The blogger, Sarah Crown of *The Guardian* newspaper, ends by asking the question: 'Which is the best Roddy Doyle novel to start with?'
>
> Make an argument for why she should read *Paddy Clarke Ha Ha Ha*. (Word limit: approximately 1500 words)
>
> Module assessment weighting: 20%[2]

Figure 8.5 BLL Assessment on Extensive Reading for EFL Context in Republic of Ireland (Mishan and Timmis, 2015: 109)

Identified on the materials dimension schema (Figure 8.2), this material was fairly 'static' and 'narrative'. The interactive potential of the blog in this case was not really exploited (as it was for reference only), illustrating that, as remarked above, interactivity is not inherent to the tool but depends on how it is used.

To broaden the perspective of this case study, the potential of using BL formats for L2 literature study was flagged as early as 2006 by Chambers and Gregory in their review of teaching English literature. There are a number of tools which are particularly well-adapted for this, offering frameworks for interpretation and critical or linguistic analysis. For example, makebeliefscomix.com, a comic strip generator current at the time of writing, includes 'teacher tips' suggesting that students can use comic strip characters as a way of 'inhabiting' literary characters as part of their interpretation of a novel. Turning to linguistic analysis, the word cloud[3] generator wordle.com (popular at the time of writing) is effectively a concordancer that represents word frequency visually, by font size (see example in Figure 8.6 below). It is particularly suitable for short texts – poems, passages from novels, or indeed for other genres such as newspaper articles, and can provide work on noticing patterns of collocation, colligation, word frequency in specific genres and others (see also Brindle, 2012 on exploiting Wordle for language learning). The word cloud in Figure 8.6 was generated for the poem *What teachers make* (Taylor Mali, 2002). This could be used, for instance, to draw out colligations with 'make' ('make kids work', 'make kids read') in tandem with a reading of the poem (see Appendix, p. 137) or a viewing of the poet performing it.[4] Also useful for literature, counter-intuitive though it may seem, is the micro-blogging site Twitter, for training students in the skill of synthesising (summarising, including all the essential points): postgraduates at University College Cork (UCC), Ireland, for instance, competed in submitting their thesis synthesised as a (140-character) tweet (a 'Tweesis').[5]

Figure 8.6 Word Cloud of the Poem *What teachers make* (Mali, 2002). (See full text in Appendix, p. 137.)

Having looked at some of the more 'static' and 'narrative' materials used in BLL programmes, it is useful to balance these with some from the opposite end of the spectrum, the 'dynamic' and 'productive' poles. Of the tools offering this type of learning material, the authorable website, the wiki, remains probably the most popular (e.g., Eydelman, 2013; Fleet, 2013; Ingham, 2013; Ducate et al., 2014; Young and Pettigrew, 2014). BLL programmes have also popularly used blogging (Gruba and Hinkelman, 2012: 120; Young and Pettigrew, 2014), online chat (e.g., Blake, 2014), Skype (e.g., Mishan, 2013) and, increasingly, mobile phones (e.g., Kern, 2013, discussed above).

A representative case study among these to use as an illustration here, on the basis of the range of tools and materials it used, is the BL programme for beginner Spanish devised at a college in the United States and reported in Young and Pettigrew (2014). The BL curriculum was based on a textbook (see also below) that had an e-platform on which the BL programme 'piggybacked', with 'input-based' materials, vocabulary, grammar, cultural content and related listening materials, added to the platform to form an e-book (Young and Pettigrew, 2014: 110). These 'static', 'narrative' materials were complemented, though, with a range of tools which 'fomented interpersonal communication' (Ibid.: 111), wikis, blogs and podcasts, and the blend was completed with two 50-minute sessions a week F2F teaching. The wiki was used to create a class profile, with students giving personal details relevant to their learning, which could be accessed by classmates. Students were also asked to write an introductory blog, for the instructor's eyes only, with the aim of helping him/her personalise learning and providing clues to proficiency needs. A more classic use of a blog though was the second one, 'talking about myself', which students shared with classmates on topics such as their families and university experience, amongst others. The third tool, the podcasting software Wimba, was used for the classic communicative activity in which one student gives instructions or a description which has to be reproduced by another. In this case, students recorded descriptions of a classroom layout as podcasts, then listened to those of others and reproduced them as drawings. The final element of the programme was a cultural project, an 'e-Portfolio', based on a choice of topics (such as exploring local Hispanic communities, creating a personalised online art gallery) and in which students were encouraged to use a range of media suitable to their project (e.g., video cameras, the internet).

This case study has some significant features as regards its materials, ones which help us look to one possible future for BL. First of all, in terms of the materials model (Figure 8.2), this blend nicely illustrates materials from the 'dynamic' and 'productive' ends of the texts and actions dimensions respectively. Noticeably, while there was a varying degree of collaboration depending on the tool and its use (greatest, say, with the wiki and the class blog), communication was in all cases asynchronous. This appears to be quite representative of BL environments, where, despite their promise for BL (there are four theoretical chapters on it in Nicolson et al., 2011, for example), tools with the potential for synchronous communication (such as video-conferencing applications, mobile phones) are sparsely used at present. BL via the mobile phone is certainly 'one to watch', particularly thriving, as mentioned earlier, in emergent countries lacking reliable internet connectivity, and there is a growing body of research in mobile learning or m-learning (see, for example, Hockly, 2013 and Dudeney and Hockly, Chapter 13, this volume). Nonetheless, the phone is often still reduced to a mere content delivery platform (Kukulska-Hulme and Shield, in a 2008 overview), which highlights the importance of recognising the distinction between 'mobile learning activities that focus on consumption of content, and activities that encourage the production of language' (Hockly, 2013: 82).

Conclusion

This brings us, in concluding this 'snapshot' of case studies in BL materials, to draw some general conclusions as to how well the materials used in BLL environments are fulfilling the potential offered by technologies, and by Web 2.0 tools in particular. In fact, a lot of the BLL experiences reported in the research to date tend to be disappointingly conservative as regards materials, with few of them using networking tools or synchronous ones, as noted above (exceptions include the use of Facebook in a French online programme [Blyth, 2014] and of 'oral discussion boards' in an EAP course [Pardo-González, 2013]). The tertiary institutions which are the main adopters of BL all have the technological infrastructure for BL: LMSs. But because, as Godwin-Jones points out, 'the core design of most LMSs in use today has not changed much from their origins in the mid-90s' (2012: 4), these platforms can be limited in the tools they provide and in the interactive exercise types they offer. Hence, a lot of the materials on them tend to be either 'static' (linked or uploaded materials such as podcasts, YouTube videos) or 'interactive' only insofar as they use the 'interactive' quizzes (e.g., multiple choice, matching) available as the LMS's default exercise types. This is somewhat of a backward step – back to Web 1.0. tools, in effect, whose activity types emulated those in coursebooks (see, for example, Vogel, 2001); and more alarmingly, to the prevailing transmission-mode pedagogical model these embodied (Godwin-Jones, 2012). That language curriculums in tertiary education are 'fundamentally linked to the textbook' (Young and Pettigrew, 2014: 109), particularly at beginner and intermediate level, may be a factor of this (or may be a result). Either way, there seems to be a worrying disconnect between BL and developments in technology and language teaching in general. In this field, research and practice extensively exploit the potential of collaborative tools for language learning, matching them to communicative and task-based pedagogies and sociocultural and social constructivist theories of learning (see, among the mass of research in the area, Thomas's [2009] compilation of studies on Web 2.0 and language learning). All this might lead us to suspect that in many cases, opting for BL is more a question of financial convenience than of pedagogical choice informed by the knowledge of what technology can offer to language learning. For teachers who are reluctant to integrate technology into their teaching in the first place, 'top-down' blended initiatives can be an unwelcome imposition – ultimately dooming them to failure.

There is a great deal of scepticism surrounding BL in the literature. Many do indeed warn against the adoption of BL merely as a cost-saving measure (e.g., Rubio and Thoms, 2014; Young and Pettigrew, 2014), or without keeping students' interests, needs and learning preferences central to pedagogical decisions (e.g., Stracke, 2007; Tomlinson and Whittaker, 2013). The need for a principled approach to BL course design is stressed (e.g., Gruba and Hinkelman, 2012; Tomlinson and Whittaker, 2013) as is the danger of the 'bandwagon' effect: not all programmes which use technology in some of their teaching involve the careful integration of F2F work with technology that characterises best practice in BL (Sharma, 2010). It would seem that, as happened with the communicative and task-based approaches to language teaching, we are seeing the development of a 'strong' form of BL, implemented at institutional level and devolved through the curriculums, and a 'weak' version developed at syllabus or course level on a more *ad hoc* basis. From the materials perspective, perhaps the greatest concern is that too often BL remains wedded to LMSs which use outmoded Web 1.0 design parameters, and to the pedagogies from which they sprang. Therefore, it is essential that BL programme developers look beyond the limitations and convenience of the LMS, to the wealth of research on technology and language learning, in order to find tools and create materials to fulfil the potential of BL.

Suggested Resources

Dudeney, G., Hockly, N., & Pegrum, M. (2013). *Digital Literacies*. Harlow: Pearson Education.

Gruba, P., & Hinkelman, D. (2012). *Blending Technologies in Second Language Classrooms*. Basingstoke: Palgrave Macmillan. (A second edition of this is forthcoming 2016.)

Kiddle, T. (2013). Developing digital language learning materials. In B. Tomlinson (Ed.), *Developing Materials for Language Teaching*, 2nd edition (pp. 189–206). London: Bloomsbury.

Rubio, F., & Thoms, J. (2014). *Hybrid Language Teaching and Learning: Exploring Theoretical, Pedagogical and Curricular Issues*. Boston: Heinle, Cengage.

Tomlinson, B., & Whittaker, C. (2013). *Blended Learning in English Language Teaching: Course Design and Implementation*. London: British Council.

Discussion Questions

1. I have referred in this chapter to the need for a principled approach to BLL course design. What sort of 'principles' need to be adhered to?

2. Kiddle says that developments in digital education have meant 'a shift from the concept of creation of "materials" (as in content created for learners' use), to harnessing and exploitation of "tools"' (Kiddle, 2013: 192). Discuss how far you agree with this, if possible illustrating with materials/tools you have used or are familiar with.

3. 'By expanding the notion of language learning materials in the blended environment from "products" to encompass "processes", we risk losing sight – and control – of the basic principles of second language pedagogy.' Discuss how far you agree with this statement, with reference to pedagogical principles and to language learning 'materials' with which you are familiar.

4. Working in small groups or pairs, outline suggestions for 'materials' (along the materials spectrum from 'static' to 'dynamic'/'product' to 'process') that could be generated using a social networking site such as Facebook.

5. Practitioners have predicted that BLL will increasingly take place via mobile devices (such as mobile phones and tablets) as use of these continues to grow.
   (a) Discuss the benefits and/or drawbacks of using mobile devices for BLL.
   (b) Generate some ideas for 'materials' for mobile devices (using the expanded definition of materials offered in this chapter).

References

Blake, R. (2014). Best practices in online learning: Is it for everyone? In F. Rubio & J. Thoms, *Hybrid Language Teaching and Learning: Exploring Theoretical, Pedagogical and Curricular Issues* (pp. 10–26). Boston: Heinle, Cengage.

Bloom, B., Engelhart, M., Furst, E., & Hill, W. (1956). *Taxonomy of Educational Objectives, Handbook I: The Cognitive Domain*. New York: David McKay.

Blyth, C. (2014). Opening up foreign language education with open educational resources: The case of Français interactif. In F. Rubio & J. Thoms, *Hybrid Language Teaching and Learning: Exploring Theoretical, Pedagogical and Curricular Issues* (pp. 196–218). Boston: Heinle, Cengage.

Bonk, C., & Graham, C. (2006). *The Handbook of Blended Learning: Global Perspectives, Local Designs*. San Francisco, CA: Pfeiffer Publishing.

Brindle, M. (2012). A Wordle in your ear. *Folio*, 15(1), 25–27.

Chambers, E., & Gregory, M. (2006). *Teaching and Learning English Literature*. London: Sage.

Chapelle, C. (2009). The relationship between second language acquisition theory and computer-assisted language learning. *The Modern Language Journal*, 93, 741–753.

Chapelle, C. (2010). The spread of computer-assisted language learning. *Language Teaching*, 43(1), 66–74.

Crystal, D. (2001). *Language and the Internet*. Cambridge: Cambridge University Press.

Delialioglu, O., & Yildirim, Z. (2007). Students' perceptions on effective dimensions of interactive learning in a blended learning environment. *Journal of Educational Technology and Society*, 10(2), 133–146.

Doughty, C., & Long, M. (2003). The scope of enquiry and goals of SLA. In C. Doughty & M. Long, *The Handbook of Second Language Acquisition* (pp. 3–16). Malden: Blackwell Publishing Ltd.

Doyle, R. (1993). *Paddy Clarke Ha Ha Ha*. London: Vintage.

Ducate, L., Lomicka, L., & Lord, G. (2014). Hybrid learning spaces: Re-envisioning language learning. In F. Rubio & J. Thoms, *Hybrid Language Teaching and Learning: Exploring Theoretical, Pedagogical and Curricular Issues* (pp. 67–91). Boston: Heinle, Cengage.

Ellis, R. (2011). Macro- and micro-evaluations of task-based teaching. In B. Tomlinson, *Materials Development in Language Teaching* (pp. 212–236). Cambridge: Cambridge University Press.

Eydelman, N. (2013). A blended English as a foreign language academic writing course. In B. Tomlinson & C. Whittaker, *Blended Learning in English Language Teaching: Course Design and Implementation* (pp. 43–50). London: British Council.

Fleet, L. (2013). A blended learning approach to soft skill training at Al Azhar University, Cairo. In B. Tomlinson & C. Whittaker, *Blended Learning in English Language Teaching: Course Design and Implementation* (pp. 201–206). London: British Council.

Godwin-Jones, R. (2012). Emerging technologies: Challenging hegemonies in online learning. *Language Learning and Technology*, 16(2), 4–13.

Gruba, P., & Hinkelman, D. (2012). *Blending Technologies in Second Language Classrooms*. Basingstoke: Palgrave Macmillan.

Hampel, R. (2006). Rethinking task design for the digital age: A framework for language teaching. *ReCALL*, 18(1), 105–121.

Hockly, N. (2013). Technology for the language teacher: Mobile learning. *ELT Journal*, 67(1), 80–84.

Ingham, L. (2013). Using a wiki to enhance the learning experience on a business English course. In B. Tomlinson & C. Whittaker, *Blended Learning in English Language Teaching: Course Design and Implementation* (pp. 163–174). London: British Council.

Kern, N. (2013). Blended learning: Podcasts for taxi drivers. In B. Tomlinson & C. Whittaker, *Blended Learning in English Language Teaching: Course Design and Implementation* (pp. 131–140). London: British Council.

Kukulska-Hulme, A., & Shield, L. (2008). An overview of mobile assisted language learning: From content delivery to supported collaboration and interaction. *ReCALL*, 20, 271–289.

Laurillard, D. (1993). *Rethinking University Teaching: A Framework for the Effective Use of Learning Technologies*. London: Routledge.

Laurillard, D. (2002). *Rethinking University Teaching: A Framework for the Effective Use of Learning Technologies* (2nd Edition). London: RoutledgeFalmer.

Mali, T. (2002). 'What Teachers Make.' In *What Learning Leaves*. Newtown, CT: Hanover Press.

Mayer, R. (2005). Introduction to multimedia learning. In R. Mayer, *The Cambridge Handbook of Multimedia Learning* (pp. 1–16). Cambridge: Cambridge University Press.

Mishan, F. (2010). Task and task authenticity: Paradigms for language learning in the digital era. In F. Mishan & A. Chambers, *Perspectives on Language Learning Materials Development* (pp. 149–171). Bern: Peter Lang.

Mishan, F. (2013). Demystifying blended learning. In B. Tomlinson, *Developing Materials for Language Teaching* (pp. 207–223). London: Bloomsbury Academic.

Mishan, F., & Timmis, I. (2015). *Materials Development for TESOL*. Edinburgh: Edinburgh University Press.

Motteram, G. (2011). Developing language-learning materials with technology. In B. Tomlinson, *Materials Development in Language Teaching* (2nd Edition) (pp. 303–327). Cambridge: Cambridge University Press.

Nicolson, M., Murphy, L., & Southgate, M. (Eds.) (2011). *Language Teaching in Blended Contexts*. Edinburgh: Dunedin Academic Press.

Neumeier, P. (2005). A closer look at blended learning – parameters for designing a blended learning environment for language teaching and learning. *ReCALL*, 17(2).

Pardo-González, J. (2013). Incorporating blended learning in an undergraduate English course in Colombia. In B. Tomlinson & C. Whittaker, *Blended Learning in English Language Teaching: Course Design and Implementation* (pp. 51–60). London: British Council.

Reinders, H., & White, C. (2010). The theory and practice of technology in materials development and task design. In N. Harwood, *English Language Teaching Materials* (pp. 58–80). Cambridge: Cambridge University Press.

Rossomondo, A. (2014). Integrating foundational language and content study through new approaches to hybrid learning and teaching. In F. Rubio & J. Thoms, *Hybrid Language Teaching and Learning: Exploring Theoretical, Pedagogical and Curricular Issues* (pp. 219–238). Boston: Heinle, Cengage.

Rubio, F., & Thoms, J. (2014). *Hybrid Language Teaching and Learning: Exploring Theoretical, Pedagogical and Curricular Issues*. Boston: Heinle, Cengage.

Sharma, P. (2010). Key concepts in ELT: Blended learning. *ELT Journal*, 64(4), 456–458.

Stracke, E. (2007). A road to understanding: A qualitative study into why learners drop out of a blended language learning (BLL) environment. *ReCALL*, 19(1), 57–78.

Thomas, M. (2009). *Handbook of Research on Web 2.0 and Second Language Learning*. London: Information Science Reference.

Thomas, M., & Reinders, H. (2010). *Task-Based Language Learning and Teaching with Technology*. London: Continuum.

Tomlinson, B. (2011). Introduction: Principles and procedures of materials development. In B.Tomlinson, *Materials Development in Language Teaching* (2nd Edition) (pp. 1–31). Cambridge: Cambridge University Press.

Tomlinson, B., & Whittaker, C. (2013). *Blended Learning in English Language Teaching: Course Design and Implementation*. London: British Council.

Vogel, T. (2001). Learning out of control: Some thoughts on the World Wide Web in learning and teaching foreign languages. In A. Chambers & G. Davies, *ICT and Language Learning, A European Perspective* (pp. 133–142). Lisse: Swets and Zeitlinger Publishers.

Vygotsky, L. S. (1981). The genesis of higher mental functions. In J. V. Wertsch, *The Concept of Activity in Soviet Psychology* (pp. 144–188). Armonk, NY: M.E. Sharpe.

Warschauer, M. (2005). Sociocultural perspectives on CALL. In J. Egbert & G. M. Petrie, *CALL Research Perspectives* (pp. 41–51). Mahwah, NJ: Lawrence Erlbaum Associates.

Young, D., & Pettigrew, J. (2014). Blended learning in large multisection foreign language programmes: An opportunity for reflecting on course content, pedagogy, learning outcomes and assessment issues. In F. Rubio & J. Thoms, *Hybrid Language Teaching and Learning: Exploring Theoretical, Pedagogical and Curricular Issues* (pp. 92–136). Boston: Heinle, Cengage.

Appendix

WHAT TEACHERS MAKE

by Taylor Mali

He says the problem with teachers is
What's a kid going to learn
from someone who decided his best option in life
was to become a teacher?
He reminds the other dinner guests that it's true
what they say about teachers:
Those who can, do; those who can't, teach.
I decide to bite my tongue instead of his
and resist the temptation to remind the dinner guests
that it's also true what they say about lawyers.
Because we're eating, after all, and this is polite conversation.

I mean, you're a teacher, Taylor.
Be honest. What do you make?

And I wish he hadn't done that – asked me to be honest –
because, you see, I have this policy about honesty and ass--kicking:
if you ask for it, then I have to let you have it.
You want to know what I make?
I make kids work harder than they ever thought they could.
I can make a C+ feel like a Congressional Medal of Honor
and an A-- feel like a slap in the face.
How dare you waste my time
with anything less than your very best.
I make kids sit through 40 minutes of study hall
in absolute silence. *No, you may not work in groups.*
No, you may not ask a question.
Why won't I let you go to the bathroom?
Because you're bored.
And you don't really have to go to the bathroom, do you?
I make parents tremble in fear when I call home:
Hi. This is Mr. Mali. I hope I haven't called at a bad time,
I just wanted to talk to you about something your son said today.
To the biggest bully in the grade, he said,
'Leave the kid alone. I still cry sometimes, don't you?
It's no big deal.'
And that was noblest act of courage I have ever seen.
I make parents see their children for who they are
and what they can be.

You want to know what I make? I make kids wonder,
I make them question.
I make them criticize.
I make them apologize and mean it.
I make them write.
I make them read, read, read.
I make them spell *definitely beautiful, definitely beautiful, definitely beautiful*
over and over and over again until they will never misspell

either one of those words again.
I make them show all their work in math
and hide it on their final drafts in English.
I make them understand that if you've got *this*,
then you follow *this*,
and if someone ever tries to judge you
by what you make, you give them *this*.

Here, let me break it down for you, so you know what I say is true:
Teachers make a goddamn difference! Now what about you?

Mali, T. (2002). 'What Teachers Make' in *What Learning Leaves*. Newtown, CT: Hanover Press. Reproduced with permission.

Notes

[1] See also Mishan (2013) and Mishan & Timmis (2015), each of which presents different aspects of this BLL course, e.g., use of corpus-based materials (in Mishan, 2013).

[2] This assignment devised by Dr Elaine Vaughan, University of Limerick, co-tutor on this programme, and reproduced with her permission.

[3] A word cloud is a representation of a text in graphic form. An example is shown in Figure 8.6.

[4] 'What Teachers Make', written and performed by Taylor Mali. Online at: www.youtube.com/watch?v=RxsOVK4syxU.

Use of this poem with permission from the author.

[5] The UCC doctoral showcase website set this challenge to its doctoral students: 'We are looking for UCC's best **Tweesis**. This one is simple – just describe your thesis work in 140 characters maximum in such a way that anyone can understand what you are doing.' Online at: www.ucc.ie/en/graduatestudies/current/showcase/

CHAPTER 9

Developing Activities and Materials to Support Effective Interaction Online

Ildikó Lázár

INTRODUCTION

Developing activities and materials to support and encourage authentic interaction among learners in blended learning (BL) courses is challenging but not impossible. This chapter examines why the blended approach requires some general 'rethinking' of commonly held notions, and explores the advantages and drawbacks of a variety of activities and materials used in three different BL contexts to help paint a more detailed picture of the pedagogical implications of BL in different settings.

The chapter begins with the assumption that BL is not only meant to supplement, but also to transform the learning process with the additional aim of improving its quality. In other words, using a computer and an interactive whiteboard to show exactly the same old reading passage with the same old reading comprehension questions as teachers did two decades ago on the blackboard cannot be considered to be BL. According to *Education Elements* (educationelements.com), successful BL occurs when technology helps carefully selected dynamic materials (see also Mishan, Chapter 8, this volume) reach and motivate students of varying learning styles. As opposed to a traditional course, in a 'flipped classroom' teachers and trainers use online media to share presentations, documents or audio-visual materials with their learners and to give them tasks that they can do at home at their own pace (*Education Elements*). As a result, in a blended course, classroom periods are ideally transformed into interactive practical sessions where teacher and students are free to engage in small group or whole class discussions, role-plays or other performing activities for which personal presence is essential (Johnson and Marsh, Chapter 4, this volume).

RETHINKING RULES AND ROLES WITHIN THE BLENDED LEARNING CONTEXT

If both the face-to-face and online materials and activities are well planned and implemented, then this practice seems to reinforce student-centred learning as in the settings described in this chapter, allowing students to master most of the content in their own preferred way. Instead of traditional frontal teaching and a linear transmission and regurgitation of knowledge, active involvement is expected from learners in creating course content, and the responsibility for their own progress will be to a much greater extent in their own hands. By promoting independent learning, active participation and cooperation, this type of BL scenario in a course, especially as described in contexts 2 and 3 below (see Figure 9.1, pp. 142–143), not only ensures collaborative construction of knowledge but also develops essential communication and cooperation skills as well as attitudes of openness, curiosity and acceptance, components that are all essential for successful intercultural communication in a foreign language.

Rethinking the rules of the game, accepting new teacher roles and empowering students in the negotiation of content and tools, developing their autonomy and thus reducing teachers' power in the traditional sense might seem frightening to many. However, sound instructional design, classroom management (Walsh, Chapter 3, this volume) and the selection of the most appropriate tools for the intended learning outcomes are just as essential in BL as in traditional settings. As can be seen in the description of some successful activities below, the teacher's role remains central to providing a structured and engaging learning environment. This has also been pointed out by Marsh (2012) and Pacansky-Brock (2012) among others, and by King (Chapter 6, this volume).

Teachers who wish to provide a rich learning environment with a variety of communicative tasks, lots of authentic input and materials with an intercultural communication focus in their language courses will realise the need for BL in a world where email, social networks, podcasts and short videos are part of nearly all students' and most teachers' everyday life. New editions of old classics in English language teaching methodology acknowledge this phenomenon, and they all include chapters on the use of technology and task design for online or BL (Brown, 2007; Harmer, 2007; Ur, 2012; Scrivener, 2011; Larsen-Freeman and Anderson, 2011). The use of computers, tablets, electronic chat, video clips, social media and interactive whiteboards in the classroom are among the tools described in the new sections of these books for teachers on the use of modern technology.

POTENTIAL BARRIERS TO THE BLENDED APPROACH

Naturally, as has been shown by a European Union report (European Commission Report, 2013) cutting edge technology is not available everywhere at the time of writing. Not all schools have interactive whiteboards, computer labs or tablets. But even in places where these pieces of equipment and gadgets are not available in the educational institutions, many teachers seem to want to try and get them or want to make students use their own mobile phones or desktop computers to stay connected and carry out tasks outside school that will help them develop in the given subject area, as described in context 2 below (see Figure 9.1, pp. 142–143).

Many other teachers, however, are still afraid of using online tools for teaching even if they use a number of them in their lives outside school. This may happen when they do not see the learning potential, do not have experience in designing appropriate web-based tasks, have limited experience in blending, or are not confident enough in their computer skills (see the discussion in Comas-Quinn, Chapter 5, this volume). Some of this relates to the fact that, despite using web-based tools in their private everyday lives, many teachers still do not see the potential of using the same tools for learning, a problem called 'digital dissonance' by Clarke and his colleagues (2009: 57). Another obstacle in the way of planning BL courses is that they are not always compatible with national curriculums and standardised examinations that emphasise knowledge consumption and reproduction (Dowling, 2011). For teachers who already have the necessary digital skills or those who consider their developing e-literacy as an added value, an article based on a large-scale study by O'Dowd (2013) gives many useful recommendations on how to overcome the barriers when organising an international web collaboration project at university level. The activities and approaches in this chapter attempt to show how the above obstacles can be overcome in any BL course from secondary level language classes to professional development courses and projects for young adults and experienced teaching professionals.

BACKGROUND TO THE CONTEXTS

The first context described was a five-month international web collaboration project set up between four secondary school intermediate-level English classes in four different countries. In this international project, most of the activities and materials had been designed prior to the start of the project by the project team both for the online and the face-to-face work with the learners, and only a few changes were made during the actual web collaboration in order to better meet the learners' needs and interests. The project team consisted of English teachers and English teacher trainers. The second type of context the chapter will draw examples from is blended methodology courses for English teacher trainees who meet their tutor in class twice every week or once every two weeks for a semester and work together online quite intensively in between the face-to-face meetings. Although some of the online materials are also prepared in advance in these courses, many activities have to be designed, redesigned or adapted as the EFL methodology courses progress. The third context examined is an online community of practice that aims to provide professional development opportunities for teachers and teacher trainers working in a variety of countries in Europe. The community of practice is supported by the Pestalozzi Programme of the Council of Europe, which, in addition to inviting teachers and trainers to attend workshops, also offers an online platform to allow participants and facilitators to exchange ideas, co-write and pilot materials and continue to learn from each other between and after face-to-face workshops. The chapter aims to analyse what activities and materials support authentic online collaboration best in these three different settings and will attempt to shed light on pedagogical implications beyond the three contexts described.

The activities presented in this chapter have been taken from courses and projects that are usually closer to the 'strong' blend category on a continuum from significant to very small amounts of e-learning as defined by Littlejohn and Pegler (2007: 29) or 'real blended courses' according to reports of the Sloan Consortium, the leading online learning society devoted to advancing quality e-learning into the mainstream of education in the United States. According to one of the Sloan-C reports, a blended/hybrid programme is one where between 30 and 79 percent of the content is delivered online (Allen, Seaman and Garrett, 2007: 5).

The examples for activities described below come from three different contexts in which English is the primary means of communication. In addition, in the secondary school and the teacher training contexts the development of English proficiency is also one of the most important learning objectives. In the professional development community of practice, for many participants the development of their language skills in English as a lingua franca is also among their priorities, especially as many of them are language teachers.

MEASURING THE SUCCESS OF BLENDED LEARNING ACTIVITIES AND MATERIALS

The debate about the appropriate method of investigating online and BL interaction and acquisition has been long and complex as many fields of study come into play, including the psychological and cognitive aspects of acquisition, the methodology of facilitating on- and offline processes, and the social aspects of interaction and learning. Reinhardt advocates a framework towards the middle ground between input-interactionist and socio-cognitive frameworks, in other words a combination of the psychological processing of language input and cognition as inseparable from social interaction (Reinhardt, 2012: 45). The methods of analysis in the present chapter may be open to interpretation but efforts have been made to follow this middle ground approach, consider both etic, or outsider, and emic, or insider, perspectives and use both quantitative and qualitative techniques. The success of the activities described below was measured by the teachers' or facilitators' perception of learner or participant involvement and progress, as well as by the feedback received from the participating learners, teachers and trainers themselves. As all the activities and tasks were compulsory for the participants in the first two types of settings, the length, depth and frequency of their contributions, as well as the perceived investment and creativity in the participants' work were assessed by the present author and her colleagues. In the third setting, in the online community of practice for professional development, the majority of tasks were optional. Nevertheless, similar assessment criteria were used when selecting the tasks and activities seen as the most inspiring and beneficial both by the facilitators of the programme and the participants of this community of practice.

The examples of successful BL activities and materials described in the present chapter have been taken from three different contexts, as summarised in the table below.

	INTERNATIONAL BLENDED WEB COLLABORATION PROJECT AT SECONDARY SCHOOL LEVEL	LOCAL BL COURSES FOR TRAINEE TEACHERS AT UNIVERSITY LEVEL	INTERNATIONAL BL MODULES AND PROJECTS FOR EDUCATION PROFESSIONALS
Online tasks and in-class activities designed and implemented by	Team members in the icEurope Comenius project See project website www.ic-europe.eu	Teacher trainers at the Department of English Language Pedagogy See description of the study programme of the Department of English Language Pedagogy of Eötvös Loránd University http://delp.elte.hu/MAinELT.htm	Moderators and members of the Pestalozzi Online Community of Practice See description of the Pestalozzi Programme's online community of practice on the Council of Europe website http://www.coe.int/t/dg4/education/pestalozzi/home/howto/Cdp_en.asp
Online platforms provided and maintained by	Moodle CMS (course management system) Applied English Linguistics Department, University of Tübingen	Moodle CMS (course management system) Eötvös Loránd University, Budapest	Ning (social network) platform of the Pestalozzi Programme, Council of Europe, Strasbourg
Number of countries involved in the course or project	4 (Bulgaria, Hungary, Italy and Turkey)	1 (Hungary)	50 (Council of Europe member states and other countries)

(continued)

Participants	Secondary school learners of English	Pre- and in-service teachers of English	Teachers and teacher trainers of any subject
Number of participants	4 groups of 19 to 21 learners (total 80) working together	3 separate groups of 16 to 18 (total about 50)	Several groups of 15 to 35 (total about 200)
Age of participants	16–17	23–45	25–70
Length of project or course	6 months	3 months	18 months for modules and 2 to 3 months for follow-up projects
Use of technology	Primarily outside class	Primarily outside class	Primarily outside the training room
Estimated proportion of the online element in the course	30% to 40%	30% to 70%	70% to 90%
Estimated time spent face-to-face in classrooms vs. online individually per week	3 hours: 1 hour	Depending on the type of course: 4 hours: 1.5 hours 2 hours: 1 hour 30 min: 2 hours	Intensive 4–5 day face-to-face meetings once every six months, and online collaboration in between, plus online projects as follow-up activities
Learning objectives	• to develop English language proficiency • to develop intercultural communicative competence	• to acquire knowledge about the theoretical background to teaching and learning languages • to discuss and try out new approaches to teaching English, and develop teaching skills • to further develop trainees' English language proficiency	• to have access to professional development opportunities in intercultural education, cooperative learning, education for the prevention of violence and discrimination • to build an international community of practice
Features used	Moodle e-learning system: course template, course management, discussion forums, wikis, journals, assignments, grading, storage and embedding of audio-visual files, personal messaging, chat, calendar	Moodle e-learning system: course template, course management, discussion forums, wikis, journals, assignments, storage and embedding of audio-visual files, personal messaging, calendar	Ning social network platform: member map, 'pages' to store documents, photo and video library, open and closed rooms (groups), comment wall, discussion threads (forums), blogs, personal messaging, chat, Skype conference calls

Figure 9.1 Overview of the Three Projects under Analysis

ACTIVITIES IN A WEB COLLABORATION PROJECT FOR SECONDARY SCHOOL STUDENTS

The first set of activities are taken from the European Lifelong Learning Comenius project entitled *icEurope – Intercultural Communication in Europe*, the primary goal of which was to explore intercultural competence development within web-enhanced English classrooms in 2010: for a more detailed description of the web collaboration, see Chapter 3 in the project publication (Warth, 2011) and an article on the intercultural competence development of the participating learners (Lázár, 2014). Four groups of 16-year-old intermediate level learners of English living in four different countries worked together online for five months on a variety of tasks with their local English teachers' guidance. Every week the students had three face-to-face English classes with their own English teacher but spent some of this time practising how to write forum posts, discussing how to react to their partners' questions and comments, at the same time improving their English accuracy and the appropriateness of their expression. In addition to the class time spent on preparing for the online component of the collaboration, they also spent approximately one hour per week working online individually or in small groups.

DEVELOPING PRINCIPLES, MATERIALS AND TEACHING STRATEGIES

The actual international web collaboration among learners was preceded by several months of preparation. An English teacher from each of the four countries (Bulgaria, Hungary, Italy and Turkey) was invited to participate in the training and materials development in 2009. The project team, led by the German consortium from the University of Tübingen, was assisted by the teachers in the development of online teaching materials that were later used for the intercultural project work with their secondary school learners of English. Contact was established on the platform of an open-source learning management system (Moodle) between the participating classes for five months in 2010. A group of 80 learners from these four classes worked together online in four mixed, international teams to discuss and reflect on a variety of topics in order to get to know each other's cultural backgrounds and multiple perspectives and develop their English proficiency at the same time.

The main themes students were asked to study and collaborate on during the project were adjusted to local curriculums and were typical language exam discussion tasks and topics that teenagers would probably find engaging. They included presenting themselves, discovering the other students' home towns, discussing typical meals and table manners, selecting, discussing and then translating popular songs, and writing a newsletter for visitors. The teaching materials in Moodle included uploaded texts, pictures and videos with accompanying tasks and language notes. The materials were mostly based on short videos found on YouTube and activities adapted from Peace Corps learning and training materials (*Culture Matters*) and the intercultural communication textbook *Mirrors and Windows* (Huber-Kriegler et al., 2003). Features of Moodle that were used included discussion forums, journals, wikis and assignments, embedded videos, chat sessions and questionnaires.

The learners were to spend one lesson a week of face-to-face class time on language and cultural preparation with their local teacher's guidance, usually in a computer lab, and they were also grouped into four international 'classes' (of about 20 students) that consisted of four or five students from each country. Each of the four participating teachers was in charge of one of these international classes in addition to their own class. The teachers agreed to incorporate the project into their syllabus and to assess the students' web collaboration work and incorporate it in their final course grade. Although there had been an agreement between the four teachers and the project team about aims, timeframes, assessment methods, and in general, about a principled approach to this BL project, not all of the four teachers managed to keep to these agreements throughout the duration of the project because of time constraints due to other commitments, as well as changes in local pedagogical programmes, staff, equipment and timetables. The consequences were that some of the groups of learners spent more time working together on the materials both face-to-face and online than the others.

ANALYSIS OF THE PROJECT: LESSONS LEARNT

Many data collection methods were used to enrich the following description of the most successful activities in the web collaboration. To supplement the data gained from the learners' posts, online questionnaire responses, the teachers' written and oral accounts, additional lesson observations and interviews were conducted with students of English in the Hungarian class.

STATE YOUR AIMS AND EXPECTATIONS

In three of the participating classes, the English teachers felt it was important to ask whether the students wanted to participate in such a project and to explain what they were supposed to do and why the teachers thought it would be beneficial for their learning. These classes gave their consent and were looking forward to the experience. The great majority of them had never used their English outside class – except perhaps at an exam – but definitely not with people from other cultures. In the fourth class, the students did not have a choice whether to participate or not and many of these students seemed less involved in the project, especially in the first month of the web collaboration.

USE PERSONALISED TASKS TO BUILD A SENSE OF COMMUNITY

After a few lessons devoted to familiarising students with Moodle and after a few technical difficulties such as forgotten passwords and out of sync schedules at the start, the first really successful activity was when each of the four classes had to produce a class wiki with photos and texts to introduce themselves to the others. As the Turkish class still had technical and timetable problems at this stage, only three class wikis were prepared but these showed many signs of creativity and enthusiasm. The Hungarian class even prepared a video that they had recorded and edited with a technician's help. Such materials can later be used as samples in subsequent collaboration projects.

By contrast, when the students had to introduce their own towns and cities, practically all of them copied passages and pictures from Wikipedia and as they later reported, they felt it was just an uncreative 'copy-paste' job with too much information to collect and read about the other three cities. Such comments and the project team's observations about interaction in the forums in the first few weeks of the project informed the team about the need to pay more attention to task design as well as online and offline support as described in the project's publication by Enyedi, Lázár and Major (2011).

REFLECT ON SUCCESSES AND FAILURES TO INFORM FUTURE CHOICES

Having learnt from the first few weeks of successes and failures, the project team decided to insert an activity here that had originally not been part of the online materials. This added task was meant to make the topic of 'Where do we all come from?' a little more personal and challenging for the students: they were asked to upload a picture and a description of their own personal top five places in their towns or cities. The instructions asked them to share photos about places other than the well-known tourist attractions, with a short explanation about why they liked these hidden corners. The personal touch and the challenge of having to show and describe 'secret places' worked wonders. Most students seemed to enjoy these tasks and put a lot of effort into uploading pictures and writing short, informative and often funny texts. However, they did not comment on each other's top five places until they were instructed to do so later, and even then, their comments were really short. It seemed that they were either afraid of initiating deeper discussions or did not feel proficient enough in English to do more than what their teacher had asked them to do.

The next interesting topic supplemented by short videos about meals and table manners generated a lot of enthusiasm and produced some lively discussions among the students in the observed face-to-face class despite the heavy vocabulary work. In response to a short film about a traditional English breakfast there were also many reflections in several journal entries and in the forum discussions in Moodle. As some of the students in the Italian class had already been to England on a study trip with their teacher, the traditional English breakfast was not surprising for most of them. In the other classes, however, many students found the quantity and the quality of a traditional English breakfast puzzling. Some expressed their astonishment politely and with curiosity or at least acceptance while others were less polite and considerate and clearly displayed a negative attitude when expressing their opinion (*'disgusting'*, *'unhealthy'*, *'horrible'*, *'my breakfast is the best'*). These learners seemed to be moving from the 'denial' phase to the 'defense against difference' phase as described by Bennett in his developmental model of intercultural sensitivity (1993).

At this point in the collaboration, one of the teachers expressed concerns about the usefulness of the project, claiming that some of the students in the other classes were ethnocentric and offensive and that there seemed to be no way of changing this attitude with the planned activities. However, it was clear from the students' entries in their learning diaries as well as from the lesson observations in the Hungarian class that it was worth discussing these issues. Although only a few students used the learning diaries regularly, it was also obvious from their forum contributions that many started to use comparison, and some also took a relativist view, meaning that beliefs and social practices are relative to the individual within his or her own context. These developing skills of comparison and critical cultural relativism are described by many in the literature as essential for intercultural competence (e.g., Byram, 1997; Fantini, 2000), which was one of the most important learning objectives of the project. In addition, in the last month of the collaboration continued online exchanges and an increased knowledge about each other and about differences in values and social practices generated a friendly community spirit, which might also have helped most learners to refrain from posting anything that others may find offensive.

THE AAA OF 'GOOD' COMMUNICATION

Although the project team had made efforts to design inspiring tasks and discussed in-class and online tutoring with the teachers as recommended by many in the literature (for example Boettcher and Conrad, 2010; Dooly, 2008; Hopkins et al., 2008; O'Dowd, 2008; Sharma and Barrett, 2007), it was noticeable that many learners still refrained from expressing their thoughts, and others tended to give very short responses, often repeating or even simply copying and pasting their peers' posts. At this stage, the project team included an activity called the 'AAA of good communication' to raise awareness of the ingredients of rich and respectful discussions. Learners were shown what it feels like when you do not get a response (A for answer), when there is no acknowledgement of the value of their words (A for appreciate), and how eager we are for others to ask questions from us (A for ask). As mentioned earlier, in this BL project the four teachers could hold in-class preparatory and debriefing sessions between phases in which the learners worked in the computer lab or from home alone. The lesson observations in the Hungarian class showed that the learners were carefully assisted by their English teacher in the preparation of forum posts and wiki contributions before they had to work on such tasks individually.

More than two months into the project the first real interactions appeared in a forum probably at least partially thanks to this AAA activity and perhaps also to a developing sense of belonging to a new learning community, an advantage pointed out by Starkey and Savvides (2008) in connection with similar online collaboration courses. These conversations appeared in the students' reactions to questions raised after they had watched a thought-provoking short video about an Englishman having difficulties at a dinner table in China. In the forum discussions that followed the viewing of the video, it could be seen that students in the international teams actually reacted to what the others had to say. For example, in a forum discussion a Bulgarian student is admittedly happy to finally have a fellow student to discuss table manners with and even adds a personal postscript expressing concern about a recent earthquake in the Turkish students' region. In yet another thread, we see accounts of the Hungarian students' account of a long face-to-face discussion with their teacher in class about the issue of acceptable reactions to unwanted food at a table before they posted their response. We could also see some students formulating questions to elicit more information about the others, which was a welcome sign of developing skills of discovery and online interaction (Belz, 2007). Finally, some learners openly acknowledged that they were learning, and that their ideas were changing as a result of the activities and discussions.

USING AUTHENTIC MATERIALS CREATIVELY

The most popular topic and task came towards the end of the web collaboration project in the form of a guessing game about songs from the other three countries. Students in all of the four countries had to agree on a popular song in their mother tongue that they would recommend to the other classes as representative of their culture. First, relying only on the music and the video clip and without understanding the lyrics, the students in the other classes had to guess what the meaning or the message of the song was. They were also asked to write down their general impressions about the song and the video before they received the 'cultural translation' of the song from the 'owners'. After about a week of reading their peers' interesting and sometimes funny guesses about meanings and messages, students were given instructions to produce a translation of the lyrics of their own song to allow the other classes to verify if their guesses were correct. Other than a good English translation of the lyrics, cultural translations had to include explanations of potentially unfamiliar culturally-loaded concepts and references in the text. One group of students, for example, translated the lyrics including the explanation of two puns in the text and they also shared the English translation of the original legend, which the song, full of historical connotations, had been based on.

The lesson observations as well as the final product in the form of a nicely illustrated cultural translation suggested that their English teacher's guidance in the face-to-face class was invaluable. Her attempts to make the students guess what might be difficult to understand for someone from another culture and how to mediate the message of the song as accurately as possible would not have been so successful without these face-to-face discussions. In addition, from the teachers' accounts of this activity, it turned out that the Hungarian class had been led through a democratic process already at the start of this activity: students had to bring their own suggestions for local songs to class and having listened to the eight nominated songs, they all voted to decide which one should be the finalist. The fairly long lyrics and the original legend were also divided up among the students for translation and they spent an entire English lesson under their teacher's helpful guidance producing a coherent and linguistically correct final version of the song in English. Having gone through a democratic process of selection and decision making about the division of work and being responsible for their part of the final joint product probably resulted in their feeling ownership of and responsibility for the final outcome of the task.

Many of the students in all four classes also started to ask more questions for clarification in the music forum, which was a welcome proof of their developing curiosity and tendency to suspend judgment (Byram, 1997; Fantini, 2000) and of their developing skills of discovery, interpretation and interaction. Some learners were still quite blunt in their reactions, but others, while sometimes also critical, managed to find good points to praise in an effort not to offend their peers abroad: *'Um... don't get me wrong, but it seems a bit stilted and silly for me. Well, it's possible that it has to be. Otherwise, I like the costumes very much, especially the first ones. Was it based on a traditional dance? Amazing language! I like the way it sounds.' 'Although it's certainly different from my own world, I really like this strange (probably very traditional) voice and style of singing.'*

GIVE A CHOICE OF TOPICS

After two optional synchronous chat sessions in which many students participated and wanted to connect, one of the last tasks for the four classes of EFL learners towards the end of the project included a 'Visiting forum' and a 'Newsletter' where they had to discuss what they would do when visiting a family in a culture different from their own and what they would show to foreign students visiting their hometowns. This was done in preparation for an imagined visit at the house of one of their new international classmates and for future generations of similar web collaboration projects. Many of the students elaborated on their thoughts, gave examples, reacted to what the others had said and asked questions noticeably more often than at the beginning of the project. The Newsletter is another product of the project that can be part of the teaching-learning material in a similar course or project.

ADVANTAGES OF THIS APPROACH AS PERCEIVED BY THE STUDENTS

The learners' journal entries and their responses to the final questionnaire indicated that the majority felt comfortable using English for task completion, communication and culture learning. This has also been pointed out by Godwin-Jones:

> Reflective journals offer a means to analyze experiences and feelings and view one's own experience in the context of other encounters or in conjunction with cohorts. Providing students with examples of blogs or journals – particularly those from students having completed a successful study abroad experience – can provide helpful modeling, to encourage moving beyond simplistic descriptions and superficial reactions. For students who are experiencing first-hand a different culture, this can be a personally disorienting and potentially disturbing experience. (2013: 5)

Writing about it and sharing their thoughts with the teacher or peers might help them overcome any potentially disturbing or unpleasant feelings.

The student interviews also highlighted the positive feelings about having real contacts with real people for the first time and the sense of achievement in communicating in the foreign language. As for the advantages of the project and their overall impressions about the web collaboration for the development of intercultural competence, the students' evaluation was overwhelmingly positive. Many of the learners appreciated the language practice opportunity and this fairly new approach to learning in a web collaboration. Perhaps the most obvious advantages for the majority of the participating students were the new friendships they had made and their discoveries in terms of culture-learning. Considering all these aspects, the web collaboration was clearly in line with the students' expectations and interests. Despite some initial difficulties in communication, the majority perceived their international classmates very positively and suggested that the final task should be for them to visit each other.

ACTIVITIES FROM PRE- AND IN-SERVICE ENGLISH TEACHER TRAINING COURSES

The examples for BL activities described in this section have been taken from several different courses taught by instructors with different personalities and teaching styles at the same university. The activities described below were considered some of the most effective ones based on the views expressed by the instructors and their summary and interpretation of the feedback given by the trainees. It was felt that these activities managed to engage trainees, produced interesting and deep discussions or joint products that could be used in other courses to motivate and inspire future teachers of English. The activities were all designed for an audience of pre-service teachers, most of whom had stated in their needs assessment questionnaires that they would appreciate a practice-oriented approach, tips and tricks for the English language classroom and opportunities for reflection.

As can be seen in the summary table above (see Figure 9.1, pp. 142–143), the proportion of online and offline content varied in these courses but the online element outside the classroom was an integral part of each. Eötvös Loránd University introduced an e-learning system in 2008. However, because our faculty is not well equipped with the latest tools technology can provide, the online components of all courses have to be managed from outside the classrooms. As we could safely assume internet access in the students' homes and dormitories as well as in the library, many instructors at the Department of English Language Pedagogy decided to gradually build increasing amounts of online work into their courses, especially for the correspondence students who usually have one face-to-face session with their instructor every two weeks.

USING JOINT PRODUCTS CREATED OFFLINE DURING FACE-TO-FACE SESSIONS

One of the first tasks in most EFL Methodology courses at our department is a visit to a secondary school. A group of 14 to 18 trainees and their methodology instructor go to a secondary school, observe an English lesson and then sit down in the teachers' room to ask questions of the teacher about the aims of the different stages of the lesson, his or her ideas about planning, discipline, the use of the mother tongue, and so on. A successful online task after such a visit usually exploits the experience of the lesson observation even further. The instructor opens a wiki in the e-learning course, inserts a table with two columns and asks trainees to describe three things they would steal from the observed teacher (anything from the voice through to a smile or to tricks for disciplining) in the left column and three things they would do differently (activities, instructions, seating) in the right column. Trainees have to use different colour texts to do this and also sign their entries in the table. When the wiki is closed, the comments are collated together in the form of a colourful chart which is used during the next face-to-face session for trainees to discuss what was remarkable or surprising in their peers' posts and why. Alternatively, in courses with fewer face-to-face sessions, a forum is opened to discuss the same. The time spent thinking and writing individually when composing the wiki entries allows trainees who are less outspoken and confident to spend more time reflecting about their experience and to feel more secure when doing so.

USING CONTROVERSIAL STATEMENTS TO PROVOKE ONLINE AND OFFLINE DISCUSSIONS

Another activity leading to deep engagement with a topic is a very simple one. The instructor posts a few controversial statements of 'popular wisdom' about a topic in methodology into the introduction to a forum discussion, e.g., 'Children should start learning a foreign language in nursery. Young children learn languages faster than teenagers or adults.' The trainees were asked to select one or two and state whether they agree with them or not. They were also asked to justify their answers by making their own beliefs explicit and by using examples from their own experience or from stories heard from friends and family. Some examples that worked well in this topic area included 'If you don't start learning a foreign language before age 12, then reaching a high level of proficiency is hopeless' or 'The parent who speaks good English in a family should speak to their babies/children in English all the time and then the children will be bilingual.' In the majority of cases, there is no need to intervene for a while as people usually have very strong convictions about teaching and can get into an intensive phase of reflection when tactfully provoked. This technique can also prove to be very effective in overcoming teachers' resistance to change in their thinking about teaching and their established practices in the classroom as suggested by several research studies (Harris and Lázár, 2011; see also Comas-Quinn, Chapter 5, this volume).

In other groups, it is occasionally necessary to establish the rules of online discussion by specifying the minimum of expected contributions that trainees have to post (own ideas, reactions and questions to peers). Finally, when a discussion has been going on for a while and when, as a result of the discussion based on beliefs and personal experiences, trainees become more receptive and interested in the topic, the instructor's role is to quote from or point them to relevant book chapters and research articles and ask them to check their ideas against research results in the given area. Ideally, before summarising the online discussion, a face-to-face session is very useful to appreciate the thinking and writing invested in the online discussion and to clarify, highlight and summarise the issues that emerged in the online phase.

USING VIDEOS FOR RESEARCH AND PEER REFLECTION

Unfortunately, in our context the use of video is limited because possession of video cameras or other filming devices cannot be taken for granted. Nevertheless, correspondence students on a specialised course in EFL for intercultural competence could select from a number of optional assignments, and one of these was to record themselves teaching an English lesson, select a 15-minute scene, and analyse it from multiple perspectives, including the point of view of missed opportunities for the development of intercultural competence. The few students who chose this option shared their recordings and their reflections on the e-learning platform and the group enjoyed viewing the videos and brainstorming first in a forum discussion on the platform and then face-to-face in class about the potential for developing intercultural competence in the recorded scenes.

Other uses of videos included tasks where trainees had to do some research on the internet to find an appropriate two-minute video on YouTube about one of the many English accents spoken in the UK, the US or Australia. As a next step, they had to plan a lesson for learners of English where these videos could be exploited. Lesson plans based on three or four selected videos were uploaded and compared. Trainees reflected on each other's lesson plans and admittedly learnt a lot from the experience. The final discussion and evaluation of the exercise took place in a face-to-face session. Trainees who normally do not contribute a lot in class because they are less confident and assertive wrote some very long and deeply reflective accounts of the uploaded lesson plans based on the selected videos (this is a nice complement to Hojnacki's study, Chapter 7, this volume, where less confident and assertive students seemed to blossom online in the oral context). Their accounts could be highlighted as excellent examples and praised by the trainer in the face-to-face session. The opportunity to be reflective online was a clear advantage to many. Students have different learning styles and personalities. As in all classrooms, some people are more active and outspoken in discussions and some are shy or reserved and usually need more time to think and pluck up enough courage to contribute. These students often prefer expressing themselves in writing at their own pace.

ACTIVITIES FROM AN ONLINE COMMUNITY OF PRACTICE FOR EDUCATION PROFESSIONALS

As can be seen in the table in Figure 9.1. (see pp. 142–143), the online component of the professional development modules and projects of the Pestalozzi online Community of Practice was around an estimated 80% in 2014. This is understandable, considering that the members (teachers, teacher trainers and other education professionals) come from about 50 countries, and groups usually meet once in a face-to-face workshop and can only keep in touch and continue the follow-up discussions and tasks online. Even in the trainer training courses that last as long as 18 months, the face-to-face workshops when participants can meet are usually six to eight months apart.

THE GROWTH FROM ONLINE STORAGE SPACE TO ONLINE COMMUNITY

The Pestalozzi Programme started to develop this online Community of Practice as defined by Wenger (1999) on a Ning social-network platform (see www.ning.com) in 2009 to facilitate an exceptionally long (2.5 years) training module for 35 teachers living in different regions of one of the Balkan states. There were six workshops spaced about six months apart and in between the face-to-face meetings teachers and the team of six trainers from different European countries had a chance to continue to work together thanks to the online platform. This was the only way to ensure continuity between face-to-face meetings. Although at the time the Pestalozzi Programme had no explicit and principled approach to BL, without the online tasks, sharing of materials and exchange of ideas on the Ning platform, the professional development of the participating teachers would not have been as effective. The trainers in the project were nearly all beginners in the use of online tools but as they felt the need to keep in touch with the participants and because they were interested in the possibilities offered by the Ning platform, they decided to experiment with it. At that time, the platform was mostly used to store activities and materials and to exchange ideas and experiences in forum discussions.

The number of similar working groups on the platform grew from just a few in 2009 to about 30 in 2011 and to over 100 in 2014. Currently over 1,500 members of the Pestalozzi Community of Practice are registered users of the community's Ning platform. Obviously, not all of these members are active all the time. Participants' online activity depends to a large extent on whether they are immediately involved in a training course or a project to produce tangible results at a given time and on the extent to which they feel a sense of belonging to the community. Similarly, a review article of research studies in this area by Owston, York and Murtha (2013) highlights students' need to develop close associations or friendships with each other face-to-face or online and to promote the development of a strong learning community. It is probably this sense of belonging that makes many members of the Pestalozzi Community of Practice remain active even when their training event or project has closed. The head of the programme estimates the number of active or very active members to be around 180, while another estimated 200 people are occasionally active, and several hundreds are 'lurkers', meaning that they go online, look around and read posts, resources and reports but do not contribute to the discussions.

With such a large and growing number of active participants, the Pestalozzi Programme realised the need to hire and train ten platform moderators (former workshop facilitators and participants) in 2011 in order to introduce a more principled approach to this BL professional development opportunity open to hundreds of education professionals all over Europe. The platform moderators' task has been to welcome new members, give online training in platform use, initiate and moderate discussions, map out and organise resources, and connect people with similar interests.

TANGIBLE AND REUSABLE PRODUCTS OF ONLINE COOPERATION

For a few examples of the tangible results of teachers' cooperation in this BL community, full reports on trainer training courses and their results and activities can be found on the programme's website. For instance, a report on the course on education for the prevention of violence in schools not only provides information about what happened during the course and what the suggested readings are for someone interested in the topic, it also contains references to teaching and training materials that can be downloaded by interested readers. Another example of a tangible product is a newsletter on local dissemination and regional networking based on the reports, photographs and exchanges on the online platform. (For further details, all reports and articles can be found on the programme website http://www.coe.int/en/web/pestalozzi/reports-articles)

The newsletter is not the result of a learning activity in the traditional sense but a networking activity that can be a very important learning field for education actors, blending face-to-face on the local level with online elements at the international level. The short report about the online work of the group of members who are interested in disseminating the programme's results is supplemented by 19 country reports written by and about members who even formed their own local Pestalozzi networks to take the idea of professional development for collaborative knowledge construction and experiential learning further in order to contribute to the development of educational institutions and practices where the rule of law, human rights, education for democracy and respectful intercultural communication are important and become an integral part of the curriculum. Finally, a full description of the theoretical underpinnings of the programme, another one of the tangible products of joint collaborative BL efforts of ten Pestalozzi trainers and authors, has also been published in the form of a comprehensive book entitled *Teacher Education for Change* (Huber and Mompoint-Gaillard, 2011). Such joint products are based on BL and produce further authentic materials through authentic, life-like tasks as recommended by Mishan (2005).

BUILDING A COMMUNITY: A SENSE OF BELONGING

On such a large and complex online platform, moderators play a very important role in establishing personal contact when welcoming new members and helping them get to know their way around both in the technical sense and as regards content. This is usually done by two moderators, sometimes in addition to the team of facilitators if the new member is a participant in a workshop or module. This consists of a welcome message, a few pointers for interesting content, and some questions about the person who has just joined the community.

When participants in a training event meet in one of the member states of the Council of Europe for a three- or four-day workshop for the first time, they are introduced to the online platform through tasks that they can work on in small groups in the face-to-face sessions. One such activity is a synchronous treasure hunt in which groups of three or four participants sit around a computer in the training room somewhere in Europe and five or six of the community's moderators who are all sitting in front of their computers in different places in Europe send them five carefully designed questions one after the other in the private or public chat room of the Ning platform. Some of the questions are simple (How many subjects does X teach? Where will the next face-to-face workshop on cooperative learning take place? Who else is online at the moment from your country?) and some are more complicated (Find the final report of the module on Education for the Prevention of Discrimination and write down their top five recommendations). Participants need to navigate through the platform to find the answers to the questions and if necessary, they are assisted by the facilitators on site. By the time they accomplish the task, they will have discovered the online community enough to feel fairly confident about using the platform and they will have made personal synchronous online contact with some moderators to whom they can turn with increased confidence with any questions or problems in the future. The activity is usually ended by one of the moderators greeting the participants on Skype to thank them for playing along and to encourage them to look for other useful information and resources on the platform.

MAINTAINING ACTIVITY: ENCOURAGING MEMBERS TO PARTICIPATE ONLINE

Within each small group on the platform the team of facilitators of the given training activity is in charge of coordinating the online work of the 25 to 35 members participating in that particular training event. In addition, a small group of nine moderators (living in seven different countries) assists the head of the programme and the general rapporteur residing in Strasbourg in encouraging people to remain active and continue to stay involved in the collaborative knowledge construction and professional development they initially started working on in their small groups. Moderators have found that encouraging participants to stay or to become active (again) is best done in private personal emails, for example by drawing their attention to finished products or ongoing discussions that they may have missed. Participants often refrain from answering posts in an open space on the platform but nearly always respond to personal emails.

A successful BL activity was born out of a question raised in one of the most popular discussion rooms of the platform called Coffee Shop. This room is there for socialising and sharing ideas about personal and professional interests. One of the moderators shared a story of a conflict in a school and asked colleagues to do the same because she wanted to use them in a training activity. In a few weeks' time, there were about 15 stories of conflicts described in detail from the members' own teaching contexts from all over Europe. When the moderator finished developing the activity based on members' contributions, she shared the lesson plan with the group and asked for feedback. A lively discussion ensued involving even more members of the community. Several people suggested modifications or variations on the original plan and asked for recommendations of resources and videos. In the next few months, some of the members adapted and tried out the activity in their own contexts and reported back to the online group. As a result of sharing a story and asking for colleagues' own personal experiences, giving and gratefully receiving feedback and suggestions, and aiming for a final product useful for all teachers, this discussion turned into a rich source of learning for many more teachers and trainers than had been expected.

Similar successful discussions evolved from a trainer posting controversial statements and provocative questions about cooperative learning, and a participant in a training event taking the initiative to start a discussion about parental involvement in schools, asking for advice to elicit colleagues' experiences and receive ideas and links to resources on how to organise and what activities to plan for a parent-teacher meeting in her school to ensure that cooperation between all parties involved becomes stronger.

Meaningful and goal-oriented discussions seem to be the most successful, and moderators play a very important role in scaffolding ideas, landscaping resources, and setting an example of respectful and constructive online communication. In addition, before discussions are closed, moderators are in charge of uploading a summary illustrated with quotations from members' contributions and a collection of useful tips and resources that were mentioned during the weeks or sometimes months while the discussion was going on. Individual members of the community often take the initiative and continue sharing their experiences in personal blogs.

CHALLENGES: LANGUAGE AND COMMUNICATION STYLE

Obviously, since activity in this community of practice is about 80% online and there are over 1,500 members, there are many challenges that participants have to overcome, from learning to use new technology to developing an online voice. Practitioners who may not be used to all the available online tools often experience technical problems. Moreover, it is often more difficult to give critical feedback in asynchronous online communication than face-to-face without offending the other. When face-to-face meetings are rare, it is also important to remember that there can be many reasons why people do not answer a post immediately. It is exactly the 'turn delay', or not having to respond immediately and 'textual trace', or leaving a mark in writing afforded by technology that gives many participants the ability to self-repair and save face, as also pointed out by Reinhardt in his review article (2012). In addition, even if most members have expressive writing skills in the languages used on the platform (in this case English and French primarily), as these languages are second or third foreign languages for the majority of the participants, it is sometimes very difficult to get a point across, and it is very easy to misunderstand each other. This is one reason why the rules of online communication have to be negotiated, established and made available to all members of the community. Two of these rules that seemed to make the biggest difference in this large BL community were 'Refrain from automatic assumptions, interpretations and judgments' and 'Always be ready to explain the obvious'.

PEDAGOGICAL IMPLICATIONS FROM THE MOST SUCCESSFUL ACTIVITIES FROM THE THREE DIFFERENT SETTINGS

The suggestions for teachers and trainers embarking on a BL course or project based on the experiences described above echo other researchers' findings (Boettcher and Conrad, 2010; O'Dowd, 2013; Starkey and Savvides, 2008; Stacey and Gerbic, 2008; Godwin-Jones, 2013; Hopkins et al., 2008). It is very important to note that no BL activity can be successful if it is not implemented at the right time, for the right aims and with the right teaching tools and strategies. This is why the pedagogical implications based on the examples described in this chapter start with organisational and planning issues to establish how we can most effectively integrate BL elements into any teaching-learning process, lessons learnt from some of the experiences described above.

A PRINCIPLED APPROACH TO PLANNING AND ORGANISING THE BLENDED TEACHING-LEARNING PROCESS

The following criteria are important:

- Base your aims on learners' needs, aims and possibilities.
- State your aims and expectations for the BL course clearly and negotiate the rules with your students.

- Incorporate the online element so it is clearly an integral part of the course and not just an add-on.
- Always leave enough face-to-face class time to prepare, discuss and assess online content.
- Plan very carefully which tasks or course components are more effectively done online and which ones should definitely be integrated into the face-to-face sessions.
- Think about the interplay between the online and face-to-face elements: do they coherently complement each other and do they build on each other?

TEACHING STRATEGIES

- Work towards building a sense of community during and between classes.
- Show that you are interested in your learners' thoughts and preferences by asking about opinions, beliefs, experiences, favourites, secrets and 'what ifs'.
- Give a choice of topics and tools in the online tasks that learners can select from.
- Appreciate and display outstanding individual contributions or joint products during the face-to-face final evaluation and validation of any task especially if submitted by less confident and assertive students.

ONLINE MODERATION

- Specify the minimum number of expected contributions if a discussion does not take off without intervention.
- Intervene in discussions when they get stuck, diverted or when a summary of the main points would be helpful for learners/participants.
- Send private email messages to ask or encourage inactive participants to contribute.
- Organise (scaffold) ideas and landscape resources.
- Quote from or point to interesting materials, relevant research or theoretical background reading in 'magic moments', in other words, when students or participants are most receptive to learning more about an issue that they have been discussing.

MATERIALS AND ACTIVITY TYPES

- Select age-appropriate topics and interesting online resources.
- Design tasks that elicit personal experience, require imagination and promote creativity and cooperation.
- Use and produce authentic materials.
- Aim for joint online products in which everybody's contribution is essential.
- Use videos and photos to inspire and build on your learners' imagination.
- Use the AAA activity or similar activities in the face-to-face class to raise awareness of communication styles and strategies, potential differences in rules of politeness, the difficulties of establishing an online voice, especially when giving feedback if your learners have no or little experience in online communication (or when using a foreign language).
- Provoke online (and offline) discussions and debates with controversial statements to raise awareness of the richness to be gained from analysing multiple perspectives.
- Encourage learners to do research on the internet and find and use texts, pictures and videos to design their own products and reflect on each other's.

- Incorporate the use of learning diaries or blogs both for developing writing skills and raising awareness of the benefits of reflecting about learning.
- Where possible and appropriate, ask learners to record themselves when doing a task or teaching a lesson and select and share an extract for peer evaluation and reflection with their fellow learners in the BL course.
- Incorporate an occasional 'treasure hunt' type activity when students or participants would benefit from some guided and playful discovery of the online learning environment.
- Incorporate themed chat sessions (on Skype/video calls if possible) to help learners connect in real time, especially if the face-to-face component of the course is minimal.

Conclusion

Although, like many researchers and materials writers, Sharma and Barrett claim that 'a blended learning course is potentially greater than the sum of its parts' (2007: 7), they repeatedly and rightfully warn the reader that this can only be true if teachers strive for a principled approach with clear roles assigned to the teacher and to the employed technology, and if the planning of the in-class and online materials and activities is very thorough and thoughtful but flexible at the same time.

There is a surge in blended courses in institutions of primary, secondary and tertiary education in Europe. According to a press release from the European Commission in April 2013, students and teachers in Europe are keen to 'go digital', computer numbers have doubled since 2006 and most schools are now 'connected' (European Commission Report, 2013). This is in line with the conclusions drawn in other publications on online and BL (e.g., Marsh, 2012; Owston et al., 2013). Despite the increasing interest of learners and teachers, the European Commission's findings, based on a large-scale survey drawing on responses from 190,000 people in 27 countries, reveal that the use of ICT tools and digital skill levels vary from very low to considerably high in Europe. As we have seen, the use of technology and good digital skills have to go hand in hand with pedagogical approaches that make BL effective. Finally, the European Commission Report also recommends, but perhaps does not emphasise enough, that support for teachers to use technology and their digital skills in a pedagogically appropriate manner needs a strong boost in the coming years. This chapter has aimed to contribute to boosting this support.

Suggested Resources

Boettcher, J., & Conrad, R.-M. (2010). *The Online Teaching Survival Guide*. San Francisco, CA: Jossey-Bass.

Dooly, M., & O'Dowd, R. (Eds.) (2012). *Researching Online Interaction and Exchange in Foreign Language Education: Current Trends and Issues* (pp. 45–77). Frankfurt: Peter Lang.

EDUTOPIA: What works in education? Online at: http://www.edutopia.org/blog/blended-learning-getting-started-lisa-dabbs

EDUCATION ELEMENTS: Can technology accelerate student learning? Online at: http://educationelements.com/

EDUCAUSE: a nonprofit association and community of IT leaders and professionals committed to advancing higher education. Online at: http://www.educause.edu

EMERGINGEDTECH: Online at: http://www.emergingedtech.com/2013/12/7-excellent-free-blended-learning-resources-understanding-the-whys-and-hows-of-mixed-mode-instruction/

Marsh, D. (2012). *Blended Learning. Creating Learning Opportunities for Language Learners*. Cambridge: Cambridge University Press.

Pacansky-Brock, M. (2012). *Best Practices for Teaching with Emerging Technologies*. New York: Routledge.

Sharma, P., & Barrett, B. (2007). *Blended Learning. Using Technology in and beyond the Language Classroom*. Oxford: Macmillan.

TEACHTHOUGHT: 37 Blended Learning Resources You Can Use Tomorrow from TeachThought. Online at: http://www.teachthought.com/teaching/37-blended-learning-resources-you-can-use-tomorrow/

Discussion Questions

1. What principles do you need to consider when you start planning a BL course?

2. If you wish to run a BL course or if you would like an existing face-to-face course to become blended, can you list which course components would be more effective online and which ones should definitely be integrated in the face-to-face sessions? How can you ensure that there is coherence between the two types of components?

3. Which recommended teaching strategies and online moderation techniques have you tried before and/or which ones are you planning to experiment with?

4. Do you have favourite materials and activity types for face-to-face or online learning courses? Can you analyse them to see what exactly makes them work well in your teaching? Would you be able to adapt them to a BL course?

References

Allen, E. I., Seaman, J., & Garrett, R. (2007). *Blending in. The Extent and Promise of Blended Education in the United States*. Needham, MA: Sloan Consortium.

Belz, J. A. (2007). The development of intercultural communicative competence in telecollaborative partnerships. In. R. O'Dowd (Ed.) *Online Intercultural Exchange: An Introduction for Foreign Language Teachers*. Bristol: Multilingual Matters.

Bennett, M. J. (1993). Towards ethnorelativism: A developmental model of intercultural sensitivity (revised). In R. M. Paige (Ed.), *Education for the Intercultural Experience*. Yarmouth, Me: Intercultural Press.

Boettcher, J., & Conrad, R.-M. (2010). *The Online Teaching Survival Guide*. San Francisco, CA: Jossey-Bass.

Brown, H. D. (2007). *Teaching by Principles. An Interactive Approach to Language Pedagogy* (3rd Edition). White Plains, NY: Pearson Education.

Byram, M. (1997). *Teaching and Assessing Intercultural Communicative Competence*. Bristol: Multilingual Matters.

Clarke, W., Logan, K., Luckin, R., Mee, A., & Oliver, M. (2009). Beyond Web 2.0: Mapping the technology landscapes of young learners. *Journal of Computer Assisted Learning* 25, 56–69.

Culture matters. Peace Corps learning and training materials. Online at: www.peacecorps.gov/culturematters

Dooly, M. (Ed.) (2008). *Telecollaborative Language Learning: A Guidebook to Moderating Intercultural Collaboration Online*. Bern, Switzerland: Peter Lang.

Dooly, M., & O'Dowd, R. (Eds.) (2012). *Researching Online Interaction and Exchange in Foreign Language Education: Current Trends and Issues* (pp. 45–77). Frankfurt, Germany: Peter Lang.

Dowling, S. (2011). Web-based learning – Moving from learning islands to learning environments. *TESL-EJ*, 15(2).

Enyedi, Á., Lázár, I., & Major, É. (2011). Moderating web collaboration and supporting learning online. In K. Kurt & C. Warth (Eds.), *Web Collaboration for Intercultural Language Learning* (pp. 50–56). Münster: Monsenstein und Vannerdat.

European Commission Report (2013). Survey of Schools: ICT in Education. Benchmarking Access, Use and Attitudes to Technology in Europe's Schools. A study prepared for the European Commission DG Communication Networks, Content and Technology. Online at: http://europa.eu/rapid/press-release_IP-13–341_en.htm

Fantini, A. E. (2000). A central concern: Developing intercultural communicative competence. *School for International Training Occasional Papers Series*, Inaugural Issue (pp. 25–42). Brattleboro, VT: School for International Training.

Godwin-Jones, R. (2013). Integrating intercultural competence into language learning through technology. *Language Learning and Technology*, 17(2), 1–11. Online at: http://llt.msu.edu/issues/june2013/emerging.pdf

Harmer, J. (2007). *The Practice of English Language Teaching* (4th Edition). Harlow: Pearson Education.

Harris, R., & Lázár, I. (2011). Overcoming resistances and ways to bring about change. In J. Huber and P. Mompoint-Gaillard (Eds.), *Teacher Education for Change*. Pestalozzi Series (pp. 91–116). Strasbourg: Council of Europe.

Hopkins, J., Gibson, W., Ros, I., Solé, C., Savvides, N., & Starkey, H. (2008). Interaction and critical inquiry in asynchronous computer-mediated conferencing: A research agenda. *Open Learning*, 23(1), 29–42.

Huber, J., & Mompoint-Gaillard, P. (Eds.) (2011). *Teacher Education for Change*. Pestalozzi Series. Strasbourg: Council of Europe.

Huber-Kriegler, M., Lázár, I., & Strange, J. (2003). *Mirrors and Windows – an Intercultural Communication Textbook*. European Centre for Modern Languages. Strasbourg: Council of Europe.

Kohn, K., & Warth, C. (Eds.) (2011). *Web Collaboration for Intercultural Language Learning*. Münster: Monsenstein und Vannerdat.

Larsen-Freeman, D., & Anderson, M. (2011). *Techniques and Principles in Language Teaching* (3rd Edition). Oxford: Oxford University Press.

Lázár, I. (2015). EFL learners' intercultural competence development in an international web collaboration project. *Language Learning Journal*, 43(2), 208–221.

Littlejohn, A., & Pegler, C. (2007). *Preparing for Blended e-Learning*. London: Routledge.

Marsh, D. (2012). *Blended Learning. Creating Learning Opportunities for Language Learners*. Cambridge: Cambridge University Press.

Mishan, F. (2005). *Designing Authenticity into Language Learning Materials*. Bristol: Intellect books.

O'Dowd, R. (2013). Telecollaborative networks in university higher education: Overcoming barriers to integration. *Internet and Higher Education*, 18, Special Edition. Online at: http://www.sciencedirect.com/science/article/pii/S1096751613000110#bb0060

O'Dowd, R. (2008). *Online Intercultural Exchange: An Introduction.* Bristol: Multilingual Matters.

Owston, R., York, D., & Murtha, S. (2013). Student perceptions and achievement in a university blended learning strategic initiative. *Internet and Higher Education*, 18, Special Edition. Online at: http://www.sciencedirect.com/science/journal/10967516/18

Pacansky-Brock, M. (2012). *Best Practices for Teaching with Emerging Technologies.* New York: Routledge.

Pestalozzi Newsletter on Dissemination in Europe. Online at: http://www.coe.int/t/dg4/education/pestalozzi/Source/Documentation/casc_newsletter.pdf

Pestalozzi Programme website with reports, articles and books. Online at: http://www.coe.int/en/web/pestalozzi/reports-articles

Reinhardt, J. (2012). Accommodating divergent frameworks in analysis of technology-mediated interaction. In M. Dooly & R. O'Dowd (Eds.), *Researching Online Interaction and Exchange in Foreign Language Education: Current Trends and Issues* (pp. 45–77). Frankfurt: Peter Lang.

Scrivener, J. (2011). *Learning Teaching* (3rd Edition). Oxford: Macmillan.

Sharma, P., & Barrett, B. (2007). *Blended Learning. Using Technology in and beyond the Language Classroom.* Oxford: Macmillan.

Stacey, E., & Gerbic, P. (2008). Success factors for blended learning: Concise paper. *Proceedings of the Ascilite Conference.* Melbourne, Australia.

Starkey, H., & Savvides, N. (2008). Learning for citizenship online: How can students develop intercultural skills and construct knowledge together? *Learning and Teaching. The International Journal of Higher Education in the Social Sciences*, 2(3), 31–49.

Warth, C. (2011). The icEurope project. In K. Kohn & C. Warth (Eds.), *Web Collaboration for Intercultural Language Learning.* Münster: Monsenstein und Vannerdat.

Ur, P. (2012). *A Course in Language Teaching* (2nd Edition). Cambridge: Cambridge University Press.

Wenger, E. (1999). *Communities of Practice: Learning, Meaning, and Identity.* New York: Cambridge University Press.

SECTION 4

CASE STUDIES

Chapter 10, by Seedhouse, Preston and Olivier, transports us very firmly outside of the conventional classroom and into a digital world where the familiar worktops, tools and appliances of the modern kitchen are implanted with computer technology, making it possible to replicate the real world of getting your fingers dirty with the cooking. It is a prime example of 'language-in-action'. In this case, what is 'blended' is the instructional methods and the computer as mediator. The blend brings together ideas from language pedagogy (task-based learning), technology (the computer interface), communicative skills (reading and speaking) and real-world outcomes (preparing food). The technology and the pedagogy constrain and enhance one another, and there is a built-in element of adaptive feedback, i.e., feedback from the machine tailored to the behaviour of the user at any given moment. The digital kitchen provides a unique opportunity for flipping a typical classroom-based, or at least classroom-generated and controlled, context, to an environment where the learners act autonomously. The chapter shows the potential of technology for creating innovative learning environments and suggests that BL can embrace a range of computer-assisted experiences reassuringly commonplace and akin to the real thing. Central to the authors' conception of how such a techno-methodological blend should operate are the same issues as would be involved in classroom task-based learning: what competences and skills relevant to language acquisition do the tasks set out to foster, and what types of learning result? The project offers linguistic pay-offs as well as skill gains in terms of noticing key language (as discussed by McCarthy in Chapter 1 of this book), the opportunity to use known language in a real context and expanding the language and interactive repertoire. The project is offered as an example of collaboration between teachers and technology experts, blending the best of both worlds.

In **Chapter 11**, Moloney and O'Keeffe take us through a blended course for trainee language teachers in a College of Education in Ireland, showing how the selective use of computer-mediated resources can ease some of the stresses of conventional learning in higher education settings, and provide trainee teachers with the necessary first-hand experience of learning in a blended context, as well as looking at learning management systems as an addition to, and a transformative element for, the conventional classroom. For example, one of the long-standing stresses of learning in the higher education context is the pressure of absorbing lecture content, often on quite complex subjects. Moloney and O'Keeffe show how the Learning Management System (LMS) can provide a recorded resource that removes the problem of the short-lived nature of the live lecture, providing a space that students can return to and absorb content at their own pace in their own time. Additionally, resources such as vodcasts can supplement the more difficult subject content (in this case, grammatical knowledge) and provide extra learning opportunities for students. Central to this chapter is the commitment to building a positive environment for learning by harnessing technological resources and for transforming the LMS resource from being a static vessel into a space for the creation of a collaborative learning community, one that involves both lecturers and students in new, more active roles. A significant spin-off is also noted in the potential for lecturers to use the record of their teaching to self-evaluate and progress professionally. Student satisfaction with the programme offered speaks for itself, and it is clear that, within their institutional context, the blended learning (BL) menu has gone a long way to satisfy the micro-, mid- and macro-level requirements outlined at the start.

Chapter 12, by McCarten and Sandiford, who are co-authors with McCarthy of a blended English language programme, takes the reader through the problems and prospects of transferring to the online environment some of the central features of the print version of their course, in this case inductive learning and interactive strategies for conversation. This case study, in a sense, confronts all the challenges raised by the authors of other chapters in this volume. These questions include: what does one transfer from a conventional, print-based set of classroom and self-study materials to an online environment and what does one best leave in the classroom? How does one maintain a balance between, on the one hand, flexibility and the freedom for the learner to work at his/her own pace and, on the other, a sense of connectedness and community between teacher and learner and among learners themselves? In the case of the particular project described here, there is the further complication of an unconventional and somewhat innovative methodology (involving corpus-informed content, noticing and figuring out of grammar, along with conversational strategies), which neither teachers nor students may be familiar with from their prior language learning and teaching experience. And in the case of conversational strategies, how does one simulate verbal interaction on learning platforms that may not have the technological capability of providing synchronous conversation and/or adaptive (tailored to the individual user) feedback? The project discussed in this chapter was, above all, one where the pedagogy could not be sacrificed to technological or institutional demands, and much detailed design was required to maintain the ethos of the print- and classroom-based course. The authors present their solutions and the results of their work as steps towards answering some of the challenges.

CHAPTER 10

Blending Pedagogy, Technology, Skills and Food: The French Digital Kitchen Project

Paul Seedhouse, Anne Preston and Patrick Olivier

INTRODUCTION

In this chapter we report on the French Digital Kitchen project, a situated language learning environment where the kitchen communicates with users, instructing them step-by-step in how to cook French cuisine and teaching them aspects of the French language. From the blended learning (BL) perspective, this project links to broader definitions of 'blended learning' which commonly describe 'blending' as the combining of instructional methods and modalities with the inclusion of the computer as mediator (Graham, 2006). It is novel in that language learning takes place using digital technology in a kitchen, and in that cooking and language skills are learned simultaneously by pairs of learners while carrying out a task. The aim is to blend language learning principles with technological design and to see if it is possible to teach two sets of skills at the same time in a situated learning environment outside the classroom. More specifically here, blending involves the combination at the design and implantation stages of theory and methodology from language learning pedagogy (in this case Task-Based Language Teaching or TBLT), technology (digital interactive systems), skills (communicative skills in the L2) and food (cooking techniques and procedure – following a digitised recipe). In the following sections, we firstly describe the project background, then the design principles on which it is based in terms of TBLT and Human Computer Interaction (HCI). We then move on to describe how the French Digital Kitchen works in practical terms. Finally, we present evidence of the kinds of learning which occur in this environment. The discussion is based on accounts of the system in Seedhouse et al. (2013), Hooper et al. (2012) and Preston et al. (2012).

PROJECT BACKGROUND

The French Digital Kitchen project was the result of collaboration between computer scientists working on the development of assistive technology (Pham and Olivier, 2009) and

Figure 10.1 The Purpose-built French Digital Kitchen

applied linguists working on how digital technology can be combined with a task-based approach to language learning (Seedhouse and Almutairi, 2009). Our project involved taking a normal kitchen and adapting it for French language learning using activity recognition and digital sensor technology. We constructed a purpose-built kitchen (see Figure 10.1) that communicates with learners in French and gives them step-by-step instructions on how to prepare French cuisine and learn aspects of French language, developing two sets of skills simultaneously. We chose cooking as a relevant task as there is currently huge interest throughout the European Union (EU) in cooking, as can be seen in the number of cookbooks sold and the number of cooking programmes on TV. Many adult learners are motivated to learn European languages through their interest in cuisine and culture, and this project exploits this motivation.

There are a number of well-known problems relating to classroom foreign language teaching tackled by this project. These include, firstly, the universal problem of classroom language teaching, namely that students are rehearsing using the language, rather than actually using the language to carry out actions such as buying a train ticket; secondly, there is the difficulty of bringing the foreign culture to life in the classroom. In the digital kitchen environment, we intend that learners will be able to learn aspects of the language whilst performing a meaningful real-world task and will simultaneously experience the cultural aspect of learning to cook a foreign dish.

There are a number of principles from the field of Human Computer Interaction (HCI), Computer Assisted Language Learning (CALL) and Second Language Acquisition (SLA) (see McCarthy, Chapter 1, this volume) which can inform the design of technologically enhanced learning environments. The French Digital Kitchen draws on pedagogical principles from CALL and TBLT as part of its blended design, specifically, the use of multimedia glosses (see Figure 10.4), which are an established area of CALL research, and the 'pre-during-post' task structure of TBLT. Principles from HCI (see p. 166) inform the different kinds of decisions we made about how the real-world learning-based activities could be adapted and supported through our sensor technology. The technological part of the design both limits and enhances how these pedagogical principles are applied. It is not possible to separate the two as both are mutually dependent.

DESIGN PRINCIPLES

In this section, we explain our design methodology for constructing and trialling the kitchen, which blends pedagogy and technology, specifically CALL, TBLT and HCI.

COMPUTER ASSISTED LANGUAGE LEARNING PRINCIPLES

The field of CALL has a long tradition of blending learning theory and research findings from SLA with the different possibilities offered by computer-based applications. Through the design and evaluation of different applications under different conditions for SLA have emerged a number of CALL principles (see Chapelle, 1998 for more detailed discussion of this development). CALL principles can be viewed in a similar way to other areas of language learning methodology like TBLT, as a commonly accepted set of values informing decision making around CALL design. CALL principles differ according to whether theory or technology are seen to take the lead in the development of approaches to pedagogical design (Colpært, 2006). For example, first, there are technological and design-based approaches where the pedagogical design could be based on selecting features of a new technology which are seen to benefit the learning process. Second, is a more theory-based approach to design, which might look to specific technological features to meet specific needs and purposes of language learning defined by principles of language learning theory and existing theory-based research.

The design of the French Kitchen can be seen as sitting at a midpoint between being informed by technology and by theory-based CALL principles. The technology used in the kitchen, drawing on activity recognition and sensor technology, is what enables learners to complete the independent language learning task in the real-world environment of a kitchen. Unlike what is often found in technology-led CALL design, the technology is not designed to play a mediating role, but to interact directly with humans. Principles from theory-driven CALL, which include the benefits of negotiation of meaning and interactional modification for learning and acquisition, inform our decision making in how people interact with the system and how learners access the different kinds of situated support available via the system.

TASK-BASED LANGUAGE TEACHING PRINCIPLES

The pedagogical design of the French Digital Kitchen employs TBLT, a well-established approach to language learning which prompts learners to achieve a goal or complete a task (Skehan, 1998; 2003). Much like real-world tasks, such as asking for directions, TBLT seeks to develop students' language through providing a task and then using language to solve it. Some of the main features of TBLT are that:

- meaning is primary (language use rather than form).
- there is some communication problem to solve.
- a classroom task relates directly to real world activities.
- the assessment is done in terms of outcomes.

Willis (1996: 1) suggests that tasks aim to provide a genuine purpose for language production. It is generally assumed (Ellis, 2003: 263) that tasks are carried out in pairs or small groups in order to maximise interaction and autonomy. Ellis (2003: 320) claims that 'task' provides both strong theoretical and empirical underpinnings for pedagogical design. Skehan (1998: 95) suggests that transactional tasks stimulate natural processes of second language acquisition, stretching the learner's abilities. TBLT has so far principally been based on tasks to be undertaken within the classroom which simulate real-world tasks. Some innovations in TBLT have combined language learning with other, non-linguistic skills in a similar way to this project. Paterson and Willis's (2008) *English through Music*, for example, aims to help children to absorb English naturally as they enjoy making music together. However, there have been few attempts to employ TBLT in naturalistic settings outside the classroom; the project described here is innovative in combining TBLT and digital technology in a naturalistic kitchen setting outside the classroom.

In order to operationalise TBLT in this setting we adopted Skehan's (1998) framework in which tasks are divided into three phases: pre-task, during-task and post-task. This provided a clear design structure for materials. The pre-task functions as a preparation stage for the activity to be carried out in the during-task phase. This may include the presentation of new language, the employment of existing language knowledge and clarification of the type of knowledge that would be required (Skehan, 1998: 138). The during-task phase involves the performance of the task set. It is in this phase of the task that Skehan claimed learners' attention can be specifically manipulated through a range of features such as time pressure, support and surprise. The post-task phase is designed as a period of evaluation and consolidation after the completion of the task through the analysis of during-task performance and reflection. This is similar to the 'plenary' section of a school lesson where a teacher goes through the learning objectives of a lesson and pupils identify 'what they have learned'.

HUMAN-COMPUTER INTERACTION DESIGN PRINCIPLES

Human Computer Interaction (HCI) employs 'bottom-up' approaches, where development of the technology is based on direct observation and investigation of usability of an initial prototype. Abras et al. (2004: 763) suggest that designers should aim to clarify tasks and their usage from the user's perspective, to enable them to engage with the task as easily as possible. To do this, HCI designers go through a range of iterative processes to produce a design which is based on user activity. In the French Digital Kitchen, HCI design focused on 'ambient displays' on the kitchen walls (Figure 10.1) and the provision of a Graphical User-Interface (GUI) (Figure 10.2), as well as an inbuilt hidden speaker system. How did the HCI design support the TBLT framework? The 'ambient displays' provided a location from which to show recipe preparation videos and vocabulary slideshows, and the inbuilt speakers streamed the audio information attached to this visual information. The speaker system also provided a list of ingredients in the pre-task. The GUI was specifically designed to support learning processes. In the pre-task, the GUI offered three types of scaffolding: translation request, repetition request and the option of moving back and forwards through the list of ingredients. In the during-task phase, the GUI provided learners with translations, repetitions and the option to move around the cooking instructions. In classroom-based TBLT, the learners carry out tasks themselves, but can call on the teacher as a resource if they require some kind of help or support. In a similar way, the GUI provides scaffolding for learners if and when they require it (see Walsh, Chapter 3, this volume, on the potential for machine-based scaffolding).

Learning was also supported through the activity recognition sensor technology, which was designed to provide the different steps of the cooking instructions in a timely manner, that is, as and when learners were ready in terms of how they were progressing through the recipe operations. Further scaffolding was provided in terms of prompts, consisting of alternative versions of instructions, often reformulated in terms of 'tips' about cooking technique. The prompts were designed in such a way as to occur in response to two alternatives: a) after a period of non-activity where the sensor technology was able to detect that an operation had not been carried out even though a cooking instruction had been communicated or b) if the incorrect food item or kitchen equipment had been moved as a result

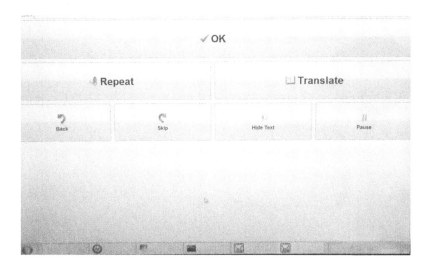

Figure 10.2 An Interactive Screen or Graphical User-Interface (GUI)

of miscomprehension. A final part of the physical design of the kitchen was the addition of labelling in French on all items associated with the cooking task (tub of flour, peeler, etc.) as well as the kitchen itself (cupboards, chopping board, tap, etc.). In a similar way to the technological design of the pre-task, the post-task exercises were also embedded in the kitchen using the 'ambient displays' (Figure 10.2). The design of the kitchen was therefore based on a careful blend of pedagogical and technological principles.

How does the French Digital Kitchen Work?

In the previous section, we explained our design methodology for constructing and trialling the kitchen. In this section, we describe the practical application of this methodology and the functioning of the kitchen.

Constructing the French Digital Kitchen involved drawing on an existing technologically-enhanced kitchen (the Ambient Kitchen) which was originally developed to support older people and those with dementia in their everyday kitchen activities. The term 'ambient' refers to the nature of the technology used in the kitchen, which is absorbed or hidden in that environment and, similar to a car satellite navigation system, is designed to guide and support the user in an everyday setting. In the French Digital Kitchen, this technology was developed so that the kitchen speaks to the learners in French, providing step-by-step cooking instructions in relation to learners' completion of the cooking steps. It can also detect what the learners are (or are not) doing and this information is used by the kitchen programme to provide feedback, such as a reminder, or to provide more details about a certain cooking action in French, or to know when to move to the next question. Embedded or hidden digital sensors were developed and inserted in or attached to all the equipment (for example, a peeler, a mixing bowl, a whisk or even the oven door) and ingredients (for example, a bag of flour, sugar or a tub of butter) as in Figure 10.3. The sensors use a technology similar to the Nintendo Wii™. The sensors hidden in the knife, for example, were designed to detect whether a 'chopping' action' or a 'scraping' motion is being made and to provide appropriate feedback. Learners are also able to communicate with the kitchen, using an interactive screen or Graphical User-Interface (GUI), where they

Figure 10.3 Sensors Embedded in Utensils and Attached to Ingredients

can request audio and textual help along the way in the form of repetitions, translations and the ability to move back and forward between the cooking instructions, as in Figure 10.2.

Following standard practice in TBLT, kitchen users work in pairs; we normally paired users with skills in French together with users with skills in cookery so that they were able to exchange skills. Users followed the three-stage task cycle detailed in the following section.

The pre-task phase involved a dual focus on cooking and French skills and was divided into presentation and preparation of French and cooking. First, learners could watch a purpose-made video recording with optional subtitles of a native-French speaker making the chosen dish for the project, *Clafoutis aux poires* (a pear dessert). This familiarised them with both the cooking procedures required and with the French language to be employed. They were able to choose to watch without subtitles, with French or with English subtitles, depending on the level of support they required (see Walsh, Chapter 3, this volume). Next, the learners were able to watch an audio-visual slideshow of the different utensils and ingredients they would need to make the dish, in order to familiarise themselves with the specific vocabulary required for the task. Figure 10.4 shows how each slide contained a photo of the kitchen utensil or ingredient, the corresponding word written in French and the option to listen to an audio file of the word being spoken. These first two activities were displayed on specially designed 'ambient' display screens on the walls of the kitchen (see Figure 10.1). The final stage of the preparation involved listening to the kitchen, which verbally communicated the ingredients and quantities required via the speakers. At this stage in the task, the learners also had the opportunity to use the interactive screen to request help such as a translation into English or the repetition of a phrase.

Blending Pedagogy, Technology, Skills and Food

Figure 10.4 An Example of a Slide in the Audio-visual Vocabulary Slideshow

The during-task phase involved step-by-step instructions on how to prepare the dish, together with a range of relevant feedback. The instructions and the feedback were communicated by the kitchen's audio speakers as and when required according to the learners' actions. The cooking task instructions were expressed in such a way as to include cooking-specific vocabulary on which we expected learners would focus most of their attention. Some examples of these instructions are shown in Figure 10.5 and cooking-specific vocabulary is highlighted in bold.

> ***Beurrez** un plat allant **au four***
>
> ***Épluchez, dénoyautez** et **coupez** les **poires** en quartiers et en tranches*
>
> ***Saupoudrez** le fond du plat d'un peu de **farine** et de **sucre***

Figure 10.5 Examples of Cooking Instructions with Specific Cooking Terms

Feedback included creating alternative versions of instructions, often reformulated in terms of 'tips' about cooking technique, which acted as prompts; Figure 10.6 shows a sample of these. English translations were also created using cooking-specific vocabulary. The final design of the cooking task instructions and feedback came about after a series of pre-trialling of different task instructions.

> *Saupoudrez le fond du plat avec un peu de farine et de sucre*
>
> Prompts: *Il vous faut un peu de farine*
>
> *Il vous faut un peu de sucre*

Figure 10.6 Examples of Prompts for the Learners

The post-task phase focused on evaluation of what the users had learned. Targeted vocabulary was reintroduced to the learners through a series of short exercises. The exercises

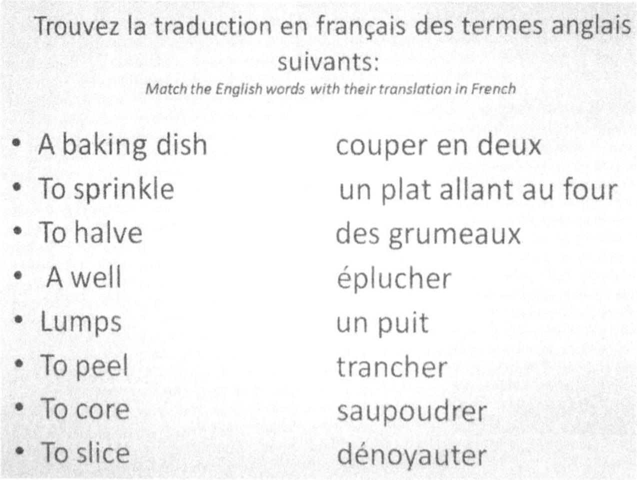

Figure 10.7

Trouvez la traduction en français des termes anglais suivants:

Match the English words with their translation in French

- A baking dish — couper en deux
- To sprinkle — un plat allant au four
- To halve — des grumeaux
- A well — éplucher
- Lumps — un puit
- To peel — trancher
- To core — saupoudrer
- To slice — dénoyauter

Figure 10.7 Example Exercise from the Post-task

were designed to be completed orally and presented on the 'ambient' display screens in the kitchen. So whilst the focus during-task was on meaning and task completion, the focus post-task was mainly on linguistic form and on which language items learners had acquired through the task. An example of one of these exercises is given in Figure 10.7 above.

WHAT IS LEARNED IN THE FRENCH DIGITAL KITCHEN?

In this section we illustrate how learners use the resources of the kitchen to carry out their tasks and analyse the types of learning which can occur. A guide to the transcription symbols can be found in the Appendix, p. 175. 'AR' is the kitchen giving instructions; S1 and S2 are students.

TRANSCRIPT 1: MAKING A HOLE

```
1    AR: mélangez ces ingrédients
2    S2: °mix them together°
3    AR: et réalisez un puits dans la farine
4    S2: when you mix them (.) you've got to make a hole in the
         centre=
5    S1: =a well in [ the cen]tre
6    S2:            [yeah]
7    S1: yeah (2.1) need to break them up
8    (2.1)
9    S2: is that
10   S1: yeah they'll break up (.) if you just give em a (1.0) .hh mix
         around
11   (1.2)
12   S1: what's mix (.) in f-
13   S2: mélanger
14   S1: mélanger (.) mélanger oeufs
15   (1.5)
16   S2: and then to make (0.4) faire un trou au milieu (.) is another
         way of
17       saying what do you do to them
```

- In lines 1-4 S2 translates instructions
- In lines 5 to 10 S1 offers cooking advice
- In lines 12-14 S1 and S2 focus on language
- In lines 16-17 S2 offers reformulates French

Transcript 1 is an extract from a session which involved a catering student (S1), who had very little prior knowledge of French, and an advanced learner of French (S2). In the opening to this episode, we see that when the instructions are provided by the kitchen (AR), S2 immediately offers a translation. From lines 5 to 11, we then see that S1, the catering student, offers his own input into the task. First he introduces a catering term, 'well' and then goes on to give S2 (who is making the well) more information about the technique and guides her in the cooking action. After a short gap, in line 12, S1 then asks S2 to provide the French word for 'mix'. Here, we see the movement or rather, return, to a new focus on language. Importantly, this switch to a focus on language form has prompted a further action from S1 to reuse this knowledge to create a new phrase 'mélanger oeufs'. In line 16, S2 offers further feedback about the French instruction 'réalisez un puits' by reformulating it as 'faire un trou' (make a hole), thus breaking down the instruction to make it clearer.

What is especially noticeable in this example is how learning in the French Digital Kitchen has the potential to provide for productive cross-curricular opportunities in French with other areas of the curriculum and more specifically here, Food Technology. Both learners, or 'experts' (one in catering and one in French) support each other through this particular stage of the task. S2, as the French expert, demonstrates and practises her knowledge of French whilst at the same time developing her ability to apply language skills (for example, by helping S1). S1, as the catering expert and French novice, guides S2 through the cooking task activity and also develops his language skills by asking questions and manipulating the language to create new phrases.

TRANSCRIPT 2: PEELING THE PEARS

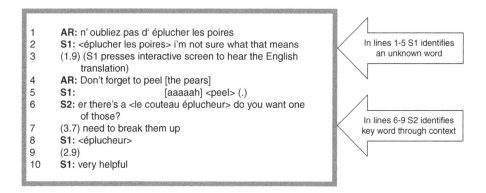

```
1    AR: n' oubliez pas d' éplucher les poires
2    S1: <éplucher les poires> i'm not sure what that means
3    (1.9) (S1 presses interactive screen to hear the English
         translation)
4    AR: Don't forget to peel [the pears]
5    S1:                      [aaaaah] <peel> (.)
6    S2: er there's a <le couteau éplucheur> do you want one
         of those?
7    (3.7) need to break them up
8    S1: <éplucheur>
9    (2.9)
10   S1: very helpful
```

In lines 1-5 S1 identifies an unknown word

In lines 6-9 S2 identifies key word through context

This episode involves an advanced level learner (a university undergraduate student) and beginner level learner of French. Neither has any professional cooking experience. The episode opens with a prompt from the kitchen (AR) to 'peel the pears'. This type of prompt demonstrates how the sensor technology in the kitchen is designed to guide the learners and appears when the inbuilt programme has registered that an action has yet to be performed, even though an instruction has been previously been provided. In line 2, S2 identifies the action 'éplucher les poires' as an unknown phrase. She uses the translation facility on the interactive screen to assist her. As a result of help, she then identifies the word causing her the problem, 'éplucher' and acknowledges the translation. Next, S2 notices the 'peeler' as the utensil needed to complete the action and reads the words 'couteau éplucheur' off the label attached to the 'peeler'. In line 8, S1 returns to the conversation by reusing the word 'éplucheur' and adds the comment 'very helpful'. The real-world nature of the task means that the users need to access the right equipment to carry out the right actions for the task; it is not just a question of understanding the input provided in the audio messages. From line 8, we can see how, in this task-based learning environment, knowledge of language and cooking is interdependent. This sequence shows how S1 has both confirmed the learning of 'éplucher' and is additionally able to apply it to a new (but related) linguistic context. S1 applies the recently noticed verb 'éplucher' to identify the adjective 'éplucheur' in the noun phrase 'couteau éplucheur' (peeler, or directly translated, 'peeling knife'). S1 does this by using a visible support provided by the kitchen, namely the labelling of utensils and ingredients in the target language. S1's turn demonstrates a dual focus on the continuing cooking action, where a peeler is now needed, and a self-initiated focus on language.

Transcript 2 demonstrates how the pedagogical and technical design supports the autonomous learning processes engaged in by the users. It also illustrates how learning in the French Digital Kitchen involves using language skills and strategies to complete a stage in the task. These skills and strategies are applied by S1 through the use of the interactive screen to make links with English and by S2 through the use of the labelling of the utensils. In this vocational context the learners are focused on the dual pedagogic goals of the task (language and cooking) and their production demonstrates their different levels of expertise in cooking and French. Thus, the language focus of this particular activity becomes one of 'talking about the language' rather than through it as might happen in a traditional classroom set-up.

The example also shows the collaborative nature of strategy use in that both learners pay attention to and benefit from each others' learning behaviours. Observations from this session allowed us to see how the task provided learners with an appropriate context for autonomous learning where they could experiment with French and both use and develop language learning strategies and skills. Transcript 2 also shows how the pedagogical and technological design allows for the initiation and application of new language which can be made potentially relevant at any point in the during-task phase.

A summary of learning behaviours observed is provided in Figure 10.8:

Learners **noticed** key words and phrases by:

- *Listening* to the instructions provided by the kitchen.
- *Using* the learning supports (labelling of equipment and ingredients in French).
- *Listening* to the appropriate or 'timely' feedback from the kitchen in the form of reminders and reformulations.
- *Hearing* their partner use words or phrase in their own creative use of French.
- *Using* the translation or repetition facility on the interactive screen.

Learners then **manipulated** these key words and phrases whilst talking with their partner, which involved:

- *Reusing* key words during a cooking action.
- *Creating* new phrases from key words during a cooking action.
- *Creating* new phrases from existing knowledge to communicate personal meanings about a cooking activity and food.

Learners also **demonstrated existing knowledge** of French, including key words and phrases, which involved:

- *Using* language to communicate personal meanings about food or a cooking activity.
- *Repeating* words and phrases communicated by the kitchen.
- *Helping their partner* to understand words and phrases by offering feedback on meaning and pronunciation.

Figure 10.8 Summary of the Learning Behaviours Identified by Observing the Learners in the French Digital Kitchen

Conclusion

The main innovation of the French Digital Kitchen is its ability to provide a real-life situated language learning environment outside the classroom in which learners become immersed in a physical task which involves them in learning aspects of a language at the same time as cooking a dish. 'Blending' has proved to be a relevant concept for applied linguistics and computing science staff working on the project at all stages of design and iterative development. On the theoretical level, principles of TBLT and HCI have proved to be compatible (particularly with the pre-task, during-task and post-task cycle and scaffolding) and were blended to provide design principles for technology and pedagogy. The design has also involved the blending of skills (communicative skills in the L2) and food (cooking techniques and procedure – following a digitised recipe). The data analysis above has shown that students have refined existing knowledge as well as proving able to learn two skills simultaneously. Further information on the project can be found on: http://europeandigitalkitchen.com.

Although the project described does not conform to the classic definition of 'blended', it is a successful example of 'blending' of technology with applied linguistics using a blend of HCI, CALL and TBLT principles. From a broader perspective, the sensor technology developed in this project can be applied to a range of professional skills across the curriculum. A range of tools can be designed to incorporate sensors in areas such as gardening, childcare, nursing or in the science laboratory, settings in which learners have to learn precise movements. Although developed specifically with and for the French language, the model has been easily transferred to other languages beyond this specific case study. The Newcastle team has now received funding from the European Union for a three-year project. We are working with partners across Europe to produce a network of seven functioning portable kitchens, each of which will be able to teach seven languages and cuisines from Catalonia, England, Spain, Italy, Finland, Germany and France. Information can be found on http://europeandigitalkitchen.com/. This study has exemplified the collaboration between computer scientists and applied linguists envisioned by McCarthy in Chapter 1, and has resulted in the emergence of a new learning mode. For the present, this is very restricted in availability, but many of the techniques, principles and procedures could be applied in other BL settings.

Suggested Resources

Ellis, R. (2003). *Task-based Language Learning and Teaching*. Oxford: Oxford University Press.

Hooper, C., Preston, A., Balaam, M., Seedhouse, P., Jackson, D., Pham, C., Ladha, C., Ladha, K,. Ploetz, T., & Olivier, P. (2012). The French Kitchen: Task-Based Learning in an Instrumental Kitchen. In *14th International Conference on Ubiquitous Computing (Ubicomp)*. Pittsburgh, PA: ACM.

Pham, C., & Olivier, P. (2009). Slice & dice: Recognizing food preparation activities using embedded accelerometers. In *European Conference on Ambient Intelligence*. Salzburg, Austria.

Seedhouse, P., Preston, A., Olivier, P., Jackson, D., Heslop, P., Plötz, T., Balaam, M., & Ali, S. (2013). The French Digital Kitchen: Implementing task-based language teaching beyond the classroom. *International Journal of Computer Assisted Language Learning and Teaching*, 3(1), 50–72.

Seedhouse, P., & Almutairi, S. (2009). A holistic approach to task-based interaction. *International Journal of Applied Linguistics*, 19(3), 1–28.

Discussion Questions

1. This chapter described one way of teaching aspects of language and culture at the same time. Try to identify other ways in which the integration of learning of language and culture might be achieved.

2. This chapter described a BL project in which the pedagogical design was based on task-based language learning and teaching. Evaluate the advantages and disadvantages of using task-based language learning and teaching in BL projects.

3. The study provides some evidence of learning in the French Digital Kitchen. How convincing do you find this evidence? Are there other kinds of evidence of learning which you think should have been gathered?

4. Apart from cooking, can you think of any other skills which could be learnt at the same time as language learning? If so, outline a project which might achieve this.

5. Based on the technologies with which you are familiar, identify ways in which you might use these technologies to teach aspects of language and culture.

References

Abras, C., Maloney-Krichmar, D., & Preece, J. (2004). User-centred design. In B. Sims (Ed.), *Berkshire Encyclopaedia of Human-Computer Interaction* (pp. 763–767). Great Barrington, MA: Berkshire Publishing Group.

Chapelle, C. (1998). Multimedia CALL: Lessons to be learned from research on instructed SLA, *Language Learning and Technology*, 2(1), 22–34. Online at: http://llt.msu.edu/vol2num1/article1/index.html

Colpært, J. (2006). Pedagogy-driven design for online language teaching and learning. *CALICO Journal* 23(3), 477–497.

Ellis, R. (2003). *Task-based Language Learning and Teaching*. Oxford: Oxford University Press.

Graham, C. R. (2006). Blended learning systems: Definition, current trends, and future directions. In C. J. Bonk & C. R. Graham (Eds.), *Handbook of Blended Learning: Global Perspectives, Local Designs* (pp. 3–21). San Francisco, CA: Pfeiffer Publishing.

Hooper, C., Preston, A., Balaam, M., Seedhouse, P., Jackson, D., Pham, C., Ladha, C., Ladha, K., Ploetz, T., & Olivier, P. (2012). The French Kitchen: Task-based learning in an instrumented kitchen. In *14th International Conference on Ubiquitous Computing (Ubicomp)*. Pittsburgh, PA: ACM.

Paterson, A., & Willis, J. (2008). *English Through Music*. Oxford: Oxford University Press.

Pham, C., & Olivier, P. (2009). Slice and dice: Recognizing food preparation activities using embedded accelerometers. In *European Conference on Ambient Intelligence*. Salzburg, Austria.

Preston, A., Seedhouse, P., Olivier, P., Jackson, D., Heslop, P., Wagner, J., Ploetz, T., Ali, S. (2012). Can a kitchen teach me French?: Using digital technology to learn French language and cuisine. *Francophonie*, 46, 3–10.

Seedhouse, P., Preston, A., Olivier, P., Jackson, D., Heslop, P., Plötz, T., Balaam, M., & Ali, S. (2013). The French Digital Kitchen: Implementing task-based language teaching beyond the classroom. *International Journal of Computer Assisted Language Learning and Teaching*, 3(1), 50–72.

Seedhouse, P., & Almutairi, S. (2009). A holistic approach to task-based interaction. *International Journal of Applied Linguistics*, 19(3), 1–28.

Skehan, P. (1998). *A Cognitive Approach to Language Learning*. Oxford: Oxford University Press.

Skehan, P. (2003). Task-based instruction. *Language Teaching*, 36, 1–14.

Willis, J. (1996). *A Framework for Task-Based Learning*. Harlow: Longman.

APPENDIX

A GUIDE TO THE TRANSCRIPTION SYMBOLS

Punctuation marks are used to capture characteristics of speech delivery, not to mark grammatical units.

AR	audio recording from the digital kitchen
S1	student no. 1
[	indicates the point of overlap onset
]	indicates the point of overlap termination
(3.2)	an interval between utterances (3 seconds and 2 tenths in this case)
(.)	a very short untimed pause
word	underlining indicates speaker emphasis
e:r the:::	indicates lengthening of the preceding sound
-	a single dash indicates an abrupt cut-off
?	rising intonation, not necessarily a question
!	an animated or emphatic tone
,	a comma indicates low rising intonation, suggesting continuation
.	a full stop (period) indicates falling (final) intonation
CAPITALS	especially loud sounds relative to surrounding talk
° °	utterances between degree signs are noticeably quieter than surrounding talk
↑ ↓	indicate marked shifts into higher or lower pitch in the utterance following the arrow
><	indicate that the talk they surround is produced more quickly than neighbouring talk
(S1 presses screen)	non-verbal actions or editor's comments
<>	indicate that the talk they surround is produced slowly

CHAPTER 11

A Case Study in Language Teacher Education

David Moloney and Anne O'Keeffe

INTRODUCTION

This chapter looks at the potential of blended learning (BL) in the context of higher education teaching, in particular in relation to language teacher education. BL offers new opportunities for learning and it can enhance learning by complementing the traditional classroom method with computer-mediated activities and electronic resources. It also enhances flexibility of learning as students can access material from different locations, and at any time that is convenient. In this chapter, we will examine a case study of the use of BL tools and activities in two undergraduate English Language Teaching modules. We will show how some of the challenges of real-time face-to-face learning environments can be overcome (for example, the short-lived, or what is often referred to as 'ephemeral' nature of live lectures and the stress of capturing what is being said in a lecture). The case study will also evaluate the use of a Learning Management System (LMS) in tandem with the traditional classroom, including the use of lecture-capturing software, uploaded to an LMS (in this case, Moodle), and the use of related activities, such as quizzes and discussion forums. We will show that these strategies have enhanced opportunities for learning and increased student engagement with content. We will draw on LMS participation statistics, student evaluations of teaching (SETs) and questionnaire data for our analysis.

Young (2002: A33) quotes the president of Penn State University (at that time) as saying that the convergence of classroom and online learning is 'the single greatest unrecognized trend in higher education today'. With hindsight, this was undoubtedly prophetic. Many factors have driven the move in mainstream higher education from solely presenting courses in traditional face-to-face contexts to offering a range of formats for learning, from face-to-face lectures or small groups to online and even Massive Open Online Courses (MOOCs). This paper focuses on BL as a format of enhanced teaching and learning. BL entails both face-to-face teaching and learning and the use of a LMS, within which teaching and learning also takes place. We do not see BL and traditional learning as being in a mutually exclusive binary relationship. In fact, we contend that one enhances and complements the other (see also King, Chapter 6, this volume).

Specifically, the focus of this paper is on an English Language Teacher Education undergraduate course in an Irish Higher Education (HE) institution. It is worth setting this course in context. At a macro-level, an Irish Higher Education Authority (HEA) policy context, *The National Strategy for Higher Education to 2030* (Higher Education Authority, 2011) stresses the importance of building more flexible learning opportunities within the Irish higher education sector. It notes that while there are isolated examples of programmes and courses available on a flexible and online basis, these are the exception rather than the rule. It acknowledges that, for most institutions, launching blended and online learning courses represents a significant cultural and operational challenge. At a meso-level (i.e., a middle level between *macro* and *micro*), within the managerial context of our institutional Strategic Plan, there is an overt statement regarding targets to increase the number of flexible programme delivery options and the greater use of our Virtual Learning Environment (VLE) (Mary Immaculate College, 2012). This aspiration mirrors the goal of enhanced flexible learning options by the Higher Education Authority at a macro-level, as detailed above (see Higher Education Authority, 2011). Therefore, it is within the context of these macro- and meso-level imperatives that our case study is situated. At a micro-level, within the context of the course team, there were also factors which drove change. These were more pedagogically based motives, as we shall detail below.

The course that we focus on is one year in duration and comprises two sequential modules in English Language Teaching. It is open to second year undergraduate students within a liberal arts degree programme (i.e., humanities and social sciences) who have no prior knowledge in relation to Initial Teacher Education in any context. Therefore, the programme has to induce them into the essentials of teaching in general (e.g., classroom management, assessment, motivation, lesson planning, and so on); it has to cover the essentials of language teaching (teaching vocabulary, teaching grammar, teaching pronunciation, skills development, using games and role plays, language teaching methods, and so on) and it has to cover the essentials of the English language as a system (i.e., morphology, syntax and phonology). The latter is quite challenging. Though the students are native speakers of English, they are *ab initio*, 'beginner' level, in terms of their grammatical and general language awareness. Annual Student Evaluations of Teaching (SETs) conducted by the Centre for Teaching and Learning consistently generated the following pressure points:

- There was too much content covered in the face-to-face contact time and not enough time to discuss it.
- Students found the grammar component particularly dense and challenging (and their results confirmed this).
- Students felt that they could understand the grammatical explanations in class but then struggled with the end-of-semester grammar assessment (an exam).
- Students did not feel adequately prepared for the classroom in terms of their content knowledge.

The overhauling of the programme, at a micro-level, came about in the context of trying to address these concerns raised by students on the course. These can be essentially summarised as:

1. a need to provide more opportunities for students to engage with the course content;
2. a need to enhance how grammar is taught and how it is consolidated;

3. a need to re-examine how grammar is assessed; and
4. a need to integrate content knowledge from the course so as to build students' confidence in their expertise as teachers of English as a Foreign Language[1].

The move from a solely traditional delivery format was a gradual one and the present chapter aims to reflect on this from the perspective of the lecturers and the students, as well as from a theoretical perspective. We will outline the process of moving to a blended format on this undergraduate course. We will detail the learning activities and online resources that were used and report on the varying degrees of success which each had.

We are keen to recognise that moving from a traditional classroom to a virtual one is a major challenge. To begin with, traditional classrooms do not crash or freeze, as computers and websites can, and you do not usually need a username and password to get into them. Faculty need training and a support team to make the virtual classroom happen (see Comas-Quinn, Chapter 5, and Lázár, Chapter 9, this volume). First and foremost, they need an LMS in place. Students also need training on how to use new online tools despite their seeming 'knowingness' in relation to technology. All in all, we recognise that innovation is challenging and time-consuming but it brings many new teaching and learning opportunities that could not have been envisaged in a traditional classroom context (McCarthy, Chapter 1, this volume). Most of all, using a BL format has brought a multiplication of both teaching and learning opportunities. Through this, teachers have more opportunities to engage with learners, and vice versa. Additionally, in the spirit of constructivist models of education where learners are actively involved in building understanding and knowledge, BL offers far more opportunities for formative and peer-to-peer learning (see below).

Before we detail the innovations that we put in place and how these were evaluated by the students, we will first explore further the rationale for BL approaches.

TRADITIONAL LEARNING AND BLENDED LEARNING

RATIONALE FOR BLENDED METHOD

The turn of the millennium saw the landscape of higher education change markedly due to the increased presence of and access to technology. Information communications technologies (ICT) have been absorbed in almost all sectors. The present authors have grounded this case study in instructional theory which, in the context of BL, focuses on the structuring of e-learning materials to improve and manage learning. The theoretical framework underpinning the constructivist-based instructional design of two English Language Teaching modules will be presented (the next section will detail these modules).

Conventional Irish higher educational institutions offer face-to-face course delivery. However, since the turn of the century, progression towards integrated learning approaches in Higher Education (HE) has become a significant priority (Department of Education and Skills, 2003). BL constitutes the integration of face-to-face, mobile and e-learning delivery methods in no predefined ratio. Each method is recognised as having distinct advantages and disadvantages. The social and pedagogical advantages and disadvantages of face-to-face teaching and learning are well documented. Numerous researchers (Al-Qahtani and Higgins, 2013; Akkoyunlu and Soylu, 2006; Klein and Ware, 2003) identify a range of advantages of e-learning including the following:

- Learning can be branched to meet individual learner needs (for example, online quizzes can use adaptive feedback to enhance formative learning for individuals who need it).

- The Virtual Learning Environment (VLE) caters for individual learning preferences (for example, learners can access materials when and where they choose).
- Synchronous and asynchronous learning provides flexibility and enhances student interaction.
- Access to knowledge and information is enhanced and increased.
- E-learning can be cost effective to both students and institutions, alleviating the need, on one hand, for students to travel, and on the other, for physical classrooms.

Disadvantages are also readily identifiable, such as:

- The possibility of student isolation.
- Success in this environment is dependent on IT and communication skills and it is acknowledged that many parts of the world still have sub-standard internet bandwidth speeds and/or lack of appropriate hardware, platforms and infrastructures.
- E-learning may be less effective than face-to-face learning with regard to providing explanation and clarification to student questions.
- The apparent prospect of online cheating in certain circumstances.

In order to capitalise upon the advantages of each method while simultaneously overcoming the negative aspects associated with each (Al-Qahtani and Higgins, 2013; Garrison and Kanuka, 2004), a blended approach to learning may be employed.

Research on the major theories of learning needs to be reflected upon in relation to BL and, in our case study, the work of Ertmer and Newby (1993) was very apt. Essentially, Ertmer and Newby contend that major learning theory strategies overlap.

They suggest that for varying levels of learner task-knowledge and required cognitive processing, different learning strategies can be applied to produce optimum return. According to this, instruction for a new learner or novice to a topic could be appropriately delivered for a low-level cognitive task by employing a behaviourist learning strategy, while a higher level task might employ a cognitivist or constructivist strategy. It is suggested by this model, as the level of knowledge that the learner has of a particular task and as the cognitive processing required by that given task increases, the more inclined a learner is to benefit from a gradual shift along the continuum from a behaviorist to a cognitivist and, furthermore, to a constructivist strategy for learning. Higher education settings typically require these high levels of learner task-knowledge and cognitive processing skills to achieve higher order skills, such as those skills associated with learning a language (Bloom et al., 1956). The concept of a gradual shift and employment of a constructivist approach was borne in mind during development and implementation of the present BL study.

THEORETICAL FRAMEWORK

Piaget and Vygotsky are credited with the foundation of constructivist learning principles (Palincsar, 1998). Constructivist principles are founded upon the most basic premise that learning environments should be designed with a focus on facilitating students in the process of knowledge creation, not merely knowledge transmission and reproduction.

In order to aid in the design, development and structure of constructivist learning environments (CLEs), Gómez and Duart (2012) suggest incorporating a theoretical framework. In their paper on designing CLEs, Jonassen and Rohrer-Murphy (1999) argue that activity theory, as proposed by Vygotsky (1978) and subsequently supplemented by Engeström (1987), provides a suitable theoretical framework to analyse needs, tasks and outcomes when designing CLEs. Activity theory acts as a lens through which many forms of sociocultural human activity can be analysed. The framework is particularly relevant to those activities that form part of the teaching and learning process (Gómez and Duart, 2012; Jonassen and Rohrer-Murphy, 1999).

Vygotsky's proposed activity system (Figure 11.1 below) includes the subject, object and mediating artefacts (materials and activities designed to promote learning) as respective components. Learning, as an activity, can be described as the interactive process that a group of people (subjects) go through in order to achieve a specified purpose (object) (Gómez and Duart, 2012). Peer interactions and student-lecturer interactions are achieved, as outlined at the top of Figures 11.1 and 11.2, through the use of mediating artefacts and instruments. In the BL context of this study, mediating artefacts and instruments are understood as the face-to-face and online factors – lecture and tutorial content, use of an LMS, activities and resources (discussion forums, wikis, blogs, other collaborative online activities) – through which communication, collaboration and ultimately constructivist intervention to facilitate knowledge creation is achieved. Jonassen and Rohrer-Murphy (1999) contend that little meaningful activity can be accomplished individually. Leont'ev (1981) substantiates this, stating: 'The human individual's activity is a system of social relations. It does not exist without those social relations.' (Leont'ev, 1981: 46–7) Figure 11.2 outlines that rules, community and division of labour also play key roles in the learning process when the aim is to produce favourable outcomes. Community, and in particular how to create a sense of community

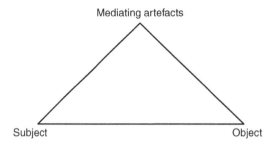

Figure 11.1 Vygotsky's Activity System (Dixon-Krauss, 1996)

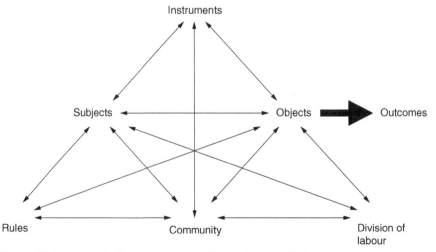

Figure 11.2 Engeström's Activity System (Dixon-Krauss, 1996)

online, will be discussed later in further detail. Elements of this sociocultural activity theory framework were used as a reference to support the design and development of the CLE for this BL case study.

ROLE DEFINITION

In a blended CLE, with particular regard to a higher education setting, the roles of the traditional lecturer and student change to assume diverse attributes. The traditional classroom lecturer takes on many roles to successfully function in a blended CLE. In line with constructivist strategies, the student role within a blended CLE also shifts from a passive to a more active nature (Jonassen, 1991). At present, the Irish primary and secondary education system is based predominantly around behaviourist and cognitivist approaches to learning indicated by a passive classroom-based approach with little focus on community and collaboration. This is changing; however, it can still pose difficulty when trying to facilitate undergraduate student integration into a CLE at the third level. In terms of an asynchronous online discussion forum, Ruey (2010) proposes that the lecturer occupies a facilitator role where the primary focus is on mentoring while students themselves are seen as moderators. This is contested by Salmon (2000) who associates the teacher, instructor, tutor or facilitator with the e-moderator role. Both of these perspectives on the role of the online lecturer, as both a mentor and moderator, were adhered to at different stages during the learning cycle of the present study, as would be expected within such a flexible approach.

'DEEP LEARNING' AND 'COMMUNITIES OF INQUIRY'

'Deep learning' and 'surface learning' (Marton and Säljö, 1976; Chin and Brown, 2000) can ultimately be compared to the processes by which students approach their learning. Deep learning promotes critical understanding and application of knowledge while surface learning refers to a more passive approach to knowledge where it is memorised and often not processed critically and not linked to previous learning. Deep learning lends itself to a constructivist approach to learning in which students are compelled to ascertain an ownership of their own education. If a student actively relates new knowledge to existing knowledge, thereby creating associations between new and existing concepts and theories, he/she is undertaking a much deeper approach to learning. Relevant prior knowledge exists to create correlations between learned concepts and new ones. In the context of this BL case study, the active construction of one's own meanings, consistent with prior knowledge, was advocated above the passive acquisition of knowledge to generate a learning experience.

In their study on understanding cognitive presence in an online and blended community of inquiry, Akyol and Garrison (2010) place substantial emphasis on both deep and surface learning approaches and outcomes and on the Community of Inquiry (CoI) framework (Garrison et al., 2001) with particular reference to the dynamics of online and BL environments. A CoI refers to an active learning experience within a group of individuals, involving collaborative engagement with materials, usually in a problem-solving situation. The importance of both of these structures to the success of a BL initiative was taken into account in the present study.

Weigel (2002) establishes a deep learning model categorising deep learning into three stages:

1. Conditionalised knowledge – essentially the ability to use existing knowledge and relate it to a number of different scenarios.

2. Metacognition – reflective thinking about your own cognitive processes.
3. Communities of Inquiry (CoI) – different elements that must be present in order for an educational experience to happen.

A deep approach requires a student to be motivated and interested in learning about the subject matter. Without this motivation or interest in a subject, students may only skim the surface and learn what is thought to be necessary. In the context of the present study, there was a feeling on the part of the lecturers, especially in the case of grammar, that students were only operating at a surface level. The authors were aware that this can often be driven by exam-based summative assessment. For this reason, continuous assessment was discussed as an alternative. Surface learning may be demonstrated through rote memorisation of facts about the subject matter and through placing pressure on oneself due to feeling obliged to complete a task for someone else's purposes. This surface learning, learning for the sake of meeting a demand, suggests that a student might know certain things about a subject without ever really fully understanding it. With this in mind, the focus of CLEs should be to bring about a dynamic and motivating learning and assessment context to promote deep learning.

A CoI consists of three fundamental elements that must all be present in order for an educational experience to take place: a social, cognitive, and teaching presence (see Figure 11.3).

It is favourable for both the lecturer and student to be active within each presence, fostering student-lecturer interactions and student-student interactions which in turn facilitate a deeper approach to both group dynamics and individual knowledge construction. In online environments it is especially important to foster each presence among students. One avenue is through the promotion of peer-to-peer mentoring. In a study on the impact

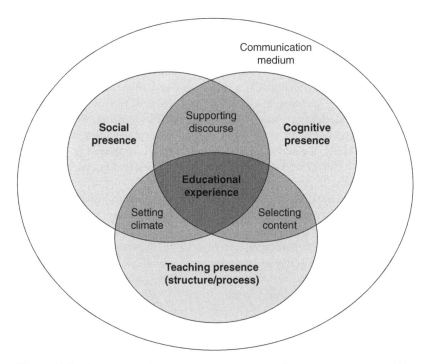

Figure 11.3 Community of Inquiry Model Cited from Garrison and Vaughan (2008)

of BL on students' achievement, as compared with both face-to-face and e-learning respectively, Al-Qahtani and Higgins (2013) found that BL supported students' learning more effectively than either of the elements on their own. It was suggested that course co-ordinators aim to foster these CoI presences to redress limitations of the traditional face-to-face approach.

In this section, we have presented the theoretical backdrop underpinning the rationale and frameworks which enabled the design and development of this blended CLE. We will now provide the context in which our case study took place.

Moving from Traditional Teaching to Blended Format

As we mentioned above, the move from traditional learning to BL was gradual and, in all, it took three semesters, i.e., a year and a half. In that period, the following graduated staging took place in terms of how the VLE actually moved from being a file repository, replacing the shared network folder which we had used, to being a collaborative learning space. This gradual building of confidence on the part of the lecturers is also linked to a building of competency in relation to how to use the new learning tools offered by the LMS. Figure 11.4 illustrates the four steps that we took over the three semester period. Note that Semester 1 in this diagram refers in fact to the second semester of the academic year 2011/12. In other words, halfway through that academic year, we decided to stop using the shared network folder as a repository for our course notes and PowerPoint presentations and instead to move over to the LMS, in this case Moodle. For this cohort of students, there was not any major change in their teaching and learning. The LMS, in this semester, was used as a file repository in the same way that we had used the network folder. However, it was a crucial stage for the lecturers in that it allowed them to become confident in the basic processes of the LMS. Without this stage, the real innovation that we embarked on in Steps 3 and 4 could not have taken place. These changes were introduced with a completely new cohort of undergraduates in the academic year that followed, 2012/13 (see Steps 3 and 4, Semesters 2 and 3).

Steps 1 and 2 These first steps in our path were the most basic but the most crucial: simply to learn how to log onto the LMS and go through the procedures of loading files.

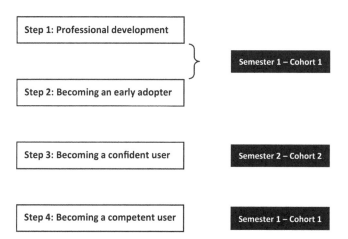

Figure 11.4 Overview of Stages of Transition from Traditional Learning to Blended Learning

This was achieved through a combination of professional development courses and trial and error. For faculty, the multi-functionality of the LMS can be daunting and we decided to take things slowly and to learn the basics of how to use the LMS in Semester 1 of the academic year 2011/12. The basic competencies to be acquired by the end of Steps 1 and 2 were:

- how to create a course and enrol the learners;
- how to load lecture files and other supporting notes and materials;
- how to add basic hyperlinks to web-based material on video upload sites such as YouTube or blogs; and
- how to use the discussion forum facility as a class bulletin board.

These were achieved in Semester 1 (Figure 11.4), and were essentially about overcoming the fear of clicking on the wrong link and losing everything and about becoming familiar with the routine and processes of just doing the most basic of functions properly. By the end of Steps 1 and 2, we felt that we had become accomplished in the basics and were ready to learn more in terms of the added potential of this space. For learners on this course, apart from having to log into the LMS, not much had changed for them compared to when they went to the shared network folder to download our lecture notes and handouts.

Step 3 A new student cohort began in the academic year 2012/13 and for this cohort, we were able to take the next steps towards BL and, in doing so, try to address some of the issues raised in our 2011/12 Student Evaluation of Teaching (SET). As mentioned earlier, this feedback had told us that students felt that there was too much content covered in the face-to-face contact time and not enough time to discuss it. They particularly felt that the grammar component was dense and taxing and their results confirmed this. Some students felt that they could understand the grammatical explanations in class but then struggled with the assessment (an exam). Overall, it was clear that students did not feel adequately prepared for the classroom in terms of their content knowledge in ELT, especially in relation to grammar. We wanted to move away from solely using the LMS as a file repository to using it for content delivery. To this end, in Semester 2 of the process of moving from traditional face-to-face teaching to blended mode, the following steps were taken:

1. We recorded all lectures and loaded them to the LMS (via YouTube). This meant that learners could watch them again at any time, in any place. It also meant that we were able to overcome some of the ephemerality of the traditional classroom by capturing it for the students. Student feedback on this simple change was overwhelmingly positive. Examples of feedback and further discussion of this and the following points can be found in the Evaluation section.

2. We created additional offline content in the form of short video recordings, known as 'vodcasts', to supplement class content and we loaded these to the LMS. This meant that we were not trying to squeeze too much into one face-to-face lecture. We were able to break content up into more manageable amounts. It particularly allowed us to take grammar lectures at a slower pace. 15-minute vodcasts were made on specific grammar topics and students then accessed these via the LMS in their own time. Again, feedback on these was very positive (see Evaluation section for more detail).

3. We created grammar quizzes within the LMS so as to give additional formative practice for learners and we also used them as a means of assessment to replace

the final summative examination in grammar that we had previously used and which had caused a lot of anxiety. The previous assessment instrument entailed an end-of-semester exam, part of which was a section on grammar, worth 20% of the total module grade. Learners, in their formal Student Evaluation of Teaching (SET), in 2011/12, detailed how they struggled with this task at the end of the semester. In our revised format, these quizzes were directly linked to the grammar lectures and vodcasts (e.g., a vodcast on prepositions had a corresponding quiz on prepositions). They were also phased over the 12-week semester period so as to make them more manageable. For each topic there were two grammar quizzes, one for practice and one for assessment. These are discussed further below in our evaluation.

Step 4 By Semester 3 (academic year 2012/13), buoyed by the positive feedback from the previous semester (see Step 3 above) and having gained further in confidence and competency in terms of using the LMS, the lecturers decided to use even more of the LMS's functionality both to enhance the course itself and also as an innovative assessment tool. To this end, the use of grammar vodcasts and quizzes was continued and increased (see Step 3). Vodcasts linked to practice and assessment tasks were also developed for areas other than grammar. These are detailed below.

DISCUSSION FORUMS

Discussion forums were used to integrate various language teaching methodologies that had been covered in detail on the course and in vodcasts. The task set for students, which was part of their assessment, was to review the lectures and vodcasts on language teaching methods and, in their randomly assigned groups of six, to make one post of 500 words on the following and to make at least one reply to another class member's post (maximum 200 words):

> **Topic for discussion**: In the lectures and vodcasts on Language Teaching Methods, we looked at the *Grammer Translation Method, Direct Method, Audio-Lingual Method* and *Communicative Language Teaching*. We can learn something from each of these in terms of how best to teach a language.
>
> You can use URL links to support your points (e.g. a YouTube clip of a class).
>
> **You will not see anyone else's post until you have made a post. You will then be able to reply to another post. You only have to reply to one post (200 words max.)**
>
> **Marks are given individually based on your posts.**

Figure 11.5 An Example of a Topic Used in a Discussion Forum

WIKIS

Wikis were used as an integrating assessment tool for the materials design component of the course. They also served an independent study function: the course was focused on teaching English to adult learners rather than young learners. In previous years, the best that we could hope to fit into the schedule was one two-hour lecture on Teaching Young Learners and we were conscious that this really was not ideal. Therefore, we gave one two-hour lecture as a starting point and loaded a number of vodcasts, YouTube clips, blog links, readings (pdf format) and infographics on the topic of Teaching English to Young Learners. The integrating task for the learners was to create a wiki, in randomly formed groups of six, to address the following:

Wiki Task

In your group, choose **one** theme and then select **four** activities or resources that you could use to teach English to children based on this theme. Choose an age group for your activities (under 7 or between 7 and 11/12).

Theme: any theme appropriate to children can be used (e.g. talking about myself, talking about my family, food, hobbies, my house, the weather, clothes, travel and transport, different cultures, actions, likes and dislikes, holidays, toys, etc.);

Activities and resources: these can be anything that you will base a lesson on (e.g. song with movements, rhyme with movements, chant with movements, dialogue to act out, mime, game, YouTube clip, arts and crafts, pictures, matching tasks, sports activity for outdoors, game, etc.);

You must use four different types of activities or resources (e.g. you can't have two songs and two picture matching activities)

What you need to do for each activity:
1) In your group, pick one theme. All of the activities will have to link to this theme.
2) Find the **four** best activities that link to that theme. Provide the URL to link to that material.
3) Write up your entry using these headings:

Theme: (say clearly what theme you are using for all of your activities)
Age group: (under 7 or between 7 and 11/12)
Activity 1: (say what it is: a song, a rhyme, a game, a puzzle, etc.)
Link to activity URL: (give the website link)
Why we chose it: (explain, in a sentence or two, why this was chosen. This will probably tell what the activity is and how it links to the theme and why this is a good choice)

Figure 11.6   An Example of a Topic Used as a Basis for a Wiki Task

Students had one month to complete this task. The wiki function on Moodle has a 'behind-the-scenes' chat area which they were able to use as a place to 'meet' and plan, so in theory they did not physically need to meet to do this collaborative task over that time. An example of this chat function in action is show below:

EXTRACT I (MID-WAY THROUGH THE DISCUSSION)

Student 1 [Friday, 17 May 2013, 1:28 PM] Okay so this could be the general format of the activities. We could start with Michael's song to teach the children the basic animal sounds and the names of the animals. Then using Mark's Old MacDonald song with pictures as said by Marion, we could teach the children of animals in certain places and settings as well as further teaching them their names and sounds. The third game could be Marion's card game as this would be perfect for recognition and ensure they fully recognise certain animals and it is a fun group activity. For the fourth activity I think we could use this as it is interactive and fully checks they recognise certain animal sounds. http://www.youtube.com/watch?v=cLTSNbNvv1s. So what do you think?

Student 2 [Friday, 17 May 2013, 2:38 PM] Ya that sounds good! Perfect. Should we put it together now so?! :) A small introduction naming the theme etc. as well at the start!

Student 3 [Friday, 17 May 2013, 4:27 PM] I'm happy with everything guys. I think we've done a good job. Now, how shall we put this together? I think we put each activity under the 'Edit' heading!!

Student 4 [Friday, 17 May 2013, 10:05 PM] Everything looks great guys. We have everything we need so that's great. We just need to put the activities under the edit heading I think.

Extract 1 is just a short excerpt from a much longer discussion. As the time stamps show, this collaborative work was done over a period of time thus illustrating the benefit of the LMS as a collaborative learning space, at a time and place that suits the learner. The other spin-off of this task was that the end results (i.e., the wikis) would make a resource for the students which they could use in year 3 on their teaching placement if they were teaching young learners. Hence, it had a real-world dimension as an activity (see Seedhouse et al., Chapter 10, this volume).

EVALUATION

Two evaluations points took place. The first was at the end of Semester 2 (see Figure 11.4), coinciding with the introduction of a number of innovations in terms of BL, namely the introduction of recordings of all of our lectures onto the LMS and the use of vodcasts and quizzes. The second was at the end of Semester 3, when the 2012/13 cohort had completed their one-year programme. By the end of this semester, we had added further BL innovations, including the use of wikis and discussion forums as well as continuing the use of quizzes, video recordings of face-to-face lectures and vodcasts. Both surveys were conducted online using Google Drive and this was linked via URL to the LMS course page. The response rates were: 44% (of a sample of 39 students) for Survey 1 at the end of Semester 2 and 45% (of a sample of 40 students) for Survey 2 at the end of Semester 3. Both surveys were given to the same class cohort. In summarising the findings, we will focus on the video recordings and vodcasts in relation to Semester 2 and discuss the remaining innovations in relation to Semester 3.

VIDEO RECORDINGS AND VODCASTS

In Survey 1 we asked students:

- how often they watched video recordings on the LMS (both lecture recordings and vodcasts);
- if they had a preference for the live recordings or the shorter vodcasts, which contain voiceovers on PowerPoint slides;
- to evaluate the usefulness of these resources;
- to consider whether video recording and vodcasting was something that they would like their other lecturers to use as a teaching aid; and
- what their learning purpose in relation to their use of the recordings and vodcasts was.

Figures 11.7–11.11 illustrate the findings.

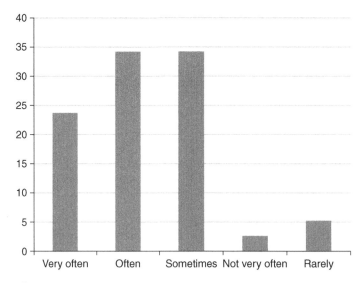

Figure 11.7 'How often do you watch the videos and videocasts on the TEFL Moodle page?' (results as percentages)

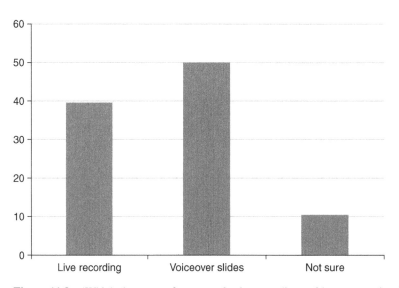

Figure 11.8 'Which do you prefer to watch, the recordings of lectures or the slides with voiceovers?' (results as percentages)

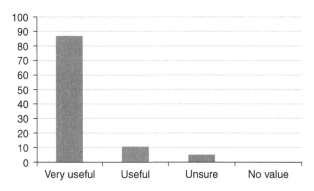

Figure 11.9 'Evaluate how useful the video recordings and vodcasts were for you as an aid to learning?' (Very useful; Useful; Unsure; or No value) (results as percentages)

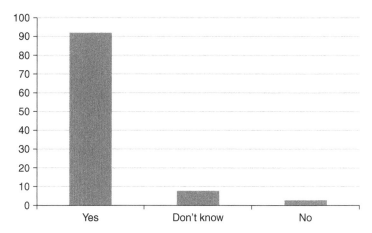

Figure 11.10 'Are video recording lectures and vodcasting something that you would like other lectures on your degree programme to use?' (results as percentages)

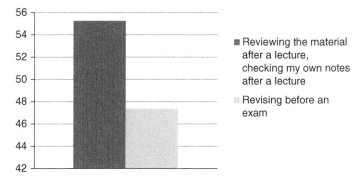

Figure 11.11 'How do you use the video recordings and vodcasts as an aid to learning?' (results as percentages)

By way of qualitative questioning, we asked the cohort the following question: 'If you were trying to persuade your lecturer to do this, what is your best argument from the point of view of the student?' Some typical responses were:

- *Because lectures are recorded I am able to listen in class. I learn best by listening and sometimes find that by taking notes I miss out on what the lecturer says because I am focused on writing and not listening... I know that I cannot possibly miss anything and if I happen to miss a lecture it is comforting that I will not miss any course material and can catch up straight away.*
- *This method of teaching provides a service for students who are shy and wouldn't like to speak up and ask a question in the lecture. I find it allows me to go at my own pace and double check anything I didn't understand as the majority of the class including me would say they understood the material or subject even if we didn't.*
- *Being able to listen more in the lecture and take fewer notes and then catch up on the video and take down notes if needed. This would be very beneficial in my opinion.*

The first survey focused on the use of video recordings and vodcast materials. In the second survey, we wanted to explore in detail students' opinions on the use of the quizzes, wikis and discussion forums, especially as assessment tools. Using online assessment as an alternative to the traditional end-of-semester exam through the following question: 'The class had a choice between an exam or online assessments and opted for online assessments.

Now that you have done the grammar quiz, discussion forum and wiki, are you happy with this decision?' See the responses in Figure 11.12 below.

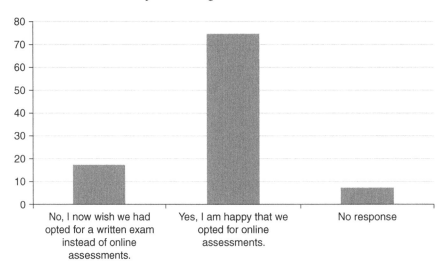

Figure 11.12 Opinions on online assessment choice versus traditional end-of-semester exam (results as percentages)

Asked whether they used lecture recordings or vodcasts when revising for grammar quizzes, the following mixed response was elicited, probably reflecting various learning styles. See the responses in Figure 11.13 below.

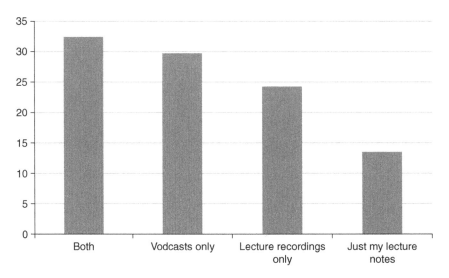

Figure 11.13 'When preparing for the grammar quiz, did you use the recorded class lectures or the shorter summary recordings? Explain your choice.'

Some explanations about use give further insight.
Both lectures and vodcasts:

- *I watched both but I found the shorter summaries to be much more to the point. It really showcased the beneficial aspects of this method of teaching to a large body of students. I think it is something that should be pursued by more lecturers.*
- *I watched the recorded class an hour or 2 before doing the quiz, then a few minutes before the quiz I revised using the shorted summary recordings.*

- *When preparing for the quiz, I first of all used the class lectures. I took notes from the class lecture, after I had done this I used the shorter summary recordings and the lecture notes for any areas I needed help clearing up.*

Vodcasts only:

- *I use the recorded lectures. Everything important as well as extra information is included in them. The summaries are simply a summary and do not go into the detail of the lectures.*

Lectures only:

- *During the lectures I had taken down the slide notes as we went along so when I went to prepare for the quiz, I looked at the notes.*

DISCUSSION FORUMS

We asked students: 'What did you like most about the Discussion Forum activity on Language Teaching Methods?' Figure 11.14 summarises their responses thematically.

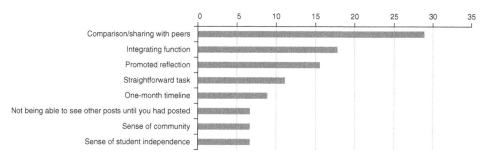

Figure 11.14 Student Responses to Discussion Forum Task (results as percentages)

Indicative examples are presented below for each theme.

Comparison and sharing with peers:

- *That we could exchange ideas and opinions and gain valuable insight into the subject by learning from others. Competition among students.*

Integrating function:

- *It prompted the student to independently go back over what he/she had learned over the semester. It also gave the student a chance to compare their work against that of their fellow students.*

Promoted reflection:

- *I liked that you could express freely what you thought about each method, exploring the different styles and approaches there are, in turn this allowed me to discover the language teaching method that I would use in the classroom.*

Straightforward task:

- *I liked the forum as we got to discuss our opinions on these methods yet it was shorter than an essay.*

One-month timeline:

- *I liked that it was a broad question and could be completed in my own time. It was not like an exam that you were rushing trying to get everything done.*

Not being able to see other posts until you had posted:

- *I liked how it was private until you posted to stop others copying, etc.*

Sense of community:

- *It is a good system and I believe it fosters a sense of community as well as competition among students.*

Sense of student independence:

- *It inspires you to read and to research the topic further in order to be able to contribute something in the forum. There is a level of student independence and freedom of purpose.*

WIKI ASSIGNMENT

We also addressed the use of a wiki to assess their understanding of designing materials for young learners, as detailed above. We posed two questions: 1) 'What did you like least about the wiki activity?' and 2) 'What did you like most about the wiki activity?' These elicited the following responses (see Figures 11.15 and 11.16 below).

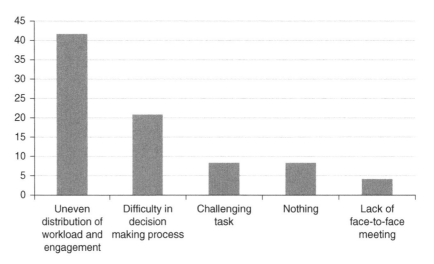

Figure 11.15 'What did you like least about the wiki activity?' (results as percentages)

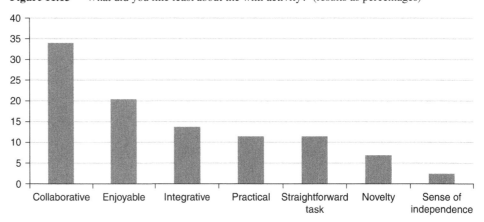

Figure 11.16 'What did you like most about the wiki activity?' (results as percentages)

These results from the wiki activity are interesting. On one hand, we find that there were quite a few negatives for the students, including: the sense of uneven distribution of workload within groups; the difficulty of the task; the difficulty of bringing it to a conclusion through decision making. On the other hand, this is offset by highly positive comments about how enjoyable it was and how much they liked the opportunity to work collaboratively. It was highly encouraging to see that they found it practical and could see its application to their future classroom contexts and also the integrating function of the activity, where they could see the application of so many areas of the course and how they inter-related. Some of the comments extracted from the data illustrate these contrasts between the positive and the negative (all responses from the same students).

'WHAT DID YOU LIKE LEAST ABOUT THE WIKI ACTIVITY?'

Uneven distribution of workload:

- *Some people didn't join the discussion until two days before it was due. This maddened me as we had already done most of the work... Also, I don't like group work much but that's only me.*
- *I found that there were only a few in the group that were doing most of the work. It depended on all the members logging in daily and the decision process was slow.*

Difficulty in decision-making process:

- *Some people seemed to take up leadership without it being discussed. This, I disliked.*
- *We could not contact one member for quite a while which meant we had to take decisions upon ourselves and hoped it would be okay.*

'WHAT DID YOU LIKE MOST ABOUT THE WIKI ACTIVITY?'

Collaborative:

- *The fact that it was group work and we had to make decisions based on each post.*
- *I especially liked the way we were able to discuss our opinions as a group and see what everyone else was thinking.*
- *I liked the interactive aspect. I have never participated in any exercise like this in college before so I found it interesting. It's slightly similar to the tutorial experience but the 'online' element renders it new and refreshing.*

Integrative:

- *It makes you more aware of the differences between teaching children and adults and the different techniques you have to use to keep them interested etc.*

Enjoyable:

- *Enjoy chatting through wiki.*
- *I really enjoyed doing the wiki page.*
- *It was fun.*

GRAMMAR QUIZZES

We asked the learners what they liked least and what they liked most about the grammar quizzes. Figures 11.17 and 11.18 show their responses.

It is highly encouraging that nearly 10% of learners had nothing negative to say about the quizzes. However, over 55% felt that the questions were very challenging and over 30% felt that the weighting of questions was a concern. In order to promote integration between the quiz questions and the recommended reading, class notes, lecture captures and vodcasts, the questions were quite challenging and there were only six in each quiz. This meant that students had to revisit the learning materials a number of times and this iterative process between assessment and learning materials meant that they worked much harder to understand and engage with the task. Each question required a lot of consideration and, to reflect and promote this, each question carried a lot of marks. However, the students felt that more questions with a spread of weighting would have been more favourable as

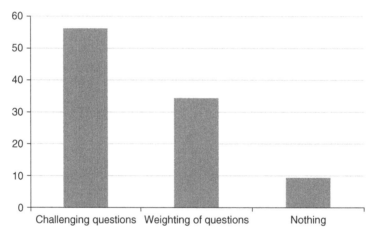

Figure 11.17 'What did you like least about the grammar quiz?' (results as percentages)

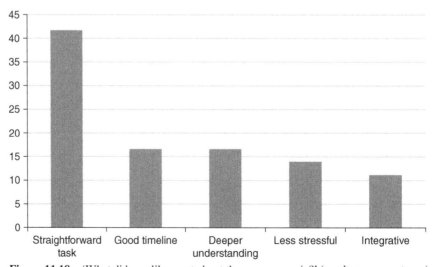

Figure 11.18 'What did you like most about the grammar quiz?' (results as percentages)

they felt that each question carried a high risk for them (in terms of its percentage of their overall module grade).

The most positive result in response to this question was that the task of answering online questions was very straightforward as a format of assessment. They also greatly appreciated having long timelines in terms of quiz deadlines, usually one month, and within the quiz itself, students could save their attempts and change them until they finally submitted. This meant that they would often reconsider answers on reviewing material (this 'process' information is available to the teacher for analysis in terms of learning analytics). For us, this was evidence of an iterative learning process, where learners moved between course materials and assessment task in a self-regulated attempt to arrive at an understanding. This promoted deeper learning (as discussed in 'Deep Learning' and 'Communities of Inquiry' section, p. 181). In fact, a number of students overtly referred to the instrument of assessment affording them a deeper understanding of the material and almost 15% referred to this form of assessment being less stressful than an end-of-semester grammar exam. There was also reference made to the integrative element of the assessment.

Straightforward task:

- *I liked the way that the questions were based on sentences and we had to guess the verb structure.*
- *As we did the grammar quizzes in the first semester, I was familiar with this exercise. I liked these from the start as it is a little different from the usual exam layout.*
- *There were not too many questions and it was well structured in terms of the questions themselves.*

Good timeline:

- *I liked it because there was no time limit on the activity. This gave you plenty [of] time to complete the quiz.*
- *It was a black and white way of getting marks but you were not pressured by a time limit to see how much you know, which is one of the biggest faults in exams.*

Deeper understanding:

- *It helped me to be able to differentiate between the different tenses and helped me to grasp more of an understanding of the tenses. I really liked the idea of a grammar quiz.*
- *I finally learned for myself the differences between tenses, especially within the past tense and how to use them.*

Less stressful:

- *It is a less pressurised way of examining.*

Integrative:

- *It was a great method of revision for such a theory-based part of the course.*

Conclusion

This chapter has outlined the transition from a purely face-to-face delivery of a course on Teaching English as a Foreign Language to a blended format, combining traditional face-to-face elements and enriching them through the use of a Virtual Learning Environment

(VLE). We have moved from a situation where traditional instructional formats were used (namely lectures and tutorials in tandem with end-of-semester written exams and other written and classroom-based assignments) to a situation where some of these still apply but have been enhanced by the flexibility afforded to us and our learners by virtual learning applications such as wikis, quizzes and discussion forums. Additionally, we have been able to overcome the ephemerality of our classroom presence by recording our lectures and further add to their value by making vodcasts. These provide an opportunity to both summarise face-to-face lectures (and in so doing provide an extra embodiment for learners) and they allow us to add more content in manageable amounts, which learners can then access at a time and place that suits them best. We feel this has promoted deeper learning through more manageable content for learners.

Our evaluation shows that while there are challenges and things that we can improve upon, our learners have responded very positively to these innovations and that there is certainly enough evidence that this is something to continue with on our programme. For us, it has been an interesting journey and it could not have happened without the appropriate professional development to bring our e-learning skills into the 21st century. We, in turn, had to provide learner training for our students so that they too could engage with new learning tools. Along the way, there were many frustrations and it was, with hindsight, important to have taken a one-semester lead-in (see Figure 11.4) where we simply became confident in the new virtual learning space.

For our learners, we could see, in comparison to previous years on the programme, that we had provided much more depth of content. We had fostered a level of collaborative learning that we had never before achieved. We had given students the chance to learn independently of us in a scaffolded environment. We have been able to address the challenge of trying to cover extensive content on grammar without properly affording our learners time to engage fully with it. We could watch their work from within the LMS and see how their collaborations were progressing (or not) and yet we did not intrude on their work.

A spin-off that we had not anticipated is that by capturing our lectures and recording vodcasts, we have been able to scrutinise closely our own teaching and reflect on how we could better present our material and construct more learning opportunities. We have done this both individually through personal reflection but also through Peer Observation of Teaching (POT).

All in all, despite the challenges of becoming a competent user of e-learning tools, we have found this a highly rewarding experience and cannot see a reversion to solely using face-to-face teaching and exam-based assessment as our key platform for learning.

At a theoretical level, through observance of the instructional strategies laid out earlier in this study, the successful design, development and deployment of two English Language Teaching (ELT) modules was accomplished. A gradual shift along Ertmer and Newby's (1993) continuum from a behaviourist model of learning to a more constructivist one was realised, aided by consistent and moderated use of the student-centred activities available on the Moodle LMS. Allied to this was the implementation of activity theory as a sound framework for designing a CLE both in the classroom and online. Communities of Inquiry (CoI) were fostered among students where a deeper and more self-regulated approach to learning replaced more superficial and summative exam-driven engagements with the course and its content. The issues outlined in Student Evaluations of Teaching (SETs) have been addressed and assessment now has a formative as well as summative dimension.

This chapter documents a process of change and transition, which had many challenges and many rewards. At an institutional level, other colleagues followed a similar path and we are now at a point where there is a critical mass of academics who have moved from traditional face-to-face to BL teaching modes. Crucial to this transition has been the establishment of a support unit called the Blended Learning Unit (BLU) and the existence of a stable and supported VLE. With the help of Educational Technologists in this BLU, we have been able to sustain this change within our institution (as advocated by McCarthy, Chapter 1, this volume). On this particular module, we have continued to survey and tweak our materials and assessments every semester. Through the cycle of innovation and evaluation, we can keep learning from our students and improving what we do. Overall, we have learned that both students and lecturers need a lot of support in the transition to BL.

Suggested Resources

Akkoyunlu, B., & Soylu, M. Y. (2006). A study on students' views on blended learning environment. *Turkish Online Journal of Distance Education*, 7, 43–56. Online at: http://tojde.anadolu.edu.tr/tojde23/pdf/article_3.pdf

Conole, G. (2013). *Designing for Learning in an Open World*. New York: Springer.

Garrison, D. R., & Kanuka, H. (2004). Blended learning: Uncovering its transformative potential in higher education. *The Internet and Higher Education*, 7(2), 95–105.

Ruey, S. (2010). A case study of constructivist instructional strategies for adult online learning. *British Journal of Educational Technology*, 41(5) 706–720.

Salmon, G. (2000). *E-Moderating: The Key to Teaching and Learning Online*. London: Kogan Page Limited.

Discussion Questions

1. Reflect on your current teaching context: is there any aspect of what you do in a face-to-face classroom environment that might be supplemented by an online task? For example, grammar revision or developing writing skills.

2. If you were to introduce this online supplementary activity, what would be the most suitable type of task, for example, an online quiz, a discussion forum, a wiki, a blog or something else?

3. What challenges do you think your students would face in the transition from a face-to-face to an online task and how would you support them?

4. What challenges would you as a teacher foresee in this transition to an online task and how would you address these in terms of professional development?

5. When you make a change in your teaching or design new materials, it's always important to find out or evaluate whether it has worked and whether your students liked it. If you were to make a change, such as to use a discussion forum, how would you evaluate the transition from a face-to-face discussion task to an online forum?

References

Al-Qahtani, A. A. Y., & Higgins, S. E. (2012) Effects of traditional, blended and e-learning on students' achievement in higher education. *Journal of Computer Assisted Learning*, 29(3), 220–234.

Akkoyunlu, B., & Soylu, M. Y. (2006). A study on students' views on blended learning environment. *Turkish Online Journal of Distance Education*, 7, 43–56. Online at: http://tojde.anadolu.edu.tr/tojde23/pdf/article_3.pdf

Akyol, Z., & Garrison, D. R. (2010). Understanding cognitive presence in an online and blended community of inquiry: Assessing outcomes and processes for deep approaches to learning. *British Journal of Educational Technology*, 42(2), 233–250.

Bloom, B. S., Engelhart, M. D., Furst, E. J., Hill, W. H., & Krathwohl, D. R. (Eds.) (1956). *Taxonomy of Educational Objectives: The Classification of Educational Goals*. Handbook I: Cognitive Domain. New York: David McKay Company.

Chin, C., & Brown, D. E. (2000). Learning in science: A comparison of deep and surface approaches. *Journal of Research in Science Teaching*, 37(2), 109–138. Online at: http://onlinelibrary.wiley.com/doi/10.1002/%28SICI%291098-2736%28200002%2937:2%3C109::AID-TEA3%3E3.0.CO;2-7/abstract

Department of Education and Skills, Ireland (2003). *The Future of Higher Education*. Online at: http://www.dfes.gov.uk/hegateway/strategy/hestrategy/pdfs/DfES-HigherEducation.pdf

Dixon-Krauss, L. (1996). *Vygotsky in the Classroom: Mediated Literacy Instruction and Assessment*. White Plains, NY: Longman.

Engeström, Y. (1987). *Learning by Expanding: An Activity-theoretical Approach to Developmental Research*. Helsinki, Finland: Orienta-Konsultit Oy.

Ertmer, P. A., & Newby, T. J. (1993). Behaviorism, cognitivism, constructivism: Comparing critical features from an instructional design perspective. *Performance Improvement Quarterly*, 6(4), 50–70.

Garrison, D. R., Anderson, T., & Archer, W. (2001). Critical thinking, cognitive presence, and computer conferencing in distance education. *American Journal of Distance Education*, 15(1), 7–23.

Garrison, D. R., & Kanuka, H. (2004). Blended learning: Uncovering its transformative potential in higher education. *The Internet and Higher Education*, 7(2), 95–105.

Garrison, R., & Vaughan, H. (2008). *Blended Learning in Higher Education: Framework, Principles and Guidelines*. San Francisco: Jossey-Bass.

Gómez, L. U. O., & Duart, J. M. (2012). A hybrid approach to university subject learning activities. *British Journal of Educational Technology*, 43(2), 259–271.

Higher Education Authority, Ireland (2011). *National Strategy for Higher Education to 2030*. Dublin: Higher Education Authority. Online at: http://www.hea.ie/sites/default/files/national_strategy_for_higher_education_2030.pdf

Jonassen, D. H. (1991). Objectivism vs. constructivism: Do we need a new paradigm? *Educational Technology: Research and Development*, 39(3), 5–14.

Jonassen, D., & Rohrer-Murphy, L. (1999). Activity theory as a framework for designing constructivist learning environments. *Educational Technology Research and Development*, 47(1), 61–79.

Klein, D., & Ware, M. (2003). E-learning: New opportunities in continuing professional development. *Learned Publishing*, 16, 34–46.

Leont'ev, A. N. (1981). The problem of activity in psychology. In J.V. Wertsch (Ed.), *The Concept of Activity in Soviet Psychology*. Armonk, NY: Sharpe.

Marton, F., & Säljö, R. (1976). On qualitative differences in learning – 1: Outcome and process. *British Journal of Educational Psychology*, 46, 4–11.

Mary Immaculate College (2012). *Strategic Plan 2012–2016*. Limerick, Ireland: Mary Immaculate College. Online at: http://www.mic.ul.ie/presidentsoffice/Documents/Strategic%20Plan%202012-2016.pdf

Palincsar, A. S. (1998). Social constructivist perspectives on teaching and learning. *Annual Review Psychology*, 49, 345–375.

Ruey, S. (2010). A case study of constructivist instructional strategies for adult online learning. *British Journal of Educational Technology*, 41(5), 706–720.

Salmon, G. (2000). *E-Moderating: The Key to Teaching and Learning Online*. London: Kogan Page.

Vygotsky, L. (1978). *Mind in Society: The Development of Higher Psychological Processes*. Cambridge, MA: Harvard University Press.

Weigel, Van B. (2002). *Deep Learning for a Digital Age*. San Francisco, CA: Jossey-Bass.

Young, J. R. (2002). Hybrid teaching seeks to end the divide between traditional and online instruction. *Chronicle of Higher Education*, 48(28), A33–34.

NOTE

[1] In year 3 of the four-year degree programme, undergraduates take a one-year work placement. Many of those who take the modules in English Language Teaching teach English in private and state schools in Europe.

CHAPTER 12

A Case Study in Blended Learning Course Design

Jeanne McCarten and Helen Sandiford

INTRODUCTION

This chapter will describe the process of creating a blended English language teaching product based on a successful published course series. It will discuss the challenges of designing a product whose use was intended to be entirely flexible between print and online and how these challenges were met. In addition, it will outline the benefits and limitations posed by the online learning environment for highly interactive materials that emphasise inductive learning (where learners notice language patterns and start to formulate rules about them) and the teaching of conversation management skills. At the heart of creating the product was the need to address one of the most significant differences between the print and online media. The print material assumes the role of a teacher as the interpreter of the content, using methods of instruction learned from their professional training and experience which are prompted by the content or suggested in the accompanying Teacher's Book. In the online world, on the other hand, the material needs to provide content, method and teacher roles; the computer is both tutor and tool (Levy, 1997). This chapter will describe the principles behind the design of the material, with particular reference to teaching grammar and conversation management strategies, and set out solutions that were chosen to meet the many challenges. Finally, some preliminary results from studies after the adoption of this particular blended learning (BL) programme by a number of institutions are briefly reported on.

BACKGROUND TO THE BLENDED LEARNING PRODUCT

The motivation to create a blended product was a joint partnership between the Laureate International Universities network (http://www.laureate.net/) and the publisher of this book, Cambridge University Press, as part of a larger, much more ambitious programme on the part of Laureate to redefine and restructure the Laureate English Programme (LEP).

The need for a blended approach to their English language programmes became apparent largely because of the difficulty for universities in the network to provide sufficient face-to-face classroom instruction to enable students to reach a B1 (CEFR) level of language proficiency, which was a clearly defined objective of the LEP. It was clear that a blended approach to learning – with students using print material in the classroom, and online material out of class in their own time – would potentially address the challenge, though in many ways a blended solution would also present many challenges of its own.

Since Cambridge University Press had not previously developed a Learning Management System (LMS) for blended product, Laureate was able to collaborate closely in the development of the platform (see Johnson and Marsh, 2013, for a description). With the LMS platform being designed and built from scratch, the partnership team then focused on the issue of developing the language content for the online programme. It was determined to use existing print material as a basis for the online product, because this meant there was ready access to a rigorous, multi-syllabus course structure, which would provide the foundation for the online content. Based on its global success and popularity with large numbers of teachers and students, as well as its corpus-informed approach to language learning, *Touchstone,* (McCarthy, McCarten and Sandiford, 2005a, 2005b, 2006a, 2006b) was selected.

At the time of developing the *Touchstone Blended* product, starting in late 2007, BL was already an established concept in many areas of education, though relatively few English language programmes were using fully integrated blended product. The impact of e-learning or computer-assisted learning (CALL) in language programmes was well-researched (e.g., Coryell and Chlup, 2007), and the potential of these 'new' technologies in enhancing language acquisition had attracted keen interest. Other research at this time focused on learners' experience of blended programmes, for example reasons for student dropout from such programmes, which included lack of support (Stracke, 2007), while other research considered how best to design BL environments (Neumeier, 2005).

While many individual teachers were experimenting with using e-learning tools in their classrooms, much teacher feedback expressed at professional conferences and seminars indicated that teachers were confused by products available on the market, had little knowledge of how to effectively use the technologies then available, or how to integrate them in their classrooms, and were struggling with restrictive institutional budgets. Nevertheless, there was a perceived interest in blended product. The Cambridge-Laureate partnership was an opportune moment to develop a truly integrated learning programme, drawing on the range of Web 2.0 tools on the market (e.g., voice tools, message boards, blogs, etc.). The vision was to not only incorporate all these tools into one LMS platform, but to create a platform and online course that were user-friendly, that provided rigorous content, and that supported teachers in what would be a very different approach to language teaching – one that we realised teachers could possibly find threatening or beyond their current level of expertise.

THE STARTING POINT: *TOUCHSTONE* PRINT EDITION

The starting point was, as noted above, *Touchstone* print edition, which had been published for just under two years. This is a four-level English Language Teaching (ELT) series in North American English for adults and young adults, which takes students from beginning to intermediate levels (CEFR: A1–B2). The Student's Book was designed for use in the classroom, assuming a teacher as the interpreter or mediator of the material together with a group of students who would work variously as a whole class, in pairs, in groups and independently. Further practice material for student homework is provided in a Workbook and the teacher is supported by the Teacher's Edition, which offers a suggested teaching approach, extra activity ideas, tests, answer keys and scripts for the audio material. Informed by the North American sub-corpora of the Cambridge English Corpus (www.cambridge.org/corpus), its language and skills syllabuses are widely acknowledged to have broken new ground, not least in the area of conversation management skills. Extensive research into conversational data was the basis of an innovative and unique syllabus strand of conversation management development (see McCarten, 2010; McCarten and McCarthy, 2010).

The development of conversational fluency, as described by McCarthy (2010) and which is central to the material, needs a high degree of in-class pair- and group-work to practise the strategies and language items taught. In terms of methodology, *Touchstone* employs a number of techniques including 'noticing' (Schmidt, 1990; McCarthy, Chapter 1, this volume). After studying a conversation for its informational content, students are exposed to a strategy employed by one or more speakers and are then required to find further examples of it within the same conversation. Inductive and noticing learning techniques also extend to the teaching of grammar. After comprehension checks and discussion of the main language presentation vehicle (e.g., a conversation, an article), *Figure it out* activities focus students' attention on one or more aspects of a target structure. Students must notice something about a structure's form (e.g., simple present third person verb endings, the use of relative pronouns) or meaning (e.g., the hypothetical meaning of some conditional structures), applying what they 'figure out' to form or complete new sentences or answer questions correctly. Figure 12.1 shows one such activity, which follows on from an interview article in which Christopher talks about his circle of friends.

Figure it out C   **How does Christopher express these ideas? Underline the sentences in the article.**

1. Nina is an interesting woman. She sits across from me at work.
2. Jen plays in a rock band. It's really hot right now.
3. Angela is a new friend. I met her through Mike.
4. Jen calls me a lot to talk about things. She's doing a lot of things.

Figure 12.1   Extract from *Touchstone Second Edition* Student's Book 3 (McCarthy, McCarten and Sandiford, 2014: 66)

Students are guided through this process by a teacher, who draws attention to the main issues and works through an example before students attempt the whole exercise. This carefully planned learning sequence, which is 'scaffolded' by the teacher (Lantolf, 2000), then leads into a grammar chart, which the teacher can then use to explain the structure(s) in full (see Figure 12.2 opposite). The Teacher's Edition fully supports the teacher in this process. It contains both explanations of each grammar point for the teacher's own reference as well as explicit guidance on how to teach the *Figure it out* exercise sequence, including possible scripts which can be used verbatim in class.

Throughout, students are required to personalise the material, comparing their experiences to that of the exercise content, telling true anecdotes and expressing their own views. The material is thus highly interactive in terms of its content – with the emphasis on conversational language and skills, as well as how students engage with this content and with each other. In addition, these interactions are set up, guided, supervised and monitored by the teacher. This use of the print product encompasses the four modes of classroom discourse identified by Walsh (2006): the teacher's *managerial mode* of classroom and activity organisation; *materials mode*, as students are doing the activities; *skills and systems mode*, as teachers elicit, explain or correct a particular language item or skill; and

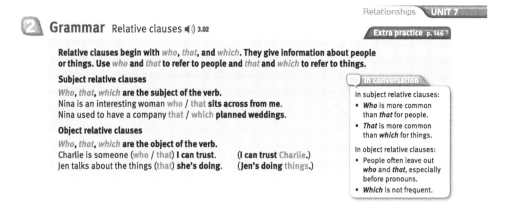

Figure 12.2 Extract from *Touchstone Second Edition* Student's Book 3 (McCarthy, McCarten and Sandiford, 2014: 67)

classroom context mode, as students relate personal experiences in what are often termed 'freer practice activities' (see also Walsh, Chapter 3, this volume). This is the nature of the material which had to be delivered as far as possible in an online, self-study medium as part of the blended programme.

THE KEY CHALLENGES

MACRO-LEVEL CHALLENGES

The challenges in creating online activities and writing online material that captured the essence of the pedagogy and underlying methodology of *Touchstone* were not to be underestimated. In the broadest sense, we were tasked with writing online material that could truly be used in self-study mode, supporting the student in the absence of real-time input or feedback from a teacher in the classroom, and without interaction with peers.

Equally challenging was determining which activities from the print material could be recreated online, and which could not. Some activities simply wouldn't translate into a self-study environment, and were best left in print for purely classroom use, for example, *Talk about it* group discussions and debates, and *Free Talk* type information-gap activities and class 'games'. Other activities (e.g., those with one or a limited number of correct answers) lent themselves better to the principles of online and translated well into online tasks, while a third subset of activities were created to enhance the online learning experience and were only suited to an online format, such as video role-play tasks, etc. In essence, it was critical to ensure that a print page was not simply being recreated in a simplified online format, but rather enhanced and fully utilising all the benefits that come with an online medium (see also McCarthy, Chapter 1, and Mishan, Chapter 8, this volume). In addition, it was important to create as many print tasks as possible online to ensure that face-to-face classroom time could be used to focus on tasks that did not translate well into an online environment.

Language activities needed to be engaging and compelling, ensuring that students would not lose interest or indeed find the activities childish or intellectually demeaning. Furthermore, we had to ensure that students were actually learning language, and not simply enjoying a variety of fun activities without building language skills.

Whilst the ability to create an enjoyable and motivating experience along with the ideal of ensuring a steady progression in language skills was perhaps the major challenge in creating online materials for English language learners, there were other factors to consider. Flexibility of time is certainly a benefit for students when studying under a BL model (see Moloney and O'Keeffe, Chapter 11, this volume). However, many students can experience difficulty in managing their time, and the obstacles that accompany being a more independent learner can potentially impact a student's progress (Vaughn, 2007). These issues needed to be addressed in the online programme to ensure that students could easily navigate the material, manage their time, and train to be an independent learner, responsible for their own learning. As Johnson and Marsh (2013) found in the preliminary results of an ongoing study, 'The confident "digital native" is not necessarily a confident "digital learner"'; we have to enable learners to access the information they need effectively.

A further challenge was to ensure that the activity types we created for online learning did not reinforce 'passivity' (Filipczak, 1995) or a lack of engagement and activity, especially in students who were perhaps also reluctant to participate in face-to-face interactions in the classroom. Being out of a classroom environment could potentially impact those students who, for whatever reason, including shyness or cultural pressures not to speak out, may avoid speaking English as much as possible. Studying online for these students could potentially provide an environment where they could easily 'hide' and avoid verbal tasks altogether.

MICRO-LEVEL CHALLENGES

One of the underlying pedagogical approaches of *Touchstone* is inductive learning. In its approach to grammar and conversation strategies students are asked to notice patterns of language or expressions that are used in a conversational or writing strategy, for example. Clearly, in a classroom, a teacher is instrumental in making such an approach work effectively for students, guiding them to look in the right place, helping them figure out patterns, and helping explain the basic underlying grammar point or strategy. In an online environment, students have to navigate the same inductive approach successfully by themselves. The activity types had to be specially designed, to allow students to readily refer back to presentation material to search for the target patterns within the constraints of a single screen.

Another typical feature of *Touchstone* is that students have multiple opportunities to speak, react and respond in meaningful ways to content throughout a lesson. Invariably, students are required to personalise the language also. This is extremely challenging when dealing with an online format, since activities tend to have to be 'closed down' (i.e., they can have only one or a limited number of correct answers, which can be easily marked by the software), and largely require students to select correct answers in a variety of ways. Designing activities that allow for personalised responses, and a similar degree of meaningful input, was a key challenge, as was finding a way to replicate some kind of interaction with other students. Clearly, while it is possible in an online medium to record your own voice, for example, that in no way replicates the true experience of interaction in class with a partner.

In the classroom the teacher has a fundamental role in explaining grammar, conversation strategies, pronunciation, etc. With the teacher absent in an online medium, we had to find ways to simulate the role of the teacher, finding ways to explain often abstract concepts without the use of a student's first language, and without overwhelming students by using difficult meta-language. Additionally, there needed to be ways for students to revisit the explanations if they did not understand at the first attempt – much as students would ask a teacher in class to explain something they did not understand, the kind of classroom interaction advocated by Walsh (Chapter 3, this volume).

CHALLENGES FOR TEACHERS

In developing online materials, many of our concerns rested with addressing student needs and determining how best to make the experience successful for a wide variety of learner types and individual differences (Skehan, 1991; Oxford and Anderson, 1995; McCarthy, Chapter 1, this volume). However, we were also keen to address the issues that would face teachers in adopting a BL model. For many teachers, getting to know the basic technologies would be the first challenge. Countering teachers' reluctance to use a new approach to teaching – and in some cases the resulting feeling of loss of control, especially in cultures where teachers are expected to transfer knowledge to their students – was another (Lam, 2000; Demetriadis et al., 2003). But technological capabilities and cultural perceptions apart, the primary concern was largely: would teachers know *how* to implement a blended programme in their classrooms?

At a very basic, practical level, blended programmes require teachers to reconsider their lesson plans, and decide exactly what they wish to teach or manage in class vs. what they want students to do on their own, whether that be preparation work prior to class, completing activities started in class, extra revision work or additional practice work. Juggling a blended approach was not likely to be as straightforward as simply assigning traditional homework at the end of a lesson. There is an almost infinite variety of ways to use BL programmes in class. This fact presented a challenge in terms of guiding teachers to discover the blend that worked best for them. Factors to consider included the teacher's unique teaching style, maximising the use of class time and creating the best possible blend for students' needs. This challenge had to be addressed not only in the development of the actual online student materials but also in additional support and training guides for teachers themselves (see also Comas-Quinn, Chapter 5, and Lázár, Chapter 9, this volume).

One of teachers' most common requests to course developers is for assistance with testing and monitoring progress of individual students. Teachers with particularly large classes are often concerned that they do not have sufficient time to read and mark large quantities of written work regularly (Hayes, 1997). Developing an online programme that can help teachers with these difficulties is not necessarily straightforward. Enabling teachers to track and monitor students' progress was just one part of the equation; testing and marking work – especially more extended pieces of writing – was quite another, which would still require teacher input and time. Managing teacher expectations about the benefits and limitations of a BL programme was also an issue (Larsen, 2012; Mendieta Aguilar, 2012).

DESIGN CRITERIA

The creation of online material presents many of the same issues as print material. In both media, writers seek successful learning to take place, by offering material which is engaging, varied, clear, reliable and accurate in content, well-paced and pitched at the right level. In both there should be a sense of progression through recycling and a sense of purpose through setting tasks that students perceive they can successfully achieve. The online environment presents new challenges as the material provides not only the learning content, but also the means of delivery of that content (methodology) as well as guidance through it, feedback and explanation (tutor) (see Mishan, Chapter 8, this volume). It addresses a sole learner for whom the learning environment must additionally supply support.

The overriding aim for the design of the online course was to retain the key principles on which the material was based: to use natural, corpus-informed language (see McCarthy, Chapter 1, this volume), to incorporate inductive learning, to teach conversation skills explicitly, to encourage autonomous learning and to be as enjoyable and engaging as the print material was with users. It should also include as many of the key principles of good language instruction as identified by various researchers in second language acquisition studies (see Ellis, 2005).

Initially, the print Workbook was converted into an online format for a limited number of Laureate universities in 2009. User feedback from the Laureate pilot programme was closely monitored and informed the development of the final product, which included the more challenging Student Book.

FLEXIBILITY AND 'CONNECTEDNESS'

A first step was to analyse the learning outcomes of the material to determine which outcomes would be part of which element of the blend: the print for in-class use or the online for (largely) self-study use. It was soon decided that there should be a one-to-one correlation between the print and online learning outcomes. No type of activity would be off limits in the online format with the exception of synchronous interactions between teacher and student and student and classmates. The capabilities of social networking were not sufficiently built into the LMS to allow for this.

The primary aim was to achieve the same standard of material in the online material as in the print. Secondly, it was important to make the links or connections between the print and online material obvious to student and teacher. Third, teachers should be free to decide which parts of the material were for in-class use and which for online use. In other words, there should be clear 'connectedness' as well as 'flexibility' (see Nagel and Kotzé, 2011). These notions of flexibility and connectedness were important. With such an innovative product, we had no preconceptions about how institutions and teachers might wish to create their own blends, or how students would access and even explore the material. It was therefore vital that the *Touchstone Blended* project offer complete flexibility with regard to the proportions of the content being delivered online from 100% to 1% and all points in between. Many modes of use were envisaged, as were different institution types, course lengths, structures and aims, teacher preferences and student needs. For example, in some settings, teachers might assign whole lessons for online use whereas others might assign specific sections. Some might have students prepare for class online and others might use the online material for consolidation. Any and all options were to be made possible, giving teachers the choice of how to develop and exploit their individual blends. Furthermore, as such forms of BL were relatively new, it was also important to offer teachers the potential to change and further develop their chosen blend at any point.

Connectedness was an important criterion as we wanted teachers to know exactly what the online content contained by reference to the print rather than produce a separate set of different and 'less visible' online materials. For teachers who were new to *Touchstone* there would already be a steep learning curve in terms of several aspects of the syllabus, particularly the spoken interaction, its corpus-informed ethos and noticing methodology, as well as all that is involved in becoming familiar with a new course. The concept of BL would also be new to many, further complicating the task of getting to know the new material. Further, having the print and online material closely matched would more readily facilitate flexibility of use. Students too would benefit from being able to see the connection between their print and online materials, aiming at the sense of integration supported by Johnson and Marsh, Chapter 4, by King, Chapter 6, and by Mishan, Chapter 8, in this volume.

PUTTING THE LEARNER AT THE CENTRE

Successful use of the material would rely on the student-user experience being positive in the broadest sense. This would not just be a matter of general enjoyment, but ease of use and, perhaps most importantly of all, measurable success in achieving learning outcomes. The design of the online material had to provide a simple, clear navigational system, which clearly showed the best route through the material. The sequential nature of much of the material and inbuilt recycling meant there were few options to depart greatly from this route and adaptive learning design was still some way off. Nevertheless, students would need a measure of control over, for example the number of times they listened to some of the audio material, or did an exercise. Options to skip over sections were incorporated, as were options to review reference material.

The privacy of the self-study environment would allow for repeated practice attempts, especially valuable for face-threatening activities in class, such as speaking, including pronunciation, and listening. In this way, it was hoped that students with Foreign Language Classroom Anxiety (Horwitz et al., 1986), or simply students with lower confidence levels in speaking out in class, would be more than adequately supported.

At each stage it was a principle that students were to be carefully guided through the material as if by an unseen teacher, the design of the activities incorporating the teacher role as far as possible. The material would have to provide the different modes of discourse (Walsh, 2006), extra activities and good models that the classroom teacher would. The important point was that students should not feel disadvantaged in any way by the lack of a teacher. Quite the opposite.

STUDENT ENGAGEMENT AND PRODUCTION

Many of the activity types, or templates, that were available for use in computer-based learning necessarily relied heavily on closed-item response activities. Students click True or False answers, choose the correct answer in multiple-choice, drag and drop labels or matching items, and so on. Some allow for limited and highly predictable written responses. This enables the software to check and record answers and provide basic feedback. Activities that require freer and less predictable, personalised written or spoken production of students need greater teacher involvement and could not at the time be accurately assessed by the software. Thus, in designing computer-based materials bound by such software constraints, there is great danger of creating a degree of passivity in learners. Creating opportunities for active student engagement with the material as well as freer student production would be a challenge, but absolutely necessary (see, for example, the case discussed in Moloney and O'Keeffe, Chapter 11, this volume).

However, interaction with the language through the guided noticing and inductive techniques in the print material, especially in teaching grammar instruction and conversation, was to be kept as a key principle of the methodology. Some of this could be achieved through the traditional templates described above, but other aspects required the design of new templates.

The explicit teaching and practice of spoken interaction skills was firmly rooted in the print Student Book though practice in written exercises was also to be found in the print Workbook. The online material would have to find a way of creating further opportunities for meaningful use and to enable interaction even if asynchronous. As a key principle, all language presentations were to be followed by meaningful interactive activities that gave opportunities of use of target items (Buttery and Caines, 2012).

PRACTICE IS LEARNING

A further issue arose as to whether it would be necessary to distinguish between different types of activities in the reporting mechanisms for teachers. Some activities were designed as presentation to be part of the teaching/learning sequence and others served as practice activities following a presentation or explanation. In the online self-study environment, the format of activities with both these functions could well be the same; for example matching words with pictures could equally function as a way of presenting vocabulary as well as practising or even testing it. One question was: should students be graded on inductive learning activities in the same way as on activities that practised their knowledge of a language item? Another question related to whether students should be allowed to redo the practice activities as many times as necessary to score 100%. The final view was that the online course was a learning not a testing environment, that all activities contributed to learning, and students would not be penalised for not getting the answers correct at their first attempt. Testing would be done under other conditions outside of the main lesson material.

Creating the Blend
Implementing the design criteria

As noted previously, one of the key aims in creating the blended product was to allow for 100% flexibility in use and connectedness by ensuring a one-to-one correlation between the learning outcomes for print and online. Therefore the online material was designed to follow the progression of activities in the print textbook, mirroring its content and organisation with the exception of freer pair and group discussion activities. The aim was that learners could move seamlessly from print to online and vice versa. Simple numbering and use of the textbook headings also contributed to the familiarity with the online units.

Accommodating the student at the centre of the learning experience resulted in various features designed specifically for the online programme. Additional lesson aims were provided online as well as the unit aims that were in the textbook, ensuring that students could clearly identify the purpose of every set of activities. The material was easy to navigate, allowing students to move easily between screens, and offered degrees of control in enabling students to check answers, redo activities, replay the audio and skip parts of the presentation material (see below).

To encourage independent learning, both progress tracking and 'help' features were included. Students were provided with a 'See my progress' feature, enabling them to track their progress and get immediate feedback. Student self-monitoring of progress has been seen as a relevant feature of online learning; see, for example, the discussion in Dahinden and Faessler (2011). In addition, teachers are able to release students' grades through an online grade book feature, allowing students to track their progress through the course. Access to help mechanisms were provided, such as: 'hints' for activity answers; help notes with explanations such as a teacher might offer; dictionary definitions; and model answers, where appropriate, for freer writing activities. A record and compare function enabled students to compare their spoken production in conversation and pronunciation practice with the audio.

Giving students opportunities to practise language without the presence of a partner was accomplished in several ways. To simulate conversation practice with a partner, a video role-play function was included so that students could practise the conversations 'with' one of the actors. The group and pair discussion activities were not included online because the software functionality was not available, but asynchronous communicative activities were devised to replace in-class exchanges and provide students with opportunities to use the language for meaningful communicative exchanges, rather than for learning display purposes. Most lessons end with students writing a blog based on a specific question related to the lesson, which is posted for classmates to read. Students are then encouraged to read others' blogs and respond, thus setting up an exchange and creating a sense of community (Yang, 2009). Forum discussion threads were set up, which students are encouraged to participate in and add to, and voice tools allow students to leave spoken messages for the teacher and each other. These opportunities to write and speak to others were an important part of reducing passivity and engaging students.

To this end, much of the presentation material in the textbook, e.g., conversations, 'on the street interviews', telephone messages, etc. were video recorded for the online presentations, occasionally with additional script for the purposes of setting context, especially in the 'on the street interviews' where an interviewer was included. Additionally, a series of fun, interactive vocabulary and grammar games were developed as a way to recycle language and increase motivation. Often the games were timed to provide additional tension and challenge and 'game-like' quality (see the discussion on the relationship between computer games and language learning in Petersen, 2013). Students are able to attempt these activities again and can also see their progression through a game as well as their scores.

To guide students through a scaffolded sequence of activities, new warm up, vocabulary pre-teaching and preview activities for the presentation material were added online. These activities were of the type that teachers would use typically in class and ensured that students had sufficient support as they tackled the main teaching and practice activities. In addition, multiple photos were added online, to give visual support for vocabulary and to create context. Further, additional practice was provided so students not only had the exercise items in the textbook, but additional items were added for further reinforcement. Many whole new activities were added throughout for the grammar, which was often broken down into smaller 'chunks', and new listening activities were created to help in an area which students often find problematic.

LANGUAGE INSTRUCTION

In terms of explicit language instruction, the inductive nature of the content was retained. In teaching conversational language, for example, it was necessary to devise an activity template that allowed students to highlight examples, as a way of showing that they had found further examples of the strategy employed, as required in the print material. The *Figure it out* approach to grammar was also retained. However, in order not to overwhelm the self-study learner, grammar structures were often broken down into smaller chunks (e.g., statements and questions), so that different aspects could be figured out and then presented separately. This is one example of how the online material was able to build and improve or enhance (see Sharwood Smith, 1993) the print material, where space restricts what can be done. The online material was able to give increased attention to certain items by such separation to facilitate noticing and attention (see also McCarthy, Chapter 11, this volume, as well as the caveat mentioned by Hojnacki, this volume).

Animated presentations for language explanations, much as advocated by Garrett (2009) for grammar, were created not only for grammar structures, but also for conversation strategies, pronunciation, writing tips and vocabulary learning strategies. These arose out of a close collaboration between the authors and the designers. A 'typescript' was written for every screen of every sequence of every presentation, organised into three simultaneously-developed parts. These were 1) the text students would read on screen, 2) a detailed description of the art and/or animation that accompanied or were applied to the text and 3) the audio students would hear when reading the screen. See Figure 12.3 below for an example.

Alongside this, one of the first tasks of the designer was to design a screen template which would be flexible enough to deliver a range of explanatory content in an accessible way. The result was a screen that was divided into three areas. At the top was the 'Narrator area,' which showed the type of presentation (e.g., Grammar), the name of the target structure or language (e.g., Relative clauses) and the 'Narrator line.' This was where the main

TEXT ON SCREEN	ANIMATION	AUDIO
Listen. Nina is a woman. She sits across from me at work.	Narrator explains. Pick up photo of Nina (#4) from SB 3 p. 66. Male character speaks. Split dialog into two speech balloons.	[N] Listen. [M1] Nina is a woman. [M1] She sits across from me at work.

TEXT ON SCREEN	ANIMATION	AUDIO
You can make this into one sentence like this. 1 Nina is a woman. She sits across from me at work. 2 Nina is a woman She *who* sits across from me at work 3 Nina is a woman *who* sits across from me at work.	Narrator explains. Animation: 1 Same sentences from previous screen appear. 2 Erase the period. Use tombola to have *she* replaced by *who* to make one new sentence. 3 New sentence is read aloud.	[N] You can make this into one sentence like this. [M1] Nina is a woman who sits across from me at work.

Figure 12.3 Excerpt from Typescript for an Animated Grammar Presentation from McCarthy, McCarten and Sandiford, 2010: *Touchstone Online*

explanation appeared and it was accompanied by an icon that represented the teacher. (Different icons and colours for each type of language explanation were accompanied by different voices: grammar, conversation strategies, and so on.) The middle part of the screen was where the animation was to take place and any accompanying art shown. This might consist of people and speech balloons containing target structure examples, sentences with coloured and/or moving parts, charts that showed structures in a dynamic way. The bottom part of the screen was the navigational area, where students could start or pause a presentation, go backwards or forwards, skip a section, or fast forward to the final 'summary' screen, which was a dynamic audio-visual form of the print grammar chart. See Figure 12.4.

To enable students to understand the explanations, all text which was heard also appeared on screen. Most of the language explanations were also written in simple English at the learner's level and to fit one or two lines in the narrator area. All the explanations remained on screen for the required duration of following examples. In the animations area, most of the examples referred back to the language presentations students had just studied, using the same context and characters. In most cases where a new structure was being taught, one example would appear at a time until it was appropriate to build up a pattern or contrast with other examples.

The explanations were all newly conceptualised and written to be delivered to a self-study student. To achieve the objective of aligning the learning outcomes of print and online, the end point of each grammar section was an animated version of the grammar chart in the print material, which was called the 'Summary' screen. This was recorded and gave

Figure 12.4 Excerpt from Grammar Presentation in McCarthy, McCarten and Sandiford, 2015: *Touchstone Online*

opportunities for students to listen and repeat the examples. It also served as a reference, which students could locate easily when doing the exercises.

Leading up to the final summary screen was the majority of the teaching content. It was often necessary to change the order of teaching points in the print chart or break them down into smaller sections so that the material could be more appropriately sequenced and paced for self-study. Each section had its own *Figure it out* and following practice activities before the whole chart was brought together in a final section. The narrator typically explained the context for the new structure and then gave examples, which were often animated. The space restrictions of the printed page meant that not every permutation of a structure or relevant issue could be shown in one easy-to-read, 'manageable' chart. Freed from such restrictions, where it was considered useful, further explanations and examples, such as a teacher might introduce, were added. For example, structures and terms were always defined at some point; before the present simple was taught, a short explanation of verbs was given. Similarly, if the example sentences in a verb paradigm began with pronouns, examples with noun subjects would be added online. Also animated were the corpus information *In conversation* boxes, which showed, for example, relative frequencies of items. The importance of careful design of self-study elements and the general relationship between online materials development and the fostering of learner autonomy is discussed in Hafner and Miller (2011).

Conclusion

An ongoing programme of research was carried out at a number of Laureate universities in Europe, Asia and South America to investigate the impact of implementing *Touchstone Blended Learning*. Classes were benchmarked in 2010 and 2012, i.e., before and after the implementation of *Touchstone Blended Learning* in 2011. An initial survey by Johnson and Marsh (2013) reported on a number of positive findings in terms of more student interaction and participation in class with reduced teacher talking time; teachers also reported that their own teaching experience improved. Further, the implementation of blending learning was found to increase student learning efficiency and autonomy. With regard to learning achievement, early studies (see, for example, Laureate International Universities Case Study, 2013) found that the students in the blended programme achieved higher levels of attainment than those who had been taught using only print materials with previous courses. There was a marked progression with a shift up the CEFR scale to the intermediate (CEFR B1) and upper-intermediate (CEFR B2) levels, and fewer at beginner levels (CEFR A1/A2), as shown in Figure 12.5.

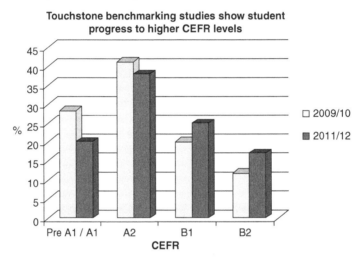

Figure 12.5 Chart Showing Progression Shift Observed in the Laureate International Universities Case Study

The effectiveness of the *Touchstone Blended Learning* product will, it is hoped, be increased through a continuing programme of future enhancements based on user feedback. At the present time, these might include clearer labelling of online activity sets to make the connectedness with the print material even closer, more varied forms of delivery of the animated language presentations with interactive concept checking elements as well as the development of templates to enable more extended student production. However, initial results illustrate that by providing increased opportunities for use of English outside of the classroom and making more effective use of classroom time (i.e., focus on production skills), BL can be more effective than classroom-only based instruction.

Suggested Resources

Dahinden, M., & Faessler, L. (2011). Monitoring blended learning environments based on performance data. Online at: http://www.cta.ethz.ch/publikationen/pdf/11_iadis_rom_dahinden

Mendieta Aguilar, J. A. (2012). Blended learning and the language teacher: a literature review. *Colombian Applied Linguistics Journal*, 14(2).

Nagel, L., & Kotzé, T. G. (2011). Choosing the best from blended and online e-learning. *Progressio*, 33(2), 151–173.

Neumeier, P. (2005). A closer look at blended learning – parameters for designing a blended learning environment for language teaching and learning. *ReCALL*, 17(2), 163–178.

Vaughn, N. (2007). Perspectives on blended learning in higher education. *International Journal on E-Learning*, 6(1), 81–94.

Discussion Questions

1. If you were to implement a BL programme in your institution using your current textbook, which aspects of the course would you like to be delivered online and which in the classroom?

2. What criteria would you use to decide on the right blend for your situation?

3. What training, if any, would you need to give students to make them confident digital learners?

4. What training, if any, would teachers need and how might their role(s) change?

5. If you were assessing a new BL publication, what criteria would you use to assess it and to decide whether or not to adopt it for your institution?

References

Buttery, P. J., & Caines, A. (2012). Normalising frequency counts to account for 'opportunity of use' in learner corpora. In Y. Tono, Y. Kawaguchi & M. Minegishi (Eds.), *Developmental and Crosslinguistic Perspectives in Learner Corpus Research* (pp. 187–204). Amsterdam: John Benjamins.

Coryell, J. E., & Chlup, D. T. (2007). Implementing e-learning components with adult English language learners: Vital factors and lessons learned. *Computer Assisted Language Learning*, 20(3).

Dahinden, M., & Faessler, L. (2011). Monitoring blended learning environments based on performance data. Online at: http://www.cta.ethz.ch/publikationen/pdf/11_iadis_rom_dahinden

Demetriadis, S., Barbas, A., Molohides, A., Palaigeorgiou, G., Psillos, D., Vlahavas, I., Tsoukalas, I., & Pombortsis, A. (2003). 'Cultures in negotiation': Teachers' acceptance/resistance attitudes considering the infusion of technology into schools. *Computers & Education*, 41, 19–37.

Ellis, R. (2005). Principles of instructed language learning. *System*, 33(2), 209–224.

Filipczak, B. (1995). Putting the learning into distance learning. *Training*, 32(10), 111–112, 114–118.

Garrett, N. (2009). Computer-assisted language learning trends and issues revisited: Integrating innovation. *The Modern Language Journal*, 93, 719–740. doi: 10.1111/j.1540-4781.2009.00969.x

Hayes, D. (1997). Helping teachers cope with large classes. *ELT Journal*, 51/2, 106–116. Oxford: Oxford University Press.

Horwitz, E. K., Horwitz, M. B., & Cope, J. (1986). Foreign language classroom anxiety. *The Modern Language Journal*, 70(2) 125–132.

Johnson, C., & Marsh, D. (2013). The Laureate English Program: Taking a research informed approach to blended learning. *Higher Learning Research Communications*, 3(1).

Johnson, C., & Marsh, D. (forthcoming). Research Report December 2013 Laureate Teachers. *Higher Learning Research Communications*.

Hafner, C., & Miller, L. (2011.) Fostering learner autonomy in English for Science: A collaborative digital video project in a technological learning environment. *Language Learning and Technology*, 15(3), 68–86.

Lam, Y. (2000). Technophilia vs. technophobia: A preliminary look at why second-language teachers do or do not use technology in their classrooms. *The Canadian Modern Language Review*, 56(3), 389–420.

Lantolf, J. P. (2000). *Sociocultural Theory and Second Language Learning*. Oxford: Oxford University Press.

Larsen, L. J. E. (2012). *Teacher and Student Perspectives on a Blended Learning Intensive English Programme Writing Course*. Online at: http://lib.dr.iastate.edu/etd/12375

Laureate International Universities Case Study (2013). Online at: http://www.cambridge.org/servlet/file/Laureate+Case+Study+Ecuador+-+July+2013.pdf?ITEM_ENT_ID=7434197&ITEM_VERSION=1&COLLSPEC_ENT_ID=7

Levy, M. (1997). *Computer-assisted Language Learning: Context and Conceptualization*. Oxford: Oxford University Press.

McCarten, J. (2010). Corpus-informed course book design. In A. O'Keeffe & M. J. McCarthy (Eds.), *The Routledge Handbook of Corpus Linguistics* (pp. 413–427). Oxford: Routledge.

McCarten, J., & McCarthy, M. J. (2010). Bridging the gap between corpus and course book: the case of conversation strategies. In F. Mishan & A. Chambers (Eds.), *Perspectives on Language Learning Materials Development* (pp. 11–32). Oxford: Peter Lang.

McCarthy, M. (2010). Spoken fluency revisited. *English Profile Journal*, 1, e4. doi:10.1017/S2041536210000012

McCarthy, M. J., McCarten, J., & Sandiford, H. (2005a). *Touchstone* Student's Book 1. Cambridge: Cambridge University Press.

McCarthy, M. J., McCarten, J., & Sandiford, H. (2005b). *Touchstone* Student's Book 2. Cambridge: Cambridge University Press.

McCarthy, M. J., McCarten, J., & Sandiford, H. (2006a). *Touchstone* Student's Book 3. Cambridge: Cambridge University Press.

McCarthy, M. J., McCarten, J., & Sandiford, H. (2006b). *Touchstone* Student's Book 4. Cambridge: Cambridge University Press.

McCarthy, M. J., McCarten, J., & Sandiford, H. (2010). *Touchstone Online* Cambridge: Cambridge University Press.

McCarthy, M. J., McCarten, J., & Sandiford, H. (2014). *Touchstone Second Edition* Student's Book 3. Cambridge: Cambridge University Press.

Mendieta Aguilar, J. A. (2012). Blended learning and the language teacher: A literature review. *Colombian Applied Linguistics Journal*, 14(2).

Nagel, L., & Kotzé, T. G. (2011). Choosing the best from blended and online e-learning. *Progressio*, 33(2), 151–173.

Neumeier, P. (2005). A closer look at blended learning – parameters for designing a blended learning environment for language teaching and learning. *ReCALL*, 17(2), 163–178.

O'Keeffe, A., McCarthy, M. J., & Carter, R. A. (2007). *From Corpus to Classroom*. Cambridge: Cambridge University Press.

Oxford, R. L., & Anderson, N. J. (1995). A crosscultural view of learning styles. *Language Teaching*, 28, 201–215.

Petersen, M. (2013). *Computer Games and Language Learning*. New York: Palgrave Macmillan.

Schmidt, R. (1990). The role of consciousness in second language learning. *Applied Linguistics*, 11, 129–158.

Sharwood Smith, M. (1993). Input enhancement in instructed SLA: Theoretical bases. *Studies in Second Language Acquisition*, 15, 165–179.

Skehan, P. (1991). Individual differences in second language learning. *Studies in Second Language Acquisition*, 13, 275–298.

Stracke, E. (2007). A road to understanding: A qualitative study into why learners drop out of a blended language learning (BLL) environment. *ReCALL*, 19(1), 57–78.

Walsh, S. (2006). *Investigating Classroom Discourse*. London: Routledge.

Vaughn, N. (2007). Perspectives on blended learning in higher education. *International Journal on E-Learning*, 6(1), 81–94.

Yang, S.-H. (2009). Using blogs to enhance critical reflection and community of practice. *Educational Technology and Society*, 12(2), 11–21.

SECTION 5

THE FUTURE OF BLENDED LEARNING

The title of **Chapter 13** includes the words: 'new tools, new learning experiences', which represents the core of Dudeney and Hockly's vision for the potential of mobile technologies in language learning. This vision is that the smartphones, tablets and other mobile devices which play such a routine part in the daily lives of many people can not only provide new channels and media for the kinds of language learning we are familiar with but also new types of learning experience not previously envisioned. The challenge, as in many of the other chapters in the present volume, is the successful integration of such new tools and what they can offer into the world of teachers and learners in an unthreatening and motivating way, so as to provide learning outcomes that lead to success. Most notably, Dudeney and Hockly see such outcomes extending beyond the classroom into lifelong learning in the world outside, and, in reverse, the technology offering new ways of bringing the outside world to the classroom. By engaging the users' natural, daily use of mobile devices (e.g., to take photographs, make videos, record audio, send text messages, etc.) in the service of language-learning tasks, the mobile devices become more than bolt-on extras to the existing technologies, and offer new and unforeseen possibilities for blended learning (BL) and for 'flipping' classroom practices. As with other chapters in this volume, exploiting the technology should be grounded in robust learning theories, and learners will need guidance and help in the transition from more behaviourist uses of their devices towards more creative, constructionist contexts, and uses which integrate seamlessly into best-practice language teaching. Mobile learning is a 'new literacy', offering the potential for new life skills as well as enhanced and motivating language learning.

In **Chapter 14**, San Pedro and Baker examine the benefits of adaptive learning, that is to say, the ability of the machine to give tailored, personalised feedback to the user in computer-mediated learning. Although personalisation is possible without technology, technology can enhance the potential for individual feedback, as well as offering institutions economically viable ways of providing learning programmes for large populations of learners in ways that would be impossible in conventional classrooms. Flexibility is at the heart of adaptive learning; the ability of the machine to adapt quickly to the circumstances of its users and provide moment-by-moment feedback based on what it knows and what it can learn about its users is its greatest asset. In good adaptive systems, cognitive science, educational psychology and artificial intelligence come together to solve problems. The machine effectively creates a model of its users; it cannot adapt 100% to every individual's characteristics but it can base its decisions on what is known about key aspects of learning. Not only whether the student is getting things right or wrong forms the basis of effective feedback, but also the student's preferences, their learning strategies, their motivation and degree of engagement all become part of what the machine should learn about its users. As with other aspects of BL discussed in this book, adaptive technology releases time for different, more complex activity in the face-to-face classroom. At the time of writing, San Pedro and Baker admit the limitations of current systems but foresee developments that will result in systems having a more subtle, complex and enriched understanding of their users.

McCarthy concludes the book in **Chapter 15** by bringing together the preoccupations of all of its authors and attempting to draw the complex threads of BL together. While there is no definitive theory or agreed best practice for BL at the present time, it is clear that some basic approaches are emerging, with the multitude of blends in existence falling into some overall major types. Although BL programmes in various disciplines have much in common, language learning is special, in that language is both the medium and the goal of the teaching and learning. This brings us squarely back to the importance of understanding second language acquisition and the central role of interaction as observed in good face-to-face classrooms. Without such an understanding, decisions as to what to 'flip' to the world of computer-mediated learning will lack the solid grounding needed and will just become arbitrary and technology-led instead of pedagogy-led. While on the one hand notions such as learning through interaction, the scaffolding provided by teachers and peers, the moment-by-moment exploration of learning opportunities that good teachers enact might be best carried out in the face-to-face classroom, on the other hand, the technology itself is providing ever new ways of communicating and the ability to use these forms part of a new literacy that can be a transformative feature of technology-assisted language learning. Challenges remain, planning is all important and a proper understanding of the transformative nature of the teaching 'material' BL brings about. Questions such as how learners learn best, how we can provide authentic language learning experiences, how pedagogies such as task-based learning can be enhanced through technology, the growing importance of mobile technology and how language learning can be embedded in a sense of community are all exciting avenues for the future of BL.

CHAPTER 13

Blended Learning in a Mobile Context: New Tools, New Learning Experiences?

Gavin Dudeney and Nicky Hockly

INTRODUCTION

The increasing popularity, ubiquity and affordability of mobile or 'handheld' devices has profound implications for language learning and in particular for blended learning (BL). Mobile devices are not just mobile in the sense of 'portable'. They can make the learning experience itself mobile if the teacher is able to design pedagogically sound and imaginative communicative tasks that take the learning experience beyond the classroom walls.

These mobile-based 'bridging' activities can link learning that takes place inside the classroom with both formal and informal learning outside the classroom. Well-designed bridging activities exploit the unique affordances or capabilities of handheld devices to encourage learners to engage with their surroundings, and to both process and produce language, based on their experiences.

Features such as geolocation and augmented reality are already present in 'smart' mobile devices, and can support language learning. 'Geolocation' refers to the ability of an internet-connected device to pinpoint where you are geographically; 'augmented reality' technology superimposes information on the real world, via apps that can access a device's camera to provide an enhanced or 'augmented' view of reality. However, few teachers feel confident in designing tasks that utilise these features, which can present unique learning opportunities. It remains for teachers to both understand how these mobile device affordances can link to language learning objectives, and how to design effective classroom-based tasks around them. These mobile-based classroom-based activities may then, in turn, serve as a springboard to a more blended approach, using bridging tasks as a connecting principle between what happens in class, and what happens outside of it.

This chapter takes as its starting point Laurillard's (2012) observation that classroom practitioners need to become designers of effective learning experiences (see also the discussion of Laurillard's ideas in Mishan, Chapter 8, this volume), and explores that assertion in the light of a short action research project carried out with two different multinational classes of EFL learners studying in the UK over the summer of 2013. The project led – via an implementation of mobile-based tasks – to the development of six parameters for consideration with regard to effective design and sequencing of tasks in mobile contexts.

In this chapter we describe the study and mobile-based tasks, and explore the six key parameters for designing mobile-based tasks for the communicative language classroom that emerged from the study: parameters which may be applicable to other fields of education, and are of particular relevance to models of BL that seek to include the use of mobile devices.

The chapter finishes by examining how a classroom-based implementation of mobile-based activities can provide the necessary skills and experience to encourage a wider adoption of mobile and handheld learning, where 'bridging activities' serve as a mobile version of BL, encouraging a link between activity and learning inside and outside the classroom.

Brief Literature Review

Defining Mobile Learning

One aspect of blended education which is proving itself difficult to outline or even accurately describe is the very concept of 'mobile learning' (mLearning). Indeed, many of the principle researchers in the field have yet to reach agreement on the issue (Kulkulska-Hulme, 2009a; Traxler, 2009). The very concept of 'mobility' is, in itself, a complex one, being open to a wide variety of interpretations of what exactly constitutes a valid use of the word in educational settings. In short, 'who' or 'what' is mobile? In one approach, mobile may refer to the mobility ('freedom of movement') of the participants, both teacher and learner, and to the possibility that they can take their learning with them, studying in any location, and at a time of their choosing, using mobile devices.

Yet the term 'mobile' can also refer to the tools themselves: feature phones and smartphones (feature phones can access the internet and have camera functionality, but lack the advanced features of smartphones), digital cameras, video cameras, games machines, MP3 players, e-readers and a number of other gadgets which are themselves mobile by definition: they are (or can be) operated solely on battery power and can, where appropriate, access the internet wirelessly or through mobile phone data. This view might best be described as a technocentric one, having at the centre of the discussion the technologies themselves.

Although both features and affordances are clearly important, there is another layer to mLearning: the layer of context. mLearning can be experienced in more formal and traditional classroom settings, but also in less formal surroundings, allowing for a smooth transition between the four walls of the classroom and the world outside those four walls. In short, this is what we refer to as 'bridging activities', and these activities lend themselves well to a blended approach. In a more rounded view of mLearning, materials may be consumed or produced on a wide variety of tools (see above), experienced in a variety of physical and temporal arenas and involve collaboration and networking (Sharples et al., 2009; Kulkulska-Hulme et al., 2009b; Hoven and Palalas, 2011). mLearning then is perhaps the most modern incarnation of BL, and a key characteristic of one of the most modern varieties of BL, the flipped classroom.

Pegrum (2014) explores this tension of mobility between tool, location and learning further, dividing mLearning into three distinct categories and thus providing a helpful way of conceptualising these interrelated aspects. He suggests that that the use of mobile devices in education as a whole, and language learning in particular, frequently falls into one of his three categories, each of which corresponds to a different emphasis, i.e., devices, learners and learning experiences:

1. Learning that takes place when the *devices* are mobile.
2. Learning that takes place when the *learners* are mobile.
3. *Learning experiences* which are mobile.

It is helpful for a greater understanding of this distinction to dig deeper into these three categories. The first – describing learning that takes place when the *devices* are mobile – is typical of what Pegrum (Ibid.: 16) refers to as 'connected classrooms' where students use their own mobile devices, or class sets provided by the institution, to create and consume content, access the internet, etc. Here, clearly, 'mobile' does not refer to actual mobility, since the learners are confined to the classroom (or, in a flipped mode, working at home) and are not physically mobile. In this model some of the more 'mobile' characteristics and affordances of mobile devices (geolocation being a prime example) are not generally exploited, and the learning is firmly rooted in the physical space of the classroom or other interior space.

In Pegrum's second category of mLearning, we see an opening up of the classroom to the world outside. In this category it is the *learners* themselves who are mobile: moving around the classroom or the wider institution whilst engaging with learning opportunities, or taking advantage of quieter moments in their lives outside the classroom, perhaps the daily commute or similar moments, to engage with short chunks of language-based content as a revision or extension activity carried out in self-study mode. This might take the shape of discrete content applications such as flashcards for reviewing vocabulary or test preparation materials such as those produced by the major ELT publishers, or more rich content such as downloaded audio or video, or online reading material in the target language. What does not change in this category is the learning experience itself – this remains fundamentally the same, wherever the learning materials are accessed from, and wherever the learners themselves may be.

Moving briefly to consider the third category – where the *learning experiences* themselves are mobile – this describes opportunities for learners to use their devices in an extensive range of real-world contexts, accessing real-time information as needed, creating multimedia records of learning on the move and recording and extending their knowledge and learning in situ, wherever that learning may take place. Tasks using more sophisticated mobile affordances (GPS, augmented reality, weather forecasts, time and date, etc.) are typical of this kind of learning where the device can customise the experience through an awareness of the user's location, time, the local weather, day of the week and more. Such tasks suggest a greater degree of memorability, being based in real-life experiences at concrete times and locations. This kind of mLearning is perhaps the most disruptive, and the most difficult to implement consistently and in a principled and strategic manner.

This then is a brief overview of what mLearning is. We now move on to consider how it fits with current education practice.

mLEARNING AND NEW LITERACIES

mLearning is becoming fixed into new approaches to learning, and new concepts of what it means to be literate today. It is now not uncommon to read of 'twenty-first century skills' in curriculums worldwide, as changes are made to more traditional educational approaches in order to equip learners with a new range of skills for the new millennium (see for example the 'Partnership for 21st Century Skills' initiative: http://www.p21.org/). These skills do not themselves replace the traditional 'three Rs' (reading, writing, and 'rithmetic or maths), but rather complement them and extend them, giving learners skills they will need to enter the workplace and participate in our increasingly connected world, preparing them for new jobs and new ways of working.

The discourse around these skills varies considerably globally: in the United States one most commonly encounters 'twenty-first century skills' or 'new media literacies', whilst in the UK we tend to refer to them as 'digital literacies' and in Australia they may be 'digital literacy skills'; further afield in countries as far apart as Finland and Spain one can readily find references to 'digital competences' (Belshaw, 2011).

But whilst the terminology varies, the core concept is remarkably unchanged on the journey: digital literacy refers, in its basic form, to the understanding and best use of technology. This is not a concept that focuses on the acquisition of discrete skills connected to individual technologies, such as the ability to make a presentation using PowerPoint; digitally literate learners (and teachers) know what it means to use PowerPoint, and what PowerPoint can achieve, or help them to achieve. Knowing how to use Facebook is a skill; knowing how to use it to build an effective learning community for yourself is a literacy. This, in a nutshell, is the essential difference. Being digitally literate involves not just 'technical' or 'technological' skills, but a deep awareness of the social practices that surround the effective use of technology, as well as understanding how technology can help develop critical thinking skills.

HOW THEN DO MOBILES AND MLEARNING FIT INTO THE NEW LITERACIES?

Dudeney, Hockly and Pegrum (2013) explore digital literacies in some detail, dividing them into four main areas: literacies focused on language, on information, on connections and on (re)design. Mobile literacy itself is placed in the language category: digital literacies that focus on communication via the language of text, image and multimedia. And mobile literacy is considered a key skill of the twenty-first century: 'Teaching mobile web literacy seems to me to be as crucial as teaching basic literacy' (Parry, 2011). But what exactly does this literacy involve?

In its most basic form, mobile literacy involves an understanding of how mobile technology is transforming our world, from issues of hyperconnectivity (always being connected to the internet, and the personal and wider social implications of this), to understanding how to use mobile affordances such as geolocation and augmented reality. Yet mobile phones and similar devices are still most often perceived as somewhat problematic in education, where issues of focus and concentration appear to clash with having connected devices in the hands of learners. This is exacerbated in the language class, where perceptions of an erosion in the quality of language produced by learners are coupled with teacher anxiety that an over-reliance on translation and phrasebook style apps and resources may impact negatively on the independence of learners. Many of these concerns are a result of teachers simply misunderstanding how mobile devices can be used by learners, but they also arise from draconian and outdated policies that prohibit the use of such devices in schools. Key to acquiring mobile literacy and integrating it into the classroom are school policies regarding acceptable mobile use, as well as negotiation between teachers and learners as to best practice in and out of class.

mLEARNING IN ENGLISH LANGUAGE TEACHING

mLearning in the language teaching profession, or MALL (Mobile Assisted Language Learning), to give it its more specific title, is a relatively new field in a long line of CALL (Computer Assisted Language Learning) or TELL (Technology Enhanced Language Learning) developments and, consequently, currently suffers from a lack of robust and reliable research. Even the umbrella term 'MALL' has come under some scrutiny (Jarvis and Achilleos, 2013), with proposals for an alternative 'MALU' (Mobile Assisted Language Use) as representing a more accurate reflection of how mobile and handheld devices may be used for learning. As Pachler (2009: 4) notes, longitudinal mLearning studies are particularly challenging due to the ever-evolving nature of the devices themselves. Additionally, like CALL, MALL suffers from a lack of a single unifying theoretical framework on which to hang any evaluation of its effectiveness and this can lead to a wide range of mainly anecdotal studies which contribute little to a solid research base (Egbert and Petrie, 2005). However such studies are set up, the underlying driver behind many mLearning projects and initiatives remain budget constraints and, ultimately, the hardware itself, and these inevitably impact on the approach chosen and the results uncovered.

As we have already noted, there is a wide variety of devices that can potentially fall under the term of 'mobile device' (MP3 players, video cameras, games consoles and more) but it should be noted that there has been a trend in recent years towards the concept of convergence, with the average smartphone or tablet computer incorporating – and therefore replacing – many other devices and their functionalities such as video recording, digital photography, audio recording, note taking, drawing and sketching, mind-mapping and beyond. Whilst first inroads into mLearning in mainstream education may have been made using XO laptops under the auspices of projects such as the One Laptop Per Child (OLPC) initiative, it is far more likely these days – where technologies are being implemented – to see examples of One Tablet Per Child (OTPC) projects in action. A look at recent or current international mLearning projects being implemented would seem to confirm this trend towards smaller, more converged devices (see, for example, UNESCO's reports on global mobile projects: http://www.unesco.org/new/en/unesco/themes/icts/m4ed/mobile-learning-resources/unescomobilelearningseries/).

Examining more closely the literature reviewing mLearning initiatives within the field of English Language Teaching we can identify three different types of project, each with a different level of funding, scalability, timeframe, etc.:

1. Large-scale projects, often, but not exclusively, undertaken in developing countries and jointly funded by a combination of non-governmental organisations (NGOs), Ministries of Education (MoEs), hardware providers, software providers and communications infrastructure companies, often mobile phone operators. These are sometimes also partnered with educational institutions such as the British Council or a particular university (see Pegrum, 2014, for examples).
2. Small-scale projects carried out in institutions, chains of language schools or universities. These take place in both developing and developed countries and tend to focus on the strategic implementation of mobile devices to support more traditional language learning. Examples of good practice in this respect range from individual language schools such as the Anglo European School of English in Bournemouth (where the authors have had some experience with the project) to larger institutions such as the Cultura Inglesa or Casa Thomas Jefferson schools in Brazil or the British Council in Hong Kong (see Hockly and Dudeney, 2014, for more on these case studies).
3. Projects initiated by individual teachers who are both early adopters themselves, and enthusiastic users of mobile technologies. These teachers experiment with the technologies on an ad hoc basis with small groups of students, often with little or no institutional support. Exponents of this kind of approach at the time of writing include Anne Fox in Demark, Paul Driver (formerly working in Portugal, now in the UK, see - http://digitaldebris.info/) and Karin Tiraşim and Çigdem Ugur in Turkey (see Hockly, 2012 for a brief overview of some of these).

AN ACTION RESEARCH PROJECT

This then is the current terrain. We turn our attention now to look briefly at a small-scale action research project carried out by one of the present authors (Hockly) in the summer of 2013 to explore factors influencing task design for mobile activities. This project serves as a springboard to considering a more strategic adoption of mobile technologies and the creation of mobile-based bridging activities to extend learning outside the classroom in a more blended model.

The research project itself was carried out with two small multinational groups of learners studying English as a Foreign Language (EFL) at a private language school in Cambridge, United Kingdom, over a period of two weeks in July 2013.

The first group of 12 learners (Week 1) were mainly of Arabic origin, with one Chinese and one Russian speaker, with approximately half of the class being under 18 and the rest ranging between 20 and 45 years old. Their proficiency level was measured at A1 on the Common European Framework of Reference (CEFR). The second group (Week 2), at B1 level, was comprised of eight learners between the ages of 16 and 27, and was more mixed, with the learners coming from Kuwait, Italy, Brazil, Turkey, Argentina and China. Each of the two groups received three hours of classes with the researcher in the morning, and a further 1.5 hours in the afternoon with a different teacher. The afternoon teacher did not make much use of technology, aside from some IWB (Interactive Whiteboard) use.

The principal aim of the study was to explore the possible integration of the learners' own mobile and handheld devices into a prescribed coursebook-driven approach (administered at institutional level) as a possible supplement to, and enhancement of, the communicative task elements, and to evaluate the learners' reactions to such an approach. The notion of integration has been much discussed in the present volume (e.g., by Mishan, Chapter 8, King, Chapter 6, and Johnson and Marsh, Chapter 4, this volume). In short, then, it was to generate theory from practice, to create a practical framework for the design and implementation of mobile communicative tasks in the language classroom as a stepping-stone to bridging activities in a secondary implementation. Thus the project attempted to generate a 'mobile specific' theory (Vavoula and Sharples, 2009; Viberg and Grönlund, 2012) with potential wider implications for task design beyond the physical language classroom itself.

Based on the general demographic of learners coming to the school in summer months, a BYOD (Bring Your Own Device) approach was chosen, relying on the learners to come to the school with a smartphone or tablet computer of their own. It should be noted that this type of institution tends to attract affluent learners (or learners from affluent families). Complementary to this approach was the institution's reliable connectivity and available wi-fi for the learners, an important consideration for any mobile implementation.

Due to external factors around rolling enrolment, not much information about the learners was available in advance, and this factor necessitated activity redesign as the project progressed. Because of this, the research design changed from concentrating on affective factors to matters more closely linked to task design and sequencing. Indeed, two research questions surfaced over the two weeks:

- **Research question 1:** Is there any observable evidence for affective improvements with the use of mobile devices in language learning tasks (e.g., increased motivation, greater learner participation)?
- **Research question 2:** What pedagogical models of task design and sequence work best to facilitate learning through mobile devices, and to enhance its benefits?

STAGE 1: CLASS SURVEY

In the first week of the project each group was asked to complete an online mobile use survey to evaluate any previous experience with learning on mobile devices and their attitudes to the same. The survey also uncovered more practical considerations such as details of their devices, connectivity in the UK for their courses, etc.

Results between the two groups were remarkably similar: all of the learners had smartphones, but were mainly relying on the availability of wi-fi both at the school and, where provided, with their host families. With this in mind, task design had to concentrate on activities to be carried out in and around the institution only. In terms of learning on their mobile devices, the learners had only ever used bilingual dictionaries or translator apps, suggesting that the introduction of mobile-based activities would need to be gradual, carefully staged and closely supported. The learners themselves, however, were open to trying out this approach; no surprise perhaps, as learners' positive attitudes towards the idea of integrating mobile devices into their learning is reflected in the literature (e.g., Woodock et al., 2012; Mueller et al., 2012).

IMPLEMENTATION

Given the results of the initial survey, it was decided to implement a carefully-staged set of activities with each group, moving from simpler to more complex as the week progressed. The activities themselves – designed to develop or improve communicative competence appropriate to the linguistic level of the learners, and therefore focused on language production rather than consuming information via mobile devices – also had to have a real and noticeable connection with the coursebook. Consequently, activity design concentrated on open-ended tasks which encouraged the learners to produce spoken and/or written language; this had the added advantage of making some of the tasks suitable for both levels, with the output dependent on the their actual linguistic capabilities. Thus tasks were developed and aligned to the syllabus and coursebook content where appropriate, and learner feedback then impacted on the approach taken and the development of the tasks for the following day. In each case the coursebook and syllabus provided the backbone of the work, with the mobile activities giving learners the opportunity to further develop their competence whilst, hopefully, being stretched and challenged.

Figure 13.1. (below) provides a short summary of the mobile-related tasks undertaken with each group. More detailed descriptions can be found on the researcher's blog 'E-moderation Station' (http://www.emoderationskills.com/), and other links are provided below.

It should be noted that the activities above did not constitute the entire set of tasks the learners engaged with over the week. Much of the time was spent with coursebook content and these activities had to be fitted into this institutional requirement. This, however, is not far removed from the situation in which a typical teacher in any country in the world might find themselves, so it was a useful and beneficial exercise to ensure that the activities integrated well into an essentially externally-imposed syllabus, and were matched to the syllabus in terms of language content and topic.

RESEARCH QUESTION 1: INCREASED MOTIVATION AND PARTICIPATION

A survey administered at the end of the week found that an overwhelming majority had enjoyed using their mobile devices and would like to continue using them. However, the one learner who clearly did not feel that there were any benefits to mobile tasks (comments such as 'useless' and 'it doesn't work') was also the learner who had previously expressed

	BEGINNER GROUP (A1 LEVEL)	**INTERMEDIATE GROUP (B1 LEVEL)**
Monday	**Letter dictation** *The teacher dictated review questions letter by letter, while learners typed the letters into their mobile phones. The questions then formed the basis for a short speaking activity in pairs.* **Online mobile use survey** *Described above*	**Online mobile use survey** *Described above* ***QR code review** *The teacher created 4 QR (Quick Response) codes, each one containing a different question that reviewed language and vocabulary from previous classes. The students used their mobile phones to read the QR code questions, and provided short written responses on slips of paper.*
Tuesday	**We've got it** *The teacher provided a list of 10 photos for learners to find on their phones. Learners shared their photos in pairs, as a speaking activity.*	**We've got it** *The teacher provided a list of 10 photos for learners to find on their phones. Learners shared their photos in pairs, as a speaking activity.* ***Water photos** *The teacher gave the learners 10 minutes to go around the school and take two or three photos (with their mobile devices) of things they could relate to the coursebook topic of 'water'.* ***Water interviews** *Based on the coursebook topic, in pairs learners used their mobile phones to record each other telling a personal anecdote about an experience in the sea or a river.*
Wednesday	***QR code review** *The teacher created 4 QR (Quick Response) codes, each one containing a different question that reviewed language and vocabulary from previous classes. The students used their mobile phones to read the QR code questions, and provided short written responses on slips of paper.*	***Bombay TV** *Learners used a website to create subtitled videos.*
Thursday	****My mobile day** *The teacher read a short text about her use of her mobile phone in a typical day. The learners reconstructed the text from memory, then created their own 'My mobile day' texts.*	**16-18-20 Selfies** *After school, learners took 'selfie' photos at 16h, 18h and 20h. They brought their photos to the next class and shared them in small groups ('At 4pm I was ...'). The aim was to give meaningful and personalised practice with the past continuous (a language point in the current unit of the coursebook).*

(continued)

	BEGINNER GROUP (A1 LEVEL)	**INTERMEDIATE GROUP (B1 LEVEL)**
	**Mobile English *The teacher gave the learners 10 minutes to take photos (with their mobile devices) of examples of English around the school. They shared their photos in small groups as a short speaking activity.*	*** QR code treasure hunt** *The teacher created 10 QR (Quick Response) codes, each one containing a different instruction, and placed them in different parts of the school. The students used their mobile phones to read the QR code, and to carry out the instruction. The instructions included carrying out and recording short interviews with school personnel, taking photos of objects, reading information, asking questions.*
Friday	***QR code treasure hunt** *The teacher created 10 QR (Quick Response) codes, each one containing a different instruction, and placed them in different parts of the school. The students used their mobile phones to read the QR code, and to carry out the instruction. The instructions included carrying out and recording short interviews with school personnel, taking photos of objects, reading information, asking questions.*	**Guide to Cambridge** *Learners used their mobile devices to research a favourite place in Cambridge. They then each prepared an 'audio guide' with information about the place, and recorded it in Woices (a geolocation audio app – see http://woices.com/)*

* E moderation Station blog (posts for July–August 2013)
** See Hockly and Dudeney, 2014

Figure 13.1 Short Summary of the Mobile-related Tasks Undertaken with Each Group Participating in the Study

to other teachers a dislike for communicative tasks in general, preferring structured written grammar activities in class. This suggests that mobile tasks do not appeal to all learning styles or preferences but, perhaps more importantly, that there is a real need for explicit learner training in the benefits of using mobile devices and, possibly, the advantages of the communicative approach itself. This idea is supported by research (Stevenson and Liu, 2010; Çelik et al., 2012) which has shown that some learners online often prefer traditional activities such as vocabulary exercises to more social-networking oriented activities. This learner aside, the majority felt that the activities had improved both their English and their mobile literacy, though it should be noted, of course, that there is no solid evidence for their perceived improvement given the range of factors involved in second language acquisition (see McCarthy, Chapter 1, this volume).

To what extent, then, do the survey results address the first research question connected to affective improvements through the use of mobile devices for language learning tasks? Learner responses do seem to support this notion, with noticeably increased motivation and participation during some tasks (QR code tasks, as one example). Indeed, increased motivation can occur through meaningful deployment of BYOD initiatives, and this is borne out in the literature generally (e.g., Swan et al., 2005; Rau et al., 2008; Hwang and Chang, 2011). Clearly this is a small, informal, qualitative survey without statistical significance, but its results provide useful, positive feedback on the affective impact of the tasks.

RESEARCH QUESTION 2: TASK DESIGN AND SEQUENCING

The second question focused on identifying what pedagogical models of task design and sequencing facilitate learning with mobile devices and enhance its benefits. The initial survey (see above) was instrumental in defining a set of task design parameters. Key elements of these parameters were: hardware (what devices learners had access to) and connectivity (where learners had access to data connections). As also noted above, given the data connected to those two, it was clear that tasks would need to be based in and around the classroom itself and that, where implemented, mobile-based homework would not be feasible if it required an active connection. Referring back to Pegrum's (2014) three categories of mLearning, it was concluded that any attempt to address all three would, inevitably, be limited to the institution and its grounds, and this had a profound effect on mobile task design for the duration of the project.

The survey also revealed the range of devices in the group (a majority of iPhones coupled with two Android devices and one Blackberry – at the time of writing, the three most widely used platforms) ensuring that, at the very least, tasks that relied on the internal affordances of the devices (audio, video, geolocation, etc.) could be included. Other device-specific issues such as screen size were also considered, ensuring that any planned activities were based on taking photographs and recording audio and video, rather than on asking learners to produce lengthy written texts on small keyboards and small screens.

Given the relative lack of experience among the learners, at least in terms of using their devices for learning, tasks started small and at a low level of technological complexity so as not to overwhelm the learners. From the first day, which featured simple tasks such as short text dictation and online surveys (see Figure 13.1. above), tasks slowly increased in complexity and challenge to allow the learners to move through smaller comfort zones en route to a higher degree of mobile literacy. This process happened far more quickly with the intermediate group, as is to be expected, since they had both greater levels of technological competence to carry out the tasks, and also a higher linguistic level for interpreting task instructions and stages.

These considerations suggest two more important parameters for successful mobile task design: technological complexity and linguistic/communicative competence. Putting learners in a position where they are struggling with both the technology and the language would make task completion almost an impossibility.

Four discrete types of MALL are proposed by Pegrum (2014), each with its own particular focus:

- Content: e.g., self-study apps, often with audio/video content.
- Tutorial: e.g., non-communicative 'behaviourist CALL' activities such as vocabulary tests or flashcards, pronunciation, grammar quizzes and games.
- Creation: e.g., creating text, audio, video, presentations, comics.
- Communication: sharing digital materials and content via mobile devices either locally and/or globally via groups and shared spaces.

The first two types correspond closely to behaviourist models of learning in which content is largely consumed and reproduced in closely defined contexts, whilst the second two would appear to fit more closely to task-based or communicative approaches (see also the discussion in Moloney and O'Keeffe, Chapter 11, this volume). They are of course not mutually exclusive, and may indeed be used in conjunction with each other in the course of any class or activity. What this small study suggests, however, is that the guidance of some kind of expert or teacher is necessary, at least in the beginning, to ensure successful implementation of 'creation' and 'communication' MALL and that starting or setting up these activities in a class setting can be highly beneficial. This then suggests the fifth parameter for task design: the extent to which the task allows for creation or communication, or relies on content or tutorial approaches.

It seems fair to suggest that in a communicative language classroom all four approaches may be present at one and the same time, though ideally with an emphasis on creation and communication MALL. However, for learners with little or no experience of using their mobile devices for learning, or in more behaviourist educational contexts, it may be less disruptive initially to concentrate on content and tutorial MALL tasks, both in and outside class, before moving on to the second two. The learner in the study who did not relate to the approach taken may well have reacted more favourably if the introduction had been more carefully staged, time permitting. This gives us the sixth and final parameter for effective task design: the educational/learning context and 'best fit'.

We now have six key parameters for the effective design of communicative MALL tasks in the classroom:

- Hardware (device affordances – features and size – and connectivity).
- Mobility (devices, learners or learning experience).
- Technological complexity (related to the learners' technological competence).
- Linguistic/communicative competence.
- Content, tutorial, creation or communication MALL.
- Educational/learning context (related to learners' expectations and preferred learning styles).

This study strongly suggest that all six parameters must be considered – and coupled with more traditional elements such as syllabus fit and coursebook relevance (see McCarten and Sandiford, for example, Chapter 12, this volume) for effective MALL task design.

RESEARCH ISSUES

Clearly there are a number of caveats connected to this project, and these should temper any over-reliance on the results suggested above. As already noted, the research was both short and involved only small groups of learners in a very specific EFL environment and each group was only exposed to this combination of methodologies and approaches for 15 hours over the course of a week. This multicultural and multilingual context is not typical of much of the teaching that occurs globally, and it is also less stable in many ways – higher teacher turnover, higher learner turnover and temporary surroundings can lead to a more complex environment where experimentation is, at best, more difficult and unpredictable. Monolingual groups in stable school environments may produce significantly different results, and, more importantly, allow for more context-specific feedback about task design and sequencing.

Indeed, the low language proficiency of both groups made it difficult to solicit detailed feedback from the learners about their experiences. In monolingual contexts where the teacher speaks the learners' L1, much more complex and detailed feedback can be gathered.

Perhaps most significantly, the ad hoc nature of the research is its major drawback. Successful integration of mobile devices needs trained teachers, enthusiastic learners but, most importantly, institutional support, forming part of a wider and systemic mobile strategy. See Hockly and Dudeney (2014) for a detailed description of how to implement a mobile strategy at institutional level.

However, we do feel that this study, with its limitations kept firmly in mind, highlights some of the key parameters involved in designing and sequencing classroom-based communicative tasks for mobile and handheld devices.

IMPLICATIONS

MALL/MALU research is still very much a young research area, and more research is needed into developing robust frameworks for the design of mobile-based classroom tasks. We hope that the six parameters suggested above will make a contribution towards effective mobile task design and issues of sequencing, in some contexts.

What is still a stumbling block in most institutions is the lack of teacher training in technologies, with a resultant poor level of technical and technological competence amongst the teaching profession in general. A study into the use of handheld devices among graduate business students in the US, for example, found that 'the limited use [of handheld devices in class-related activities] may reflect pedagogical limitations as perceived by the instructors and lack of professional training and support around the implementation of mobile technology as a learning tool' (Mueller et al., 2012). To overcome this, teacher training programmes (both in-service and pre-service) need to ensure that the technological competence described in Mishra and Koehler's TPACK (Technological Pedagogical Content Knowledge) model (2006) is addressed on an equal basis alongside the more traditional content and pedagogical competences. Teachers also need to feel comfortable with a wide range of digital literacies and their integration in the classroom (Dudeney et al., 2013). And teachers need to feel that they have the opportunities for dialogue and collaboration with technology experts to provide the right kinds of educational breakthroughs that mLearning promises (see McCarthy, Chapter 1, this volume). Mobile is one of those key literacies: 'The future our students will inherit is one that will be mediated and stitched together by the mobile web' (Parry, 2011). Equipping teachers with these skills will ensure that learners receive the education they need for the twenty-first century.

CONCLUSION

We have seen that effective task design, coupled with strategic introduction and implementation can lead to a perceived increase in motivation and language production, as well as helping learners develop mobile literacy. It is from this starting point that we move on to consider the future of BL mediated by mobile devices and content, turning to the concept of bridging activities.

Once learners have worked through a set of initial classroom mobile-based tasks, as described above, they should be in a position to appreciate the potential impact of using their mobile devices in their learning and be ready to extend that learning beyond the comfort and support of the class into the rest of their lives, using the bridging activities previously suggested. These bridging activities are conceived as a way of enabling two-way communication between the class and the outside world, whereby learners take content from the language class and work on it outside, on their devices, but also collect content and experiences outside of the class and bring them back to class for further exploration and language production. Essentially, we are enabling our learners to 'go mobile' with their language learning (see Hockly and Dudeney, 2014).

In this context, content and tutorial MALL are again a familiar and comfortable place to start, giving learners an opportunity to further their study outside of class on their mobile devices, but in a more controlled and comprehensible manner: activities started in class can be extended and completed out of class. Apps from major publishers, for example, can provide more extensive grammar, listening and reading practice, freeing up more class time for activities where communication takes centre stage, or where teacher support and correction are more useful. This model works well, both in terms of the basics of BL itself but also of its more radical incarnation, the flipped classroom.

Extending the model further, and moving more towards creation and communication MALL, devices can be used to capture content outside of the classroom which can then be used as a springboard for more creative language production in class – bringing the outside in. This may involve collecting photographs, audio and video of places and people who are not connected with the classroom, but also content which is geolocated, or connected to a particular place and time. In this way, learners can easily work with the motivation of their own content, but with the guidance of the teacher to interpret this content and these experiences, pinning their language production on real-life experiences and needs. As Kulkulska-Hulme pointed out in her 2006 review of mobile language learning, the potential of mobile devices to provide learning experiences across a range of *contexts*, and to create a sense of *continuity* between formal and informal learning – both in and outside of class – is something that language educators would do well to take into account.

It is here, then, that we see one possible future of BL. With so many people now no longer tied to desks for the technological part of the blend, there is equally no longer a need for the blend to be based on static experiences. Taking the mobile device, which has the potential to become the most common, accepted and 'normalised' (Bax, 2003) piece of technology in the history of educational technologies, and putting that centre stage in the blend seems both obvious and desirable.

Suggested Resources

Dudeney, G., Hockly, N., & Pegrum, M. (2013). *Digital Literacies*. New York: Routledge.

Hockly, N., & Dudeney, G. (2014). *Going Mobile: Teaching with Hand-held Devices*. London: Delta Publishing.

Kukulska-Hulme, A., Sharples, M., Milrad, M., Arnedillo-Sánchez, I., & Vavoula, G. (2009). Innovation in mobile learning: A European perspective. *International Journal of Mobile and Blended Learning*, 1(1), 13–35.

Pegrum, M. (2014). *Mobile Learning: Languages, Literacies and Cultures*. London: Macmillan.

Traxler, J. (2009). Learning in a mobile age. *International Journal of Mobile and Blended Learning*, 1(1), 1–12.

Discussion Questions

1. Do you think there is a place for teaching 'digital literacies' in language classes? How might you go about integrating them with your normal materials and approaches?

2. Which of Pegrum's three categories of mLearning would work best in your context? Why? Is there one that simply would not work for you at all?

3. How might you go about introducing the use of mobile devices in your current teaching? What issues and challenges do you think you might encounter and how might you deal with them?

4. How might you deal with an institutional ban on mobile devices in your workplace?

5. When considering a blended approach in your context, how much of a blend would be right? What would you keep as classroom content and activities, and what might you hand off to homework and technology-mediated study?

References

Bax, S. (2003). CALL – past, present and future. *System*, 31(1), 13–28.

Belshaw, D. (2011). What is 'Digital Literacy'? A Pragmatic Investigation. PhD Thesis, Durham University. Online at: http://bit.ly/RbYK6W

Çelik, S., Arkin, E., & Sabriler, D. (2012). EFL learners' use of ICT for self-regulated learning. *The Journal of Language and Linguistic Studies*, 8(2), 98–118. Online at: http://www.jlls.org/vol8no2/98-118.pdf

Dudeney, G., Hockly, N., & Pegrum, M. (2013). *Digital Literacies*. London: Routledge.

Egbert, J. L., & Petrie, G. M. (Eds.) (2005). *CALL research perspectives*. Mahwah, NJ: Lawrence Erlbaum Associates. E-moderation Station blog (Posts for July–August 2013). Online at: http://www.emoderationskills.com

Hockly, N. (2012). Tech-savvy teaching: BYOD. *Modern English Teacher*, 21(4), 44–45.

Hockly, N, & Dudeney, G. (2014). *Going Mobile: Teaching with Hand-held Devices*. London: Delta Publishing.

Hoven, D., & Palalas, A. (2011). (Re)conceptualizing design approaches for mobile language learning. *CALICO Journal*, 28(3), 699–720.

Hwang, G. J., & Chang, H. F. (2011). A formative assessment-based mobile learning approach to improving the learning attitudes and achievements of students. *Computers and Education*, 56(4), 1023–1031.

IATEFL 2013 conference presentation 'Moving with the times'. Online at: http://iatefl.britishcouncil.org/2013/sessions/2013-04-11/moving-times-mobile-literacy-elt

Jarvis, H., & Achilleos, M. (2013). From computer-assisted language learning (CALL) to mobile assisted language use. *TESL-EJ*, 16(4), 1–18. Online at: http://goo.gl/Uuq5dr

Kukulska-Hulme, A. (2006). Mobile language learning now and in the future. In P. Svensson (Ed.) *Från vision till praktik: Språkutbildning och Informationsteknik (From vision to practice: language learning and IT)* (pp. 295–310). Sweden: Swedish Net University (Nätuniversitetet).

Kukulska-Hulme, A. (2009a). Will mobile learning change language learning? *ReCALL*, 21(2), 157–165. Online at: http://goo.gl/Pbv5n

Kukulska-Hulme, A., Sharples, M., Milrad, M., Arnedillo-Sánchez, I., & Vavoula, G. (2009b). Innovation in mobile learning: A European perspective. *International Journal of Mobile and Blended Learning*, 1(1), 13–35.

Laurillard, D. (2012). *Teaching as a Design Science: Building Pedagogical Patterns for Learning and Technology*. New York: Routledge.

Levy, M. (forthcoming 2015). Researching in language learning and technology. In F. Farr & L. Murray (Eds.), *Routledge Handbook of Language Learning and Technology*. New York: Routledge.

Mishra, P., & Koehler, M. J. (2006). Technological pedagogical content knowledge: A framework for teacher knowledge. *Teachers College Record*, 108(6), 1017–1054.

Mueller, J., Wood, E., De Pasquale, D., & Cruikshank, R. (2012). Examining mobile technology in higher education: Handheld devices in and out of the classroom. *International Journal of Higher Education*, 1(2), 43–53.

Mwanza-Simwami, D., Kukulska-Hulme, A., Clough, G., Whitelock, D., Ferguson, R., & Sharples, M. (2011). Methods and models of next-generation technology enhanced learning. In *Alpine Rendezvous*, March 28–29, La Clusaz, France. Online at: http://goo.gl/G5bLod

Pachler, N. (2009). Research methods in mobile and informal learning: Some issues. In G. Vavoula, N. Pachler, & A. Kukulska-Hulme (Eds.), *Researching Mobile Learning: Frameworks, Tools, and Research Designs*. New York: Peter Lang.

Parry, D. (2011). Mobile perspectives on teaching: Mobile literacy. *EDUCAUSE Review*, 46(2), 14–18. Online at: http://goo.gl/AKizd

'Partnership for 21st Century Skills' initiative. Online at: http://www.p21.org/

Pegrum, M. (2014). *Mobile Learning: Languages, Literacies and Cultures*. London: Macmillan.

Rau, P. L. P., Gao, Q., & Wu, L. M. (2008). Using mobile communication technology in high school education: Motivation, pressure, and learning performance. *Computers and Education*, 50(1), 1–22.

Sharples, M., Milrad, M., Arnedillo-Sánchez, I., & Vavoula, G. (2009). Mobile learning: Small devices, big issues. In N. Balacheff, S. Ludvigsen, T. de Jong, A. Lazonder, S. Barnes, & L. Montandon (Eds.), *Technology Enhanced Learning: Principles and Products* (pp. 233–249). Dordrecht, Germany: Springer.

Stevenson, M. P., & Liu, M. (2010). Learning a language with Web 2.0: Exploring the use of social networking features of foreign language learning websites. *CALICO Journal*, 27(2), 233–259.

Swan, K., van 't Hooft, M., Kratcoski, A., & Unger, D. (2005). Uses and effects of mobile computing devices in K-8 classrooms. *Journal of Research on Technology in Education*, 38(1), 99–113. Online at: http://www.eric.ed.gov/PDFS/EJ719939.pdf

Traxler, J. (2009). Learning in a mobile age. *International Journal of Mobile and Blended Learning*, 1(1), 1–12.

UNESCO reports on global mobile projects. Online at: http://www.unesco.org/new/en/unesco/themes/icts/m4ed/mobile-learning-resources/unescomobilelearningseries/

Vavoula, G., & Sharples, M. (2009). Meeting the challenges in evaluating mobile learning: A 3-level evaluation framework. *International Journal of Mobile and Blended Learning*, 1(2), 54–75.

Viberg, O., & Grönlund, A. (2012). Mobile assisted language learning: A literature review. In M. Specht, M. Sharples & J. Multisilta (Eds.), *mLearn 2012: Proceedings of the 11th International Conference on Mobile and Contextual Learning 2012* (pp. 9–16). Helsinki: Finland. Online at: http://goo.gl/mPOFs2

Woodcock, B., Middleton, A., & Nortcliffe, A. (2012). Considering the smartphone learner: An investigation into student interest in the use of personal technology to enhance their learning. *Student Engagement and Experience Journal*, 1(1), 1–15.

CHAPTER 14

Adaptive Learning

Maria Ofelia Z. San Pedro and Ryan S. Baker

INTRODUCTION

As discussed throughout this book, blended learning (BL) has become an increasingly important part of modern education, from schoolchildren to higher education and adult learners. In a BL environment, students learn in part at their own time and pace through instruction and content delivered online, as well as learning in part through supervised face-to-face instruction in a school or higher education context (Garrison and Vaughan, 2008; Graham, 2006). This blend can vary in the degrees of face-to-face and online instructional content depending on the subject matter, students and instructor.

One of the key opportunities of BL is to support better personalisation for the range of individual differences which students bring to learning situations. For example, students may vary in terms of their aptitudes, interests and motivations (Cordova and Lepper, 1996; Grant and Basye, 2014). To help students achieve their optimal learning potential, educators must be able to offer personalised learning experiences that customise the instruction given to students to meet their individual needs and goals for learning. Such differentiation of instruction must then address each student's ability, interest and motivation.

Personalised learning in instruction development does not necessarily require technology (e.g., Clarke and Miles, 2003), but the arrival of modern computerised learning environments increases the potential for individualisation, both through providing better data to teachers and instructional designers, and by making it economically feasible to design student models and interventions that may apply to a relatively small proportion of students (Ben-Naim et al., 2007; Graesser et al., 2007; Koedinger and Corbett, 2006; Mayer et al., 2004; VanLehn, 1996). In integrating technology within a traditional classroom instruction model, BL takes advantage of these opportunities for personalised learning, while maintaining the affordances of classroom activities. Within well-implemented BL, students are provided with technology that enables them to learn the material at their own pace, lets them individually experience success and failure with the material and informs them about their learning progress. The affordances of such technology include capturing student learning experiences in real time and reporting on students' performance to the teacher, giving the teacher opportunities to provide more immediate feedback relevant to the students' learning state. Also, to the degree that BL can take over the rote or practice-based parts of the curriculum, teachers are able to focus their time on more complex instructional content, such as critical thinking or project-based activities.

It is important to note that to be truly effective, BL's use of technology for instruction must be integrated in a way that it can enhance teaching, customising instruction and providing flexible options for the student users, and not merely as a method for providing learning content. And one great potential for technology in classrooms is the ability for this technology to be adaptive, able to change quickly to suit varying situations or conditions, such as the students' learning.

Adaptive educational software has been adopted in recent years in classrooms worldwide, with particularly intense usage within the United States. This type of educational software adapts to assessments of a student's attributes, their individual differences in terms of a wide range of attributes influential in the learning experience – student knowledge, academic emotions, behavioural engagement and disengagement, motivation and interest. Within this chapter, we will present examples of adaptive learning systems developed with these aspects in mind.

An adaptive learning system attempts to select content and instruction that best fit a particular student based on a model that represents what the system knows about a student's current knowledge and other key information, towards the goal of facilitating deep, meaningful and effective learning. In this chapter, we will define adaptive learning and describe its essential components. We will consider which learner attributes are feasible to identify and adapt to in an automated fashion and discuss examples of how existing systems tailor learner experiences based on these attributes. We conclude with a discussion of the limitations of the current generation of adaptive learning systems, and areas of potential for future progress.

What is Adaptive Learning?

Adaptive learning in educational settings is a method for personalising learning experiences for students. Using technology such as online systems where students learn, and the data on student performance collected within these systems, adaptive learning tailors instruction, remediation (error correction and feedback) and other aspects of the learning experience, to better support the student's individual needs. Adaptive systems are designed to evaluate the student's understanding of the material and other aspects of their performance, such as learning strategies, to identify their limitations in understanding and other needs for support, and to provide instruction and content that will aid students to learn the material and succeed, until the learning objective is achieved. The goal of adaptive learning is to provide the best possible learning content and resources for the student's needs at a particular point in time. Adaptive learning utilises findings and methods from cognitive science, educational psychology and artificial intelligence in order to achieve these goals. Adaptive learning takes what an expert teacher does with students in classrooms and scales it up via technology-enabled learning systems. Effective teachers have always been able to gauge individual students and personalise their learning in classrooms without technology; adaptive learning systems scale this ability beyond the contexts where teachers can be present (i.e., homework), and make it possible to pay attention to every student at once. As will be discussed below, modern adaptive learning systems can identify what a student knows and does not know, their skills and strategies, and can identify the source of a student's misunderstanding or error. They can sense a student's learning goals, level of engagement and their motivation to learn. This information can be used by the system itself, or can be provided to teachers, enabling the teacher and the learning system to work together to select what the student should be working on, to support the student in learning that material, and to support the student in becoming more engaged and motivated in their learning experiences. In this chapter, we focus largely on the potential of adaptive learning systems to support the learner through their own actions, as this is the sense in which these systems are themselves adaptive. However, systems that inform instructors on student success and help the instructors adapt their instructional practices (e.g., Razzaq et al., 2005) are also a valuable innovation in twenty-first-century education.

As such, adaptive learning systems are able to constantly evaluate students and dynamically change the content and instruction presented to students in response to information acquired during the student's course of learning with the system (US Department of Education, 2013), beyond just pre-existing information such as student test scores and demographic information. This 'assessment-driven' approach (Newman et al., 2013) to adaptive learning allows individual students to work through learning objectives in a variety of ways, using personalised instructional content provided by the system without the need for direct intervention by the instructor. Another approach is to have the instructor direct which instructional content is given to the students. In this approach, instructors are provided with data on the student along with tools that enable them to adapt the instruction and content at varying degrees of scale. While the 'assessment-driven' approach is more common within adaptive learning technology, the two approaches are not necessarily mutually exclusive; adaptive learning systems can embed elements of both in their design and development (see, for example, Razzaq et al., 2005).

One core aspect of most adaptive learning systems is the explicit use of a student model (Sottilare et al., 2014; Sottilare et al., 2013; Woolf, 2010) that consists of measures of the student's knowledge, interests, goals, engagement and other pertinent attributes that enable the system to make informed decisions in adapting to individual students. These student models contain assessments of each of these attributes and update them in real time, so that they can be used in adaptation or provided to the instructor.

Another aspect of adaptive learning systems is how a system adapts its instructional or pedagogical components to the individual student. According to the taxonomy for pedagogy within adaptive learning systems proposed by Newman and colleagues (2013), systems can be characterised in terms of several dimensions: student profile (information about the student used for personalisation, e.g., prior knowledge, interests, motivation, etc.), the unit of adaptivity (from a single problem step to a whole course), instruction coverage (the amount of content to include in instruction), assessment (infrequent to continuous), content model (closed to open), and coverage of educational objectives according to Bloom's Taxonomy (1956) (representing the depth of understanding covered; from rote knowledge to synthesis and evaluation). Each adaptive learning system can vary in its level of adaptability based on these components.

FRAMEWORK FOR ADAPTIVE LEARNING SYSTEMS

While there are several approaches to adaptability in adaptive learning systems, most of the currently implemented adaptive learning systems are characterised by inferring student knowledge and then adapting in an immediate, low-level fashion to that inference, for example by providing a hint to a struggling student.

At their core, online or digital learning systems are made adaptive by being built with three major components: a domain model, a student model, and a pedagogical or instructional model (see Figure 14.1). This is broadly the same set of components that has been used to describe intelligent tutoring systems, a specific type of adaptive learning system

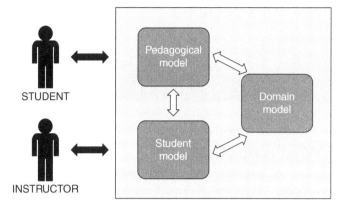

Figure 14.1 Adaptive Learning Systems Framework

(Sottilare et al., 2014; Sottilare et al., 2013; Woolf, 2010). The domain model refers to the content domain to be taught by the system, containing the set of topics and the corresponding learning objectives or outcomes, skills, knowledge, strategies and sequencing needed to learn them (Nkambou et al., 2010; Sottilare et al., 2013; Woolf, 2010). The student model assesses the student users' cognitive state, as well as other states (such as affective, behavioural and motivational states) based on the student's interaction with the learning system. The model not only contains general information about the student, but it can also incorporate educationally relevant student attributes (e.g., knowledge, behaviour, affect [emotion in context], interests, etc.) within the system (Sottilare et al., 2013). Data about these attributes can be used to continuously update inferences about each student. The information from the student model is what adaptive learning systems consider in selecting the content and instruction to present to the student user. The pedagogical or instructional model selects the specific content, tutoring strategies and feedback for an individual student at a specific time. It takes information from the domain and student models as inputs and decides the next activity the system will provide to the student user based on that information (Murray and Arroyo, 2002; Sottilare et al., 2014; VanLehn, 2006). The pedagogical model's behaviour is generally designed based on theories in pedagogy and instruction.

Examples of adaptive learning systems that have successfully emerged over the years include intelligent tutoring systems, adaptive hypermedia (systems that resemble a text but incorporate additional materials such as text, image, video and audio), and adaptive platforms developed by educational publishers. Two popular instances of successful intelligent tutoring systems currently in large-scale use in the United States are the Cognitive Tutor from Carnegie Learning/Apollo and ALEKS (Assessment and Learning in Knowledge Spaces) from McGraw Hill Education. These systems are used by hundreds of thousands of students a year throughout the United States, and the Cognitive Tutor is also being used in substantial numbers in several Latin American countries. Both these systems were designed using cognitive and pedagogical principles, to teach maths skills. They are used by schools and districts all over the United States, with a user base in the hundreds of thousands each year. Both systems have been shown to promote positive outcomes. Cognitive Tutors have been shown to lead to better performance on standardised examinations (Corbett and Anderson, 1992; Koedinger et al., 1997), and subsequent maths courses (Koedinger et al., 2000). ALEKS implemented in after-school programmes has been shown to increase class attendance and maths performance (Craig et al., 2011). Beyond this, the combination of maturing technological affordances and government educational initiatives has led to a growth in the number of adaptive learning systems used by schools. Some systems have been designed to provide a platform for instructor users to develop and import their content and pedagogical practices (e.g., Smart Sparrow, CogBooks, ASSISTments), while others provide instructional content created by the provider (e.g., Adapt Courseware and LearnSmart). In the next sections, we will discuss what student attributes are adapted to by these systems (what is adapted?), as well how these systems enable adaptation (how is it adapted?).

ADAPTIVE LEARNING – WHAT IS ADAPTED?

As mentioned earlier, an adaptive learning system takes into account learner attributes through a student model. Developing a good student model is usually seen as the starting point in the development of adaptive learning systems, as it is difficult to adapt effectively to individual differences if the system does not know how specific students differ. An effective adaptive learning system tailors its provision of instructions to the individual student's needs related to their learning experience. Across research and real-world systems, many learner attributes have been proposed for incorporation into student models. However, it would be unrealistic to expect that any real-world system could fully model and represent all possible learner attributes. Hence, there has been considerable research to determine which learner attributes can form the basis of meaningful and effective intervention, while at the same time be easily inferred from the data available within a real-world system. The following subsections present examples of systems which adapt to a variety of learner attributes.

STUDENT KNOWLEDGE

Perhaps the most commonly modelled learner attribute is student knowledge. One category of adaptive learning systems that model student knowledge is intelligent tutoring systems (Woolf, 2010). These systems represent student knowledge as skills, facts or concepts, and track student progress from one problem or activity to the next, building a skill mastery profile for the students. A skill mastery profile is an assessment of the probability that the student has learned each of the skills the system is attempting to support the student in. By modelling what a student knows, and updating that profile in real-time, the system can then organise instruction around what the student knows, as well as provide feedback on the student's problem-solving.

One example of an adaptive learning system that takes student knowledge into account is the Cognitive Tutor (Koedinger and Corbett, 2006), discussed above. The systems make use of a cognitive model (the ACT-R model, Anderson, 1983) that assesses student knowledge in real-time. Specifically, the model follows the actions made by students within the system to determine which knowledge (or incorrect knowledge) the student is demonstrating or failing to demonstrate. With each student action linked to the skill (or other knowledge component) needed to solve a problem, the system collects and integrates student performance into evidence about which skills the student has (Corbett and Anderson, 1995), and displays this information to students and teachers. The system provides the student with further practice on the current skill until the student demonstrates mastery of that skill. When a student has been assessed to have mastered the skills in a problem set, the system will introduce a new problem set with a new set of skills to master.

Another example of an adaptive learning system is AutoTutor (Graesser et al., 2007), an intelligent tutoring system that simulates a human tutor through a conversation with the student in 'natural' language (i.e., interaction through text-based conversation rather than filling in worksheets or other user interfaces). The system presents a question that requires the student to provide a set of sentences or a paragraph of information that answers the question. After an initial response, there is a back and forth of questions and answers between the system and the student, supporting the student in constructing an improved answer to the problem. This process helps the student clarify and refine their knowledge about the domain (content or topic) and adapts the conversation (through prompts and hints) to the student's knowledge so as to fill in the gaps in student knowledge and address misconceptions.

Andes is an adaptive learning system that teaches Newtonian physics using coached problem solving (VanLehn, 1996) where the system and the student collaborate in solving a problem. When a student offers a correct solution, the system agrees; when the student makes an error, the system provides assistance, guiding the student towards the correct solution. Within this process, the tutor interprets the student's actions and reasoning by looking at its student model to decide on what kind of instructional content (feedback prompts or help) it will provide. This student model uses a probabilistic framework (based on the theory of probability, where inferences take into account the possibility that a student's actions do not perfectly reflect their knowledge) that assesses a student's plans in solving the problem, predicts the student's goals and actions, and provides a long-term evaluation of a student's domain knowledge. The tutor updates its student model based on the problems the student has worked on and the student's interactions with the system during problem solving, assessing the probability and uncertainty of the student's knowledge state (Conati et al., 1997).

Another example of an adaptive learning system that evaluates student knowledge in its student model is the SQL-Tutor, an intelligent tutoring system used in classroom instruction on database theory and a commonly-used programming language for database queries (Mitrovic, 1998). It gives the student an SQL problem to work on and intervenes when the student is having difficulties answering or asks for help. It selects a problem based on a constraint-based student model (Ohlsson, 1994), a type of model that represents correct knowledge in solving a problem as a set of constraints – aspects a correct solution must have. If a student's solution violates a constraint, the system intervenes through feedback attached to that constraint. This feedback informs the student what is incorrect, why it was incorrect and points out the corresponding domain principle attached to that constraint.

STUDENT AFFECT

Another popular area for adaptive learning systems focuses on efforts to address negative affect (emotion in context), also called 'academic emotions'. These systems identify the emotions that students experience during learning and classroom instruction. Through patterns of student activity, student interactions with pedagogical agents, conversational cues, and sometimes physiological sensors, adaptive learning systems detect and infer students' affective states, focusing particularly on those known to influence learning. For example, many systems detect and attempt to respond to boredom, which is unfortunately a prominent part of many students' experiences in middle-school classrooms (Ahmed et al., 2013; Goetz et al., 2006; Pekrun et al., 2007). Boredom has been found to correlate to short-term learning outcomes (Craig et al., 2004), long-term learning outcomes (Pardos et al., 2014), and long-term academic outcomes, such as whether students attend college (San Pedro et al., 2013). At the other end of the spectrum are students who are more engaged in school and tend to have higher academic motivation and achievement (Fredricks et al., 2004). Students who experience greater amounts of engaged concentration tend to achieve better short-term learning outcomes (Craig et al., 2004; Rodrigo et al., 2009), better long-term learning outcomes (Pardos et al., 2014), and are more likely to enrol in college years later (San Pedro et al., 2013).

Adaptive systems such as the Affective AutoTutor (D'Mello and Graesser, 2012; D'Mello, et al., 2007; Graesser et al., 2008) have designed and developed interventions that respond when students experience boredom, frustration and confusion. Affective AutoTutor makes use of the AutoTutor architecture, discussed above, but extends it to detect students' affect during their interaction with the system. It utilises an embodied conversational agent (a computer-generated character with a visual form including a body, that demonstrates similar characteristics to those of humans during conversations) that simulates a human tutor to respond when students display negative affect, adjusting the difficulty and pace of the learning activity. Affective AutoTutor also responds to negative affect through facial expressions and motivational or humorous messages (D'Mello et al., 2009).

STUDENT BEHAVIOUR AND SELF-REGULATION LEARNING

Student behaviours associated with difference in engagement and self-regulated learning are also considered by developers of adaptive learning systems. As with affect, disengaged behaviours and self-regulated learning behaviours can be associated with student outcomes. Take, for example, the behaviour of 'gaming the system', where the student exploits the properties of a learning environment to succeed in the learning task rather than by actually learning and using knowledge to answer correctly. This includes rushing through problems without reading them, or repeatedly requesting hints until the system gives the student the answer. It has been shown that this behaviour is related to poorer short-term learning (Cocea et al., 2009), poorer long-term learning (Pardos et al., 2014) and lower probability of college attendance (San Pedro et al., 2013). Models have been developed that can identify this behaviour from student log files (Baker et al., 2008), and have been incorporated into a pedagogical agent for the Cognitive Tutor that provides interventions when it detects students exhibiting this behaviour (Baker et al., 2006). If the agent detects that the student is gaming the system, it provides supplementary exercises to the student on the material that the student bypassed with this behaviour; these supplementary exercises have been found to be associated with significantly better learning (Baker et al., 2006).

Learning systems have also been made adaptive by identifying students' metacognitive skills and self-regulated learning (SRL) strategies, such as goal setting, self-monitoring, help-seeking or self-questioning, and then attempting to support students in developing these skills. For example, Roll and colleagues (2011) have modelled student help-seeking behaviour in developing the Help Tutor, a plug-in agent added to a Cognitive Tutor. The Help Tutor tracks student actions that involve (or should involve) help-seeking behaviours and aims to teach students to become better help-seekers through feedback. When a student exhibits help-seeking errors (such as requesting help when it is not needed, or failing to ask for help when it is needed), they receive feedback messages that advise the student how to seek help effectively (Roll et al., 2011). With a metacognitive component in the Help Tutor feedback, students' hint usage improved significantly – decreasing the instances of asking for bottom-out-hints (hints that provide the answer) and increasing the time the student took to read the hint text. However, at the time of writing, the Help Tutor changes student behaviour but does not appear to impact domain learning (Roll et al., 2011).

Another system that responds to differences in self-regulated learning (SRL) is Betty's Brain (Biswas et al., 2005; Leelawong and Biswas, 2008), a teachable agent system that gives feedback about self-regulated learning in promoting deep understanding in science concepts. The system is based on the 'learning by teaching' model where students create concept maps and then use these to 'teach' Betty, the agent. Betty answers questions based on what was taught, and through this process the implications of the student's concept map are explored and the student's misconceptions are revealed. While doing this, Betty in turn evaluates the students' action sequences as they teach Betty, providing metacognitive and self-regulated learning prompts (i.e., scaffolds, accessible resources that contain all information about the topic) designed to help the students develop better SRL strategies.

ADAPTIVE LEARNING – HOW IS IT ADAPTED?

As the examples in the previous section indicate, once learner attributes are incorporated into an adaptive learning system, the pedagogical model is designed to select problems or customise instructional content for the learner. Adaptive systems take into account the information in the student models and behave differently in terms of pedagogical mechanisms for different students or groups of students, aimed at providing individualised support for better learning. As seen above, several aspects of the learning experience can be adapted, including the content's complexity or difficulty (AnimalWatch, Murray and Arroyo, 2002; Andes, VanLehn, 2006), scaffolding and support (ASSISTments, Razzaq et al., 2005; Cognitive Tutor, Koedinger et al., 2006), the visual interface (Adaptive VIBE for TaskSieve, Ahn and Brusilovsky, 2009; DEPTHS, Jeremic et al., 2009), feedback prompts such as hints, prompts or pedagogical agents (Betty's Brain, Biswas et al., 2005; ASSISTments, Razzaq et al., 2005; Scooter the Tutor, Baker et al., 2006; AutoTutor, Graesser et al., 2007). In its simplest form, an adaptive learning system uses predetermined rules to evaluate the student actions within the system and determine what type of instructional content it will present. For example, in a simple adaptive learning system, if a student gets a question right, the student is provided with the next activity; if the student gets it wrong, they are given additional support to assist them, such as scaffolding, hints or supplementary materials. Depending on the design of learning material and amount of related supporting materials or the scope of the rules established, the instructional process of rule-based systems may vary in difficulty or complexity. Benefits of rule-based systems include the ability for instructors to create content or use existing content, with the system features being relatively easy for instructors to use. Adapt Courseware is a publisher of educational courseware (interactives) in three instructional modalities: text, multimedia interactives and instructional videos (Newman et al., 2013). These materials are organised into sets or 'adaptive stacks' with corresponding predefined topics and learning objectives, aiming to provide students with instructional content appropriate to their current skill level. Based on the student's success rates with the materials, they are presented with interactive content that may be basic or complex in nature, with different types of feedback (such as hints) appropriate to the current learning task as well as the student's mastery progress through a 'mastery meter' or 'skill bar' that shows the learner their degree of progress on each skill.

Smart Sparrow (Ben-Naim et al., 2007) allows instructors to determine the level of adaptivity used in their lessons or courses through authoring tools. The system provides its instructor users 'WYSIWYG' (What You See Is What You Get) tools that allow content authoring capabilities, as well as rule-authoring interfaces where they can activate rules for content adaptivity. For example, many science-based courses have been created with Smart Sparrow where instructors create adaptive lessons that contain web-enabled content such as text and multimedia, together with virtual lab simulations (Polly et al., 2014). An instructor decides how adaptive an online lesson is, using mechanisms such as adaptive feedback, adaptive sequencing and adaptive content (Ben-Naim et al., 2009; Marcus et al., 2011). With these, Smart Sparrow promotes 'learning by doing', with students interacting with educational content and receiving adaptive instructions while they work.

Adaptive learning systems can also implement their pedagogical model by using artificial intelligence or machine learning algorithms from the educational data mining or learning analytics communities (Baker and Siemens, 2014) to analyse student performance. These methods discover unknown patterns in data and can use large amounts of student data to precisely infer student knowledge or other student attributes, or to predict the probability of student success. Some experimental systems go beyond this to use algorithms which attempt to automatically discover which types of interventions work for which students, under which conditions (e.g., Chi et al., 2011). Through this process, the system 'learns' more about the student in real-time, and what works for this student, as the student responds to the instructional or learning material presented to them.

ALEKS is a web-based assessment and learning system that uses adaptive item selection to determine what the student knows or does not know (Canfield, 2001; Hu et al., 2012); it essentially integrates computer-adaptive testing methods into an intelligent tutoring system. As discussed above, ALEKS uses a student model to track what the student knows, in this case using methods such as Bayesian Networks that relate items to prerequisite skills as well as other items with the same skill. This enables ALEKS to identify when a student is struggling because the student does not know a prerequisite skill and to switch to supporting the student in learning the prerequisite skill. As the student progresses in learning topics, ALEKS updates its student model and uses that information to make a principled selection of what skills it asks the student to work on.

Finally, some systems provide support through natural language dialogues. The best known example, as discussed above, is AutoTutor. It compares a student's input text to the text of the ideal answer to a problem, as well as sample text representing other potential answers, including both good answers and common misconceptions. By recognising a range of potential answers (and being able to do textual transformations between standard answers and alternative ways of saying the same thing), AutoTutor can respond in a flexible and sensitive fashion. It adaptively responds to the student answers, whether answers are incomplete or representing misconceptions, by engaging in a variety of tutorial strategies, including asking for more information, giving positive, neutral or negative messages, prompts for missing words, giving hints, answering questions from students and summarising answers (Graesser et al., 2007).

Conclusion

BL offers the opportunity to support better personalisation in a student's learning experiences. In particular, a system that a single learner continually interacts with has the opportunity to tailor its interaction with the student to that student's individual needs; it can study that student over time in a depth that few teachers have the opportunity to do, determine that student's needs and adapt to provide them. By adapting to student attributes during learning tasks, these systems are able to support students that come to class with different prior knowledge, adjust the difficulty of learning activities dynamically, provide motivational or affective support to students and help students develop better self-regulated learning skills.

In this chapter, we have discussed what adaptive learning systems adapt to, and how they do so. We have done so by discussing a small number of established adaptive educational systems. Although not discussed in detail here, most of the systems presented in this chapter have been shown to lead to significantly better student outcomes than traditional curricular approaches (Graesser et al., 2007; Hu et al., 2012; Koedinger et al., 1997; Leelawong and Biswas, 2008; Razzaq, et al., 2005). Especially in the United States, adaptive learning systems have achieved scale, with systems such as the Cognitive Tutor or ALEKS being used by hundreds of thousands of students.

Current Limitations and Future Opportunities

One interesting limitation to the current generation of adaptive learning systems is that with a few exceptions (such as Affective AutoTutor, for instance), most existing systems adapt to a single dimension of the learner, in a single way. Individual systems become very effective at using mastery learning, or at providing feedback when students make known errors, and perhaps giving messages as to why the student is wrong, but the full combination of support for problem selection, misconceptions, affect, motivation, disengaged behaviour and self-regulated learning is relatively rare. Personalised instruction in these adaptive learning systems could have the most benefit for students if they have a richer assessment of a range of student attributes while they are engaging with the learning system. Research studies have suggested that these different factors have separate impacts on student outcomes; for example, San Pedro and colleagues (2013) found that student knowledge, student disengaged behaviour and student affect each exert an influence on whether students will attend college several years later. As such, we envision and hope that the adaptive learning systems of the future will consider the student in a richer, more multi-dimensional fashion.

Another key area for the future of adaptive learning systems is the emerging role of 'big data' in education (Baker, 2014): extremely large datasets, bigger than those used in standard statistical analyses, involving process data from student educational experiences. As we get more and richer data on learners, we will be able to improve the quality of our models and make more differentiated assessments of how individual learners can be supported. We will be able to evaluate not just what works in general, but what works for very specific subcategories of students, in very specific situations. And we will be able to test new interventions and ideas for adaptations in a comprehensive fashion, rather than just on non-representative groups of students that are easily accessible to researchers and developers. This will help us develop a future generation of adaptive learning systems that fully realise the vision of learning technologies that help every student achieve their full potential.

Suggested Resources

Baker, R. S. (2014). *Big Data and Education*. New York, NY: Teachers College, Columbia University. Online at: http://www.columbia.edu/~rsb2162/bigdataeducation.html

Sottilare, R., Holden, H., Graesser, A. C., & Hu, X. (2013). *Design Recommendations for Adaptive Intelligent Tutoring Systems: Learner Modeling*, 1.

Woolf, B. P. (2010). *Building Intelligent Interactive Tutors: Student-centered Strategies for Revolutionizing E-learning*. Burlington, MA: Morgan Kaufmann.

Discussion Questions

1. What should adaptive learning systems respond to? Are there attributes of the student that current systems do not support, but future systems should?

2. With adaptive learning systems tailoring instructions for the students, does this create a risk of students being less able to regulate their own learning (because the system supports them too much)? How can we avoid this?

3. How could adaptive learning systems support students in becoming creative thinkers?

4. How can adaptive learning systems better support teachers as well as students?

References

Ahmed, W., van der Werf, G., Kuyper, H., & Minnaert, A. (2013). Emotions, self-regulated learning, and achievement in mathematics: A growth curve analysis. *Journal of Educational Psychology*, 105, 150–161.

Ahn, J. W., & Brusilovsky, P. (2009). Adaptive visualization of search results: Bringing user models to visual analytics. *Information Visualization*, 8(3), 167–179.

Anderson, J. R. (1983). *The Architecture of Cognition*. Cambridge, MA: Harvard University Press.

Baker, R. S. (2014). *Big Data and Education*. New York, NY: Teachers College Columbia University. Online at: http://www.columbia.edu/~rsb2162/bigdataeducation.html

Baker, R. S., Corbett, A. T., Roll, I., & Koedinger, K. R. (2008). Developing a generalizable detector of when students game the system. *User Modeling and User-Adapted Interaction*, 18(3), 287–314.

Baker, R. S., Corbett, A. T., Koedinger, K. R., Evenson, S., Roll, I., Wagner, A. Z., & Beck, J. E. (2006). Adapting to when students game an intelligent tutoring system. In *Intelligent Tutoring Systems* (pp. 392–401). Berlin/Heidelberg: Springer.

Baker, R., & Siemens, G. (2014). Educational data mining and learning analytics. In K. Sawyer (Ed.), *Cambridge Handbook of the Learning Sciences* (2nd Edition) (pp. 253–274). Cambridge: Cambridge University Press.

Ben-Naim, D., Bain, M., & Marcus, N. (2009). A user-driven and data-driven approach for supporting teachers in reflection and adaptation of adaptive tutorials. *International Working Group on Educational Data Mining*.

Ben-Naim, D., Marcus, N., & Bain, M. (2007). Virtual apparatus framework approach to constructing adaptive tutorials. In *CSREA EEE* (pp. 3–10).

Biswas, G., Leelawong, K., Schwartz, D., Vye, N., & The Teachable Agents Group at Vanderbilt (2005). Learning by teaching: A new agent paradigm for educational software. *Applied Artificial Intelligence*, 19(3–4), 363–392.

Bloom, B. S. (Ed.). Engelhart, M. D., Furst, E. J., Hill, W. H., & Krathwohl, D. R. (1956). *Taxonomy of Educational Objectives, Handbook I: The Cognitive Domain*. New York: David McKay.

Canfield, W. (2001). ALEKS: A web-based intelligent tutoring system. *Mathematics and Computer Education*, 35(2), 152.

Chi, M., VanLehn, K., Litman, D., & Jordan, P. (2011). An evaluation of pedagogical tutorial tactics for a natural language tutoring system: A reinforcement learning approach. *International Journal of Artificial Intelligence in Education*, 21(1), 83–113.

Clarke, J., & Miles, S. (2003). Changing systems to personalize learning. *Introduction to the Personalization Workshops*. (Report No. ED 482 970). Providence, RI: The Education Alliance at Brown University.

Cocea, M., Hershkovitz, A., & Baker, R. S. (2009). The impact of off-task and gaming behaviors on learning: Immediate or aggregate? *Proceedings of the 14th International Conference on Artificial Intelligence in Education*, 507–514.

Conati, C., Gertner, A. S., VanLehn, K., & Druzdzel, M. J. (1997). On-line student modeling for coached problem solving using Bayesian networks. *Proceedings of the Sixth International Conference on User Modeling*, 231–242.

Corbett, A. T., & Anderson, J. R. (1992). Student modeling and mastery learning in a computer-based programming tutor. *Proceedings of the Second International Conference on Intelligent Tutoring Systems*, 413–420.

Corbett, A. T., & Anderson, J. R. (1995). Knowledge tracing: Modeling the acquisition of procedural knowledge. *User Modeling and User-Adapted Interaction*, 4(4), 253–278.

Cordova, D. I., & Lepper, M. R. (1996). Intrinsic motivation and the process of learning: Beneficial effects of contextualization, personalization, and choice. *Journal of Educational Psychology*, 88(4), 715.

Craig, S. D., Anderson, C., Bargagloitti, A., Graesser, A. C., Okwumabua, T., Sterbinsky, A., & Hu, X. (2011). Learning with ALEKS: The impact of students' attendance in a mathematics after-school program. *Artificial Intelligence in Education*, 435–437.

Craig, S., Graesser, A., Sullins, J., & Gholson, B. (2004). Affect and learning: An exploratory look into the role of affect in learning with AutoTutor. *Journal of Educational Media*, 29(3), 241–250.

D'Mello, S., Craig, S., Fike, K., & Graesser, A. (2009). Responding to learners' cognitive-affective states with supportive and shakeup dialogues. In J. A. Jacko (Ed.), *Human-Computer Interaction. Ambient, Ubiquitous and Intelligent Interaction* (pp. 595–604). Berlin/Heidelberg: Springer.

D'Mello, S., & Graesser, A. (2012). AutoTutor and affective AutoTutor: Learning by talking with cognitively and emotionally intelligent computers that talk back. *ACM Transactions on Interactive Intelligent Systems (TiiS)*, 2(4), 23.

D'Mello, S., Picard, R. W., & Graesser, A. (2007). Toward an affect-sensitive AutoTutor. *IEEE Intelligent Systems*, 4, 53–61.

Fredricks, J. A., Blumenfeld, P. C., & Paris, A. H. (2004). School engagement: Potential of the concept, state of the evidence. *Review of Educational Research*, 74(1), 59–109.

Garrison, D. R., & Vaughan, N. D. (2008). *Blended Learning in Higher Education: Framework, Principles, and Guidelines*. Hoboken, NJ: John Wiley and Sons.

Goetz, T., Pekrun, R., Hall, N., & Haag, L. (2006). Academic emotions from a social-cognitive perspective: Antecedents and domain specificity of students' affect in the context of Latin instruction. *British Journal of Educational Psychology*, 76, 289–308.

Graesser, A. C., D'Mello, S. K., Craig, S. D., Witherspoon, A., Sullins, J., McDaniel, B., & Gholson, B. (2008). The relationship between affective states and dialog patterns during interactions with AutoTutor. *Journal of Interactive Learning Research*, 19(2), 293–312.

Graesser, A. C., Jackson, G. T., & McDaniel, B. (2007). AutoTutor holds conversations with learners that are responsive to their cognitive and emotional states. *Educational Technology*, 47, 19–22.

Graham, C. R. (2006). Blended learning systems. In C. J. Bonk & C. R. Graham, *The Handbook of Blended Learning: Global Perspectives, Local Designs*. San Francisco, CA: Pfeiffer.

Grant, P., & Basye, D. (2014). *Personalized Learning: A Guide for Engaging Students with Technology*. Eugene, OR: ISTE (International Society for Technology in Education).

Hu, X., Craig, S. D., Bargagliotti, A. E., Graesser, A. C., Okwumabua, T., Anderson, C., & Sterbinsky, A. (2012). The effects of a traditional and technology-based after-school setting on 6th grade students' mathematics skills. *Journal of Computers in Mathematics and Science Teaching*, 31(1), 17–38.

Jeremic, Z., Jovanovic, J., & Gašević, D. (2009). Evaluating an intelligent tutoring system for design patterns: The DEPTHS experience. *Educational Technology and Society*, 12(2), 111–130.

Koedinger, K. R., Anderson, J. R., Hadley, W. H., & Mark, M. A. (1997). Intelligent tutoring goes to school in the big city. *International Journal of Artificial Intelligence in Education*, 8, 30–43.

Koedinger, K. R., & Corbett, A. T. (2006). Cognitive tutors: Technology bringing learning science to the classroom. In K. Sawyer (Ed.), *The Cambridge Handbook of the Learning Sciences*, (pp. 61–78). Cambridge: Cambridge University Press.

Koedinger, K. R., Corbett, A. T., Ritter, S., & Shapiro, L. J. (2000). *Carnegie Learning's Cognitive Tutor: Summary Research Results*. Pittsburgh, PA: Carnegie Learning.

Leelawong, K., & Biswas, G. (2008). Designing learning by teaching agents: The Betty's Brain system. *International Journal of Artificial Intelligence in Education*, 18(3), 181–208.

Marcus, N., Ben-Naim, D., & Bain, M. (2011, April). Instructional support for teachers and guided feedback for students in an adaptive elearning environment. *Eighth International Conference on Information Technology: New Generations*, ITNG 2011, Las Vegas, Nevada, USA, 11–13 April 2011. IEEE Computer Society 2011, 626–631.

Mayer, R. E., Fennell, S., Farmer, L., & Campbell, J. (2004). A personalization effect in multimedia learning: Students learn better when words are in conversational style rather than formal style. *Journal of Educational Psychology*, 96(2), 389.

Mislevy, R. J., & Riconscente, M. M. (2006). Evidence-centered assessment design. In S. Downing & T. Haladyna (Eds.) *Handbook of Test Development*, (pp. 61–90). Mahwah, NJ: Lawrence Erlbaum Associates.

Mitrovic, A. (1998). A knowledge-based teaching system for SQL. *Proceedings of ED-MEDIA*, 98, 1027–1032.

Murray, T., & Arroyo, I. (2002) Toward measuring and maintaining the zone of proximal development in adaptive instructional systems. *Proceedings of the International Conference on Intelligent Tutoring Systems*, 749–758.

Newman, A., Bryant, G., Stokes, P., & Squeo, T. (2013). Learning to adapt: Understanding the adaptive learning supplier landscape. *Education Growth Advisors*. Online at: http://tytonpartners.com/tyton-wp/wp-content/uploads/2015/01/Learning-to-Adapt_Supplier-Landscape.pdf

Nkambou, R., Mizoguchi, R., & Bourdeau, J. (Eds.) (2010). *Advances in Intelligent Tutoring Systems* (p. 308). New York, NY: Springer Science and Business Media.

Ohlsson, S. (1994). Constraint-based student modeling. In *Student Modeling: the Key to Individualized Knowledge-based Instruction*, (pp. 167–189). Berlin/Heidelberg: Springer.

Pardos, Z. A., Baker, R. S., San Pedro, M., Gowda, S. M., & Gowda, S. M. (2014). Affective states and state tests: Investigating how affect and engagement during the school year predict end-of-year learning outcomes. *Journal of Learning Analytics*, 1(1), 107–128.

Pekrun, R., vom Hofe, R., Blum, W., Frenzel, A. C., Goetz, T., & Wartha, S. (2007). Development of mathematical competencies in adolescence: The PALMA longitudinal study. In M. Prenzel (Ed.), *Studies on the Educational Quality of Schools* (pp. 17–37). Muenster: Waxmann.

Polly, P., Marcus, N., Maguire, D., Belinson, Z., & Velan, G. M. (2014). Evaluation of an adaptive virtual laboratory environment using Western Blotting for diagnosis of disease. *BMC Medical Education*, 14(1), 222.

Razzaq, L., Feng, M., Nuzzo-Jones, G., Heffernan, N. T., Koedinger, K. R., Junker, B., & Rasmussen, K. P. (2005). The Assistment project: Blending assessment and assisting. *Proceedings of the 12th Annual Conference on Artificial Intelligence in Education*, 555–562.

Rodrigo, M. M. T., Baker, R. S., Jadud, M. C., Amarra, A. C. M., Dy, T., Espejo-Lahoz, M. B. V., & Tabanao, E. S. (2009). Affective and behavioral predictors of novice programmer achievement. *ACM SIGCSE Bulletin*, 41(3), 156–160.

Roll, I., Aleven, V., McLaren, B. M., & Koedinger, K. R. (2011). Improving students' help-seeking skills using metacognitive feedback in an intelligent tutoring system. *Learning and Instruction*, 21(2), 267–280.

San Pedro, M. O. Z., Baker, R. S., Bowers, A. J., & Heffernan, N. T. (2013). Predicting college enrollment from student interaction with an intelligent tutoring system in middle school. *Proceedings of the 6th International Conference on Educational Data Mining,* 177–184.

Sottilare, R., Graesser, A., Hu, X., & Goldberg, B. (Eds.) (2014). *Design Recommendations for Intelligent Tutoring Systems: Volume 2 – Instructional Management.* US Army Research Laboratory.

Sottilare, R., Holden, H., Graesser, A. C., & Hu, X. (2013). *Design Recommendations for Adaptive Intelligent Tutoring Systems: Volume 1 – Learner Modeling.* US Army Research Laboratory.

U.S. Department of Education, Office of Educational Technology (2013). *Expanding Evidence Approaches for Learning in a Digital World.* Washington, D.C.

VanLehn, K. (1996, January). Conceptual and meta learning during coached problem solving. *Intelligent Tutoring Systems,* 29–47. Berlin/Heidelberg: Springer.

VanLehn, K. (2006). The behavior of tutoring systems. *International Journal of Artificial Intelligence and Education,* 16(3), 227–265.

Woolf, B. P. (2010). *Building Intelligent Interactive Tutors: Student-centered Strategies for Revolutionizing E-learning.* Burlington, MA: Morgan Kaufmann.

CHAPTER 15

Where We Are and Going Forward

Michael McCarthy

INTRODUCTION

This book has brought together a number of chapters by different authors, all concerned, in one way or another, with good practice in blended learning (BL). At the time of writing, the field is still, relatively speaking, wide open, with no definitive theory, methodology or practice that could be said to form the 'canon' or rulebook of BL. This means that there are potentially as many ways of approaching and realising BL programmes as there are curriculum designers, materials writers, teachers and researchers who have entered the field.

This book, therefore, cannot be said to be more than exploratory, in the sense that the discipline of BL itself remains somewhat exploratory. That is not to say that successful BL programmes have not been designed and rolled out; clearly they have, as case studies reported in this book and reports elsewhere testify (e.g., Hsu and Sheu, 2008; Graham, 2013). But rapid change and progress in all aspects of the allied technology means that the situation is very fluid. This is one of the reasons why the book has tried to avoid detailed technical descriptions of tools used which might quickly become outdated and has, instead, tried to address the arguments and challenges surrounding BL in the second language context. The chapters seek to offer practical advice concerning integration of BL and solutions which can be implemented through a variety of different tools, with both theoretical and practical considerations discussed throughout the volume.

This final chapter looks back and summarises what the previous chapters tell us, considers briefly how our preoccupations concerning BL align with or should differ from BL programmes in the educational world beyond second language learning and speculates on where things might go in the future. We embark upon this chapter having constantly in mind Thornbury's Chapter 2, where he stresses the need for a proper, grounded scrutiny of BL and its technologies. Thornbury asserts that technology-driven learning cannot call upon the many years of past experience and tried-and-tested reliability that face-to-face pedagogy can claim in terms of fitness for purpose. According to Thornbury, without proper scrutiny of its theoretical underpinning and its place in pedagogy, technology runs the risk of just being a fad, a passing, short-lived phenomenon, something used just because it is on offer and because its creators have sold it with hype and overblown claims.

SLA and Classrooms

Thornbury points out, in Chapter 2, that it is often difficult to judge the efficacy of technology in an experimental way; we cannot always say what aspect of any particular tool has been the one which has 'done the trick' and produced successful learning. However, he offers the possibility of using core insights of SLA as a yardstick for measuring whether technology is doing its job properly. And that is how we began this book. We looked in detail at a variety of aspects of SLA theory and gave consideration to how they might potentially inform choices of platforms, materials and delivery methods in BL programmes. However, BL is not the exclusive domain of second language learning; designs and options for BL have been described in detail for disciplines such as maths education, engineering, computer studies, business studies and economics (Lage et al., 2000; Foertsch et al., 2002; Mackey and Ho, 2008; Kistow, 2011). These other disciplines are evolving and devising models and approaches to BL which can be equally valid for second language learning and they have given much thought to different ways of combining classroom activity with online work.

From the various disciplines, several models or approaches have emerged. These include the so-called *station-rotation* model, where BL happens within the four walls of the physical classroom, a method often preferred in the education of elementary level learners (Staker and Horn, 2012: 2; Bailey et al., 2013: 16). In this approach, a typical 90-minute class period might be divided into three 30-minute segments during which students move from one area of the classroom (where face-to-face-instruction is the main mode of delivery), to a collaborative workstation where online activities are engaged in, to a self-study zone, where the individual can work at their own pace on tasks relevant to their learning situation (ideally with some sort of adaptive feedback). At other extremes, BL might consist almost entirely of online delivery of course content with only occasional face-to-face encounters with teachers, a model often used in online training in various professions and corporate environments. In between lie a number of options combining elements to greater or lesser degrees, most of which have been enacted in one discipline or another. It is generally agreed that choices and potential mixes across those two extremes will be determined by learning objectives and/or institutional requirements. In the case of second language learning, insights from SLA theory and practice will continue to have considerable influence on the choices to be made.

All the various modes of BL delivery will have potential relevance for second language learning, though their desirability and effects will vary according to individual and institutional circumstances. Graham's (2006: 13) threefold model of *enabling* blends, *enhancing* blends and *transforming* blends can all be related to what we know about SLA:

- *Enabling blends*, defined as blends that provide the best of access and flexibility for users, are helpful for learners unable to follow conventional face-to-face programmes through pressures of time, work or domestic constraints, or for learners who do not function best or feel threatened in the exposed and public world of the physical classroom. These personal and individual factors, it was argued in Chapters 1 and 2 of this volume, must always be at the forefront of our thinking.
- *Enhancing blends* are characterised by the ways in which institutions use technology and learning management systems to enhance existing course offerings. Here

the technology is key in monitoring student performance (see also San Pedro and Baker, Chapter 14, this volume), and institutions can offer alternative or supplementary forms of teaching and assessment via discussion forums, wikis, blogs and similar media, as outlined by Moloney and O'Keeffe in Chapter 11 of this volume. In Chapter 1, we considered the pluses and minuses of machine-led monitoring of students' work and concluded that it can offer important additional evidence for the study of SLA processes.

- *Transforming blends*, according to Graham (Ibid.), have been more readily embraced in the corporate world, where technology-supported training programmes transform the learning experience itself, for example through the use of visualisation and simulation tools. A strong argument for the transformative potential of mobile learning is made in Chapter 13 of this volume by Dudeney and Hockly, as well as in the exciting developments in adaptive feedback discussed by San Pedro and Baker in their chapter. As we have seen, new learning experiences carve out new potential pathways for acquisition; consequently, SLA researchers will need to adjust their approach to the study of learning processes.

These different models of BL relate directly to aspects of SLA such as motivation, the potential for developing 'noticing', input enhancement (where the target items are made clearer and brought more to the fore), different types of feedback and issues of sequence, along with depth and durability of acquisition. SLA studies have shown us that second language learning is a complex encounter between an individual's personal and cultural identities and sense of 'self', and a repertoire of unfamiliar modes of expression; the language itself is massively complex, and so is the learner (as was discussed by Thornbury, in Chapter 2 of this volume). We have already asserted that computer capabilities such as the time-stamping of student activity do not give us the full picture of the role of affective factors, learning styles and motivation (Barrs, 2010; Lai and Gu, 2011; McCarthy, Chapter 1, this volume). Equally, students' perceptions of their learning experience and of the learning environment in blended contexts can only properly be gauged through well-designed studies that combine quantitative and qualitative evidence (e.g., Ginns and Ellis, 2007). If we are to achieve truly transforming blends, we will need to keep constantly in mind the many complex factors that play upon language acquisition, as well as welcoming the new paths to acquisition offered by transformative technologies. As Thornbury advocates in his chapter in this volume, core aspects of SLA are appropriate yardsticks for the investigation of the effectivity of technology-enhanced learning, and are not just relevant to conventional, non-technology-based learning modes.

One thing that does distinguish second language learning from the case of, say, mathematics or engineering, is that language is both the medium of instruction and the goal; the two cannot be divorced. Thus, in the case of spoken interaction in a second language, the goal of fluent and successful interaction cannot be separated from the interactions that take place in the face-to-face classroom. It is in the classroom that the development of interactional competence lays the foundations for interactional competence in the second language world outside of the classroom, with humane, sensitive teachers spotting and fostering the learning opportunities which emerge from 'talk' itself (i.e., the various different types of spoken interaction that take place – teacher-led discussion, pair work, group feedback, and so on).

This notion of talk in the classroom as the foundation of learning lies at the heart of Walsh's Chapter 3 on classroom interactional competence in this volume. Just as in the world outside of classrooms, conversational mechanisms such as turn-taking, sequential organisation (how turns in the conversation logically and coherently follow and affect one another) and repair are crucial features of interaction between teachers and learners and among learners (Markee, 2008). In short, we cannot effectively decide what types of activity should be 'flipped' out of the face-to-face classroom into the online world without a deep understanding of the relationship between language as the goal of learning and language as the medium of interaction and how the successful development and management of both go hand in hand. Even in contexts where language learning is not the goal, there is evidence that students value face-to-face peer interaction as part of their learning experience in vocational or professional training (Kistow, 2011), emphasising again the central role of interaction in classrooms.

For the time being, at least, it would seem that the delicate fabric of classroom interaction and its contribution to the fostering of interactional competence is best left undisturbed for those tasks and activities where conversation, negotiation of meaning and collaboration are essential. On the other hand, as Kenning (2007: 196) points out, competence in a second language in our time *includes* the ability to communicate via internet and phone technology, and so the notion of developing interactional competence in L2 extends outside of the classroom and is further shaped by the use of technology. It is therefore imperative, as BL develops, that practitioners remain equally aware of the ongoing research into classroom interactional competence *and* new insights into how technology changes the way people communicate in an L2. That way lies a path to properly transformative models of BL while retaining the most valuable elements of face-to-face teaching and learning.

One of the main questions requiring an effective response in the near future is how to develop interactional competence as effectively online as in the classroom. To assist in this endeavour, more classroom spoken corpora will need to be collected, preferably multimodally (i.e., recording audio and video and including a record of the materials used, etc.). Equally, we need more corpus evidence of speaking (and 'writing-as-if-speaking') in online environments such as social media, chat, text-messaging, emailing and video calling and conferencing between teachers and students as well as peer-to-peer among students. Such discourses can be examined in isolation, but they should also be set alongside and compared with classroom data (de Leng et al., 2010). This, as we have suggested above, will most probably result in a rethinking and broadening of the notion of L2 interactional competence.

Research at the Cambridge Institute for Automated Language Learning and Assessment (ALTA; see http://alta.cambridgeenglish.org/#) has set out to gain insights from learner spoken corpora as to how learners interact in oral examination settings with a view to developing automatic systems for feedback and assessment. Progress in this area will add to our knowledge of learner interactional competence and offer better prospects for adaptive feedback and automatic assessment for learners doing interactive activities and tests online. San Pedro and Baker's Chapter 14 in this volume has already indicated some impressive realisations of adaptive systems and these will undoubtedly be an increasingly important feature of BL programmes in the future.

AUTHENTICITY

This book began by emphasising (a) the importance of understanding second language acquisition processes and (b) an understanding of the crucial role played by classroom interactions. It was argued that decisions regarding appropriate blends of classroom activity and computer-mediated activity in blended (or 'hybrid' as they are sometimes called) courses should be grounded in those two understandings. Parallel with such concerns must go an understanding of the experiences of teachers and students who actually work with blended programmes, for the perceptions of the key participants will affect the success or otherwise of the offering. We cannot assume that just because something harnesses the latest technology it will be embraced wholeheartedly by its consumers.

Johnson and Marsh, in Chapter 4, began by setting out criteria for successful language learning which included factors such as performing authentic tasks, opportunities for varied, creative expression and social interaction, careful attention to the learning process, lack of stress and anxiety, and so on. As regards authentic tasks, debates concerning authenticity in second language learning have a long history (e.g., Chavez, 1998; Widdowson, 1998) but it is generally agreed that it is the learners who 'authenticate' (or otherwise) the materials and tasks they are confronted with, rather than materials and tasks possessing intrinsic authenticity. In other words, if I, as a learner, perceive a text or audio passage as a genuine example of the target language which will be useful to me, then I have 'authenticated' the material. On the other hand, no matter how real the text or audio might be, if I, the learner, see it as obscure, unnatural or of little use to me, it will be difficult for me to authenticate it. This might be the case, for example in the teaching of academic or professional English, where the student might not perceive the material as genuine or relevant to their needs.

Authentication, or lack of it, will affect response and motivation in the online environment as well as in the classroom, so continued feedback from learners will be all-important. We need to understand not only how learners work with the material they are given, but what they do and how they experience things when they explore the vast resources the online world offers them. This will require more than just automated records of students' interactions with teaching materials, but also getting direct feedback, using the students as informants and properly understanding their online experiences, where and how they encounter the target language. King, in Chapter 6 in this volume, suggests that higher-level students may come across material in the L2 (e.g., videos) on the internet beyond that prescribed for their course and experience it as authentic. This is clearly something the teacher cannot fully control but will become an increasingly common source of authentic encounters to be exploited with the target language as students access a wider range of resources and spend more time learning with technology. Materials discovered by students and perceived by them as authentic could be used as input for tasks which would have a greater chance of success.

Kramsch et al. (2000) see computer-mediated texts as the basis of a new literacy. Learners using technology need to authenticate the texts they encounter in the electronic world just as they have to in the classroom. Kramsch et al. go on to say: 'Computer learners do this by learning the language variety of their electronic interlocutors, the rhetorical conventions of electronic genres, and by interacting with people and written texts on line.' (ibid.: 82) In other words, we come back to the need to understand student interactions online not merely as face-to-face speaking and conventional writing transferred to keyboard, mouse and screen but as a new and different kind of communicative environment.

The experiences of students interacting with technology reported in Kramsch et al.'s paper are very positive; they engage in creative language use and feel that what they are doing is more meaningful and important to them as individuals. Additionally, they develop an awareness of the process of exploring and manipulating the target language. Technology-mediated activity can create (for the learner) authentic encounters with the target language and opportunities to become the authors and agents of their own language use in L2. What is more it can help to construct and reinforce their sense of identity. If this is indeed so, there is more likely to be a positive effect on motivation and involvement in those aspects of the course retained in the face-to-face classroom, as long as appropriate connections can be forged between the two learning environments. Thus the process will become two-way: classroom practices will feed into online activity, and the fruits of online activity will increasingly feed back into re-thinking classroom practices, perhaps another possible example of what King (Chapter 6, this volume) urges in the promotion of the term 'integrated' in relation to BL environments, where teaching and learning activity in the computer-mediated world should not be seen as radically different from that of the face-to-face classroom.

LANGUAGE LEARNING AS COMMUNITY

Johnson and Marsh (Chapter 4, this volume) suggest that one of the potential advantages of the inclusion of social networking in a BL programme is that students can become members of wider communities beyond that of their own classmates, both internationally and globally (see also Linniou et al., 2015). BL programmes can take advantage of the fact that the experience of global communities is not likely to be new for most people, given the extent to which social networking platforms are already an integral part of their daily life. Garrison and Vaughan (2008: Chapter 2) see the creation of a sense of a 'community of inquiry' as fundamental to any learning context and stress that students must have freedom to think and act and to develop social relationships linked to their educational goals, while still under the guidance of a teacher. In the online world, the development of such a community is independent of time and location, but the online sense of community must ideally fuse with that of the face-to-face community in the totality of the BL experience.

At the same time as fostering a sense of international community, Johnson and Marsh stressed the importance of taking local conditions into account: there is no one-size-fits-all blended solution and local communities and educational and institutional cultures should be respected (see also Morris and Miller, 2014; Tankari, 2014). The decisions taken on the Laureate Universities programme outlined by Johnson and Marsh involved teachers from different countries acting as an international community, feeding their views into the evolution of the project as a whole. Although coming from distinct local communities and cultures, the teachers identified common rewards, challenges and concerns both for them as teachers and their students, a fact which is perhaps one of the most exciting and potentially fruitful developments to emerge from BL projects. Key concerns which were raised from a student and a teacher perspective were best use of time and the pedagogical appropriateness of tasks. From the project there came a sense not only that 'flipping' the classroom was a good way to use classroom time from the student viewpoint (more active interaction, less teacher-talk), but that the experience for the teachers themselves was a more positive one. At the core of the flipped classroom experience for the teachers was the realisation that their practice in the face-to-face classroom could be as new and innovative as the technology-led elements.

The sense of community is also important in the 'vertical' domain, i.e., not just among students or among teachers but between teachers and students (Ngoyi and Malapile, 2014; Zhang, 2015). It has long been argued that an increased level of contact between students and their teachers contributes to a sense of involvement for the student (Astin, 1999). Astin was not writing within a technological framework, but his model of student involvement could be judged as gaining greatly from the incorporation of social networking and teacher-student communication into BL programmes. Across BL domains, especially in distance-learning contexts, the presence and actions of tutors/instructors in online elements is considered crucial to success (Lund and Snell, 2014).

THE ROLES OF TEACHERS AND LEARNERS

Anny King in Chapter 6 in this volume invites teachers to return to some fundamental principles of learning as advocated by thinkers of former centuries, going right back to the ancient Greeks, whose vision, she argues, is no less relevant today than in times gone by. Teachers need to be not just educators but 'listeners', says King, and must see themselves as participants in dialogues with their students. Thornbury, in Chapter 2 in this volume, sees the scaffolding and 'just-in-time' support that teachers provide as a key factor in the sociocultural context of language acquisition.

Meanwhile, Anna Comas-Quinn in Chapter 5 deals with the need for a review of teacher professional development. Implicit in her chapter title is the view that teacher education cannot simply continue as it is but has to take the characteristics of BL environments into account. Comas-Quinn points out that the online world has created a shift in the traditional hierarchy of teacher and student. Students can now take far greater control over their own learning and become 'co-creators' of their learning environment, including the easier provision of peer feedback. This represents a significant shift in the roles of teachers.

Central to the new roles and responsibilities of teachers is an understanding of the 'why' of technology (why it is suitable/unsuitable for particular purposes) and not simply the 'how' (how to manipulate the software, how to understand computer programmes and learning management systems, etc.). The imperative for teacher education is to help teachers move from seeing BL as just doing traditional pedagogy online to a new vision of their teaching. Since most teacher-training programmes are governed by top-down decisions (institutions, school managers, trainers and assessment bodies are typically the spur for their existence), one can argue that senior managers and institutional decision-makers also need to shift their perspective to a new understanding of teaching and learning.

In the online world where students may be required to collaborate with one another in group activities, the teacher has some overlapping, and some distinct, responsibilities as compared with organising the face-to-face classroom. Ernest et al. (2013) stress the importance of the skills that teachers need to successfully organise and support online collaborative learning. These include:

- adequate planning;
- effective design of activities and appropriate choice of tools to carry them out;
- encouraging students to agree on 'ground rules' for the modes of participation in online activities; and
- decisions as regards monitoring and moderating the learning activity.

Although most of these skills are already required in the effective organisation of face-to-face learning, the virtual world of online collaborative learning differs in that it takes place at times and places that suit the learners and via modes of communication quite different from face-to-face talk (e.g., email, synchronous and asynchronous chat, text-messaging, social networking). Ernest et al. (2011) remind us that the training and experience of many teachers simply may not have prepared them for these new modes of learning and their roles within them (also Lázár, Chapter 9 in this volume). This will clearly continue to be a key issue in teacher education for the foreseeable future.

TRAINING TEACHERS AND LEARNERS

A potential lack of experience and training in new modes of learning frequently coupled with increasing institutional pressures upon teachers to engage in initial or in-service training might leave teachers feeling overwhelmed by change. In addressing this issue it should be recognised that the motivation to pursue and complete training is just as important for teachers as for learners doing language courses, and this should be at the heart of training programmes. Banegas and Manzur Busleimán (2014), in reporting on an online teacher education programme, highlight some of the factors we have already discussed in connection with SLA, such as personal motivation and the sense of identity and self, as well as the perception of their own performance on the course and the motivation the innovative technology itself can generate (see also Wang, Chen and Levy, 2010).

The importance of motivating teachers is further strengthened by Comas-Quinn in Chapter 5 where she demonstrates that teachers who successfully embrace their new role in the world of e-learning motivate their own students to succeed. Teachers have a role in creating students' perceptions of the goals and importance of the various course elements, whether in the face-to-face classroom or in the computer-mediated world (Murphy et al. 2010). Understanding this link must be among the central aims of teacher education programmes. And, as in Johnson and Marsh's report of the Laureate programme (Chapter 4, this volume), teacher collaboration and reflection are vital.

Taking full advantage of the new opportunities for peer collaboration offered by social networks and global communication means that teacher education in the future can become more self-directed, creative and democratic, with less imposition from above. Synchronous (delivered in real-time) online peer observation of teaching has been shown to contribute to a sense of community and to the building of confidence and good relations among teachers in ways that might not necessarily occur in observation in the physical classroom (Harper and Nicolson, 2013). In all the various considerations we have looked at concerning teacher education, learning to use technology is not, and never will be, enough. The most important challenge is for teachers to rethink their role in the blended environment and to put themselves in the position of their learners so that they understand and experience the online learning world from both perspectives: their own and their students', once again echoing King's view of the teacher as a 'listener'.

Learners, too, need to develop a new sense of their role in the language teaching-and-learning enterprise where BL is concerned, just as teachers need to do, and learner training may prove to be just as important as teacher training with regard to BL. In an issue of the *CALICO Journal* devoted to the question of learner training in technology-enhanced language-learning environments, Hubbard (2013) makes the point that language learners' needs do not necessarily mesh with their skills in using technology. Though we might assume that learners (especially younger ones) are all 'digital natives', factors such as disorientation, anxiety and varying perceptions of the value of language learning in the computer-mediated environment still need to be taken into account (Yang, 2001). For example, doing rather static exercises online compared with the immersive experience of a virtual world using avatars can negatively affect how students rate themselves and their language-learning experience (Zheng et al, 2009).

Rott and Weber (2013) further underline some of the difficulties students may face in transferring their language learning to an online environment: they may well be at ease with social networking software but unable to see how to transfer their skill to the creation of learning media such as wikis. They also discuss problems in getting students to understand what is involved in collaborative authorship and their roles and responsibilities in it. In big classes of 30–40 students, especially teacher-fronted ones, individuals can choose to be more passive and to 'switch off'; in the collaborative online world, success depends on engagement and participation. The types of difficulty, disorientation and anxiety experienced at the time of writing may well change and decline in the future as technology becomes easier to navigate, as online language learning is seen as more 'normal' and as adaptive learning becomes more sensitive to individuals' needs and the shifting circumstances of their learning (San Pedro and Baker, Chapter 14, this volume), but monitoring of the personal and affective responses to out-of-class online work will remain important, especially as new, as yet undreamt of, technology-led modes of communication and learning are developed.

Materials

Perhaps the most vital connection between teachers and learners is that provided by teaching materials. For centuries, these were rooted in printed books, supplemented by audio and non-book-based visual material only in the latter part of the 20th century. The student's handwritten notebook provided the record of practice, note-taking and composition, and tests and examinations were paper-based. Half a millennium ago, when learners of Latin in the England of the first Queen Elizabeth sought to improve their oral skills, their only support in the classroom came from text books and whatever role-plays and classroom dialogues the teacher promoted (Carter and McCarthy, 2015). Until relatively recently, books, wall-charts and pictures, chalk and blackboard provided the hardware for language learning.

Now, as Mishan argues in Chapter 8, we need a complete reconceptualisation of teaching materials. We cannot now assume that the materials will be authored by professional material writers and published in print by major publishers, or that teachers will necessarily be the authors or originators. Learner-originated materials represent one of the most innovative trends in language learning. Furthermore, the media through which the materials will be delivered to the user now offer vastly wider possibilities compared with the environment of 30 or 40 years ago. Audio-visual delivery is now high-definition; computer-based materials may be synchronous (delivered in real-time) or asynchronous (deposited on servers and accessed at any time); they may be open-access, i.e., usable by anyone, not just those they were initially designed for; place of delivery and reception of the material can be anywhere in the world; and its life and duration may be short-term or permanent. Communication between teacher and student and among students with regard to the use of the material may happen through email, social media, video conferencing, text messaging, wikis, blogs/vlogs, etc.

Crucially, the communications generated through these new media need not simply *accompany* the materials in the conventional sense but have the potential to *become* the materials in themselves. As Mishan says, in this way the materials are not just a product; they become part of the learning process. Computer-mediated communication opens up new possibilities for language acquisition and, as we argued in Chapter 1, new windows on SLA processes. Teaching materials nowadays, therefore, can be redefined as any item that can be exploited for interaction and learning, whether print-based or digitised, and whether used in classrooms or online. This trend will continue and no doubt expand as technology offers new perspectives on learning.

The idea of learners becoming originators or (co-)authors of 'materials' in the sense we are using the word here, therefore, includes the following:

- Learners collaborating online while carrying out conventional tasks such as academic writing: the students co-own and provide feedback on the writing process and the end products (Strobl, 2014).
- Learners communicating online with other learners or target-language users. Research shows, for example, that incidental improvements in syntax can occur through email exchanges (Stockwell and Harrington, 2003).
- Learners collaborating on projects to create websites, wikis, blogs/vlogs, videos, podcasts and social media pages (Thorne and Payne, 2005; Rott and Weber, 2013).
- Learners incorporating material they have found for themselves, whether on the internet or elsewhere into their language learning environment, which they can then share with their learning community (Warschauer and Healey, 1998; Fletcher and Barr, 2008; Peterson, 2010; King, Chapter 6, this volume).
- Learners creating and/or using online games, comics, quizzes, alternative identities through avatars on virtual-world websites and sharing these (Francis Pelton and Pelton, 2009; Wang et al, 2012; Hitosugi et al., 2014).
- Learners using tools which may not (yet) be part of their institutional language-learning environment but which are a familiar part of their everyday lives (e.g., smartphones, apps and other smart technology items such as fitness-tracking wristbands, games consoles, etc.). Dudeney and Hockly (Chapter 13, this volume) explore further the potential of mobile learning, and there is no doubt that materials will become increasingly 'mobile' in the sense defined here.

UNDERSTANDING LEARNERS

In Chapter 9 in the present volume, Lázár reiterates the notion of 'transforming blends' and sees good materials as supporting transformative learning experiences and not just supplementing existing modes of learning. These transformative learning experiences are best illustrated by the kinds of collaborative learning that online activity offers to communities of learners, especially where cross-cultural communication is involved, something we can expect more of, as global communications become ever easier and more immediate. She stresses the importance of flexibility in materials design in the relatively novel environment of online work: materials may need to be redesigned and reconceptualised as the course progresses. Intelligent adaptive systems may provide some solutions to this question of flexibility; San Pedro and Baker further discuss this in Chapter 14.

Lázár also notes the importance of obtaining feedback from both teachers and learners as regards the efficacy of the BL experience and the tasks and material involved. Central to the success of the online activities was preparation of the learners both in terms of practice in writing forum posts and in ways of responding to their online partners' postings before actually engaging with the online elements of the course. Similarly, Heiser et al. (2013) prepared students for synchronous conferencing online and found that students benefited from practice in their L1 before doing the real thing in L2. BL also places new demands on learners to exercise greater autonomy, in that they will be presented with a greater range of choices regarding their communication in the L2 than they might have needed to exercise in the conventional face-to-face classroom. These examples reinforce the argument that we cannot simply assume that learners will know how to 'do' online communication in a language-learning context just because they are digital natives. Hubbard (2013) rightly sees research into the efficacy of learner training and preparation to be one of the most important tasks now and in the ongoing development of technology-based learning.

TASK-BASED LEARNING

Chapter 10 in this volume by Seedhouse and his colleagues on the digital kitchen offers an interesting perspective on BL. In the digital kitchen, interest lies in the extent to which task-based language learning can be removed from the conventional classroom to a machine-led environment, including the necessary pre-task input and post-task feedback normally provided by teachers and/or fellow-students.

Task-based learning emphasises 'pragmatic meaning' (i.e., meaning in context) rather than language forms (Ellis, 2003:16), is grounded in a philosophy of learning by doing and, in its purest form, involves the performance of real-world tasks in the service of language learning. Tasks typically operate around some sort of 'gap' (e.g., an information gap) which needs to be bridged. The successful outcome and completion of the task is the primary goal (Skehan, 1998) rather than the successful and accurate manipulation of language forms, though each may support the other (Nunan, 2004: 4; Willis and Willis, 2007). The choice of language used in the performance of the task is ideally that of the participants as the task unfolds, rather than fixed beforehand by the teacher or the material.

The transfer of classic types of task from the classroom to the online environment may not seem, on the face of it, to be entirely straightforward. This is because, in ideal circumstances, pre-task input, plus any input needed during the performance of the task itself, and post-task evaluation are negotiated in the face-to-face classroom moment by moment. Furthermore, the process by which the task is to be solved is not pre-determined. Transferring the typical tasks done in the classroom to the online environment is a considerable challenge. Normally, pre-task input is provided by the materials, under the guidance of the teacher. Often, students are given opportunities for pre-planning in pairs or groups, and while they are doing the task, they can ask for help from the teacher. When the task is complete, there is ideally a feedback and evaluation session. All of these stages offer potential learning opportunities.

One solution to this challenge has been offered via the use of computerised 'operational scripts' for collaborative learning, whereby stages and desired actions in the solution of the task are built into the computer programme. For example, the computer will give instructions as to how student groups should be organised and reorganised as the task progresses, or present grids and charts at intervals that have to be completed by the task participants. Such pre-programmed automated steps and procedures form a 'contract' between instructor and students, allowing a limited degree of freedom of action circumscribed by the constraints of the script but also offering the instructor sufficient opportunity to intervene at various stages (Dillenbourg, 2002).

In the digital kitchen, the smart technology which enables the computer programme to script and monitor the students' use of kitchen utensils and ingredients and the actions they perform with them provides structure and immediate feedback on the success or failure of specific sub-tasks. Take a wrong step at any point and the dish you are preparing will not be right. Thus, theoretically at least, the computer provides real-time responses and adaptive feedback that present learning opportunities which may feed into acquisition. There is also good evidence of such learning opportunities in the peer-to-peer collaboration in overcoming problems, as the transcribed data in the chapter by Seedhouse et al. show.

The digital kitchen is a model for task-based language learning in simulated environments and one can envisage a range of tasks other than food preparation which could take advantage of similar technology. As well as the examples given at the end of Seedhouse et al.'s chapter, one could imagine, for instance, learning a musical instrument, making and editing a video, using physical exercise equipment, learning to drive or fly a plane in a simulator, constructing a model for an engineering project. Any one of these could be mediated through a second or foreign language with real-time input and feedback. Such affordances do not necessarily exclude intervention from human teachers in a blended programme but the independence they offer the student and the potential for realising task-based learning in its strongest form are clear. Virtual-world second-language encounters such as the digital kitchen and its spin-offs may be a key element of transformative blends in the future as the technology advances and simplifies the creation of simulated learning environments.

FLEXIBILITY

King in Chapter 6 of this volume sees the flexibility of BL (where non-linearity and 'just-in-time' learning are significant features) may be seen as one of its strengths. Similarly, Moloney and O'Keeffe in Chapter 11 of this volume see the flexibility of learning options as a great strength. For example, removing lectures to the server-based world of the online environment reduces the stresses college and university students experience in listening to and absorbing the lectures in real time, delivered in large theatres. The lectures can be accessed and processed in a calmer, more personalised environment. And overall, the student complaints that there was simply too much content in the face-to-face course, too little time to discuss it and not enough preparation for classes beforehand could also be addressed in the blended solution (see also Young, 2008).

Flexibility also includes the possibility of more individual feedback, of choice of time and place for students to complete their work, interaction both synchronously and asynchronously and increased interaction and opportunities for collaborative learning, and not least, institutional and personal cost-effectiveness. However, Moloney and O'Keeffe are also realistic in seeing potential downsides to the computer-mediated solutions. These include possible isolation, technological shortcomings and inadequate feedback. This last point would seem to chime with Walsh's emphasis in Chapter 3 of this volume on the role of good teachers in making moment-by-moment decisions on monitoring and managing the learning process.

At the heart of Moloney and O'Keeffe's BL project was concern with the cognitive demands placed on students at different levels and when faced with different processing demands from different types of tasks. How the cognitive aspects could be built into a knowledge-creating approach to education instead of a transmissive one (where knowledge is simply delivered to students) and how the student body could be turned into a learning community (or community of enquiry) was one of the principles of their programme (Garrison and Vaughan, 2008; Akyol and Garrison, 2010).

Even more significant in Moloney and O'Keeffe's chapter than the flexibility provided by the technical affordances such as vodcasts and wikis and the transformation of the student body into a cohesive learning community is the belief that success in BL comes from a solid, grounded and robust theory of education and learning which really tries to understand what is involved for students in dealing with challenging teaching media such as lectures and dense content in reading and other forms of input.

'BACK TO BASICS': THE INTERACTIVE IMPERATIVE

In Chapter 1 of this volume, I devoted some space to the question of classroom interaction and its role in underpinning SLA. Thornbury, in Chapter 2, also focused on the value of teacher-learner interaction as one of his key points. Walsh's Chapter 3 then expanded upon face-to-face classroom interaction as a key element in the creation and exploitation of learning opportunities, with the expert teacher playing a central role in managing the several modes of communication in the classroom. It was argued in both chapters that reproducing in the online world the essential qualities of face-to-face spoken interaction was a major challenge for BL. The chapters by Hojnacki (Chapter 7) and McCarten and Sandiford (Chapter 12) in this volume have faced that challenge, as have other projects and research studies. Hojnacki mentions the question of whether an online medium such as asynchronous chat (i.e., chat that does not happen in immediate, real time) can not only reflect some of the characteristics of face-to-face oral interaction but whether it can also facilitate greater use of the target language for students. Clearly, as Hojnacki acknowledges, there are differences in the communication that results from synchronous (real-time) and asynchronous chat. However, the slower exchanges of asynchronous chat can offer students greater opportunities to use the L2 and output increases compared with what they manage in the face-to-face classroom. Hojnacki notes that, in comparison, voice-based online tools might reintroduce some of the anxiety that often works against oral communication in the classroom. Other research has shown little difference between asynchronous and synchronous exchanges (e.g., Pérez, 2003), while Sotillo (2000) found that synchronous discussions contained more of the discoursal features of face-to-face conversation.

Not least of the problems of the face-to-face classroom, as Hojnacki points out, is the rationing of speaking time per student, especially in large classes; online forms of communication allow more time per individual to engage in meaningful interaction, even if it is only in a 'writing-as-if-speaking' mode of communication such as text chat. In Hojnacki's project, which attempted to overcome this difficulty, speaking opportunities were enhanced by 'audio dropboxes', where learners could deposit recordings of their speech, simulated 'conversations', where students gave spoken answers to recorded oral questions and opportunities for students to record their oral responses to images and videos and respond to other students' responses, creating a kind of conversational thread. These modes had the added advantage of providing students with greater planning time before producing spoken language. The tools seem to have produced good results, with greatly increased spoken output by the students involved, including among students who were less willing in the face-to-face classroom, along with an increase in confidence. One can only speculate that the kinds of tools Hojnacki explores for online oral production will become more and more sophisticated in the future, enabling the simulated conversational worlds they generate to become more realistic.

But just how much of oral interaction online of the types Hojnacki discusses truly replicates face-to-face talk? Can online learning really replace the rich interaction of teacher-student talk and student-student talk in pair and group work? This was the challenge facing my co-authors of the *Touchstone* adult course series (McCarthy et al., 2005–2014), which puts a strong emphasis on conversational skills, when it was decided to create an online version for wholly online and blended courses. McCarten and Sandiford, in Chapter 12, reported on how they faced the challenge. They recognise the kinds of skills experienced and trained teachers bring to the task of generating interaction in class, which Walsh explored in detail in Chapter 3, and the importance of the modes of teacher communication that Walsh delineates. The printed course material destined for transfer to the online environment assumed a mediating tutor and students working in pairs or small groups. In the absence of the human tutor, where the material must simultaneously act as the content, the task, the tutor and the guide, what could be expected from a machine?

The *Touchstone* authors were required by their publisher to transfer to the computer-mediated world the best elements of a globally successful adult course which was corpus-informed, especially in its spoken language lessons, and which focused on interactive conversational strategies, and not just speaking skills in the sense of prepared monologues or recording responses to prompts and questions. In short, as McCarten and Sandiford put it, the print course offered 'multiple opportunities to speak, react, and respond in meaningful ways to content throughout a lesson'. Additionally, the *Touchstone* methodology rests upon noticing and inductive learning (working out rules and generalisations based on close observation of corpus-based examples). This aspect of the methodology, too, was to become part of the online material. The *Touchstone* authors faced the added difficulty that the learning management system they were working with was not suited to synchronous online communication between tutor and students; in essence, the learner was on his/her own while doing the learning activities. The plus-side to this was privacy for learners who may be shy or feel threatened by having to 'perform' in class.

Video role-plays, where learners could practise taking one of the parts in simulated conversations with the actors, was one way into the interactive issues. Asynchronous communication with classmates through blogs and forum discussions was another, which in the online world in general have become conventionalised as a form of writing-as-if-speaking, as we have mentioned elsewhere in this chapter. Voice tools (where students can leave recorded messages for the teacher – see also Hojnacki, Chapter 7, this volume) were another way of creating an interactive environment. In line with the *Touchstone* printed course emphasis on conversational skills, noticing activities based on corpus-informed conversational extracts were retained in the online material. Maximum use was made of graphics and audio and video support. In this way, the *Touchstone* authors attempted to remain true not only to their spoken-corpus-informed principles, but also to maintain the SLA principles outlined at the start of this book.

We can conclude from the studies in this book where the authors have tried to maximise interaction in the online world that, despite the advances in audio and video technology and enhanced graphics, in an almost completely machine-led world such as the *Touchstone* online course, pair-work, group work and the kinds of conversation managed and monitored through the teacher's sensitive social antennae are best kept in the face-to-face classroom. But that is the great advantage of the flipped classroom. By not just transferring the mechanical and static elements of the print course (e.g., grammar and vocabulary exercises, reading texts) to the online platform but carefully building in best methodological practice in the online components (e.g., guidance and scaffolding, noticing activities, inductive tasks, a good deal of listening, engagement in simulated dialogues based on real, corpus-informed language, etc.), the *Touchstone* authors release potentially great swathes of time for the face-to-face classroom to devote its energies to genuine spoken interaction. At present, this would seem to be the best recipe for a blended programme where teacher-guided spoken interaction is seen as central and where conversational competence is the goal.

THE MOBILE WORLD

Dudeney and Hockly's Chapter 13 explores the potential for learning from mobile technology: phones, tablets and other portable machines open a new world of novel learning experiences. The smartphone is not just an instrument of communication; it can become the source of new learning opportunities and entirely new types of learning (Patten et al., 2006). With access to a mobile phone, learning can happen anywhere, and at any time, and, despite the often negative connotations of the word, opportunistically, i.e., whenever opportunities present themselves (Kenning, 2007: 192). Perhaps the greatest potential of smartphones and other portable devices is their ability to develop 'seamless learning spaces' (Looi et al., 2010), wherein learners can switch effortlessly from solitary, individual learning experiences to social networking and collaborative learning, from written media to audio and visual media, from more formal learning material (e.g., encyclopedias, online pedagogical materials) to informal sources (e.g., blogs, chat rooms, videos), all as and when their curiosity prompts them. Contextual learning (i.e., learning that takes advantage of the learner's physical location when using the phone) is seen as one of the great pluses of mobile devices (Kukulska-Hulme, 2006).

That is not to say that we can, at the present time, safely assume that learners will embrace learning at any opportunity on their phone or tablet as opposed to, say, at a specific moment in front of a desktop computer, or that they will value mobile learning in the same way as more conventional classroom or other types of computer-mediated learning (Stockwell, 2013; Tossell et al., 2014). Successful design of activities, as in all modes of teaching and learning, are key to the integration of mobile learning into the student's learning environment, though, as Dudeney and Hockly point out in Chapter 13, teachers may currently lack the confidence to design activities that fully exploit smart mobile technology.

Dudeney and Hockly reiterate a point made by Kramsch et al. (2000), referred to earlier, that the notion of literacy in our time involves abilities with regard to using and getting the full benefits of technology. The screen of a smartphone is not just somewhere to 'read' things in a conventional sense, but is a new reading landscape in itself, one that can link instantaneously to both the physical environment (through GPS location services) and to the rest of the network and the entire World Wide Web. Developing new 'reading skills' in this landscape is part of the new literacy, and educators will have a prominent role in promoting and developing such skills. Dudeney and Hockly lay out the parameters for successful design and implementation of mobile learning within a new literacy framework. Most importantly, the literacies that have to be developed are not ones that only apply to professionals (e.g., computer programming skills which might be needed in certain professions) but are those that dominate our everyday lives (researching information online, reading, interpreting and evaluating such information, communicating effectively in Skype conversations, maintaining an interesting blog, and so on).

As always, in the BL context, making the vital links between what happens in the face-to-face classroom, what happens in computer-mediated environments within institutions and what happens out there, on the street, phone or tablet in hand, will be the most direct route to success. In second language learning, any encounter outside of the classroom with the target language (whether it be in a song lyric, a street sign, a food package, a restaurant menu) can lend itself to a learning opportunity by using the mobile device's built-in apps (e.g., online dictionaries and encyclopedias, search engines). The real test will be whether the student can see relevance to their educational programme and incorporate such experiences into their growing competence in the target language.

THE INTELLIGENT MACHINE

The final chapter in this present section, by Baker and San Pedro, brings us back to the individual student and how BL can best provide the kind of personalised feedback that is so important to language learners. What progress am I making? How successful am I in doing these activities? What errors am I making? How does my performance relate to other students following the same programme? These are reasonable and legitimate questions for any learner to ask, or for teachers to ask about their students or about the effectivity of their own teaching.

San Pedro and Baker see good feedback as a way of helping learners to 'achieve their optimal learning potential' and mention ways in which technology can enhance individualisation. Firstly, technology, as we have discussed elsewhere, can provide educators with useful data about groups and individuals; learning platforms can monitor student activity. Secondly, technology can offer the possibility of targeted materials for specific groups and sub-groups in an economically viable way. This latter point is an important one, because, in the past, major international publishers of printed teaching materials at best were only able to adapt their courses for major regions (e.g., Asia editions, so-called 'British English' or 'American English' markets, and so on) or broad age groups (adults, teenagers, young learners, etc.).

But greatest of the potentials of technology is the ability of the material to be *adaptive*, in that it can change rapidly according to circumstances and the varied activity of its users. San Pedro and Baker see this adaptivity as tailored not just to success or failure in doing an activity but also sensitive to the key personal factors we have mentioned in this book – motivation, affective and behavioural factors, learning strategies, personal interest, boredom and frustration, engagement and disengagement, etc. It is the job of the machine to tailor its output to what it can learn about the individual user in relation to all these factors from that person's input. This clearly takes BL further into a new domain, where, perhaps, one day, the teacher may be an irrelevant bystander in the learning experience as intelligent machines communicate with their users in an almost-human-like manner, so that everyone can enjoy a one-to-one lesson delivered by a caring, sensitive computer.

However, it has been the basic ethos of this book that the best language learning experiences are those that involve human-to-human interaction and that the greatest strength of BL is that it can release time for even more fruitful face-to-face interaction by 'flipping' to the arena of out-of-class work/homework many of the activities that used to consume class time (e.g., reading, task preparation, closed exercises, tests and quizzes, exercise correction sessions, etc.). So at the end of this book, we reiterate that ethos: good BL brings the participants together rather than separating them into a soulless world of an army of individuals in isolation working at machines or wandering the streets with their smartphones. That togetherness may come from greater face-to-face classroom interaction, but it can also come from the informed use of technology via blogs/vlogs, chat forums, email, text messaging, postings on social networks, exchanging photographs, exploring and sharing virtual worlds, synchronous and asynchronous communication between and among teachers and learners and whatever else technology can offer. Recent developments such as mobile technology and adaptive learning become, therefore, not replacements for human interaction but ways of enhancing learning, of adding something extra, exciting and new, of providing a different kind of learning experience over and above what we already know to be good educational practice. A good blend of face-to-face classwork and out-of-class computer-mediated work is not just 1 + 1 = 2; it is more like 1 + 1 = 3, with innumerable extra possibilities and often unpredicted benefits of the third dimension.

References

Akyol, Z., & Garrison, D. R. (2010). Understanding cognitive presence in an online and blended community of inquiry: Assessing outcomes and processes for deep approaches to learning. *British Journal of Educational Technology*, 42(2), 233–250.

Astin, A. W. (1999). Student involvement: A developmental theory for higher education. *Journal of College Student Development*, 40(5), 518–529.

Bailey, J., Ellis, S., Schneider, C., & Vander Ark, T. (2013). *Blended Learning Implementation Guide*. Online at: http://digitallearningnow.com/site/uploads/2013/02/DLNSmartSeries-BL-paper_2012-02-05a.pdf

Banegas, D. L., & Manzur Busleimán, G. I. (2014). Motivating factors in online language teacher education in southern Argentina. *Computers & Education*, 76, 131–142.

Barrs, K. (2010). What factors encourage high levels of student participation in a self-access centre? *Studies in Self-Access Learning Journal*, 1(1), 10–16.

Carter, R. A., & McCarthy, M. J. (2015). Spoken grammar: Where are we and where are we going? *Applied Linguistics* (2015) Online at: 10.1093/applin/amu080.

Chavez, M. (1998). Learner's perspectives on authenticity. *International Review of Applied Linguistics in Language Teaching*, 36(4), 277–306.

de Leng, B. A., Dolmans, D. H., Donkers, H. H., Muijtjens, A. M., & van der Vleuten, C. P. (2010). Instruments to explore blended learning: Modifying a method to analyse online communication for the analysis of face-to-face communication. *Computers & Education*, 55(2), 644–651.

Dillenbourg, P. (2002). Over-scripting CSCL. The risks of blending collaborative learning with instructional design. In P. A. Kirschner (Ed.), *Three Worlds of CSCL: Can We Support CSCL?* (pp. 61–91). Heerlen: Open Universiteit Nederland.

Ellis, R. (2003). *Task-based Language Learning and Teaching*. Oxford: Oxford University Press.

Ernest, P., Guitert Catasús, M., Hampel, R., Heiser, S., Hopkins, J., Murphy, L., & Stickler, U. (2013). Online teacher development: collaborating in a virtual learning environment. *Computer Assisted Language Learning*, 26(4), 311–333.

Ernest, P., Heiser, S., & Murphy, L. (2011). Developing teacher skills to support collaborative online language learning. *The Language Learning Journal*, 41(1), 37–54.

Fletcher, C., & Barr, V. (2008). Developing and adapting resources. In A. Paton & M. Wilkins (Eds.), *Teaching English to Speakers of Other Languages: A Teacher Education Handbook* (pp. 161–187). Maidenhead: Open University Press/McGraw-Hill Education.

Foertsch, J., Moses, G., Strikwerda, J., & Litzkow, M. (2002). Reversing the lecture/homework paradigm using eTeach® web-based streaming video software. *Journal of Engineering Education*, 91(3), 267–274.

Francis Pelton, L., & Pelton, T. (2009). The learner as teacher: Using student authored comics to "teach" mathematics concepts. In G. Siemens & C. Fulford (Eds.), *Proceedings of World Conference on Educational Multimedia, Hypermedia and Telecommunications* 2009 (pp. 1591–1599). Chesapeake, VA: Association for the Advancement of Computing in Education (AACE).

Garrison, D. R., & Vaughan, N. D. (2008). *Blended Learning in Higher Education: Framework, Principles, and Guidelines*. San Francisco, CA: Jossey-Bass.

Ginns, P., & Ellis, R. (2007). Quality in blended learning: Exploring the relationships between on-line and face-to-face teaching and learning. *The Internet and Higher Education*, 10(1), 53–64.

Graham, C. (2006). Blended learning systems: Definition, current trends and future directions. In C. J. Bonk & C. Graham (Eds.), *The Handbook of Blended Learning: Global Perspectives, Local Designs* (pp. 3–21). San Francisco, CA: Pfeiffer Publishing.

Graham, C. R. (2013). Emerging practice and research in blended learning. In M. G. Moore (Ed.), *Handbook of Distance Education* (3rd Edition) (pp. 333–350). New York: Routledge.

Harper, F., & Nicolson, M. (2013). Online peer observation: Its value in teacher professional development, support and well-being. *International Journal for Academic Development*, 18(3), 264–275.

Heiser, S. L., Stickler, U., & Furnborough, C. (2013). Ready, steady, speak-online: Student training in the use of an online synchronous conferencing tool. *CALICO Journal*, 30(2), 226–251.

Hitosugi, C. I., Schmidt, M., & Hayashi, K. (2014). Digital game-based learning (DGBL) in the L2 classroom: The impact of the UN's off-the-shelf videogame, *Food Force*, on learner affect and vocabulary retention. *CALICO Journal*, 31(1), 19–39.

Hsu, L., & Sheu, C-M. (2008). A study of low English proficiency students' attitude toward online learning. *Electronic Journal of Foreign Language Teaching* (Singapore), 5(2), 240–264. Online at: http://e-flt.nus.edu.sg/v5n22008/hsu.pdf

Hubbard, P. (2013). Making a case for learner training in technology enhanced language learning environments. *CALICO Journal*, 30(2), 163–178.

Kenning, M-M. (2007). *ICT and Language Learning: From Print to the Mobile Phone*. Basingstoke, UK: Palgrave Macmillan.

Kistow, B. (2011). Blended learning in higher education: A study of a graduate school of business, Trinidad and Tobago. *Caribbean Teaching Scholar*, 1(2), 115–128.

Kramsch, C., A'Ness, F., & Lam, W. S. E. (2000). Authenticity and authorship in the computer-mediated acquisition of L2 literacy. *Language Learning & Technology*, 4(2), 78–104.

Kukulska-Hulme, A. (2006). Mobile language learning now and in the future. In P. Svensson (Ed.), *Från vision till praktik: Språkutbildning och Informationsteknik* (pp. 295–310). Sweden: Nätuniversitetet.

Lage, M. J., Platt, G. J., & Treglia, M. (2000). Inverting the classroom: A gateway to creating an inclusive learning environment. *Journal of Economic Education*, 31(1), 30–43.

Lai, C., & Gu, M. (2011). Self-regulated out-of-class language learning with technology. *Computer Assisted Language Learning*, 24(4), 317–335.

Linniou, M., Holdcroft, C., & Holmes, P. S. (2015). Increasing research students' engagement through virtual communities. In R. D. Wright (Ed.), *Student-Teacher Interaction in Online Learning Environments* (pp. 50–75). Hershey, PA: IGI Global.

Looi, C. K., Seow, P., Zhang, B., Hyo-Jeong, S., Chen, W., & Lung-Siang, W. (2010). Leveraging mobile technology for sustainable seamless learning: a research agenda. *British Journal of Educational Technology*, 41(2), 154–169.

Lund, J., & Snell, C. (2014). Behave yourself! An investigation of the impact of tutor behaviour on the student experience of online distance-based learning. In T. Yuzer Volkan & G. Eby (Eds.), *Handbook of Research on Emerging Priorities and Trends in Distance Education* (pp. 14–31). Hershey, PA: IGI Global.

Mackey, T., & Ho, J. (2008). Exploring the relationships between web usability and students' perceived learning in web-based multimedia (WBMM) tutorials. *Computers and Education*, 50, 386–409.

Markee, N. (2008). Toward a learning behavior tracking methodology for CA-for-SLA. *Applied Linguistics*, 29, 404–427.

McCarthy, M. J., McCarten, J., & Sandiford, H., (2005–2014). *Touchstone*. 1st and 2nd edition Student's Books 1–4. Cambridge: Cambridge University Press.

Morris, A., & Miller, M. (2014). Adult learners online: Cultural capacity assessment and application. In J. Keengwe, G. Schnellert & K. Kungu (Eds.), *Cross-cultural Online Learning in Higher Education and Corporate Training* (pp. 134–148). Hershey, PA: IGI Global.

Murphy, L., Shelley, M., & Baumann, U. (2010). Qualities of effective tutors in distance language teaching: Student perceptions. *Innovation in Language Learning and Teaching*, 4(2), 119–136.

Ngoyi, L., & Malapile, L. G. (2014). Social presence and student engagement in online learning. In J. Keengwe, G. Schnellert & K. Kungu (Eds.) *Cross-cultural Online Learning in Higher Education and Corporate Training* (pp. 244–252). Hershey, PA: IGI Global.

Nunan, D. (2004). *Task-based Language Teaching*. Cambridge: Cambridge University Press.

Patten, B., Arnedillo Sánchez, I., & Tangney, B. (2006). Designing collaborative, constructionist and contextual applications for handheld devices. *Computers & Education*, 46, 294–308.

Pérez, L. C. (2003). Foreign language productivity in synchronous versus asynchronous computer-mediated communication. *CALICO Journal*, 21(1), 89–104.

Peterson, E. (2010). Internet-based resources for developing listening. *Studies in Self-Access Learning Journal*, 1(2), 139–154.

Rott, S., & Weber, E. D. (2013). Preparing students to use wiki software as a collaborative learning tool. *CALICO Journal*, 30(2), 179–203.

Skehan, P. (1998). Task-based instruction. *Annual Review of Applied Linguistics*, 18, 268–286.

Sotillo, S. M. (2000). Discourse functions and syntactic complexity in synchronous and asynchronous communication. *Language Learning & Technology*, 4(1), 82–119.

Staker, H., & Horn, M. (2012). *Classifying K-12 Blended Learning*. Innosight Institute. Online at: http://files.eric.ed.gov/fulltext/ED535180.pdf

Stockwell, G. (2013). Tracking learner usage of mobile phones for language learning outside of the classroom. In P. Hubbard, M. Schultz & B. Smith (Eds.), *Human-Computer Interaction in Language Learning: Studies in Honor of Robert Fischer* (pp. 118–136). *CALICO* Monograph Series.

Stockwell, G., & Harrington, M. (2003). The incidental development of L2 proficiency in NS-NNS email interactions. *CALICO Journal*, 20(2), 33–359.

Strobl, C. (2014). Affordances of Web 2.0 technologies for collaborative advanced writing in a foreign language. *CALICO Journal*, 31(1), 1–18.

Tankari, M. (2014). Cultural orientation differences and their implications for online learning satisfaction. In J. Keengwe, G. Schnellert & K. Kungu (Eds.), *Cross-cultural Online Learning in Higher Education and Corporate Training* (pp. 20–61). Hershey, PA: IGI Global.

Thorne, S., & Payne, J. S. (2005). Evolutionary trajectories, internet-mediated expression, and language education. *CALICO Journal*, 22(3), 371–397.

Tossell, C. C., Kortum, P., Shepard, C., Rahmati, A., & Zhong, L. (2014). You can lead a horse to water but you cannot make him learn: Smartphone use in higher education. Online at: http://onlinelibrary.wiley.com/doi/10.1111/bjet.12176/full

Wang, Y., Chen, N-S., & Levy, M. (2010). The design and implementation of a holistic training model for language teacher education in a cyber face-to-face learning environment. *Computers & Education*, 55(2), 777–788.

Wang, F., Burton, K., & Falls, J. (2012). A three-step model for designing initial second life-based foreign language learning activities. *Journal of Online Learning and Teaching*, 8(4). Online at: http://jolt.merlot.org/vol8no4/wang_1212.htm

Warschauer, M., & Healey, D. (1998). Computers and language learning: An overview. *Language Teaching*, 31(2), 57–71.

Widdowson, H. G. (1998). Context, community and authentic language. *TESOL Quarterly*, 32(4), 705–716.

Willis, D., & Willis, J. (2007). *Doing Task-Based Teaching*. Oxford: Oxford University Press.

Yang, S. C. (2001). Integrating computer-mediated tools into the language curriculum. *Journal of Computer Assisted Learning*, 17(1), 85–93.

Young, D. J. (2008). An empirical investigation of the effects of blended learning on student outcomes in a redesigned intensive Spanish course. *CALICO Journal*, 26(1), 160–181.

Zhang, B. (2015). Bridging the social and teaching presence gap in online learning. In R. D. Wright (Ed.), *Student-Teacher Interaction in Online Learning Environments* (pp. 158–182). Hershey, PA: IGI Global.

Zheng, D., Young, M. F., Brewer, R. A., & Wagner, M. (2009). Attitude and self-efficacy change: English language learning in virtual worlds. *CALICO Journal*, 27(1), 205–231.

LIST OF CONTRIBUTORS

Ryan S. Baker is Associate Professor of Cognitive Studies at Teachers College, Columbia University, and Program Coordinator of TC's Masters of Learning Analytics. He earned his PhD in Human-Computer Interaction from Carnegie Mellon University. Dr Baker was previously Assistant Professor of Psychology and the Learning Sciences at Worcester Polytechnic Institute, and served as the first technical director of the Pittsburgh Science of Learning Center DataShop. He is currently serving as the founding president of the International Educational Data Mining Society, and as associate editor of the *Journal of Educational Data Mining*. His research combines educational data mining and quantitative field observation methods to better understand how students respond to educational software, and how these responses impact their learning.

Anna Comas-Quinn is a Senior Lecturer and Associate Head of the Department of Languages at the Faculty of Education and Language Studies at The Open University, UK. She led the development of LORO (http://loro.open.ac.uk), a repository of open educational resources for languages, was a Fellow of the Support Centre for Open Resources in Education (SCORE), and is a long-standing member of the organising committee of the UK-based Open Education Conference (OER). She has published on technology-enhanced and mobile language learning, teacher professional development and open educational resources and practices, and co-edited the first book on open practice in language teaching (http://research-publishing.net/publications/2013-beaven-comas-quinn-sawhill/).

Gavin Dudeney is Director of Technology for The Consultants-E (www.theconsultants-e.com), working in online training and consultancy in EdTech. Former Honorary Secretary and Chair of ElCom at IATEFL, he now serves on the International House Trust Board. Gavin is author of *The Internet and the Language Classroom* (Cambridge University Press, 2000, 2007) and co-author of the award-winning publications *How To Teach English with Technology* (Longman, 2007) and *Digital Literacies* (Routledge, 2013). His new book, *Going Mobile*, was published by DELTA Publishing in 2014.

Nicky Hockly is Director of Pedagogy of The Consultants-E (www.theconsultants-e.com), an award-winning online training and development organisation. She has worked in the field of ELT since 1987, as a teacher, teacher trainer and consultant. She is an international plenary speaker, and gives seminars, in-service workshops and teacher training courses for practising language teachers all over the world. Nicky writes extensively on educational technology, and has co-written several prize-winning methodology books on the application of new technologies to language teaching. Her current research interests include mobile learning, and blended and online course design. Nicky lives in Barcelona, Spain, and prides herself on being a technophobe turned technophile.

Susan Hojnacki is a PhD Candidate in the German Studies Program at Michigan State University in East Lansing, Michigan, and an Adjunct Assistant Professor of German at Aquinas College in Grand Rapids, Michigan. Her research interests include instructional design for online language learning, the flipped classroom, and bridging the gap between research and practice in foreign language instruction. She is currently writing a dissertation based on a year-long study she completed on the flipped classroom in foreign language learning. With those results she is working on designing both hybrid and fully online German courses at the beginner and intermediate level and giving workshops to foreign language instructors on effectively designing online language instruction.

Christopher P. Johnson is currently the regional manager for Laureate Languages in Central and South America. He has taught, coordinated and directed EFL programmes in Chile for over 15 years and is keen to explore solutions to the challenge of teaching and learning EFL in blended and online formats. In an effort to understand the difficulties that students and teachers face in virtual instructional environments, Chris recently completed his online doctoral studies at Walden University and received his degree in 2014. He also holds two Bachelors' degrees, one from the University of Portland, USA (in Interdisciplinary Studies), and one from the Instituto Chileno-Británico de Cultura, Chile (in TEFL), as well as a Masters' degree in Theology (M.Div.) from the University of Notre Dame, USA.

Anny King is Emeritus Director of the University of Cambridge Language Centre and Fellow at Churchill College, Cambridge. She is a specialist in innovative, face-to-face and online language teaching and learning methods. She is also a teacher trainer. She has worked with Thames TV and the BBC for many years as a consultant, writer and co-producer of their language programmes. Anny developed the blended learning Cambridge University Language Programme (CULP) in many languages, initiated the Junior CULP programme for schools, and developed EAP programmes. She has led several development projects for online language learning materials, which have won her awards for their innovative approach, their flexibility and their appropriate use of technology.

Ildikó Lázár is senior lecturer at the Department of English Language Pedagogy of Eötvös Loránd University in Budapest. She gives lectures and seminars in English language teaching methodology, American cultural studies and intercultural communication in the BA, MA and PhD programmes. She has worked as a researcher, materials writer and trainer in Council of Europe, Comenius and Erasmus projects. She has published books and research articles on language teaching and teacher education with a special focus on online tools and ways to bring about change in teachers' beliefs and practices, especially in the field of education for democracy and intercultural competence development.

Michael McCarthy is Emeritus Professor of Applied Linguistics at the University of Nottingham, UK, Adjunct Professor of Applied Linguistics at the University of Limerick, Ireland, and Visiting Professor at Newcastle University, UK. He is co-director (with Ronald Carter) of the 5-million word CANCODE spoken English corpus project and the (co-)author and (co-)editor of 50 books and more than 100 academic articles, including the international best-seller adult course, *Touchstone* and its higher level, *Viewpoint*, as well as the *Cambridge Grammar of English*, *English Grammar Today* and several titles in the Cambridge University Press *English Vocabulary in Use* series.

Jeanne McCarten taught English in Sweden, France, Malaysia and the UK and has many years of experience publishing ELT materials, specialising in grammar and vocabulary. She was also closely involved in the development of the spoken English sections of the Cambridge International Corpus. Currently a freelance ELT author, her main interests lie in applying insights from corpus research to materials, about which she has written several academic articles. She is co-author of the corpus-informed course materials *Touchstone* and *Viewpoint*, published by Cambridge University Press, which are available in print and fully online editions to allow users complete flexibility in planning blended learning programmes.

Debra Marsh is Head of Teacher Professional Development at Macmillan Education. She has been involved in online and blended English language learning for over 20 years. She has been in the forefront of learning innovation from the early days of *Project Merlin* (1995) at the University of Hull (UK) where she project managed the development of one of the very first online EFL courses and early virtual learning environments for ELT. Debra has written and published online ELT content for all modes of delivery, including content to support a 'flipped' classroom model and more recently adaptive learning. Debra's research interests focus on exploring the needs of the online learner and teacher and the benefits, potential and constraints of the online learning environment.

Freda Mishan is course director of the Structured PhD TESOL at the University of Limerick, Ireland, where she lectures on both the PhD and MA TESOL. Her research interests and publications include problem-based learning, blended learning and materials development. Her publications include *Materials Development for TESOL* (co-authored with Ivor Timmis, Edinburgh University Press, 2015), *Designing Authenticity into Language Learning Materials* (Intellect, 2005), two co-edited books and chapters in recent volumes such as *Developing Materials for Language Teaching* (Tomlinson, Bloomsbury, 2013). She is also editor of the Materials Development Association (MATSDA) journal, *Folio*.

David Moloney works as the Co-ordinator of Blended Learning within the Blended Learning Unit at Mary Immaculate College (MIC), University of Limerick. David graduated with a First Class Honours Master's degree in Technical Communication and E-Learning from the University of Limerick. He began work in MIC as an Educational Technology Assistant at the inception of the Blended Learning Unit. Since then, David has been actively involved in developing the unit and works closely with the college's academic faculties and departments. He has helped to co-ordinate the design, development and implementation of many unique academic modules and programmes of a blended and fully online nature.

Dr Anne O'Keeffe is Senior Lecturer in Applied Linguistics and Director of Teaching and Learning at Mary Immaculate College (MIC), University of Limerick. She oversees programmes in undergraduate English Language Teaching and postgraduate research in Applied Linguistics. She is also responsible for quality assurance and professional development in teaching and learning at MIC.

Patrick Olivier is a Professor of Human-Computer Interaction at Newcastle University where he leads the Digital Interaction Group at Culture Lab, Newcastle Centre for Cross-disciplinary Digital Research. His research interests include human-computer interaction, computer graphics and artificial intelligence. Olivier received his PhD in language engineering from the University of Manchester.

Anne Preston has a PhD in Applied Linguistics and has worked in language education in the UK and France for more than 10 years. Anne works across disciplines in language education, applied linguistics, computing science and human computer interaction to develop research agendas around the design and evaluation of technology-enhanced language learning. Her interests in blended learning focus on striking more of a balance between technology-driven theory and learning theory-driven approaches to design, which has also a strong pedagogical foundation.

Helen Sandiford has over 25 years' experience as an English teacher, teacher-trainer and sales and marketing specialist. She spent nine years in Japan setting up English programmes and teaching in Japanese senior high schools and vocational colleges. She has conducted training seminars for English teachers throughout East Asia and South America. She is co-author of the course books *Touchstone* and *Viewpoint*, and also the *Touchstone Online* and *Viewpoint Online* series. She lives and works in Utah, USA.

Maria Ofelia Z. San Pedro is a PhD student and research assistant in the Cognitive Studies programme at Teachers College, Columbia University. She is a member of the university's Educational Data Mining Lab. She received her MS degree in Computer Science in 2011 and BS degree in Electronics Engineering in 2005 from the Ateneo de Manila University. Her research interests include learning analytics (LA), educational data mining (EDM), learning sciences and educational technology. She has written and presented academic papers on educational data mining and on artificial intelligence in education. Her current research work is on the longitudinal analysis of interaction data from educational software in middle school mathematics using LA and EDM methodologies.

Paul Seedhouse is Professor of Educational and Applied Linguistics in the School of Education, Communication and Language Sciences, Newcastle University, UK. His monograph *The Interactional Architecture of the Language Classroom* was published by Blackwell in 2004 and won the Modern Languages Association of America Mildenberger Prize.

Scott Thornbury is an associate professor on the MA TESOL programme at The New School in New York. His previous experience includes teaching and teacher training in Egypt, the UK, Spain and in his native New Zealand. He has published extensively in the field of language and of language teaching methodology and is series editor for the *Cambridge Handbooks for Language Teachers*.

Steve Walsh is Professor and Head of Applied Linguistics in the School of Education, Communication and Language Sciences, Newcastle University, UK. He has been involved in English Language Teaching for more than 30 years in a range of overseas contexts. His research interests include classroom discourse, teacher development and second language teacher education.

Index

accuracy, and fluency 28–9, 87–8
ACMC (asynchronous computer-mediated communication) 107, 110, 111
action research project, design of mobile-based tasks 219–20, 224–31
active learning 89–90
activities for blended learning 139–56
Adapt Courseware 238, 241
adaptive educational software 235
adaptive hypermedia 237
adaptive learning 234–43, 262–3
   definition 235–6
   goal of 235
   personalised learning experience 234–5
   utilising the affordances of technology 234–5
adaptive learning systems 3, 235–43
   current limitations 242–3
   data mining and analytics 241–2
   features of 235–6
   framework 236–8
   future opportunities 242–3
   how they enable adaptation 241–2
   intelligent tutoring systems 237–42
   modelling student knowledge 238–9
   responses to student behaviours 240
   responses to student help-seeking 240
   student affect detection and response 239–40
   student attributes adapted to 238–40
   support for self-regulated learning 240
   taxonomic dimensions 236
adaptive platforms 237–8

Adaptive VIBE for TaskSieve 241
Affective AutoTutor 239–40, 242
affective factors in language learning 14, 30, 239–40
affordances of technology
   influence on learning materials 123
   space for learning 42–3
ALEKS (Assessment and Learning in Knowledge Spaces) 237, 242
Andes adaptive learning system 239, 241
AnimalWatch 241
applied linguistics, insights for blended learning 7–9
assessment of technology *see* educational technology assessment
assisted performance notion 29
assistive technology development 163–4
ASSISTments 238, 241
asynchronous computer-mediated communication (ACMC) 107, 108, 110, 111
attention, role in second language learning 11, 88
Audiolingual teaching methods (1970s) 86, 109
augmented reality technology 219
authenticity of tasks, learner evaluation 251–2
automaticity 29–30, 32
AutoTutor 238–9, 239–40, 241, 242

Berlitz Method (Direct Method) 86
Betty's Brain 240, 241
big data in education 243
Blackboard (LMS) 127
blended approach, potential barriers to 140–1
blended environment, evaluation of 94

blended learning (BL)
   and socio-constructivist theory 125
   approaches in other disciplines 249
   as a cost-saving measure 133
   cost-effectiveness 258
   developing activities and materials 139–56
   effects of rapid change in technology 248–9
   evidence to inform decisions about 7–9
   flipped classroom model 56, 60–3
   history and development 1–3
   impact on the classroom function 68
   implications for teacher education 61–3
   increasing oral output 108
   integrated learning environment 90
   literature review 110–11
   need for pedagogy research 56
   potential benefits 56
   teaching challenges 61–3
blended learning course design 2–3
blended learning course design (case study) 200–12
   background to the blended learning product 200–1
   challenges for teachers 205
   creating the blend 208–11
   design criteria 205–8
   differences between print and online media 200
   evaluation of the course 212
   flexibility and 'connectedness' 206
   grading issues 207–8
   implementing the design criteria 208–9
   key challenges 203–5

blended learning course design (case study) (cont.)
  language instruction 209–11
  macro-level challenges 203–4
  micro-level challenges 204
  practice is learning 207–8
  putting the learner at the centre 206–7
  reporting for teachers 207–8
  student engagement and production 207
  Touchstone Blended Learning development 201
  Touchstone Blended Learning evaluation 212
  Touchstone print edition as starting point 201–3
blended learning for language teachers (case study) 72–6
  analysis and discussion 75–6
  case study context 72–3
  collaboration 74–5
  deepening learning and engagement 75
  developing further learning 75
  move towards open practices 74–5
  presenting and writing for publication 75
  sharing good practice 74–5
  sharing teaching resources 73–4
  training for online synchronous teaching 73
blended learning pedagogy research 56–60
  and the flipped classroom 56
  background 57–8
  figuring out the 'blend' 58–9
  how the 'blend' turned out 59–60
  need for research 56
  phases of the research 58
  results 59–60
  study design 58–9
blogs 3, 124, 125, 128

CALL *see* computer-assisted language learning
Cambridge Institute for Automated Language Learning and Assessment (ALTA) 251
Cambridge University Language Programme (CULP) 84, 92–3
Cambridge University Press 57, 200–1
case studies in blended learning
  blended learning course design 200–12
  French digital kitchen project 163–73
  language teacher education 176–97
CA-SLA (Conversational Analysis for SLA) 39
Center for Open Educational Resources and Language Learning (COERLL) 77
Châlon, Yves 95
chat rooms 3
Chinese University Teacher Training in English (CUTE) 84, 92, 94
Chomsky, Noam 86
CIC *see* Classroom Interactional Competence
classroom environment 90–1
  features of the learning process 36–7
  human interactions and support 2–3
  opportunities for noticing 11–12
  traditional vs. flipped classroom 89–90 *see also* flipped classroom
classroom interaction
  and spoken corpora 15–17
  comparison with general interaction 16
  exploiting mode-switching online 16–17
  features of 16
  modes of interaction 15–16
  recreating in the computer-mediated world 16–18
  reproducing online 259–61
  role in a blended programme 259–61, 262–3
  using technology to maximise 2 *see also* interactional competence
classroom interaction studies, insights for blended learning 7–9
Classroom Interactional Competence (CIC) 250–1

communicative competence 37–8
  definition 36–7
  definitions of interactional competence (IC) 38
  features of 40–9
  features of interactional competence (IC) 39–40
  interactional space 42
  L2 classroom interaction 37
  role in the learning process 36–7
  space for learning 42–8
  teacher's pedagogic goals 40–2 *see also* interactional competence
classroom observation protocols 13
classwork and homework distinction 1, 2
CogBooks 238
cognitive demands on learners 259
Cognitive Tutor (intelligent tutoring system) 237, 238, 240, 242
Common European Framework of Reference for Language Learning and Teaching (CEFR) 57, 87–8, 97
communicative approach to language teaching 87–9
communicative competence 37–8, 86
Communicative Language Teaching (CLT) 37
communities online 180
community of inquiry 182–3, 253, 257, 259
community of language learners 253
community of learning 259
community of practice for education professionals 151–4
competence, view of Chomsky 86
computer-assisted language learning (CALL) 2, 14–15, 124, 125, 164, 222–3
  development of 8–9
  learners views on 108
  principles 165
computer-mediated communication (CMC) 108 *see also* ACMC; SCMC
computer-mediated learning
  potential contributions in language learning 17–19
  potential downsides 259
  use in SLA research 13–15

concurrent think-aloud protocols 13
conditionalised knowledge stage 182
confluence (flow of spoken language between speakers) 38
constructivist learning environments (CLEs) 180–1
Contrastive Analysis Hypothesis (CAH) 86
convergence in mobile technologies 223
Conversation Analysis for Second Language Acquisition (CA-SLA) 39
cooking *see* French digital kitchen project
corpus linguistics 7–9, 28
cost-effectiveness of blended learning 258
Council of Europe 87–8
cross-cultural communication 257
CULP (Cambridge University Language Programme) 84, 92–3
cultural context *see* socio-cultural perspective on learning
curriculums, compatibility with blended learning 140
CUTE (Chinese University Teacher Training in English) 84, 92, 94

data-driven learning (DDL) 8–9
deep learning 181–2
DEPTHS (adaptive system) 241
Developing Online Teaching Skills (DOTS) project 77
digital competences 221–2
digital dissonance in teachers 140
digital kitchen *see* French digital kitchen project
digital literacies 221–2
digital literacy skills 221–2
Direct Method (Berlitz Method) 86
discourse competence 86–7
discussion forums 185, 191–2
distance learning 108

ecological approaches to learning 42
Education Elements 139
educational technology assessment 25–32
  adaptivity 31
  automaticity and practice 29–30, 32
  chunks 32
  complexity of the learner's task 28, 31
  deriving assessment principles 26–7
  feedback 31
  flow 30–1, 32
  fluency and memorised sequences (chunks) 30
  going beyond the hype 26–7
  history of exaggerated claims 26
  input 31
  input enhancement 28
  insights from SLA research 27–31
  interaction 31
  learner associations with new materials 30
  natural order of acquisition 27–8
  need for exposure to authentic input 28
  need for feedback 28, 29
  noticing salient features of the input 28, 31
  output (language production) 28–9, 31
  pedagogy-driven use of technology 25
  peer collaboration 29
  personalisation 29, 32
  practical issues 32
  scaffolding 31
  time spent on learning 30–1
  twelve observations 27–30
  twelve principles 31–2
emic perspective on language learning 108, 110–11
enabling blends 249
Engeström's Activity System 180, 181
English at Your Fingertips (E@YF) 91–2, 93, 94, 100–2
English teacher training courses, materials and activities for BL 149–51
enhancing blends 249–50
error correction 45, 47
existential competence (le savoir-être) 97
explicit versus implicit knowledge 11
extended wait-time, use by teachers 37, 43–5, 47

face-to-face (F2F) class time, oral output compared to online modules 107–19
Facebook 128, 132, 222
feedback
  from both teachers and learners 257
  role in language acquisition 28, 29
  role in learning 10, 11
flexibility, as a strength of blended learning 258–9
flipped classroom 9, 13, 55–63, 139, 251, 253
  aspects of 8, 9
  blended learning pedagogy research 56–60
  changing pedagogy with the aid of technology 60–1
  definition 9
  implications for teacher education 61–3
  model for blended learning 60–3
  optimal conditions for language learning 55–6
  potential benefits for language learning 56
  spaces for learning 43
  teaching challenges 61–3
  vs. traditional classroom 89–90
flow state in language learning 30–1, 32
fluency
  and accuracy 28–9, 87–8
  and memorised sequences (chunks) 30
focus-on-form 88
French digital kitchen project 163–73
  aims 163
  background 163–4
  computer science and applied linguistics collaboration 163–4
  design principles 165–7
  development of assistive technology 163–4
  future developments 173
  Graphical User-Interface (GUI) 166–8
  how it works 167–70
  how learners use the resources 170–2

French digital kitchen project (*cont.*)
  pedagogical principles 164
  pre-during-post task structure 168–70
  types of learning 170–2

geolocation feature of mobile devices 219
globalisation, influence of 1
grammar quizzes 185, 194–6
Grammar-Translation Method (GTM) 86
grammatical encoding and decoding 109
grammatical morphemes, acquisition of 9–10
Graphical User-Interface (GUI) 166–8
Guardian Teacher Network 77

Help Tutor 240
historical views on education 85–6
homework and classwork distinction 1, 2
human aspect of teaching and learning 2–3
Human-Computer Interaction (HCI) 163, 164, 166–7
Humbox 77
hybrid courses 2 *see also* blended learning (BL)
Hymes, Dell 37, 86, 96

identity and motivation, challenge for teachers 70–1
identity issues for the learner 12
identity theories 30
immersion 109
individual learner differences 10–11, 12 *see also* personalised learning experience
inner speech 13
input enhancement 14, 28, 109, 250
input (i+1) hypothesis (Krashen) 109
input-output loops 14
integrated learning environment 90–1
integrated learning examples 92–4
integrative processing in language tasks 109–10

intelligent machines, personalised learning opportunities 262–3
intelligent tutoring systems 237–42
interaction
  in a blended learning context 36–49
  reproducing in the online environment 259–61
  role in language learning 36–7, 259–61, 262–3 *see also* classroom interaction
interaction hypothesis (Long) 110
interactional competence 15, 250–1
  definitions 38
  features of 39–40 *see also* Classroom Interactional Competence (CIC)
interactional space 42
interactionist learning theories 29
international community of language learners 253
internet, influence on teaching and learning 2

Jorum repository 77
just-in-time support for learners 29, 88

knowledge-creating approach 259

language acquisition, natural order of 27–8
Language Box 77
language laboratories 1–2
language learning environments 84, 89–92
language teacher education (BL case study) 176–97
  communities of inquiry (CoI) 182–3
  context of the case study 177–8
  deep learning 181–2
  discussion forums 185, 191–2
  evaluation 187–96
  factors driving the BL approach 177–8
  future developments 196–7
  goal of flexible programme delivery 177–8
  grammar quizzes 185, 194–6
  move from traditional teaching to BL 183–7

online moderator role 181
possible negative aspects of e-learning 179
potential of blended learning 176–7
range of outcomes 196–7
rationale for the blended method 178–80
role definition 181
student evaluations of teaching (SETs) 177–8
surface learning 181–2
theoretical framework 180–1
transition from traditional delivery 178
use of the LMS 183–7
video recording evaluation 187–91
vodcasts 187–91
wiki assignment 186, 192–4
Languages at Your Fingertips (L@YF) 91–2, 92–3, 100
Languages Open Resources Online (LORO) 74, 77
Laureate English Programme (LEP) 57, 200–1
Laureate International Universities (LIUs) 57, 200, 212
Laurillard, D. 125–6, 127, 219
learner affect 108
learner autonomy 111
learner-centred blended learning approach 139–40
learner-driven online environment 91–4
learner role
  impact of new modes of learning 254, 255
  in a blended CLE 181
learner spoken corpora 251
learner turns, extended 43, 45–7
learners
  as originators of materials 256
  assisting one another 15
  associations with new material 30
  cognitive demands on 259
  evaluation of authenticity of tasks 251–2
  experience of using blended programmes 251–2
  feedback on the BL experience 257

importance of positive affect 30–1
individual differences 10–11, 12
learning from one another 29
personalised learning experience 29, 234–5, 262–3
preparation for online activities 257
social and cultural identity 12
training in technology-enhanced environment 255, 257
views on CALL 108
learning, approaches to 70
learning environments
  blended learning environment 90
  classroom environment 90–1
  evaluation of the blended environment 94
  integrated learning examples 92–4
  online environment 91–2
  traditional vs. flipped classroom 89–90
learning management systems (LMS) 59, 127–8, 129–30, 132–3, 176, 183–7, 201
learning materials *see* materials
learning platforms, uncovering SLA processes 13–14
learning skills and language simultaneously 164
learning strategies 11
learning styles 11, 14
LearnSmart 238
lecture-capturing technology 176, 184–5
lexical approach 30
LMS *see* language management systems
LORO (Languages Open Resources Online) 74, 77

MALL (Mobile Assisted Language Learning) 222–3, 228–9
MALU (Mobile Assisted Language Use) 223
Massive Open Online Courses (MOOCs) 176
materials for blended learning
  background to BL contexts 141
  case studies 128–32
  community of practice for education professionals 151–4

content vs. process distinction 124–5
definitions of materials 123, 124–5
developments with new technology 123
exploiting the potential of technology 132–3
flexibility of design 257
interactivity within tasks 124–5
LMS design restrictions 132–3
measuring the success of 141–3
multi-dimensional concept 127–9
pedagogical implications from successful activities 154–6
potential barriers to the BL approach 140–1
pre- and in-service English teacher training courses 149–51
process aspects 124–5
reconceptualisation for new learning modes 255–6
redefining for the technological/digital environment 124–5
rethinking rules and roles 139–40
role of language materials 123
role within BL frameworks 125–8
theoretical base 125
theoretical basis for methodology 125–8
using the BL materials framework 128–32
variations in effective use 156
web collaboration project for secondary school students 144–8
metacognition 182
Mobile Assisted Language Learning (MALL) 222–3, 228–9
Mobile Assisted Language Use (MALU) 223
mobile-based 'bridging' activities 219
mobile-based classroom activities 219–20
mobile learning (mLearning)
  action research project 224–31
  and new media literacies 221–2
  definition 220–1
  in English Language Teaching 222–3
  literature review 220–3

potential learning opportunities 261–2
types of project 223
mobile learning action research project 219–20, 224–31
  aim of the study 224
  BYOD (Bring Your Own Device) approach 224
  effects on motivation and participation 225–7
  future developments 230–1
  implementation of staged activities 225
  implications for teacher training 230
  initial online mobile use survey 225
  research issues 229
  research questions 224, 225–9
  study groups of learners 224
  task design and sequencing 228–9
mobile literacy 221–2
mobile technology 3
models of blended learning 249–50
modern pedagogical approaches in ELT 86–7
monitor theory (Krashen) 108
Montaigne, Michel de 84, 85–6, 89, 96, 97
MOOCs (Massive Open Online Courses) 176
Moodle 127, 144, 145, 146, 176, 184
motivation 12, 14
  and teacher identity 70–1
  and time spent on learning 30–1
  learner associations with new material 30
  of teachers 70–1, 254–5
multimedia glosses 164
multimedia labs 2
multi-user virtual environments (MUVEs) 17

new media literacies 221–2
Nintendo Wii™ 167
noticing, role in language learning 10, 11–12, 28, 88, 109–10
notional-functional teaching approach 11

One Laptop Per Child (OLPC) projects 223

One Tablet Per Child (OTPC) projects 223
online community of practice for education professionals 151–4
online courses, integrated learning examples 92–4
online environment
  learner driven 91–2
  training for teachers and learners 254–5, 257
online forums 3
online moderator role 181
open collaboration 77
oral output (online modules)
  advantages of CMC 108
  blended learning studies 110–11
  challenges of online course design 107–8
  comparison with F2F class output 107–19
  literature review 109–11
  oral production pilot study 111–19
  rationale for study 107–8
  role in blended learning courses 108
  role of output in the SLA process 108
oral output (traditional language classroom) 108
oral production pilot study 111–19
  conclusion 118–19
  data collection and analysis 113–16
  description 111–12
  instruments and treatment 112–13
  learners' assessment of the online modules 117–18
  methods 112
  research questions and hypotheses 112
  results 113–18
output
  and integrative processing 109–10
  functions in language learning 110
  production needed for language acquisition 28–9
output hypothesis 28–9

passive learning 89
pedagogical philosophy 85–6
pedagogical scaffolding 31
pedagogy, influence of the blended approach 2–3
pedagogy-driven use of technology 25
pedagogy-led blended learning programmes 3
peer collaboration in the classroom 29
personalised learning experience 29, 234–5, 262–3
Piaget, Jean 180
piecemeal learning theories 28
Plato 84, 85–6, 89, 97
positive affect and learner motivation 30–1
possible selves notion 71
PowerPoint (PPT) 126, 128, 222
pragmatic meaning 257–8
pre-during-post task structure 164, 168–70
presentation software 126, 128, 129–30
Prezi 126, 128, 129–30
private speech 13
'pushed output' 108, 109

real-world learning-based activities 164
Re:Source platform 77
resource-sharing platforms 77
rhetorical skills in writing 15
Rousseau, Jean-Jacques 84, 85–6, 89, 97

SCMC (synchronous computer-mediated communication) 13, 14, 17, 107, 110
Scooter the Tutor 241
second language acquisition *see* SLA
second language learning, optimal conditions for 55–6
self concept 70–1
Skype 110, 128
SLA (Second Language Acquisition) 7, 9, 164
SLA approaches in relation to BL 9–12
  acquisition of grammatical morphemes 9–10
  individual learner differences 10–11, 12
  learner's social and cultural context 12
  noticing concept 10, 11–12
  scope of SLA study 9–10
SLA processes
  limitations of using technology to reveal 14–15
  student self-reporting on 13
  using technology to 'uncover' 13–14
SLA research
  insights for educational technology assessment 27–31
  nature of what is observed 13
  use of computer-mediated language learning 13–15
SLA theory, insights for blended learning 7–19, 249–50
smart mobile devices 3, 8, 219
Smart Sparrow 238, 241
social networking 3, 14, 17–18
social networking site (SNS) 124, 125, 128
social speech 13
socio-cognitive view of learning 29
socio-constructivist theory 125
sociocultural perspective on learning 12, 13, 29, 42, 125
socio-interactional perspective on learning 110–11
space for learning 42–8
spoken corpora 251
  and classroom interaction 15–17
  interactive speaking in BL 8
SQL-Tutor 239
station-rotation model of BL 249
surface learning 181–2
synchronous computer-mediated communication (SCMC) 13, 14, 107, 110

tablets 3
task-based language learning, in the online environment 257–8
Task-Based Language Teaching (TBLT) 37
  French digital kitchen project 163–73
  principles 164, 165–6
task-based pedagogy 11
teacher education
  impact of new modes of learning 254–5

implications of new technology 61–3
teacher identity 70–1
teacher professional development
   and self concept 70–1
   applying new technologies 68–9
   approaches to learning 70
   approaches to teacher education 69–70
   approaches to the teacher's role 70
   BL for language teachers (case study) 72–6
   competences for delivering blended learning 71–2
   holistic approach 72
   implications of blended learning 68–77
   key underpinning concepts 69–72
   literature review 69–72
   meeting teachers' needs 76–7
   resource-sharing platforms 77
   teacher identity and motivation 70–1
teacher role
   approaches to 70
   appropriate use of technology 96–7
   Classroom Interactional Competence (CIC) 36–7
   description of a good teacher 94–7
   digital dissonance 140
   experience of using blended programmes 251–2
   feedback on the BL experience 257
   guiding interaction in the classroom 15–16
   impact of new modes of learning 253–4
   impact of the blended approach 68–9
   in a blended CLE 181
   interactional strategies 43–8
   listening to learners 95
   motivation of teachers 254–5
   online language teaching 68–9
   pedagogy in the flipped classroom 60–1
   promoting and supporting learning 95–7
   resistance to using online tools 140
   rethinking in the BL approach 140–1
   shaping learner contributions 43, 45–8
   understanding of mobile device affordances 219
teacher self concept 70–1
teacher-student ratio 88
teaching and learning
   complementary relationship 83–4
   historical perspective 83–4
teaching as learning 84–9
   appropriate use of technology 88–9
   background to pedagogy 84–7
   communicative approach to language teaching 87–9
   historical views on education 85–6
   modern pedagogical approaches in ELT 86–7
   pedagogical philosophy 85–6
   putting theory into practice 87–9
teaching materials *see* materials
Teaching Resources bank, TESConnect website 77
technology
   appropriate use in teaching and learning 88–9
   availability of 140
   influence on pedagogy 2–3
   theoretical base for language learning applications 125
   training for teachers and learners 255, 257
   use in teaching and learning 96–7
   views on role in language learning 1–3
Technology Enhanced Language Learning (TELL) 222–3
TESConnect website 77
The Threshold Level (Van Ek) 87
thinking aloud protocols 13
threefold model (enabling, enhancing and transforming blends) 249–50
Touchstone Blended Learning 201, 212, 260–1
Touchstone print edition 201–3
transcription symbols
   for Chapter 3 52
   for Chapter 10 175
transformative learning experiences 257
transforming blends 249, 250, 257
Tweesis 131
twenty-first century skills 221–2
Twitter 127, 128, 131

University of Cambridge Language Centre 92–4
usage-based theories of SLA 28

van Lier, Leo 42
Verlaine, Paul 97
video conferencing 107
Virtual Learning Environments (VLEs) 127–8, 177, 179
vodcasts 185–91
Voices for Openness 77
Vygotsky, Lev 42, 125, 180

wait-time, increasing 37, 43–5, 47
Web 2.0 tools 111, 123, 124, 125
web collaboration project for secondary school students 144–8
WebCT 127
What teachers make (Mali) 130–1, 137–8
wiki assignment 186, 192–4
written corpora 8

YouTube 113, 124, 128, 132, 150, 184, 186

zone of proximal development 29

Lightning Source UK Ltd.
Milton Keynes UK
UKOW07f0258241215

265224UK00003B/30/P